main

Diary of a DA

THE TRUE STORY OF THE PROSECUTOR WHO TOOK ON THE MOB, FOUGHT CORRUPTION, AND WON

HERBERT J. STERN

SKYHORSE PUBLISHING

Skyhorse Publishing books may be purchased in bulk at special discounts for sales promotion, corporate gifts, fund-raising, or educational purposes. Special editions can also be created to specifications. For details, contact the Special Sales Department, Skyhorse Publishing, 307 West 36th Street, 11th Floor, New York, NY 10018 or info@skyhorsepublishing.com.

Skyhorse® and Skyhorse Publishing® are registered trademarks of Skyhorse Publishing, Inc.®, a Delaware corporation.

Visit our website at www.skyhorsepublishing.com.

10 9 8 7 6 5 4 3 2 1

Library of Congress Cataloging-in-Publication Data

Stern, Herbert Jay, 1936-
    Diary of a DA / Herbert J. Stern.
      p. cm.
    ISBN 978-1-62087-167-6 (hardcover : alk. paper)
    1. Stern, Herbert Jay, 1936- 2. Public prosecutors—New York (State)—Biography.
    I. Title.

    KF373.S7S74 2012
    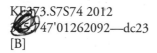47'01262092—dc23
    [B]

ISBN ~~978-1-62087-167-6~~

Printed in the United States of America

For Frederick B. Lacey
And
To the memory of my father, Samuel Stern
And
Clifford P. Case

SIGNIFICANT PERSONS WHO APPEAR

NEW YORK COUNTY DISTRICT ATTORNEY'S OFFICE

FRANK S. HOGAN – District Attorney. Entirely non-political, tough on political corruption, determined to stamp out pornography and "sexual deviancy" and to uphold decency

JOSEPH MICHAEL DONOHUE – Mass murderer hit man for "The Westies," the west side Irish mob.

LENNY BRUCE – Nightclub performer prosecuted, convicted, and incarcerated for offensive language in his performances.

PATRICK CROWE – Traffic cop who fired his gun twice at a car after a traffic stop, killing bystander Julius Ofsei.

GEORGE WHITMORE – Falsely arrested for the savage double murder in the "Career Girls" case; his false confession to the murders—which he did not commit—led to the repeal of capital punishment in New York State.

BETTY SHABAZZ – Eyewitness to the murder of her husband, Malcolm X.

DEPARTMENT OF JUSTICE

HENRY E. PETERSEN – Career Departmental Attorney who works his way up from Deputy Chief to Chief of the Organized Crime and Racketeering Section and ultimately to Assistant Attorney General in charge of the Criminal Division at the time of the Watergate break in and cover up, which investigation he oversaw until replaced by Special Prosecutor Archibald Cox.

DAVID M. SATZ – United States Attorney for the District of New Jersey during the Administration of Lyndon Johnson, who owed his appointment to the political boss of central New Jersey, David T. Wilentz. He is replaced by Frederick B. Lacey.

FREDERICK B. LACEY – Appointed United States Attorney upon the recommendation of U.S. Senator Clifford P. Case.

SENATOR CLIFFORD P. CASE – Senior Senator of New Jersey who recruits Fred Lacey as U.S. Attorney to clean up the state.

OPERATION PIPELINE

THE COLONIAL PIPELINE COMPANY – The largest privately financed project at the time—wholly owned by the nine major oil companies—extending from Houston, Texas, to Woodbridge, New Jersey; succumbs to pressure by New Jersey labor leader Peter Weber to award construction contracts and by public officials in Woodbridge to pay $110,000 in bribes.

BEN D. LEUTY – President

KARL T. FELDMAN – Executive Vice President

GLENN GILES – Vice President

PETER WEBER – President of Local 825, Operating Engineers, with jurisdiction over all construction in New Jersey and five counties of New York State; he lines his pockets by extorting monies from construction jobs—burying much of the proceeds in the name of his "secretary," Mitzi.

MAYOR WALTER ZIRPOLO and PRESIDENT OF THE CITY COUNCIL OF WOODBRIDGE, ROBERT JACKS – Members of Boss David T. Wilentz's county organization, took $110,000 in cash from Colonial for permits and easements for the Colonial facilities.

NEW JERSEY POLITICAL BOSSES

DAVID T. WILENTZ – Boss of Middlesex County, leader of one of New Jersey's largest law firms. As Attorney General of New Jersey, in the 1930s, prosecuted the Lindbergh kidnapping case; the father-in-law of Leon Hess, the principal of Hess Oil, he is the second most powerful boss in New Jersey. He made his law partner, Arthur Sills, Attorney General in the Administration of Governor Hughes, and, in later years, his son Robert Wilentz Chief Justice.

JOHN V. KENNY – Boss of Hudson County – which includes Jersey City, Hoboken, Bayonne and West New York—defeated and then replaced Frank Hague as Boss; the most powerful politician in New Jersey, leading a ring of corrupt public officials—including the Mayor and the President of the City Council of Jersey City that exacts 10% off every public contract given by the city and the county, and 3% of the salaries of city and municipal employees. He gifts $700,000 in bearer bonds – purchased for cash by the Chief of Police of Hudson County—to his grandkids.

FRANK S. FARLEY – State Senator, Republican Boss of Atlantic County; Farley, originally a member of the corrupt organization of Enoch "Nucky" Johnson (of the TV show Boardwalk Empire fame), took over when Nucky went to prison for tax evasion; Farley bosses the corrupt administration of Atlantic City Mayor William T. Sommers.

THE NEW JERSEY MAFIA

ANGELO "GYP" DECARLO – Known as "Ray," gambling, loan sharking, and entertainment—sponsor of the "Four Seasons" singing group –and a character in the Tony Award winning Broadway show, Jersey Boys. A cousin of Frank Sinatra, his extortion sentence is commuted by President Nixon.

RITCHIE "THE BOOT" BOIARDO – A mafia captain whose Livingston estate contained an incinerator used to dispose of bodies.

ANTHONY "TONY BOY" BOIARDO – Son of Ritchie, who along with DeCarlo controls the administration of Newark's Mayor, Hugh J. Addonizio.

ANTHONY "LITTLE PUSSY" RUSSO – Controls the rackets on "The Jersey Shore."

The above were sometime models for and source material for the TV series, *The Sopranos*.

SAM "THE PLUMBER" DeCAVALCANTE – Boss of New Jersey's only independent family whose illegally recorded conversations by the FBI revealed the inner workings of the mob.

THE ADMINISTRATION OF THE CITY OF NEWARK

HUGH J. ADDONIZIO – Mayor of Newark, a former U.S. Congressman recruited for Mayor by Gyp DeCarlo and the Boiardos.

PHILLIP GORDON – Corporation counsel of the City

ANTHONY LAMORTE – Director of Public Works, a collector for Tony Boy, and Mayor Addonizio.

PAUL RIGO – Civil Engineer, who pays off on numerous city projects.

IRVING KANTOR – Dying of Lou Gehrig's disease, testifies to cashing $1,000,000 in checks to pay Boiardo.

THE ADMINISTRATION OF HUDSON COUNTY AND JERSEY CITY

THOMAS WHELAN – Mayor, Jersey City

THOMAS FLAHERTY – City Council President

Members of Boss John V. Kenny's organization, who collected millions in graft, who had a joint bank account in Florida with $1,230,000 in cash and bearer bonds.

JOHN J. KENNY – No relation to Boss John V. Kenny. Former Chairman of the Democratic Party who after receiving $50,000 in cash from John V. Kenny turns witness for the United States.

WALTER WOLFE – Successor to John J. Kenny as Democratic Chairman of Hudson County.

FRED J. KROPKE – Chief of Police of Hudson County, who dispenses cash for John V. Kenny, including the $700,000 used to purchase bearer bonds for the Boss's grandkids.

THE ADMINISTRATION OF ATLANTIC CITY AND ATLANTIC COUNTY

WILLIAM T. SOMMERS – Mayor of Atlantic City, member of Republican Boss Frank Farley's ring, who takes kickbacks on public contracts.

PATRICK J. DORAN – Atlantic County Engineer who takes kickbacks on highway contracts.

THE ADMINISTRATION OF GOVERNOR RICHARD J. HUGHES

ROBERT BURKHARDT – Secretary of State who extorts payments for the Democratic Party and himself.

JOHN A. KERVICK – State Treasurer who takes $113,000 in bribes.

D. LOUIS TONTI – Executive Director of the New Jersey Highway Authority, who takes hundreds of thousands of dollars from contractors working on the Garden State Parkway.

ARTHUR SILLS – Attorney General; a former law partner of Boss David T. Wilentz, who resists efforts at reform.

THE ADMINISTRATION OF GOVERNOR WILLIAM T. CAHILL

PAUL SHERWIN – Secretary of State who attempts to get a state contract for a donor who pledges $50,000 to the Republican Party.

DAVID BIEDERMAN – Former Deputy Attorney General who reports the misconduct of Paul Sherwin to Attorney General George F. Kugler.

NELSON GROSS – Republican State Chairman who suborns perjury in the investigation into McCrane's illegal campaign activities.

JOSEPH M. McCRANE, JR. – State Treasurer who raises money illegally for the campaign of Governor Cahill.

GEORGE F. KUGLER – Attorney General who initially refuses to investigate Secretary of State Sherwin and State Treasurer McCrane.

STATE POLICE DETECTIVE JAMES CHALLENDER – Who reports the misconduct of the Cahill Election Finances, and the refusal of the Attorney General to investigate, to the United States Attorney.

FEDERAL OFFICIALS

ROBERT MARDIAN – Assistant Attorney General in charge of Internal Security Division, in charge of investigations and prosecutions of anti war demonstrators, who oversees the "Camden 28" case.

CONGRESSMAN CORNELIUS GALLAGHER – Ranking member of the House of Foreign Affairs Committee, member of Boss Kenny's Hudson County Organization, who purchases over $900,000 of bearer bonds in cash.

VICE PRESIDENT SPIRO AGNEW – Who as corrupt Baltimore County Executive and then Governor of Maryland, exacted kickbacks from contractors on public works.

GEORGE BEALL – United States Attorney for the District of Maryland who indicts Agnew.

RICHARD KLEINDIENST – First as Deputy Attorney General, then as Attorney General of the United States, supports the efforts to clean up New Jersey, and to indict Colonel Paul Fournier of the French CIA for shipping 100 pounds of heroin into the United States; resigns when his mentor, former Attorney General John N. Mitchell becomes a subject in the Watergate investigation.

ELLIOT RICHARDSON – Succeeds Kleindienst as Attorney General and appoints Archibald Cox as Special Watergate Prosecutor. Designates Stern and Cox to investigate President Nixon's release of DeCarlo from prison.

ARCHIBALD COX – Special Watergate Prosecutor replaces Henry Petersen as head of the Watergate investigation.

ASSISTANT UNITED STATES ATTORNEYS

HERBERT J. STERN – Assistant DA under Hogan; Trial Lawyer in Justice under Peterson; First Assistant under U.S. Attorney Frederick B. Lacey; later United States Attorney.

JONATHAN L. GOLDSTEIN – Chief of Criminal Division under Lacey; First Assistant under Stern; later United States Attorney.

BRUCE I. GOLDSTEIN – Appointed by Lacey as an AUSA; Later Chief of Special Prosecution under Stern.

JOHN J. BARRY – One of the defense team in the Colonial Pipeline case, appointed by Lacey as an AUSA; later Chief of Appeals.

GARRETT BROWN – Appointed an AUSA by Lacey; later Executive Assistant under Stern.

JOHN W. BISSELL – Appointed by Lacey; later Chief of Criminal Division under Stern.

RICHARD LANGWAY – Appointed by Stern; later Chief of Criminal Division.

Table of Contents

BOOK I: FOR THE PEOPLE

Chapter One: The Complaint Bureau
      February–December 1962   3

Chapter Two: The Indictment Bureau
      1962–1963   15

Chapter Three: The Criminal Court Bureau
      1963   18

Chapter Four: "Why Did You Prosecute Him?"
      1963   25

Chapter Five: The End of the Beginning
      1963–1964   30

Chapter Six: The Homicide Bureau
      1964   34

Chapter Seven: "Get Me out of Here"
      May–December 1964   44

Chapter Eight: The Beginning of the End
      December 1964–February 1965   51

Chapter Nine: Time to Move On
      January–February 21, 1965   58

Chapter Ten: The Murder of Malcolm X
      February 21, 1965   62

Chapter Eleven: The Murderers
      February–April 1965   65

Chapter Twelve: "The Kid Had the Key"
      April–August 1965   75

Chapter Thirteen: A New Beginning
      April–September 1965   78

BOOK II: FOR THE UNITED STATES

Chapter One: The Department of Justice
      November 1, 1965   83

Chapter Two: Peter Weber
      November 1–December 31, 1965   87

Chapter Three: New Jersey
      January 1966   91

Chapter Four: Operation Pipeline
      January 1966   95

Chapter Five: Price Tower
      January 1966   100

Chapter Six: The Special Grand Jury
      January–May 1966   104

Chapter Seven: The Visits
      June 1966   111

Chapter Eight: The Best Lawyers in America
      July 1966–February 1967   115

Chapter Nine: Motions and Riots
      February 1967–November 1968   119

Chapter Ten: Voir Dire
      November 13–14, 1968   126

Chapter Eleven: The Opening Argument
      November 19, 1968   135

Chapter Twelve: "That Was Very Good"
      November 19, 1968   139

Chapter Thirteen: Simon Hirsch Rifkind
      November 1968   141

Chapter Fourteen: "The Dirty Bastards are Shaking us Down"
      November–December 1968   147

Chapter Fifteen: "The Meat of the Coconut"
      December 1968   153

Chapter Sixteen: "I Swear Before My God"
December 1968   157

Chapter Seventeen: Final Argument
January 1969   162

Chapter Eighteen: "Political Money Is Cash Money"
January 1969   168

Chapter Nineteen: The Thing We Have to Fear
January 1969   171

Chapter Twenty: Verdict
January 23, 1969   177

Chapter Twenty-One: Dead Man's Testimony
January 23–April 15, 1969   182

Chapter Twenty-Two: Mugs, Jurors, and Openings
April 15–18, 1969   186

Chapter Twenty-Three: "Déjà Vu All Over Again"
April 17–18, 1969   192

Chapter Twenty-Four: A Dead Man Testifies
April 18–May 28, 1969   194

Chapter Twenty-Five: "You Were Out with a Blonde"
April 22–May 28, 1969   199

Chapter Twenty-Six: The Most Important Witness
May 28, 1969   202

Chapter Twenty-Seven: A Union Man
May 29, 1969   204

Chapter Twenty-Eight: *The Miss Mitzi*
May 30–June 5, 1969   207

Chapter Twenty-Nine: Verdict
June 5–7, 1969   213

Chapter Thirty: "No One May Pay a Public Official"—
Simon Hirsch Rifkind
June 9–27, 1969   216

BOOK III: BATMAN AND ROBIN—THE FULCRUM

Chapter One: Jersey Boys
June 27–August 14, 1969   223

TABLE OF CONTENTS

Chapter Two: Henry and Me
August 14–21, 1969   231

Chapter Three: A Letter from the Grave
August 22–September 2, 1969   235

Chapter Four: "Hughie Gave Us the City"
August 28–September 2, 1969   239

Chapter Five: "A Stench in the Nostrils"
September 2, 1969   241

Chapter Six: Stepping on Toes
September 3–December 3, 1969   245

Chapter Seven: "Let's Go"
December 4–5, 1969   253

Chapter Eight: "The Biggest Secret"
December 5–7, 1969   257

Chapter Nine: "An Efficient and Effective Government"
December 7–17, 1969   259

Chapter Ten: Gerald Martin Zelmanowitz
December 17, 1969–January 5, 1970   264

Chapter Eleven: Trials and Tapes
January 5–6, 1970   267

Chapter Twelve: A Beating and a Stipulation
January 7, 1970   270

Chapter Thirteen: Trial Within and Without
January 8–28, 1970   273

Chapter Fourteen: Confrontation, In Court and at the Bar
January 1970   275

Chapter Fifteen: The Don
January 1970   280

Chapter Sixteen: "Even the Nice People"
January 29–February 10, 1970   282

Chapter Seventeen: "A Frame Up All the Way"
February 10–March 5, 1970   288

Chapter Eighteen: "We'll All Have to Stay Home"
March 4–May 12, 1970   291

Chapter Nineteen: "The Kind of Thing Americans Don't Like"
    May 12–June 1, 1970   295

Chapter Twenty: "A Reign of Terror—Like the French Revolution"
    June 2–9, 1970   298

Chapter Twenty-One: Hero and Heroine
    June 8–16, 1970   302

Chapter Twenty-Two: "The Spaghetti Is On"
    June 16–July 1, 1970   305

Chapter Twenty-Three: "You May Sit ... Mr. Guilty"
    July 1–22, 1970   310

Chapter Twenty-Four: "For the Greater Good"
    July 23–August 31, 1970   313

Chapter Twenty-Five: "No Ordinary Crimes"
    July 27–September 22, 1970   315

Chapter Twenty-Six: "That Great Jewish Lawyer"
    September 22–October 29, 1970   320

Chapter Twenty-Seven: "Let Me Finish"
    October 30–November 1970   327

Chapter Twenty-Eight: "The President Is Entitled to the
    Lawyer of His Choice"
    November 4–16, 1970   331

Chapter Twenty-Nine: The Commission
    November 16–December 31, 1970   334

Chapter Thirty: Acting U.S. Attorney
    January 1–31, 1971   339

BOOK IV: THE LEVER

Chapter One: United States Attorney
    February 1–19, 1971   345

Chapter Two: Washington, Trenton, and Paris
    February 19–March 31, 1971   351

Chapter Three: "An X Will Be Fine"
    March 31–May 17, 1971   357

TABLE OF CONTENTS

Chapter Four: "A Way of Life"
May 17, 1971   362

Chapter Five: Trashcans and Florida Bank Accounts
May 17–31, 1971   364

Chapter Six: The Boss Is Out
May 31–June 22, 1971   373

Chapter Seven: "Quite a Saver. Quite a Housewife."
June 22–July 3, 1971   375

Chapter Eight: He Built the Garden State Parkway
July 3–4, 1971   383

Chapter Nine: Heroes
July 3–4, 1971   385

Chapter Ten: "Do You Want Me in This Job?"
July 5, 1971   387

Chapter Eleven: "You Have Eighteen Months"
July 7–August 18, 1971   390

Chapter Twelve: South Jersey Republicans and Lefties
August 18–September 1971   395

Chapter Thirteen: "Still Want the Job?"
September 1971   398

Chapter Fourteen: Fiat Justitia Ruat Caelum
September 15–28, 1971   400

Chapter Fifteen: The Jersey Shore
October 1–November 2, 1971   403

Chapter Sixteen: Jersey City; Atlantic City; Paris, France
November 2–15, 1971   406

Chapter Seventeen: Come and Stand Trial
November 15–December 3, 1971   411

BOOK V: A PLACE TO STAND

Chapter One: Full Salary
December 3, 1971   417

Chapter Two: Newsmaker
December 3, 1971–January 15, 1972   419

Chapter Three: "Foaming at the Mouth"
January 15–March 27, 1972   424

Chapter Four: "Why that's Bullshit, Mr. Gallagher."
"Try to Prove it, Mr. Stern."
March 27–April 14, 1972   428

Chapter Five: Under Attack
April 11–21, 1972   432

Chapter Six: "I'll Have to Investigate"
April 21–26, 1972   438

Chapter Seven: A Nation of Men as Well as Laws
May 1972   440

Chapter Eight: A Stench Lingers
May 2–23, 1972   448

Chapter Nine: A Matter of Privilege
May 23–July 1, 1972   455

Chapter Ten: "Sealed with a Kiss"
July 1–August 1, 1972   459

Chapter Eleven: Ghosts
August 1–November 9, 1972   462

Chapter Twelve: Looking Ahead
September 1–November 9, 1972   466

Chapter Thirteen: A Private Inquiry and a Christmas Gift
November 9–December 1972   470

Chapter Fourteen: "Mr. Stern and his Staff Merit Cooperation"
January 1–9, 1973   475

Chapter Fifteen: "We Will Summon the Wind"
January 10–February 28, 1973   478

Chapter Sixteen: Off to the Races
March 1–20, 1973   484

Chapter Seventeen: "We are Going to Tell the Truth"
March 20–April 1973   487

TABLE OF CONTENTS

Chapter Eighteen: "Don't Tell Me That!"
April–May 15, 1973 — 491

Chapter Nineteen: "Cleansed Climate"
May 15–June 5, 1973 — 493

Chapter Twenty: Watergate and Washington
May 15–June 5, 1973 — 497

Chapter Twenty-One: Law and Order
June 5–30, 1973 — 501

Chapter Twenty-Two: "Something Smells"
July 1–September 1, 1973 — 506

Chapter Twenty-Three: DeCarlo Still Speaks
September 1–October 22, 1973 — 512

Chapter Twenty-Four: The Flaming Pen
October 22–31, 1973 — 516

Chapter Twenty-Five: I Want You to Be Attorney General
October 31–December 7, 1973 — 519

Chapter Twenty-Six: A Promise
December 7, 1973–January 18, 1974 — 522

Afterword — 527
End Notes — 531
Acknowledgements — 537
Index — 538

How Did It Come to This?
February 1, 1971

"Give me a long enough lever, a fulcrum, and a place to stand, and I shall move the world."

—*Archimedes*

"**T**HIS IS A great day in your life," friends and relatives said as they surrounded me the morning after the court appointed me United States Attorney for the District of New Jersey. Yet here I am, hiding in my New York apartment, smoking cigarette after cigarette, enveloped in a cloud of smoke, shaking with apprehension. Sure, I bought a house in New Jersey a couple of months ago, but I never lived in the state until then. Why am I afraid? Because I think this job is too much for me. I became an assistant district attorney in New York right out of law school, nine years ago to the very day. Now here I am at thirty-four, the chief federal prosecutor for the entire state, and I'm not even admitted to the practice of law in New Jersey. I have forty assistant U.S. Attorneys and offices in Camden, Trenton, and Newark. I have promised to clean up this most corrupt of all of the states, and to do it with these forty kids—every one younger than I am.

The organized bar opposes me. The local politicians hate me. And the Nixon Department of Justice in Washington D.C. is moving heaven and earth to get rid of me. My only supporter is an aging United States senator, and he can't stop the president from firing me. All he can do is prevent Nixon from appointing anyone else.

In a few months my "crusade" begins: I am to try the most important criminal case in the country. My adversaries, the leading criminal lawyers in the state, represent the eight men who rule Hudson County, which includes Jersey City, Hoboken, Bayonne, and West New York. These men command the longest-standing and most corrupt political organization in the United States. A "way of life" they call it. They take ten percent from each public contract made by the cities and the county itself. They take three percent from the wages of municipal workers, who must kickback to keep their jobs. From the time of Boss Frank Hague to their present leader Boss John V. Kenny, for sixty years, democratic presidents genuflected before these men and their fore-bears, seeking political support, including votes from graves in Hudson County. Even the Mafia bows before these men, unlike Newark where the mighty mob ruled the politicians.

If I lose this case there is no place for me to go, certainly not in New Jersey. And I cannot go back where I started, the district attorney's office in New York. I burned those bridges five years ago.

I can only go forward. I smoke my last cigarette, lean on the sink to splash water on my face, then hurry out to head back to my Newark office before I am seriously missed.

As I point my car toward New Jersey, I cannot help asking, how did it come to this?

BOOK I
FOR THE PEOPLE

Chapter One

The Complaint Bureau
February–December 1962

AFTER THEY SWEAR you in as an ADA—assistant district attorney— they give you a badge a few weeks later with your name on it. It looks just like a detective shield, only it isn't. It is not official, and it entitles you to nothing. But it's good for showing friends, particularly girls.

A few months into my new job I'm riding on the subway, traveling from the courthouse to my walkup apartment in a brownstone on West 76th Street, when the train stops at 42nd Street. The doors open. I am right next to a woman standing with her bag over her arm. She is holding onto a pole near the open door. Quick as a flash, a guy jumps into the car, flips her bag open and takes her wallet out. He does it so fast she doesn't know it happened. He jumps back onto the platform.

Without thinking, I leap onto the platform just as the doors close, and follow him down the platform. The guy hustles to the stairs, which will take him up to the street.

He is chugging along. Fast walking. I keep following and looking— and praying—for a cop. This guy is on his way to the street level and I'm still following him, trying to look like I'm not. Still no cop. He hits the street, with me trailing. He takes out the lady's wallet from his pocket, goes through it, takes the cash, and I see him looking around for a trash can to dump the wallet. When he finds one there will be no evidence to corroborate that he stole anything. That is, if I ever do find such a thing as a policeman in Times Square, which has plenty of small shops selling "dirty" pictures, but no cops.

I'm trying to figure what to do, when I see that he has spied a trash can across another street and he starts heading for it. We are now two blocks away from the scene of his underground crime and I'm about to give it all up, when I remember my badge.

I run at him, grab him by the arm, show him the badge, and—trying to look like a cop—tell him he is under arrest. I hope he doesn't notice that the badge says "Stern," not "Detective." I quickly put the shield away and seize the woman's wallet from his hand. Now I have him with one hand and the wallet in the other, and still no cop. I'm plenty scared, but to my surprise he is docile, like he was expecting it, or has been there many times before.

Finally I see a patrolman. I walk the guy over, hand him to the cop, and say, "Officer, this is a DC (6)," which is code for a pickpocket, and give the cop the lady's wallet. I know this because one of my principal jobs as a new ADA is trying offenses like pickpocketing, smoking in the subway, bookmaking, and romances between men in public toilets. But on this case I am the complainant, not the ADA. That is not so good for the thief. He pleads guilty in that very court.

The next day there is a brief story in the paper about the incident, which quickly makes the rounds in the Complaint Bureau where I work, and I am a celebrity for a few hours. I never hear from the victim, but I do get a letter from somebody who had been pickpocketed on a subway and wrote that she wished I had been there at that time. I also get chewed out by David S. Worgan, the executive assistant district attorney to Frank S. Hogan—the DA—who told me not to do that sort of thing again. So that is the last time I pull my badge until the day Malcolm X is assassinated—but that comes much later.

Facing Worgan is humbling. He has been a member of the office since 1938. That means he was part of the original group headed by the legendary Thomas E. Dewey, the biggest racket buster in New York history. After hitting the mob, including Lucky Luciano and the corrupt pols, Dewey was elected DA of New York County—that's Manhattan—in 1937, then governor. He then parlayed it all into two presidential nominations, the first against Franklin Delano Roosevelt in 1944, and the second against Harry S. Truman in 1948. On his way out of the DA's office to the governorship of New York in 1941, Dewey pushed Frank Hogan into his spot.

Now, 21 years later, not only Hogan but also other Dewey men are still there.

"Let me tell you," Worgan says, "assistant district attorneys are not vigilantes. We don't arrest people. We can and do order the police to make arrests, but we do not make them ourselves."

"I understand," I say. What I don't say is that I was not going to permit that bozo to commit a crime under my nose. And I'd do it again. But I just nod, which he takes for a yes.

"Good," he says, nodding towards the door.

I get out quickly, but as I glance back I see he is grinning, so I figure it is all right. I go back to my job in the Complaint Bureau.

****

The Complaint Bureau is where all new ADAs start. We begin by taking complainants, often off the street. And you never know what will walk in cold from the streets of New York.

Joe Stone, the ADA in charge of the bureau, another Dewey original, greets and breaks in new assistants. You get the lecture about how you are going to hear about "swindles."

"There's no such a crime as a swindle," he waves his finger at me, in his office for the first time. "We prosecute larceny, we prosecute fraud," he intones, "but when they say they have been swindled, out they go." And he lays out how the bureau works.

Sometimes complainants have an appointment, sometimes not. Sometimes they have no place else to go. They complain about neighbors, even radio waves coming through the walls. But occasionally you get a real one, he explains.

Stone makes it clear that everyone, nuts or not, gets a courteous hearing. That means you sit, you listen, and then you try to ease them out. If you have a real problem, you call upstairs to the DA's office squad of detectives and you ask for assistance from one of those old hands who are capable of ending problems gently, but efficiently. And if you have a meritorious complaint, you get one of the detectives assigned.

Just a few weeks into the job, sitting in my office, the telephone rings.

"Stern," I answer.

"I'm Dr. Hugh Davidson."

"Yes, Doctor, what can I do for you?"

"I need to see you as soon as possible," he says, in a tight voice. Like the lips are moving but the vocal cords are kind of frozen.

I can't resist asking what the trouble is. He tells me he's married to a famous opera singer at the New York City Metropolitan Opera, who he thinks is being ripped off. At least he didn't say "swindled." So I ask him how. "Well, there is this gentleman named Charles Kingsley," he tells me, "who claims to be the heir to a two hundred million dollar fortune." My ears perk up, but so does my disbelief.

This Kingsley, the husband reports, is an opera lover who has promised the good doctor and his opera star wife $105,000 each—only they each have to give him $3,200 for the gift tax first.

I can't believe this Dr. Davidson is serious. I ask him if they gave this Kingsley the money. Oh yes, says he. And by the way, he says, Kingsley did the same thing with another "opera star."

Now I have my doubts about this Dr. Davidson. What kind of nut would believe such bullshit? And not just one, but two opera stars? He sounds like one of Joe Stone's promised crazies. What can I do? I make the appointment. I tell him to bring the two "stars" with him. I ask what their names are. "My wife's name is Nell Rankin," he says. The other singer is Margherita Roberti. I set the appointment for later in the day. I also call the Met and ask about Rankin and Roberti—if there are any such people. The ladies are not only for real, I'm told, but while Roberti's just started with the Met, Rankin is one of their leading singers—a mezzo-soprano who usually plays the lead in *Carmen*. I am excited and can't wait for their arrival. I even start sprucing up the office in anticipation. These are my first celebrities. I also call the DA's office squad and ask for detectives to be assigned to sit in on the interview.

In a few hours the divas show up with Rankin's husband, and I have two of the largest detectives of the DA's office squad—Henry Cronin and Joe Feeley—not only waiting, but filling half my small office. Soon I have five people stuffed around my desk/conference table, which makes for close quarters.

We go over their story. Kingsley, apparently ensconced in the social world of the opera, met Rankin first, then Roberti through her.

Pretty soon they were all hanging out together, often being driven in Kingsley's chauffeured limousine, with him pointing out various buildings that he claimed to own as they drove by them on their Manhattan jaunts. Then came the bite. Everybody gets $105,000 each. How he got to that amount is confusing—but what is clear is that everybody had to write him a check for his or her gift taxes. Rankin wrote the check, but her husband explains that he stopped payment on the way to the DA's office. By the way, he says, Kingsley just announced that he is leaving for his ranch in Brazil tomorrow.

Everyone goes quiet. The complainants are looking at me. Worse, the two senior detectives are too. What am I supposed to do now? Arrest Kingsley? What if this guy really is a multi-millionaire? I see the detectives looking back and forth at me, and then at each other, and Cronin asks Davidson to repeat the part about a ticket to Brazil. I finally get the clue and tell the detectives to go to Kingsley's hotel and invite him to my office. I figure that there is nothing to lose there: If Kingsley is for real, I'm just checking stuff out; if he isn't, I will lock him up. I tell the detectives to be sure to be polite. They nod, with their most serious faces on.

In an hour they are at Kingsley's hotel. The two giants arrest him in the lobby and drag him out to the street with him screaming and crying, his hands cuffed behind his back. By the time they get him down to the office, he has blabbered out a full confession, and I breathe a great sigh of relief.

****

On the days we are not catching complaints upstairs in the office, we are in court. And that is some court.

The organizational plan of the DA's office is quite clever. New ADAs catch complaints and lead investigations, if the complaint is worthy of it, using New York City detectives from the DA's office squad. The other part of the job is to try offenses in the magistrate court, where we cut our trial teeth, until ready to move up. The next step is the Indictment Bureau, then Special Sessions Bureau to try misdemeanors, and then, if we are lucky, on to try felonies in the Supreme Court Bureau. The idea is that you get better and better at trial work by doing it in volume, in progressively more serious courts. There is no formal training. You learn from your mistakes.

What are these offenses in the magistrate court? Along with smoking in the subways, pickpocketing, and men soliciting each other in public toilets—usually a cop claiming to be solicited—the vast majority of these prosecutions are for gambling, in the form of either bookmaking or numbers running.

We spend a lot of time and a lot of the public's money going after the various runners operating in the gambling syndicates. We view these offenses as serious violations, to the amusement of the cadre of defense lawyers, who are often teamed with bail bondsmen, providing a full line of services to various "illegal" gambling organizations.

The defense attorneys, typically older men who have been at it for years, kid us about how silly it is to prosecute people as criminals for providing a service that the public wants. It is wrong to use the criminal laws as expressions of false piety and insincere morality, they say, based on the made-up claim that gambling activity is harmful to society.

Most ADAs reject that argument. At least I do, at first. I buy into the idea that I am protecting society by vigorously prosecuting gamblers. Perhaps I should have remembered my Uncle Benny and his encounter with the blue laws, way back in the 1940s.

When I was a little boy, my Uncle Benny was a barber. He was in his sixties, a little guy who wore a beard and a yarmulke, because Uncle Benny was a big-time Orthodox Jew. He followed all the rules. His problem was that his faith forbade him from working on Saturday. His next problem was that the laws of New York forbade him from opening his barbershop on Sundays because in the view of the majority of the voters, it was immoral to allow stores to open on the Lord's Day, which for them was Sunday. They were so serious about it that they not only personally refrained, they made it an offense for anyone else to work in a store on Sunday. Oh, they found a reason to justify the prohibition without saying out loud that working was immoral. Instead, they said they were protecting the quiet enjoyment of *their* day of rest. But Uncle Benny could not support his wife and nine children working just five days a week. On top of it his shop was located directly across from the Pitt Street police stationhouse. However, he found a way to solve all his problems. He snuck into his shop on Sundays.

I loved to go there for a haircut. Not only was it free, but Uncle Benny would also give me a quarter for each haircut. The role reversal amused me, even as a kid. But what I really loved, if I was there early, would be to see my Uncle Benny sneaking into his shop, making sure all the window shades were down so that the cops would be shielded from his illegal activities of haircutting and shaving on Sunday.

It did not take me long to figure out that with all these comings and goings every Sunday, the cops across the street would have had to be deaf, dumb and blind not to know what was going on. And yet these cops—undoubtedly mostly Irish and Italian Catholics—never bothered Uncle Benny. Even as a kid, I figured out that he knew they knew, and his window shade activities were designed to make it possible for them to let a guy who wasn't hurting anyone practice his trade and keep to his faith, law or no law. It was a humane arrangement.

But as an ADA, I prosecute the violations the cops bring to me. It takes me a while to figure out that maybe it is not such a good idea to always strictly enforce all the laws; that our society relies on prosecutors to have enough common sense to know when to look away or at least to overlook. This is dangerous talk, I know, raising fear of anarchy, but I have come to learn that prosecutorial discretion enables a system to work that would otherwise be broken by its own weight. You just have to know when to do that sort of thing. And when you must not.

Gambling, we are told, is a vice harmful to society and we can stamp it out by vigorous prosecutions. Never mind that houses of worship are openly running lotteries and sponsoring gambling nights. Never mind that the newspapers publish not merely the results of the horse races at the tracks, where people can bet at will, but also the details of the pari-mutuel betting, which horse paid what, enabling bookmakers to pay off horse bets and policy banks—that is numbers organizations—to select winning lottery numbers. We even see the corruption of law enforcement by senseless prohibitions of conduct that the public wants, but is reluctant to legalize. We do not understand that because some policemen see no point to enforcing these gambling laws, they are willing to corruptly refrain from enforcing them. Unfortunately, the gates are then lowered, and the mob owns those cops.

In all fairness, novice ADAs can hardly do other than prosecute, given an office's commitment to enforcing laws against gambling, homosexuality, and, as I soon discover, "obscenity."

****

On the days I'm not in the office catching complaints, I'm in one of these tiny magistrate courtrooms trying six, eight, sometimes more cases a day. Only trouble is that I am terrible at it. At least in the beginning.

The court itself runs on an assembly line basis. Cops wait in the hall for their turn. And when it comes up, the cop hands me the complaint he has previously filed as we stand in the hallway.

Bzz, bzz, bzz, he whispers in my ear, giving me the essence of the case in a few sentences. I *bzz, bzz, bzz* back a question or two. In five or ten minutes we are ready for trial. In these cases, there is often just one witness: a vice squad cop.

However, the proceedings themselves are not informal. Small though the quarters are, there is a real judge in a robe. I get to say, "Herbert J. Stern for the People," which of course is short for "The People of the State of New York." The oath the witness takes is real, and all the rules of evidence and all the constitutional rights apply. The problem is that I don't know anything about how rules and rights apply in practice. All I have is theory.

The University of Chicago Law School, from where I graduated a half dozen months before, is a great law school. Like other great ones—Harvard, Yale, Virginia, and so forth—it taught me how to think about stuff, but not how to actually do any of it. For instance, I studied the concept of wills, but never saw an actual will. The other classes were more of the same: I never saw a search warrant in Criminal Law. I never learned how to avoid leading questions on direct examination, or how to use them on cross-examination, in a class called Evidence. I took and passed the bar exam without knowing or being tested on any practical skills. Even that exam I could not have passed without going to a special bar review course.

So I went to a great law school, and I did come out of it with real analytical skills, and the bar exam undoubtedly did weed out some who needed weeding, but none of that helps me in my early appearances in court. Standing alone, I am helpless in the face of experienced adversaries. They are slaughtering me with objections. So two minutes after I say "Herbert J. Stern for the People" for the first time, "the People" are in deep trouble while I stumble around the courtroom. These miserable performances go on for several weeks.

I just cannot do anything right. I do not even know how to mark a physical exhibit into evidence. My questions are often objected to successfully.

I'm beside myself. I don't know enough to know what I am doing wrong. After a few days of this, I get an idea. I ask the judge. And I get lucky. The one I pick to ask, Judge T. Vincent Quinn, is an old-school gentleman who has been a congressman and also the district attorney for Queens County and even a high-ranking member in Washington's Justice Department. He sees a young kid getting pushed around. He's seen it before and doesn't like it.

He peers over his horned-rimmed glasses. "Try, 'Did there come a time that you saw this defendant?'" he suggests. "Or" he adds, correcting himself "when, if at all, did you see the defendant?"

It goes on for about two weeks, Judge Quinn and his colleague, Judge Frances X. O'Brien, shepherding me through my first few dozen trials. If they hadn't done it, I would never have made it. My despair is over; now I am trying them like a pro, convicting everyone—which once you know your way around is not difficult, what with ring-wise cops as witnesses. That is, unless for some reason a cop doesn't want a conviction in a particular case. It's when I start beating up on the defense lawyers that they start trying to persuade me to lighten up. "Gambling cases are nonsense," they tell me. I don't listen, of course, because now I'm out for blood. It's not just for truth, justice, and the American way. I am out to win for me.

Then I get careless. After months of complaint bureau interviews and stints in the magistrate courts, the routine is reflexive. I'm spending less time in the hall preparing the cop. Pretty soon I'm not even reading the written complaint signed by the cop, which in that court is the formal charge, like an indictment by a grand jury in the more serious felony cases. I am just doing the *bzz, bzz, bzz* in the hall and up on the stand goes the cop. And then a case goes down the drain because of a violation of the Fourth Amendment—the prohibition against unreasonable searches and seizures—and the exclusionary rule imposed for its violation. It happens because I didn't read the court papers. I didn't see it coming.

I'm spending the day on loan upstairs in Special Sessions, handling a minor narcotics charge, possession of a small amount of heroin. Our courts are clogged with these prosecutions of small-time addicts caught with tiny amounts of heroin. In this case, there had been an earlier proceeding in which the defendant challenged the search that was made after his arrest. But he lost. The heroin has not been suppressed. It will come into evidence. Nothing to worry about. No need to read the earlier court papers on the suppression hearing. That's over. I do the *bzz, bzz, bzz* in the hall and put the narcotics cop on the stand. It's a one-witness case.

The cop begins with the arrest of the defendant in the street—no mention of pre-arrest events since this was all covered in the previous suppression proceedings, which another ADA handled a week earlier. After the arrest, the cop searched the defendant and found a needle, a cooker, which is a small bottle-cap used to cook up the dope, and a few grains of heroin in his pocket. That's all the cop told me in the hall. And that's all I need from him on the stand. I mark all of it for identification and then into evidence. No objection.

Before turning the witness over for cross, I ask the legal aid lawyer defending the case whether he will stipulate that the stuff in the pocket is heroin, or whether he wants me to put it in the lab report. He waives the need of the formality. "I'll stipulate," he says, only half out of his chair.

"Anything else," says the bored judge, who has already heard nearly a dozen cases including pleas and trials shepherded by a couple of different ADAs.

"No, Your Honor," I say.

My adversary rises and cross-examines. "You say you approached the defendant."

"Yes."

"And you arrested him in the street?"

"Yes."

"And after you arrested him, you searched him?"

"Yes."

"And you say that in my client's pocket you found this heroin," pointing to the exhibits on the table.

"That's right."

"Well, tell us, Officer, how deep in the defendant's pocket the heroin was when you put your hand in his pocket?"

"I object," I am on my feet. "This is outrageous," I am fuming. "Counsel is just badgering and ridiculing the witness, he should . . ."

I stammer to a stop because the cop has his hand up, palm facing me. The universal stop signal. It's all right. I can handle this, he seems to be saying, as he grins at me. Then, turning a smirk on to the lawyer, he says, "It was as deep in the pocket as the pocket went." Great, fabulous answer, I think, as I finish sitting back down.

But my adversary is not embarrassed. He goes to his file and takes out the original complaint signed by the cop. Holding it in his hand, he reads out how the cop swore that he spotted the defendant, and what the defendant was doing in some hand-to-hand transaction at the street corner, and then he reads, "As I approached the defendant he threw an object to the ground. I kept the object in continuous view until I retrieved it from the pavement and found that it contained a white powder, which I believed based on my experience to contain heroin." It is on that basis the cop swore he arrested the defendant with probable cause, searched him and found the rest of the stuff in his pocket.

The stillness in the courtroom is deafening. Everyone knows what is coming next, including me. I begin to rise to my feet. Can I help the cop? There is nothing I can do, so I collapse back into my chair. The legal aid lawyer, whose attention has been diverted to me momentarily, turns back to face the cop in the witness chair.

"Well, Officer," the cross-examiner bends forward and points both hands at the man in the witness chair as he delivers the blow, "which is it? Did you find the narcotics in my client's pocket or did he throw it to the ground as you approached him?"

Everyone in the courtroom is now looking at the cop. I am as well. I'm fascinated.

The cop pauses. He has to choose his perjury. "It was in his pocket," he says. The answer is spoken softly, with no more grins or smirks.

The defense attorney gives him a withering look, and then turns to me. "Your witness," he smiles. And I'm on the hook. At least I have the brains to say, "No questions," and get the cop off the stand as quick as I can.

The legal aid lawyer does not call the defendant to the stand. He offers no evidence. He simply moves for an acquittal. I am disgusted and torn, trapped between a clearly lying cop and an equally clearly guilty drug dealer. I try to find some words to resolve the issue. The defendant had the drugs, I tell the judge. Under either version of the arrest the defendant is guilty. Why let him off? The judge tosses the case, refusing to convict based on anything that cop has to say.

I'm sore at losing the case, but also sore at the defendant's walking out free. I'm livid at the cop. To me he is worse than the pickpocket that I arrested. So I go to David Worgan, the executive assistant DA, and he tells me I can report the cop if I want to. And I do want to. I call the officer in charge of the cop's command and make a formal complaint. I realize that it's probably fruitless, but I think the cop needs to be punished. I report him because I'd feel dirty if I did nothing.

That is my first experience with the dilemmas posed by the Exclusionary Rule. If you exclude the evidence, the criminal goes free, and the cop is not punished for the violation of privacy—that is, if he hasn't lied to avoid the suppression, in which case there is a conviction and he is promoted. If you allow the evidence to come in, the criminal is convicted, the policeman gets promoted, and the cops are openly incentivized to more Fourth Amendment violations. All in all, "it's a puzzlement."

Chapter Two

The Indictment Bureau
1962–1963

SEVEN MONTHS INTO my service I am promoted to the Indictment Bureau. I join half a dozen of my colleagues in processing the thousands of prosecutions that bubble up from courts where the defendants have been arraigned for purposes of bail, and the appointment of counsel if they do not have lawyers.

Some of the arrests have already been reduced. These we do not see. But the ones we get, we have to evaluate. Should the case remain a felony, or be reduced to a misdemeanor? The grand jury can reduce a felony arrest to a misdemeanor, and will if we tell it to. The grand jurors do what they are told. Are there exceptions? I've never seen a grand jury refuse a prosecutor's request to indict, or to dismiss, but I guess it's possible.

I do have one close call. In addition to presenting cases where there has already been an arrest, we are assigned some grand jury investigations. Not rackets, or heavy fraud, and certainly not a political corruption investigation. These are reserved for the senior bureaus. But we do have some lesser ones. I am assigned the "baby selling" investigation.

The adoption process in New York in 1962 is complicated and anything but swift. The would-be parents face not only the problem of qualifying to the satisfaction of the authorities, but also of finding the kind of baby that they want to adopt. As in other matters where people want to side-step rules or avoid the queue, couples are willing to pay for the babies. By the same token, some unscrupulous lawyers—and doctors—are willing to provide babies from local or even foreign sources, for a fee. And the hopeful parents are more than happy to pay for the child that they have longed for.

From our office's point of view, of course, this is a highly dangerous practice, for both the child and for the new parents. There is, after all, a point to the annoying red tape in place to supervise the process so that suitable parents receive healthy children whose natural parents are also protected. It is routine for our office to maintain ongoing investigations into "baby selling rings," and I am the ADA assigned to work on them with Detective Theresa Heath of the office squad. She brings the witnesses, mostly adoptive parents, and I present them to the grand jury where they testify against the doctor or the lawyer or both, as the case may be. These people don't want to testify, of course. They are petrified that they will lose the baby.

So I have one mother in the grand jury. It's going okay; she's giving me what I need. Then she suddenly stops testifying. She begins to shudder and shake. In a moment she's on her feet, her hands clasped in front of her in prayer, addressing the grand jurors, "Please don't take my baby," she begs, sobbing uncontrollably. "Don't take my baby," she is pleading over and over again. Tears are running down her cheeks, which she does not wipe because her hands remain steepled in prayer. I glance around the room and see that some of the jurors are also starting to cry. And some of them are looking daggers at me, like I'm responsible for taking her baby.

The foreman beckons me out of the jury room, into the waiting room, and says, "Mr. Stern, you're not going to take away her child, are you?" It's not said as a question. It's a command. I do not want to do anything of the kind. So I excuse myself and grab Theresa, who is at the other end of the waiting room. "No," she tells me. "They never take the child away if the parents cooperate." Back I go to calm everyone down. And that's as close as I ever get to having trouble with a grand jury.

In the Indictment Bureau we sift through the cases as they come in. Should they stay felonies? If so, what counts? How many counts? We present the evidence, just enough to make out a prima facie case—enough to withstand a motion to dismiss the indictment—but we do not present more than we have to. In New York the defense attorney can often obtain the grand jury testimony, and we don't want to provide pretrial previews of the case that our senior colleagues in the Supreme Court Bureau will be trying after the indictment we draw is handed up by the foreman of the grand jury. The jury votes without even seeing the written indictment. We draw it up *after* the vote, and present it to the court when we are ready.

It's not the most exciting work in the office, presenting evidence with no adversary present, and drafting indictments that conform to the legal requirements, often using language that went out of style a couple of hundred years earlier.

Although I am alone in the grand jury room with the jurors and the witness—one witness at a time because only the witness, the DA, the stenographer and the jurors can be present—I treat every presentation as though there's an adversary present, able to make objections. I do this to keep myself sharp, in training for the courtroom, because I can't wait to get out of indictments and back to the courtroom.

The bureau does have its moments. The Organized Crime Squad of the police locks up Dominick Montemarano, but they have no case. Not even probable cause. The cops tell me he is a mob killer in the Columbo family. So they bust him and they seize his car. They also tell me that the case has to be dismissed. They want the grand jury to do it so it does not happen in public in the trial court. Grand juries don't have to give reasons for dismissing cases. Prosecutors do. For the DA, the grand jury can be a shield as well as a sword. I tell the grand jurors what to do and, of course, they do it. Montemarano is "no billed," which is grand jury jargon for "case dismissed." The cops also tell me that Montemarano will be coming around my office to ask me for a slip so he can get his car released from the police property clerk. They tell me to send him over to see them. This I am not crazy about.

Next day, Montemarano shows up in my little office in the Indictment Bureau, and he and I are alone together. I don't like it, but am reluctant to call for help. He wants the form to get his car. I tell him what I've been told to tell him. Go see the arresting officers first. He does not like that, and his face gets red.

"Are you the guy who presented my case to the jury?" he leans forward with both fists on my desk.

"Yes, yes," I stammer.

"No wonder they threw my case out!" he snarls and slams the door shut on the way out.

A few weeks later I get promoted.

Chapter Three

The Criminal Court Bureau
1963

THIS SECOND PROMOTION gets me out of the grand jury routine and into the old Special Sessions—trying cases before one judge, and sometimes three judges. Only it's not called Special Sessions anymore. As I arrive, it becomes the Criminal Court of the City of New York, so I am in the Criminal Court Bureau.

We get all the misdemeanor cases. It's a very busy place, busier than the magistrate court. All kinds of cases are arraigned and set for trial. But they are usually adjourned; because someone is not ready; because the cop is not there; or because a private counsel says he is missing a witness named "Mr. Green." That's code that the lawyer has not been paid yet. The judges will almost always grant the adjournment because they know that the defense lawyer must collect his fee before trial, or he never will. Ultimately, if there is no disposition, which is the court jargon for a plea bargain, the case will be tried. There are lots of dispositions. There have to be. It is simply impossible to try all of the cases.

Many of them are drug cases, of course. We are the district attorney's office for New York County—that means just Manhattan. There's something special about Manhattan. It's varied. It has Harlem and Wall Street. There are plenty of robberies, drugs, homicides, and sophisticated financial crimes. It also has 42nd Street with the porn shops I found myself in front of when I nabbed the pickpocket. And those cases, "obscenity" cases, go to the Criminal Court Bureau, along with small narcotics cases and minor versions of the other kinds of crimes, small larcenies, minor assaults, that kind of thing. Not homicides, of course. There are no minor homicides.

The ADAs in the Criminal Court Bureau are assigned to "trial parts." A trial part is a courtroom with an assigned judge. Some parts have just one judge. Some are three-judge courts, available if a defendant requests one. These courts are more formal than the old magistrate court, but not much more. Their crowded dockets preclude formality and often even dignity. But I do get more serious cases to try, and that means getting closer to the Supreme Court Trial Bureau, which is where most of the up-and-coming ADAs want to wind up trying cases before juries. In the meantime, I am perfecting my trade.

I have one distraction: My bureau chief, Richard H. Kuh, has assigned me to be in charge of all the pornography prosecutions in the office, and that means not only all the prosecutions, but also all the investigations of pornography. I am still trying the normal stuff; it is just that I have this sideline. It's important because DA Hogan, a devout Catholic and a pal of Francis Joseph Cardinal Spellman, the Archbishop of New York, is personally committed to stamping out smut. Hogan has deputized Kuh, who wears the extra hat of administrative assistant DA, and Kuh has assigned me.

When I come up from trying cases, I can hardly get into my office; it's now crammed full of photographs and movie films, the bulk having been seized in raids of Times Square bookstores. Some of the seizures lead to prosecutions. When they do, the most important cases are assigned to the chief judge of the court, John M. Murtagh. He's another devout Catholic. Between him and Hogan, with Kuh as their lord high executioner, and now me as the assistant executioner, we are all doing the work of the Lord. We are going to stamp out smut in Manhattan.

Censors know that they can't get away with imposing what appears to be nothing more than their own morals and ideology on everyone else. It doesn't look good. They have to find some harm, or at least potential harm, in exposure to "dirty" pictures and films to justify their prohibition. So the claim is made that pornography fosters rape, or sexual deviancy. It is nonsense, of course, nothing more than a cover for some people imposing a personal code of conduct on others. Just another form of the blue laws.

What particularly amuses me are my own colleagues. My little office has become a popular spot. Lots of ADAs dropping by, undoubtedly to help stamp out the impurities that are housed there. But before they can stomp, they have to take a look. After all, you cannot fight what you cannot see.

All in all, it is a shoddy business, and I would feel better if I refused to be part of the morals police. But for the few months I have the assignment of enforcing the law against obscenity, I do it in the same spirit of competition as I had earlier with the laws against gambling. I do understand that I am not really protecting society from actual harm. But it's the job. So I do it. Full throttle. And then one day I come face to face with "enough is enough."

When I return from court, two United States postal inspectors are waiting for me in Kuh's office. Now that's a rare event, because we local types don't have much contact with the feds, not even the FBI. The federals have their jurisdiction, led by the United States Attorney for the Southern District of New York, Robert M. Morgenthau; and we have the New York City detectives. As a matter of fact, we and the feds compete. There's no enmity, we are not hitting each other, but there's no love lost either. Nonetheless, two feds are in Kuh's office when I get there.

Kuh tells me the inspectors have just filed a complaint, and he hands it to me. It is several pages long, and very detailed. They have just charged a defendant with obscenity, but not by use of the mails under the federal statute, although that is how they caught him. Instead, they charge him under the New York State obscenity law.

I am reading how this guy is sending letters around trying to arrange for orgies and wife swapping, using his own wife. After intercepting the mail, the postal inspectors got a federal warrant and raided the guy's house, then seized pictures and slides of his wife, naked, performing things, using implements. It's all laid out descriptively in the complaint, although the pictures themselves are not attached.

I am puzzled. I ask myself, why are they here rather than at the Southern District with United States Attorney Morgenthau? The answer is that Morgenthau won't prosecute. The defendant is a famous composer and conductor. The postal inspectors want him prosecuted for his use of the mail to arrange sex parties and transmit dirty pictures, but the United States Attorney refuses. The post office sleuths can't do anything about that, so they go to see Hogan. He is enthusiastic about an obscenity charge under state law. Kuh tells me that we, namely I, are the ones who are going to do it. Before they leave Kuh's office, the inspectors hand over the letters and the pictures and the slides, and finish giving me details, including the name of the defendant's lawyer.

He has a great lawyer, Ephraim London. London has had numerous First Amendment cases before the United States Supreme Court, and won them all. But I know that he can't win this one. The stuff is too raw. The solicitations are too funky. The pictures are very literal, and they show the defendant's own wife performing. If this goes to trial, I am sure that Murtagh will grab it. Even worse, I don't see how the defendant can allow this stuff with his wife to go into an open courtroom. No one can save him from a conviction, I conclude, but maybe I can save his wife and his career. It all depends on what London wants to do, and whether I can implement my plan. But first I have to get London to agree.

We meet at my office, he and I and a younger lawyer about my age, Martin Garbus, who works for London. London is an imposing figure, well over six feet tall, balding, distinguished looking. It's clear that he is the First Amendment intellectual and Garbus is the trial lawyer. From London's point of view, the First Amendment has been violated. He makes a big deal about the fact that the feds wouldn't prosecute, but I tell him that our office will, and Garbus knows that we will, knows that I cannot dismiss the case, given the priorities of the DA. But I tell them that I do want to help prevent their client's destruction over something that should be irrelevant to his music.

What I can do, I tell them, is to arrange for a quiet plea. We could go into a courtroom right at the very end of the day, when no one is there. I tell them that I would prepare the judge, and have the judge agree to waive a pre-sentence report and sentence right then and there. If it all goes well, and I tell them that I'm pretty sure it will, when it's over I will destroy the photos and all the rest, because the case will be closed and the State has no need of the evidence.

They agree. They really have no choice. But they want me to give them back the photos at the end of the case. This, I cannot do. "The Boss," which is what we call Hogan, would have a fit if that stuff were back out there. They know I'm telling them the truth, so it's a deal.

The material will be destroyed, and it will be over. It's the best I can do. As it is, I'm sticking my neck out. If Hogan gets wind of it, I figure I am toast.

I pick the judge carefully; it has to be one with both courage and heart. I know most of them pretty well by now, so that is not a problem. It takes a few days, and it is done. I get it set for the next week and tell London. He says okay.

Then the world caves in. The case is discovered by the press. New York reporters routinely go through the newly filed complaints, looking for stories. Paul Hoffman, the *New York Post* reporter covering the criminal courts, finds the filed complaint. His next stop is my office. He wants background.

Hoffman is a stranger to me. But he has what he needs from the detailed complaint. He even knows what the defendant does for a living. He probably got that from the postal guys. Of course he might have known anyway. He could have recognized the man's name. But I think he was tipped by the feds, who want to crush the musician. In any event, the whole thing is about to unravel.

I decide to take another chance. I tell him about the deal, and the effort to keep the man in his music, and I sense from Hoffman's reaction that he is sympathetic. So I gulp and pop the question. Will he agree not to print the story? That is usually a big no-no, but I ask anyway. To my surprise, he says, "Yes."

Just when I think I have everything under control, a *New York Times* reporter drops by. He, too, has read the complaint, been tipped, or both, but the point is he knows, and I'm back at square one. I don't even know what I'm doing anymore. I am acting more like the defense than the prosecution. Well, in for a penny, in for a pound. I try the same speech on the *Times*' guy. He says okay, too, but he has a price. He knows my office is packed with porn and he says he will accommodate me but he wants to take some stuff home. He doesn't mean this guy's pictures; he just wants to push a shopping cart through my supermarket.

I am so close to bringing this off that I can't bear to see the plan founder on the rocks of a *New York Times* exposé. I know I am not going to give this guy a basket of goodies. I say nothing, just kind of smile. He thinks we have a deal and goes off happy. There is no story.

And pretty soon it's the next week, and Ephraim London and his client show up at the courthouse to take the plea. Unfortunately, he comes without Garbus.

It is the end of the day. The courtroom is totally empty. The judge is ready. I look at the defendant with some curiosity. This is the first I have seen the man. He looks perfectly normal, although I think he must be nuts to have such a hobby. I shrug it off and tell London and his client to go with me right up close to the bench, and I go through the routine of taking a plea. The judge is going along with the program, and there is no hitch until we get to the part where the defendant is to enter a plea in one word, "guilty." Instead, London launches into an oration about the First Amendment and freedom of speech. He is real good at it. He must have made it or something like it many times. But the more he speaks about his client's right to do what he did, the more he is undermining the plea of guilty. I'm getting mad. Worse, the judge who agreed to do the deed is now obviously annoyed. He starts shaking his head in a "no" movement. But London doesn't seem to care. He keeps on going until the judge has had enough and stops him cold, "I don't think I can take this plea." And he can't, not when the defendant's lawyer is proclaiming his client's innocence while purporting to plead him guilty.

As for me, I'm furious. I ask for a brief recess, and the judge grants it. I leave London's client alone with the judge standing right up at the bench. "Stay right here," I tell him. I take London by the arm and lead him out into the empty hall. There, I lose it and scream at him, "You son of a bitch, I've been breaking my back and sticking out my neck to give your client a chance to have a life, me, the prosecutor, and you the defense attorney come in here and screw it up! Now go back in there and shut up before we lose this judge forever."

Large man that he is, he physically recoils. I'm sure no twenty-six-year-old freshman ever talked to him like that. Back we go. The defendant and the judge are where we left them. We start taking the plea all over again. London stays shut up. The judge concludes the plea and immediately imposes an "SS," a suspended sentence. The defendant walks out of the court and back to his life and his music, and that is that. We don't say a word to each other. He has no idea what went into all that just happened. I'm sure that from his point of view he thinks that his lawyer did a great job. And he did, if I say so myself.

The *New York Times* guy does come around a few days later. "Let's take a look around," he says pointing to the cartons piled up against my wall.

"Go take a walk on Forty-Second Street and look around there," I say.

"You gave your word!" he shouts.

"So sue me."

Chapter Four

"Why Did You Prosecute Him?"
1963

Too BAD ALL the days can't be that good. I am manning my trial part, handling case after case. Because I am nearing the end of my time in the bureau and am quite senior, I am assigned to a three judge trial part. The bench is Ben Gassman, Lester Shalleck, and the presiding judge sitting in the middle is Vincent Impellitteri, former mayor of the City of New York, known far and wide as Impy when he occupied city hall. After he lost his reelection bid to Robert F. Wagner, Jr., in 1954, Wagner appointed Impy to the bench.

There are judges who convict everybody and some who convict nobody. Given who is available, these three are regarded as a very good bench. Gassman is the very best of the bunch. Shalleck is relatively new, and Impellitteri has the standing of having been mayor, although I do note that while he treats private counsel with great consideration, he is very tough on legal aid lawyers and their defendants.

My last case of the day is a two-count misdemeanor complaint, charging petit larceny and simple assault. Each offense carries a maximum sentence of one year in prison. I see that the charges have been reduced from the original felony charge of robbery, punishable by ten years. The two misdemeanors are the junior components of the felony. This is not unusual. The office tries to keep the felony parts in the Supreme Court free for the serious cases, and I see the defendant is charged with taking "the approximate amount of five dollars" from the victim. Right, I think. The case belongs here, not in the Supreme Court.

The defendant could not make bail. He has been in custody for several weeks. He has refused any plea bargain. There will be three judges because his lawyer, Bob Ferraro, who heads the legal aid section for criminal court, has requested a three-judge panel. Bob is a pro, experienced in evaluating the worth of cases and reasonable in negotiating with our office. He and I have a solid working relationship.

The arresting officer is there with his complainant, the man who was robbed. While the judges are hearing cases scheduled before ours, I take the cop and the victim into the hall to prepare them for the trial. But when we get outside, the cop pulls me aside, away from the victim. I follow him down the hall. When we are out of earshot, the cop says to me, "I don't think he did it." Just like that. What does that mean—I want to know. And the cop explains that the complainant says he was attacked and robbed by two men at 2:30 a.m. at a street corner. They hit him and took his money, which were four one-dollar bills and some loose change. According to the victim, he found this officer within ten minutes of the assault. Cop and victim began to comb the area looking for the two men. They found them, or so the complainant said, as he pointed them out to the officer. So the cop arrested them both. When he searched them, their money totaled two one-dollar bills and a little change. That didn't match the amount the victim said had been taken from him moments earlier. The cop was not happy and asked the victim if he was really sure that these were the men. He said he was, so the cop arrested the two of them.

A few hours later the four of them were at the arraignment. As they waited, the victim approached the cop and told him that he was no longer sure of the identification of one of the men. So the officer passed the information along to the ADA at the arraignment, and the ADA cut that defendant loose.

"So what," I say to the cop. "The victim was honest, what more can you ask?" But the cop says there is more. He has been waiting around all day with the complainant, waiting for their turn in the trial part, when this afternoon the complainant tells him that because he was drunk the night he was attacked, he is not sure that the remaining guy was one of the two.

I see the cop is worried. I am sure this uniformed officer is on the up-and-up. The defendant has no money. He can't make bail. He is represented by legal aid. There can be no question; the cop simply does not want an innocent man convicted. I tell him I will check it out.

I go over to the complainant. I ask him if he told the officer earlier in the day that he was no longer sure of the identification of the defendant. He denies saying that to the cop. I ask him if he was drunk the night he was robbed. He denies that. I ask him if he told the cop that he had been drunk. He denies that, too.

I walk back into the courtroom to wait our turn. The other case is still going on, but winding down. While we wait, I go over to Bob Ferraro, who is going through a file on his lap. I put my hand on his shoulder and when he looks up I tell him not to worry about this one, I will take care of it. He nods, and pulls out the next file.

The case is called, and I put the complainant on the stand. We go over his story. I am careful to bring out his claim about the amount of money that was taken, and the arrest of the two men within minutes of the assault and theft of the five bucks from him. I want the judges to realize when they hear the cop's testimony that the money doesn't match. And then I ask him if it's true that he withdrew his identification of one of the men.

Impellitteri stops me. "Don't impeach your own witness," he rules.

I can't believe my ears, but I conclude he doesn't realize I am just bringing out the truth. So I go on. I ask the witness if he has told the officer that he is no longer sure that the defendant on trial was one of the men. He barely gets the denial out when Impellitteri barks out, "I told you not to impeach your own witness."

The practice is for the presiding judge, the one who sits in the middle, to make all the evidentiary rulings, so that is that. But I am not too concerned. The three judges obviously heard the questions and understand what I am trying to tell them. So I finish and sit down. Bob rises to cross-examine the complainant. It's a repeat of what I tried to do. Then he is done too. Then it's my turn again, and I call the cop to the stand. I elicit the events from his perspective. I am able to bring out the dismissal of the first man. I then ask the cop if the victim said that he was no longer sure about the identification of the man on trial. Impellitteri interjects again.

"Mr. Stern, I am not going to tell you again. Do not impeach your own witness."

I try to tell him that I am just trying to bring out the facts, that in my view that is my duty, but he doesn't want to hear me. He shuts me down. So I rest. Bob rests without calling his client. And then the three judges huddle at their bench. It doesn't even take two minutes. Impellitteri announces the decision. Guilty on both counts. Gassman notes his dissent. But it's guilty two to one. So that's it. Guilty. I am totally stunned.

Impellitteri asks Ferraro if he wants to waive the presentence report and proceed directly to sentencing. Ferraro says yes. I guess he figures that having extracted this pound of flesh the judges will cut his man loose. After all, he had already served several weeks.

So the judges huddle again. Then Impellitteri announces the decision. Count I, Larceny, one-year imprisonment. Count II, Assault, one-year imprisonment. Sentences to run *consecutively*.

I am beside myself. I can't believe it. They just gave the man two years! I simply can't contain myself. Improper or not, I literally run up to the bench. Standing in front of Impellitteri, I commit a contempt of court. "How could you do that?" I say to him. But he doesn't hold me in contempt. Instead, with his eyes cold and unblinking looking into mine, he says, "Mr. Stern, if you did not want us to convict him, why did you prosecute him?"

I stand frozen. There is nothing I can say. So I turn around and go back to my place, while the court officer gets ready to take the defendant back to the holding pen.

"*Mr. Stern, if you did not want us to convict him, why did you prosecute him?*"

I know I will never forget those words. They will be with me to the end. I had thought I did right, not wrong. I did not know if the defendant was guilty or innocent. I never will. I did not know if the witness was right or if he was wrong, or even if he was lying in his answers. I did not think my job was to judge credibility. I believed it was for the court to decide who was telling the truth and my function was just to present the testimony. I thought that once I had a prima facie case, my job was to put it in, warts and all, and let the tribunal determine the truth.

But standing before that cold man I see that I am wrong, and I will remain wrong as long as people like him sit in judgment. I have learned that the prosecutor must do more than determine if a judge or a jury could *legally* convict. In that moment I see that the prosecutor must do more than advocate *reasonable* positions. The power of his office is too vast to permit him to shift responsibility from himself to any tribunal for the outcome of what he alone has the authority to initiate.

As I watch the attendants lead the defendant away, I make a sacred promise. Never again will I turn over to a judge or even to a jury any person whom I believe should not be convicted.

That night I do not want to go home to be alone in my tiny one-bedroom walk-up on West 76th Street. I walk over to the Village and hit the White Horse, a bar on Seventh Avenue. Then I hit a few more. I don't remember how I got home.

Chapter Five

The End of the Beginning
1963–1964

MY YEAR IN the Criminal Courts is up, which means I can expect the next promotion soon. This is the big one. Everyone takes the same route, Complaints to Indictments, Indictments to Criminal Courts. Then the road divides into four possible paths. The Supreme Court Bureau is where you try jury cases. Most of us want to go there. The Frauds and the Rackets Bureaus are where you investigate for years using grand juries and wiretaps, and very rarely go to court. In my opinion, only the ADAs with cop-like, not trial lawyer mentalities want to go to either. And, finally Homicide, which is between the Trial and Investigative Bureaus. There is a fifth, the Appeals Bureau, in which you just write briefs and argue appeals. In our view, only the egghead types want to go there. But they don't assign anyone to appeals who doesn't request it, so I am not worried about being shipped there.

I want Supreme Court jury trials. I know I am being selfish. I know that the unique reputation of our office springs from uncovering sophisticated criminal conduct, not the crimes that the police bring to us to take to court. Since Dewey's time it has been the rackets and fraud investigations—leading to prosecutions for political corruption, the mafia and sophisticated frauds—that made the office the envy of DAs throughout the country. But I don't care. I want to try felony jury cases in the Supreme Court. That is what I have wanted since I was ten years old.

Before he became a bureau chief in the New York State Attorney General's office, my father had been a trial lawyer. I adored him. As a little boy, I listened to his courtroom stories. I found his old trial transcripts in a closet, and I read them. I could smell the smoke of his courtroom battles.

In spite of his advice to the contrary, it's all I ever wanted to do. "Son," he told me, "it's the hardest work there is. Harder than shoveling coal. After a day in court your shirt will be stuck to your back. You will smell." He advised me to become a dentist.

I had no interest in anything but a courtroom. For me, academics were a waste of time. I didn't care about high school. Stuyvesant High School was either the first or second best in the city, depending on whether you went there or Bronx High School of Science. You took a test to get into either. But I was one of its worst students. Imagine courses in woodworking and mandatory gym classes. I couldn't. So I stopped going for a while. That nearly got me thrown out.

The principal called my father in for a meeting, with me present. There was no mother to call, as she had died the summer before my senior year. The meeting was not my greatest hour. The principal was clearly preparing for my departure. He asked my father to agree that my repeated cutting of school demonstrated that I was not interested in remaining at Stuyvesant. My father then made his immortal response, "That's a stupid statement." That ended the interview, and that moment further enshrined my father as my hero. But when we got outside the building he let me have it. Not physically, just verbally. But it was enough to propel me across the finish line. Barely. I graduated 535 out of 681.

That was the culmination of the worst academic history of anyone in my family. When I first entered grade school, my mother, like all Jewish mothers, believed she had a child prodigy on her hands. So she brought me up to Hunter College Model Elementary School to be tested.

The elementary school began at kindergarten and went on to high school. It took about thirty "gifted" kids a year out of the whole city. I entered the kindergarten, but did not make it to the high school. Hunter asked me to leave after third grade. Between my performance at grade school and high school, my parents were ready to pull their hair out. "Why can't you be like your cousin Arthur?" they said to me. My cousin Arthur Greenbaum is some five years older, and perfect.

So terrific that notwithstanding these unflattering comparisons, even I liked cousin Arthur, who went on to Harvard Law School, graduated with honors, and joined a Wall Street law firm in the 1950s, when very few Jewish graduates were accepted into white-shoe establishments.

After graduating from Stuyvesant, I enrolled in Hobart and William Smith Colleges, a liberal arts college in Geneva, New York. There I finally decided to get serious, at least about academics. First, I loved the program. The college had a core curriculum. All students had to take twenty hours over four semesters in a course called HLA, which stood for history, literature and the arts. It took the student through a journey of time, beginning with the founding of Judaism in about 1800 BC, and continuing through the Greeks, Romans, Christianity, Middle Ages, Renaissance and so forth—studying each period of history in conjunction with its literature and its arts—the Old Testament and the New, even St. Thomas Aquinas and St. Augustine. I learned and studied other cultures, traditions, and faiths. It wowed me. It still does. Many of my classmates did not feel the same way. It gave me an advantage. But the biggest advantage I enjoyed over many of them was that I knew what I wanted to be—a trial lawyer.

Then it was on to law school, and an application to the Manhattan DA's office upon graduation. I figured that if I got in, I would try cases in court. It was the only DA's office in New York City that did not make political appointments, so it was the only one I could apply to. I did try the U.S. Attorney's Office for the Southern District of New York, but they turned me down flat. They said I did not have enough experience, coming right out of law school. That did not seem to stop them from taking plenty of federal judicial law clerks right out of law school. But it worked out anyway, because the DA said yes, and I would get into court earlier and more often there than with the feds.

But first it was the bar exam, then six months of active duty with the National Guard, from August 1961 to February 1962. There was no war then, but there was the draft and military training. So you had to do something. I chose six months of active duty—where I learned to be a light truck driver with close to disastrous results. I could drive the thing forward okay. I could even back it up. But then they added a trailer. When I backed up with it, there was a calamity. I was removed from transportation and made a clerk.

The first Monday after my discharge from active duty I was sworn into the DA's office, and a few days later found myself in the magistrate court getting my life's dream shattered, ready to resign not merely from the office but from trial work. Now, after a year of constant trial work in the Criminal Court Bureau, I know I am ready for the Supreme Court Bureau and the glory days of jury trials.

But I am assigned to homicide.

Chapter Six

The Homicide Bureau
1964

I'M IN MY fourth office in two years, housed with the other ADAs in homicide. We have our own wing. We even have a holding cell as part of our suite of offices. We often need to interrogate witnesses to homicides who are in jail themselves, so the cell is useful.

The bureau is led by Alexander Herman, another Dewey man. After twenty-five years in the office, Al Herman has tried more homicides and sent more murderers to the electric chair than any other prosecutor in New York. Maybe even the country. But he doesn't try them any more. There's something wrong with his throat, I don't know what, but his voice rasps. No more court. Now he runs the bureau from behind his desk, with an ever-present cigarette between the fingers of one of his very much misshapen fists. They look like the hands of a bare-knuckle prizefighter. I ask no questions. This, I say to myself as I report to him for duty for the first time, is one tough guy.

"Homicides are different than other crimes." With that lead-in, Herman introduces me to his bureau. Whenever a homicide occurs in New York County, and the police want to book a suspect, they first must call the ADA on homicide duty. A police car is sent for the assistant district attorney, another for a stenographer, and the two rendezvous at the police station where the subject is being held. The object is to get a statement from the accused, and to make sure there is enough evidence to arrest the person. If the ADA orders the arrest, from that moment the case is his.

Of course the detainee is not free to leave before the ADA gets there, and I have never heard of anyone trying to. Is he already under arrest? We don't think much about that, but I guess the answer is yes. Once we say to book the suspect, or whatever you want to call him, the police make a formal arrest. And if we say let him go, they do that too.

Every homicide has two lead detectives assigned. One is always from either Manhattan North or Manhattan South homicide, and the other detective is from the local precinct who is "catching," which is jargon for on duty at that time. Once the ADA arrives, he is in charge.

If he believes the evidence is sufficient, the ADA orders the booking and then makes sure that all the witnesses are accounted for and interviewed, that the evidence is collected, and that all the leads are followed to the end. The investigation can be over in a day, or it can take weeks. When the ADA is satisfied that all the bases have been covered, he presents the case to the Homicide Bureau of the DA's office. The bureau meets every Friday. It sits in final judgment as the ADA presents his case and fields questions. He has to satisfy his colleagues that there are no loose ends. Once he does, he makes his recommendation as to what to charge. Then the bureau votes on what to recommend to a grand jury.

The vote can go from the top charge of murder in the first degree, to second degree, to manslaughter or even less, such as involuntary manslaughter. It's a majority vote. The voting was instituted because of the possibility of the death penalty for Murder One. Herman tells me that decision is too important to entrust to one assistant.

"How often are we on duty?" I inquire.

"Every five to ten days depending on the trial schedules of the other men in the bureau," is the answer.

"Do we only get cases when the police have someone already in custody?" I inquire.

"Since you asked," he replies through a cloud of smoke, "here's a file." And he hands me a folder which he obviously had ready for me.

I see it is entitled "Joseph Michael Donohue." And it's thick. I don't want to seem pushy, and I don't even know what to ask. But I don't have to wait. Herman outlines the file.

Donohue, known on the street as Crazy Joey, is a robber and a paid killer, Herman explains. "We don't know how many people he has killed for money, but we do know about five who were his friends," and he lists them. A double murder in the Bronx, and a single homicide of a black man named Presley Wilkes in Manhattan. And then the double homicide in a Manhattan bar. There are pictures of all of the bodies. Herman comes around his desk, takes the file, and spreads the pictures of the bodies around his conference table. I have never seen anything like it.

The Castilian Room is a bar on East 75th Street. The interior in the photo is deserted, except for two bodies, a man named Robert Hannigan, who owned the bar, and the hatcheck girl, who was Donohue's girlfriend. She is spread-eagled on her back, arms outstretched on the floor of the bar. Hannigan is found shot in the head, crumpled against a wall under a public telephone affixed to the wall. He died with a dime in his hand, obviously in the process of making a call. "We think he was making a call for help after Donohue shot the girlfriend," Herman tells me.

According to neighbors, a string of firecrackers rang out at about four in the morning. The bar was closed. Shortly after the noise stopped, neighbors, drawn to their windows, see Donohue and a man identified as Ray Tobin exit the closed bar. In a matter of minutes, the police swarm in. There are no witnesses, just four people in a bar. Two wound up dead, and two walked out. Who did it?

"We know Donohue did it. We just can't prove it," Herman closes up the file, handing it to me.

"What about Tobin?" I ask.

"We tried to interview him. He told us to screw off. So we threatened to put him in the grand jury. He threatened to take the Fifth. We threatened to give him immunity. Then he threatened to testify that he did the shooting."

Check and mate. The office, appalled at the thought of putting an immunized, confessing Tobin before a grand jury, backed off. That is why Tobin and Donohue still walk the streets. I leave Herman's office with the file and instructions to do something about it.

The first is to pull everything we know about Donohue together. That's easy. He's one of the last of the criminal gang known as the "Westies." The ferocity of the Westies terrifies everyone, even mafia members who hire them as contract killers. The Westies are crazy. They kill without hesitation, anywhere, at any time. Witnesses or no witnesses. The famous Elmer "Trigger" Burke, for example, got into a fight in a bar on the West Side. He beat the man savagely. Finally, bartender Edward Walsh, a friend of Burke's, stopped Burke from kicking the helpless man to death as he lay on the floor. Burke, furious at his friend for siding against him, walked out of the bar, across the street to his apartment building, retrieved his gun from behind a toilet, walked back into the bar and repeatedly shot Walsh until he was dead, in front of everyone in the bar.

It is plain that Donohue's conduct was similar. He must have had an argument with his girlfriend. Shot her, then shot Hannigan who was calling for help. Then he walked out calmly with his pal Tobin.

I look up Donohue's record. It is substantial. One report of a prior Donohue arrest captures my attention. Donahue and a Greek mobster, Tommy "The Greek" Kapatos, were stopped by two officers in a patrol car who did not like the way the two looked. One officer got out of the car, searched Donohue, and found a gun in his pocket. Donohue said, "Okay, you got me. I give up." The cop yelled to his partner, "Watch out, this guy has a gun!" His partner, who was searching Kapatos, yelled back, "Watch out yourself. This guy's got two guns!" The cop then continued to search Donohue and found another gun stuck in the small of Donohue's back. If that officer had stopped searching with the "okay you got me," there would have been two dead cops.

But the stop-and-frisk came to nothing. There was no probable cause for the searches. All four guns were suppressed, and both men walked free. And I have a bunch of homicides with only one clue. A man named Tobin.

I call in the two detectives assigned to the Castilian Room murders. The Manhattan North homicide detective is Walter Curtaine, a tall, elegant, white-haired veteran of more than twenty-five years, going back even before Dewey's time. The 16th Precinct detective is Jack Justy, soft-spoken, highly educated, in his mid-forties, with a reputation as the best detective on the force. The department has put its very best on to Donohue. We meet in Room 603, my office on the sixth floor. I have made my decision: I am going to call Ray Tobin's bluff. I ask the detectives to find him.

They bring him in. He's a fat, sloppy, red-faced son of the owner of a bar on the Upper East Side, Tobin's East. This guy is no mobster, just a hanger-on. A small fish in a big body riding on the back of a shark.

He couldn't kill anyone, much less two people in less than thirty seconds. I never had a doubt about what happened in the Castilian Room at 4:00 a.m. Seeing Tobin does not create any.

I tell him he is going in to the grand jury. He gives me the same routine about confessing to the murders. In New York a witness gets immunity automatically, unless he waives his rights. So he thinks he will scare me off. But I have a plan. I intend to ask him just one question, "On the night of September 22, did you have a gun in your hand?" If the answer is "yes," he will be taken from the grand jury as fast as I can get him out. All he will have is immunity for gun possession, not murder. If the answer is "no," we are off to the races.

So in he goes. When he comes out, I tell Curtaine and Justy that his answer is "no," he had no gun. I sit him down with the detectives. He tells his story that the two people were alive when he and Donohue left. "They must have been killed later," he says.

I can ask the grand jury to indict him for perjury, but that will get me no place. But I have a fallback plan. I make an application to the court that, in light of his grand jury testimony, he should be held as a material witness. The judge slaps a $100,000 bond on him, which he can't make. The street knows he was called to testify before the grand jury. I hope the word on the street is that Tobin is talking. Perhaps fear of Donohue's reaction will motivate him. It's all legal. He is a material witness and he did testify before the grand jury. I know that I am fighting fire with fire, but I have five dead bodies. I do not want to have to wait for a sixth.

While I wait, hoping that Tobin will crack, I take my turn every week at catching homicides. Most of them seem to happen after midnight, and many of them are the result of domestic disputes. The sight of a police car coming to collect me in the wee hours in front of my walk-up at 46 West 76th Street becomes a regular event.

Because I am still new, my inventory of cases is light. With time on my hands, I spend some going to courtrooms to watch the senior assistants try cases. It is a way to learn. The days pass. Then nearly two weeks go by. Tobin still has not talked. I have him brought out of the holding facility and to my office. Other than losing some weight, nothing has changed. He still isn't talking. So back in he goes. I know this can't go on forever. But as it turns out it doesn't have to. A few days later, on the evening of September 24, 1964, we get the anticipated sixth body.

At 3:00 a.m. on the twenty-fifth, my telephone startles me conscious. Justy and Curtaine are on the line. "We've got him now," Jack yells into the phone.

"Who we got?" I ask groggily.

"Donohue," Jack laughs, and fills me in on the events of last night.

Donohue, driving south on Fifth Avenue in a stolen car with his buddy Lawrence Krebs sitting in the passenger seat, turns right at a light at the 79th Street transverse road through Central Park. He is heading for the west side. As he turns the vehicle, he has an argument with Krebs. While driving, Donohue shoots Krebs twice in the head. This action causes Donohue to lose control of the car, which crashes, banging and scraping against the transverse road's wall on the passenger side of the car. It finally stops. The car is immobilized. As the dust and smoke settle, Donohue calmly exits the driver's side and strolls back up the transverse road to Fifth Avenue, where he made his turn. As he does, he walks past the driver's side of a taxicab waiting at a light to exit the transverse onto Fifth Avenue. There are two people in the back seat of the cab. When Donohue reaches Fifth Avenue, he makes two throwing motions.

The police arrive at the car wreck and find Krebs's dead body in the passenger seat. The cab and the passengers have remained at the scene. The uniforms call the detectives, who quickly ascertain that the car is stolen. In the trunk they find skeleton keys and empty burlap sacks. They get the names of the people in the taxi, but they still do not know the name of the victim, much less the driver who is obviously the murderer. Examination of the body reveals the victim is Lawrence Krebs. The examination of the contents of the trunk reveals that the two men were traveling to commit a crime. Within hours they learn that Krebs is, or rather was, a pal of Donohue's.

The lab people show up. They dust the car for prints. Behind the rear-view mirror they find a fingerprint. It belongs to Joseph Donohue. Further investigation by the detectives establishes that Krebs and Donohue were close friends. A matter of hours after the body is identified, my telephone rings. Justy, Curtaine and I are back in business.

Two days later Curtaine and Justy come to my office. They have the gun, an automatic, and also the clip—the two items that Donohue tossed one after another into the bushes as he strolled away from the body of his latest victim. There are no fingerprints, but they do have the name of a woman, an English woman, who saw a man make two throwing gestures towards the bushes as he walked away from the crash.

I ask the detectives about the people in the cab. Who are they? What did they see? The cab driver saw nothing, I'm told. Just heard the crash and saw a shadowy figure walk past his cab. The fact that there is a streetlight on the corner is of no help to his ability to see. He either can't or won't help.

I ask who was in the back seat of the cab. The detectives' faces break into grins. We are in luck. A young couple was in the passenger seat. They hailed the cab in front of their west side apartment at 81st Street and were being driven through the park to a location on the east side. Stopped at the light where the transverse road exits onto Fifth Avenue at 79th Street, they see the murder car come fast down Fifth Avenue, turn right onto the transverse road, and pass them quickly. Then they hear the crash. As they turn around to look, they see a man leave the wrecked car, walk past their stopped cab in the other lane, on the driver side of the cab, and then onto Fifth Avenue. There he disappears.

And now for the best news: The husband in the back of the car, sitting behind the driver, which means he is the closest to the man walking by, is a former Hogan ADA, only a year or two out of the office.

"Great!" I say. I am rubbing my hands in glee.

"Not so fast," Justy holds up his hand. "The former ADA says he never got a look at the man's face."

I can't believe it. "You mean he saw nothing?" Justy shakes his head no. "Not even for a second?" I beg. Justy shakes his head no again.

But the detectives still look like they swallowed the canary, so there has to be more. "What about the wife?" I tentatively ask.

Justy tells me she saw the face of the man as he passed. "She thinks she can make him, but she has to see him." I ask about her background. Both men now sport wide grins, "Very pretty, a tiny little thing but . . . she has plenty of guts," Justy pauses for effect. "She's a veteran of the Israeli Navy." We are in business.

We also have the name of another witness, the English woman who was standing at the corner of Fifth Avenue, who saw a man walk out of the transverse road after the car crash and make two throwing gestures, which we think are likely the gun and the clip. But she too says she needs to see the man in person to make the identification. All we have to do is arrange for a line-up, get the IDs, and hopefully that will be that. The problem is, Donohue has disappeared.

We have two potential witnesses, but no Donohue. I can't get IDs without a lineup, I can't get a lineup without Donohue, I can't get Donohue without a warrant, and I can't get a warrant on just a fingerprint in the car. I need an ID for the arrest warrant. It's a circle of frustration.

We figure that Donohue has fled to Boston. Trigger Burke ran there after killing Walsh, his bartender pal. The detectives tell me there are still connections between the West Side Irish and the Boston Irish mobs. They also say that the word on the street is that Donohue is there. But no one can tell us for sure. We need the help of the FBI to conduct a search across state borders.

So I pack my bag and go to the FBI office in Boston with Jack Justy. Curtaine stays and continues to probe. The FBI office in Boston is nothing like the dingy police stations I have been deposited in lately. They have a reception area and a receptionist, a nice clean conference room with a big long table in the middle, with three agents standing around it. They are all very neat. All in white shirts and all are condescending. We locals don't understand that the bureau can't arrest Donohue unless he is a fugitive. And, they say, unless they can arrest him as a fugitive, they can't search for him. So they need a warrant. "Come back and see us when you get one." They get up from the conference table, and we are supposed to be polite and leave quietly.

"Just a minute," I say, and they pause impatiently.

From my briefcase, I take out pictures of dead bodies and spread them on the table. First the double homicide in the Bronx, then Presley Wilkes, then the double in the Castilian Room and, finally, the slumped body of Krebs in the abandoned car.

The agents stop moving for the door and form around the table. I'm sure they have not seen anything like that before. Bureau agents rarely see even one homicide. What gets them is the woman lying in a pool of blood on the floor of the bar. There's something that gets to men when they see a woman killed like that. And the picture of Hannigan under the telephone, which he never got to use, is the final

41

straw. The atmosphere does a one-hundred-eighty-degree turn. I see they really want to help. Maybe they will. All I need is a warrant.

So it's back to 155 Leonard Street, the DA's office. I turn Tobin loose. No point to keeping him in. You can only hold people so long. I no longer believe that I need Tobin to make my case against Donohue. All I need to do to nail Donohue is to find him.

****

While I wait, I continue my practice of going to court to watch experienced lawyers try their cases. And there is one case I particularly want to see.

Ephraim London and Marty Garbus, old adversaries from my "dirty pictures" days, are trying a hot obscenity case. They are defending the comedian Lenny Bruce. My old boss Kuh is prosecuting. Bruce has been charged with talking dirty in a nightclub act at the Café a Go Go in Greenwich Village. According to the newspaper accounts, in addition to using foul language in his act, like "motherfucker," Bruce also says, "Eleanor Roosevelt has the nicest tits of any First Lady," and that Jackie Kennedy, far from exiting the back of the assassination car to seek help, was "hauling ass to save her ass." When Hogan heard about these heresies, he was determined to shut Bruce up by arresting and convicting him of obscenity. He had Kuh send in a licensing inspector by the name of Ruhe to monitor and take notes of the offensive performance. Two nights later, April 2, 1964, Kuh, armed with the evidence of the impurities, had Bruce and the owner of the Café a Go Go arrested for obscenity. The case is on trial by mid-June.

The courtroom is packed. Because of the number of spectators, the trial is held in one of the large jury trial courtrooms. I join several ADAs sitting in the jury box. There is no jury because it is a three-judge-court trial. Judge John M. Murtagh presiding, of course. Kuh and an ADA named Vincent Cuccia are at one table. London, Garbus and Bruce are at another. I have missed the prosecution's case, which I hear was nothing more than putting Bruce's night-club act into evidence. The defense is proceeding. Garbus has a Presbyterian minister on the stand, who testifies that he is not offended by Bruce's act, including Bruce's use of words like "motherfucker."

On cross-examination, Kuh refers the reverend to the Fourth Commandment, "Honor thy father and thy mother."

> Q. Would you say the phrase, and you'll excuse me, Reverend, for using this language, but the phrase "motherfucker" is in accord with that Commandment?
> A. I don't think the term "motherfucker" has any relationship to that Commandment.
> Q. To the uninitiated, to the unsophisticated, to persons other than reverends, Mr. Johnson, might someone understand "mother-fucker" to have something to do with mothers and fucking?

I do not pay attention to the answer. I am busy thanking Providence that I am out of the Criminal Court Bureau. Imagine spending your time and resources to prosecute this nonsense. And there is Kuh, a brilliant Harvard Law magna cum laude, using his considerable gifts to commit a courtroom mugging of a decent man. My colleagues and I do not sit around in the jury box for long. Hogan sends executive ADA David Worgan into the courtroom to shoo us all out. So I return to homicides.

Chapter Seven

"Get Me out of Here"
May–December 1964

W**E HAVE A** break on Donohue. Curtaine's investigation had taken him to New Jersey. When he comes back he has a court record showing that Donohue had jumped bail on an assault charge pending in a New Jersey court. That means that he is already a fugitive! We can get a fugitive warrant for his arrest, so we do, and I call the FBI in Boston to let them know.

It doesn't take them long to bring him in. It's so quick that Justy and I wonder if the bureau didn't start on Donohue right after we left. Within a few days after we furnish the warrant, they have him, and I get a call from the FBI's Boston field office.

"Where did you get him?" I'm elated.

"We took him on the street," the agent says.

"Great!"

"Thanks," he says, "But I think you should know that when we arrested him he had a master handcuff key sewn into his underpants."

"Unbelievable," I start to say. "Yeah," he interrupts me, "and he also had a master leg-iron key in his shoelaces."

The agents turn Donohue over to the Boston cops. They house him in Charles Street Jail, the same one that Trigger Burke had been put into, and then broke out of, a dozen years before. I intend to move fast.

I go to Al Herman. We have to get the witnesses up to Boston to ID Donohue before he either makes bail or busts out of there. He is in only as a bail-jumper for an assault charge, not a murder complaint. Herman agrees, but instructs me to take the two women separately, the Englishwoman who had been standing on the street corner when Donohue walked out of the transverse road, and the former ADA's wife who had been in the back seat of the taxicab. He doesn't want any claim that there was collusion between the two of them at the ID.

I pick the Englishwoman to go first. I still have some hope that the former ADA might recall enough of the face of the man who passed by his side of the cab so I can bring him up, rather than his wife.

Justy and I take the Englishwoman up to Boston. The cops have arranged for a lineup in one of the station houses. So we bring the woman right to the Boston precinct station. She is a pleasant, educated woman in her early thirties. She seems steady, but with their accents most English people seem that way to me. We enter the precinct and the Boston Police Department has everything ready. With us standing by, they bring in four men, one after the other, to form a lineup. Donohue, number five, comes in last. It's the first time I have ever seen the man. He is not impressive. Not tall. Not muscular. Not distinctive. You would never give him a second glance. And then, as he enters, he sees a lineup forming, and he goes into action. He drops to the floor. He refuses to move. The Boston cops grab him, but he struggles with them. Soon we have three cops and Donohue wrestling and rolling on the floor.

I look over at the Englishwoman. Her mouth is hanging open in disbelief. Then it gets worse. Seeing that it is going to be impossible to put Donohue into a lineup, the cops grab his head by his hair to pull his face up so that my witness can see his features. But that doesn't work because Donohue contorts his face into grotesque grimaces in an obvious effort to disfigure his features. This is some lineup! What the hell good is this? But it doesn't matter because my witness is now beside herself. She grabs my arm hard. "Get me out of here," she says. So I do.

When we get outside I ask the question, although I'm sure that I already know the answer. "No," she says. She cannot say he was the man she saw that night with the throwing gestures. But "no," she says she cannot say that he is *not* the man. She obviously wants out. And I can't say I blame her.

It comes to mind what one of the judges told me when I was trying cases back in the Criminal Courts. During a break between cases, he said, "You know what's the second worst thing that can happen to you in New York?"

"No," I said, playing along.

"That you should walk down the street, and someone should grab you and take your money," he said.

"What's the worst thing?" I ask, although I thought I knew.

"That they should catch him," the judge said with a laugh, as we both involuntarily looked around the courtroom at the cops, witnesses, even defendants all waiting for their turn. Nobody wants to be there. Nobody.

With the departure of the Englishwoman, I have but one witness left. That is, if she can make the identification. Her husband is out of it. He is firm that he never saw the killer's face. It will be her, or we will have to turn Donohue loose and, once again, start waiting for another victim.

Back to Boston. Donohue is due to be arraigned on the fugitive warrant in the Boston court. The courtroom is crowded with all sorts of people. She and I are in the rear, her glance sweeping the room. Without any prompting, she picks him out of all the people that she sees. We have our witness.

What we have in total is a witness who saw him walk by in profile, briefly, and at dusk. We have his fingerprint in the car. And, except for the flight and the hidden master keys, that is all that we have. It will have to be enough, because we will not get more.

I present the case at our Friday homicide bureau meeting. The vote is unanimous. Murder I. We are going for the death penalty. We probably won't get it at trial. It's a classic Murder II case, murder without cold-blooded premeditation. After all, it looks like Donohue shot Krebs on the spur of the moment, but then again maybe he planned it that way. We go for the top charge, and, of course, so do the grand jurors.

Armed with a warrant for Donohue's arrest, issued after indictment, we apply to Boston for extradition, which is granted. I go to Boston for a third time, but this time with a train car full of New York City policemen. The cops are taking no chances. They tell me that the Boston authorities report, from a wire on the Boston mob, that a guard on the take tried to speak to Donohue, to help break him out. But the guard reported back that Donohue, believing it a plant, refused to speak to him, saying "Fuck you, and tell those New York cops to go fuck themselves." At the train station in Boston, a van meets up with us and Donohue emerges. The Boston PD unlocks Donohue's shackles, and the New York PD replaces them with theirs.

We bring Donohue back in a private car reserved just for us, with the New York cops openly toting shotguns. It feels like the Wild West. I can't help studying the man during the four-hour trip. I search his face for a clue to the mind of a man who has coldly killed so many people. But I see nothing but an ordinary face. When he catches me staring, I look away. I want no contact of any kind with him. When we pull into the station in Manhattan, the cops take us in a convoy to the police station in Central Park. From the time we board the train until we arrive at the police station, Donohue does not say a word. Nor did anyone expect him to.

Al Herman will decide who will try the case. It can't be me. I'm too young. But I can expect to assist.

The Homicide Bureau has the two best trial lawyers in the office, in my view. One of them, Vincent J. Dermody, is the man we all watch and learn from. He is lethal in the courtroom. But it is not his size. He is a small man, not at all physically imposing. It's not his voice. He is a "dese" and "dems" and "dose" guy, originally from the Bronx, the son of a former police inspector. It's not his style or flamboyant movements in the courtroom that is trademark. When he examines, he rises slowly, slides his chair into and under his table, and stands unmoving behind that chair, both hands resting on its back. His speech is slow, soft, and very deliberate. Almost halting. Occasionally, he lifts his hands from the back of his chair, not to thrust or to point, but as a man does when he struggles to find the right word. What makes Dermody lethal is that the jurors quickly come to believe that he is incapable of telling them a lie. He therefore wins all his cases.

I study Dermody closely. The lesson is clear. The jurors know that the lawyers for the prosecution and the defense know more than the jury is allowed to hear. That is of course true. This is constantly reinforced as objections are made, sustained, and evidence excluded. They even think that the lawyers know what really happened, which is often not true. It comes to me that with jurors believing that the disputing lawyers know the "truth," the jurors must also believe that one is truthful and the other is dissembling while each flog conflicting versions of the facts.

That is the one great advantage we have as prosecutors. When we DAs stand up and give our names and say we are "For the People," we start off being perceived by the jury as being without personal interest, while our adversaries are presumed to be paid advocates for profit. The jurors often believe that the size of these fees even depend on the outcome of the case. The perception is entirely false. Our adversaries are most often paid in advance, win or lose. As for us, we want to win as much as our adversaries do. But the best of us learn to sail before the wind of our perceived personal-disinterest rectitude, and to avoid its dissipation by shoddy conduct in the courtroom.

Few of us have learned this lesson as well as the office's other fine trial lawyer, John F. Keenan. He is our second lethal man in the courtroom. I go out of my way to watch him, too. Some fifteen to twenty years younger than Dermody, Jack Keenan is more animated, but his tone is the same. So are the words and phrases. The speech is plain and direct. The phrase "in all fairness" is one Jack uses often in court, as he offers some morsel to the defense. It's not that he is insincere. He does give the defendant something, even if not much. Then he convicts him. As far as I can see, he too convicts them all.

The real gold is studying the way senior ADAs prepare their witnesses. Not prepare them for court, I mean prepare them on the "facts." As I watch, I learn that people recall very little with accuracy. As time passes, the defects in memory grow. Then, when a trial appears on the horizon, witnesses are suddenly required to account for events that took place months or even years earlier. At the starting point, all that anyone has are a few tattered recollections filled with gaps. Even these are likely incorrect to some degree. And yet no one testifies with large holes in their account. All witnesses strive to housekeep their fragmentary recollections into well-ordered, connected accounts of events and conversations. To bring a witness to that point, the point where they have filled in gaps and interstices, is the real preparation. The ability to mine for recollections favorable to your case is the true art. That accomplished, the second step, translating the now "revived recollections" into a Q and A for purposes of trial is what most call "witness preparation." I have learned to wield a powerful tool.

Al Herman assigns the Donohue indictment to Jack Keenan. I am delighted to serve as second chair to him. I expect to learn much watching Jack, but still I am not happy about the progress of my career.

As I near the end of my first year in homicide, I evaluate where I am. I have been out on half a dozen homicide cases. I have a major investigation, and now a major trial to prepare, and will sec-ond-chair one of the best trial lawyers in the city. All of that is good. But on November 8, 1964, I turned 28. I have tried hun-dreds of non-jury cases and minor jury trials in the summer, when Supreme Court ADAs are on vacation. Although my brain tells me I have plenty of time, I grow impatient. I am not happy.

The events of Christmas weekend, 1964, convince me it is time for me to move on. The day after Christmas, I have the twenty-four-hour duty. Most of my colleagues are Christian and are with family, so I have volunteered. It is after 11:30 p.m. when I get the call. I know when the phone rings that it has to be a homicide. No one telephones me at that hour except the police. It's a police inspector, calling to tell me that a patrolman has accidentally shot a bystander after firing at the fleeing driver of a car that had tried to run the policeman down. The inspector refers to the driver as a felon. The inspector is insistent on giving details on the telephone, although we both know I will be there in less than an hour. The traffic cop, Patrolman Patrick Crowe, was on duty on the corner of 34th Street and Madison Avenue. I'm told that when Crowe attempted to pull a car over for a traffic violation, the driver attempted to strike the officer with the car. According to the inspector, Crowe reached into the window on the driver side to take the keys, but the car started going, dragging the officer whose hand was trapped.

The officer was bouncing off other cars as he was dragged, the inspector tells me, until finally he freed himself, falling to the pave-ment. As the officer got to his feet, the car sped away. Crowe then took out his gun and fired two warning shots into the air. The car did not stop. So Crowe fired another two shots at the car. He apparently missed, at least missed the car. Two full blocks away one of the bullets hit pedestrian Julius Ofsei in the head and killed him instantly. "How many passengers were in the car?" I ask the inspector. "Two, plus the driver," is the answer. "What time did this happen?" I ask. "Five-thirty this afternoon," I am told.

I put down the telephone to get dressed. But first, I open the sliding door to my little Pullman kitchen and get the coffee pot going. I know the police car will be downstairs in minutes, but I want the coffee. I need it.

I know that this one is going to be trouble. I know I have just been lobbied. That I expect. But even in the first moments, questions jump out at me. Why the hell is the cop shooting at a car containing at least two people who as passengers did nothing wrong. Not to mention shooting a couple of rounds up Madison Avenue at 5:30 in the afternoon for any reason short of protecting human life? And why have I not been called for six hours?

Chapter Eight

The Beginning of the End
December 1964–February 1965

L ESS THAN AN hour after the call, I am at the 13th Precinct. The police brass is there. So is Patrolman Crowe. The police have one witness who was at the scene, a Mr. Gerald Greenberg. When my stenographer arrives, I take a statement from him at 1:12 a.m. By that time, Greenberg has apparently been at the precinct for nearly eight hours.

I sit at a desk in the stationhouse with a container of coffee and a smoldering cigarette and question Greenberg as to what he saw.

"I saw a police officer, who was doing traffic duty at 34th Street and Madison Avenue, proceed north on the center of the street and approach a vehicle and direct that the vehicle to stop and pull over to the side."

"Do you recall seeing people in the car?"

"I thought there were two or three, I'm not certain."

The witness has the car in view from the corner of 34th Street to nearly the corner of 35th Street, moments before the shooting. So far there is nothing about any assault on the officer. Greenberg says he walked past the car on his way to 35th Street. When he is about five feet from the corner of 35th Street, almost at the corner, he sees the vehicle and the driver again.

"What did you see at that time?

"The officer chasing the vehicle on foot. The vehicle proceeding north. The officer following as rapidly as his feet would carry him."

Where is the assault? The cop seems to be none the worse as he sprints after the car. "What did you see then?"

"The car proceeded north. The officer continued to run after it covering about one third of the distance into the block. He pulled his weapon and fired a warning shot in the air. He fired a second warning shot in the air."

"Where was the vehicle?"

"At the intersection of 36th Street. When he fired, the vehicle was approaching the intersection. Then he leveled his arm and leveled his weapon and fired, apparently at the vehicle."

This is damning to the cop. What is he doing firing his gun? After Greenberg leaves, I take Donovan, the homicide detective, aside, "Are there any other witnesses?"

"Not here," he tells me, "We got the name of a priest, but he left a couple hours ago." That gets me annoyed.

"I want to speak with him."

"Okay," Donovan agrees.

There is nothing left to do tonight except to question the officer.

Patrolman Patrick Crowe is a pleasant-looking man, I judge somewhere between thirty-five and forty. Fairly tall. Stocky. Light hair. Nothing unusual in his appearance. He is still in full uniform, of course. I see no signs of bandages or serious injuries. I begin the questioning with warnings. He is not under arrest, so the law requires none. But that is our policy, and under the circumstances I think it is the right thing to do. I begin at 1:25 a.m., right after I finish with Greenberg.

He tells me he was directing traffic away from going west on 34th Street. All the cars obeyed but one.

"Well, all the cars turned north or south. One particular car, the car in question, a black Peugeot, as it approached the intersection, I motioned for it to make a right turn or a left turn."

"What happened after you gave that hand signal?"

Crowe responds that the driver shook his head "no" and "he pointed with his finger straight ahead." He obviously wanted to keep going on 34th Street. But Crowe continued to signal that he must divert his direction from proceeding west.

"After you continued to make your hand signals, what happened?"

"Well, he stopped the car, and he still indicated he wanted to go west. Then to make it understood, I took out my summons book and pointed to him."

Crowe, threatening a traffic ticket, prevailed. The driver made his unwilling right turn, heading north on to Madison. When the car was abreast of Crowe, the driver gave Crowe the finger.

"Did he make that gesture in your direction?"

"Yes," Crowe responds, and then continues, "With that I told him to pull over. I had to run up to the car, and I told him to pull over."

The motorist obeyed the cop. He made the turn and diverted his trip, but his irate gesture infuriated Crowe, who ran up to the Peugeot.

I cannot help but wonder what it was that the officer was going to ticket the driver for, an obscene gesture? But what I ask is,

"What happened then?"

"He kept going slowly towards me."

According to Crowe, the car came close to him, then, "he swerved and brushed my clothing with the car, and when I got close, I put my hand in to grab the keys." And then, according to Crowe, the driver picked up speed, and Crowe had his hand caught in the car.

"What happened then?" I ask him.

"He got to the intersection of 35th and Madison. I fell free. I fell to the pavement. I went down on my knees. I got up and took out the revolver." Crowe fired two shots in the air. Then, with the car a block away, Crowe fired two shots, totally missing the car, but hitting a pedestrian Julius Ofsei in the head, killing him instantly.

I am looking at Crowe in disbelief. Why did he fire? How could he have been dragged? The man looks completely okay. He sees me staring at him, and looks away.

"Were you injured as a result of this incident?" I ask.

Crowe points out to me a minor mark on his left arm. I put it on the record. "You're indicating a scratch, a break in the skin on your left forearm. I would say an inch over the wrist bone, would that be correct?"

"Right."

"Have you received medical aid?"

"No."

There is nothing more to be done. Not at 2:00 a.m.

Tuesday, January 7

Detective Fred Stepat, the detective carrying the Crowe case, brings Father Dunn to my office, Room 603, for a stenographic statement. The priest is a member of the Graymoor Atonement Order, and he saw the whole incident, from beginning to end. We sit at my conference table and I take his statement, with a stenographer present. He relates how he saw the officer pull the car over.

"How did he do that?"

"He just motioned the car over with his hand, left."

"What did the car do when he made that motion?"

"The car came up to him and stopped, double-parked."

This is a different kettle of fish. Not that it matters, for I have come to the conclusion that assault or no assault, Crowe was wrong to shoot his gun. But I want to be fair to the cop who says the driver drove at him, so I ask the priest, "When you say up to him, do you mean it came directly at him?"

"No," says the priest, "it moved not at him but toward the right."

"Over to the side?"

"Over to the side."

According to the priest, there had been no assault. "And what happened at that point?"

"Then the car proceeded forward and the policeman ran forward with the car." It is clear that the priest saw Crowe running sideways alongside the car, going north on Madison Avenue.

"And did he have to run or was he walking?"

"He had to run. He had to run progressively faster."

I'm satisfied that Crowe did have his hand in the window trying to take the keys. Whether it was "stuck" or he just would not quit trying to seize the keys as the car drove away is an open question. "Then what did you see?" I ask the priest.

"Then I saw the policeman disengage himself from the car, take out his revolver, and shoot twice in the air."

"Did you see him fall down at this point?"

"I did not see him fall at any time."

I look over at the detective from the 13th, but he is not making eye contact with anybody in the room. I must make absolutely sure that the witness means to stick with what he says happened.

"Now, Father, did you have the officer under observation continually, from the time that you first saw him with his palm upstretched until the time that you saw him fire the first two shots in the air?"

"Yes, he was in my view all the time."

"Continually?" I ask.

"Continually," he answers.

Father Dunn leaves with the detective. I then fill out the initial report form to Al Herman. I deliberately do not include the nonsense about the driver trying to hurt the cop with the car. I am convinced that when the driver gave Crowe the finger, the cop got furious, stuck his hand in the window to take the keys, and the driver got scared and ran, pulling Crowe along as he kept trying to get the keys. I can't know for sure, of course, but that's what it looks like to me.

And, in the end, I conclude that it really doesn't matter if the cop's story about being stuck is accurate, or if it happened as I think it did. Under any of the possible scenarios, the shooting is outrageous. The driver of the car had done little enough to warrant arrest, much less to be shot at. Even had the driver been alone in the car, the cop would not have been justified in killing him. With two completely innocent passengers, the shooting at the car is incomprehensible. And in any event, car or no car, discharging a pistol on a New York street corner, shooting up Madison Avenue at 5:30 in the afternoon, could be justified only if innocent human life was threatened. I intend to seek an indictment of Crowe for manslaughter. That is, if I can get the Homicide Bureau to vote yes. And I am sure I am going to have trouble with that.

I have reluctantly come to the belief that with all of its undeniably outstanding qualities, the DA's office is protective of police misconduct, with the exception of graft and corruption. It is disheartening to encounter pretense in any office as outstanding as ours. No other office that I know of can boast the same professionalism, the lack of political influence, and the continuity of leadership over twenty-five years. Not even the U.S. Attorney for the Southern District of New York. At a time when other DAs' offices are riddled with political appointees, ours is totally free of all such influence. Every four years, Hogan runs without political opposition. ADAs are appointed solely on merit. In contrast, the state judiciary is populated with judges who openly make political donations to their district leaders to get "nominated" in pro forma general elections in a one-party city, and then, as judges, appoint permanent "law secretaries," politically favored lawyers often selected by the clubhouse.

Our office alone is free of such taint. And yet, with the freedom to completely follow our consciences, we seem unable to deal with police misconduct as we do with all other kinds of wrongdoing. No politician of any party, no business tycoon, no matter how well connected, is immune from our inquiry or prosecution. But short of actual police corruption, which both we and the department do vigorously deal with, we seem unable to treat police brutality, perjury, or other misconduct as we would the misconduct of anyone else. The relationships are just too close.

A few days after the Crowe shooting, James A. Wechsler, a syndicated columnist for the *New York Post*, does a lengthy column on the shooting of Ofsei, using the complaint for assault that Crowe has filed in court against the driver of the Peugeot.

> At 5:30 p.m., the Sunday *Times* reported, Ptl. Patrick Crowe was directing traffic at Madison Ave. and 34th Str. A green Peugeot bearing Michigan license plates tried to cross Madison going west into 34th St. Crowe ordered it to stop; the driver defied the edict and also, the patrolman recalled, "Made an obscene gesture."
>
> In what was described as usual procedure to prevent escapes, Crowe tried to seize the ignition keys. He ran alongside the car for one block and was dragged another; finally, he said, he freed his arm, "got my gun out, and fired two times in the air and two times at the car."
>
> One of his bullets struck the head of Julius Ofsei, the inoffensive pedestrian, bringing sudden death.
>
> Even accepting every detail of the patrolman's story, the tragedy is senseless. He was not in hot pursuit of some notorious killer whose escape might have exposed others to assault before he was apprehended. He was dealing with a recalcitrant traffic violator . . .
>
> No one disputes the right of patrolmen to employ weapons where their own lives may be at stake; unfortunately . . . But there is no semblance of sanity or safety in a policy which permits a

patrolman to believe that the flight of a traffic violator is sufficient excuse for shooting things up on a major thoroughfare or anywhere else. . . .

And then in his final thrust, Wechsler draws the comparison between our failures to deal with police misconduct and our relentless pursuit of obscenity.

One dreams that District Attorney Hogan's office will display as much diligence in the case of Ptl. Crowe as it has in rescuing us from the verbal villainies of Lenny Bruce. But one offers no bets on the prospect.

Wechsler's attention is drawn to Bruce, I think, because on December 16, just ten days before Crowe fired his gun on Madison Avenue, Lenny Bruce was sentenced to four months imprisonment by Chief Judge Murtagh. At the sentencing, Kuh recommended that no mercy be granted because Bruce had shown "a complete lack of any remorse whatsoever."

The Wechsler column hits home. I intend to ask my colleagues for authority to indict Patrolman Patrick Crowe for manslaughter in the death of Julius Ofsei. But I know I don't have a chance in hell in getting their approval.

Chapter Nine

Time to Move On
January–February 21, 1965

THE **HOMICIDE** **BUREAU** meeting in February is just what I expect. There is genuine sympathy for Ofsei and his family. There is genuine outrage at the conduct of Crowe. However, the sentiment of my colleagues is that the police department should discipline Crowe, and no criminal charge should be brought. When it comes to the vote, only two of us want to recommend a manslaughter indictment to the grand jury. Only ADA Peter Koste joins with me. It is more than disheartening. It is infuriating.

I am sure I know why Koste votes to indict. On August 28, 1963, eighteen months before our meeting on Crowe, the day Martin Luther King, Jr. made his immortal "I have a dream" speech at the Lincoln Memorial, two young women were brutally murdered after a sexual assault, one of them in the third-floor apartment they shared on East 88th Street in Manhattan. There were no suspects.

I was still in Criminal Courts at the time. But the case captured my attention and much of the city's. It became the "Career Girls Murder Case." When I arrived at the Homicide Bureau, the case was still open. Janice Wylie, twenty-one-years old, niece of author Philip Wylie, and her roommate Emily Hoffert, twenty-three, were discovered dead by a third roommate. A burglar, apparently caught in the act by the girls, had violated and then savagely butchered them. There were no clues, and no suspects. Prospects for solving the crimes were dim.

The understandable concern of many thousands of women living alone in New York City apartments caused a media frenzy. The inability to solve the crime left a sense of unease in apartment-dwelling City residents. The murders remained open from August 28, 1963, until April 25, 1964. By then I was in the Homicide Bureau.

On April 24, 1964, some eight months after the Wylie/Hoffert murders, detectives in Brooklyn arrested George Whitmore, Jr., a nineteen-year-old black man, on an unrelated charge. One of the detectives in the Brooklyn precinct at Whitmore's arrest, Edward Bulger, had worked the Career Girls Murders in Manhattan the year before. He had been in the Wylie/Hoffert apartment. He knew the details of the murder scene. He also believed that a photo of a blonde white girl found in Whitmore's pocket at the time of his Brooklyn arrest was that of one of the victims, the pretty, blonde Janice Wylie, who had been slaughtered along with Emily Hoffert. They had been stabbed at least sixty-three times between them, left tied up back to back, with Janice eviscerated, her intestines on the floor, after she had been sexually attacked. Emily's neck had been sawed at. Knives taken from the apartment's kitchen had been broken during the savagery of the attack and lay on the floor next to the girls' mutilated bodies, along with Coke bottles that the assailant had used to beat his victims. These details had not been released to the public. As a member of the bureau, I was shown photographs of the scene. I have always regretted looking at them.

After a twenty-six-hour interrogation of Whitmore at the 73rd Street precinct station, the Brooklyn police telephoned Manhattan North homicide to report that Whitmore had confessed to the Wylie/Hoffert murders. The call went out to the Manhattan homicide ADA on duty to rendezvous with a police car to go to the Brooklyn precinct, meet the stenographer, and take Whitmore's statement. To my eternal relief, I was not on duty that night. It was ADA Peter Koste's turn.

It was Koste that warned Whitmore of his rights, and then took a sixty-one-page confession that itemized the circumstances and numerous details of the crimes. When finished, Koste authorized booking Whitmore for the double homicide. Had I been on call, I would have done exactly as he did.

That night, Chief of Detectives Lawrence McKearney explained to the press that Whitmore confessed that he entered the East 88th Street apartment building to go to the roof, but on impulse entered the victims' apartment. Finding two women there, he used Coke bottles and three knives to beat and carve up the victims. According to the confession summarized by the police, after Whitmore killed the girls, he bound the bodies together and, as he left the apartment, he took a picture of the blonde girl with him. McKearney told the press that the photograph was on Whitmore when he was arrested. "We got the right guy. No question about it. He gave us details only the killer could know."

We later learned that there were two things wrong with that statement. First, there was not one word of truth to the Whitmore confession. He was not the right guy. The photograph was not Janice Wylie, but Arlene Franco, a woman whose photo Whitmore had found in a junkyard and who was still alive. Whitmore had not been in the Manhattan apartment of Wylie and Hoffert; instead, he had been watching Martin Luther King's "I have a dream" speech on television along with witnesses in Wildwood, New Jersey. Beyond question, he did not commit the murders. He had never been in the apartment. He had no way personally to know a single one of the many details in his sixty-one-page statement.

The second thing wrong in the police statement was its claim that only the killer knew the details of the crime. The police who interrogated Whitmore themselves knew all the details of the killings. That, of course, we ADAs did know. What we could not even imagine was that the police would feed sixty-one pages of details to an innocent man before our ADA colleague was called to the police station in Brooklyn.

As a result of an outstanding investigation by our office, led by ADA Mel Glass (who was not in our bureau), Richard Robles was identified through informants as the real killer. That information was confirmed beyond doubt through electronic surveillance of Robles. Our office indicted Robles and exonerated Whitmore.

As for the Brooklyn police officers who "interrogated" Whitmore and undoubtedly furnished him sixty-one pages of details—they were never prosecuted by the Brooklyn DA, or by our office, or disciplined by the police department.

On January 26, 1965, one month after Patrolman Crowe shot Ofsei, the indictment of Robles for the Career Girl Murders was handed down. That same day, Hogan simultaneously announced the exoneration of Whitmore stating, "In spite of every safeguard, occasional honest mistakes are made. To eliminate even this minute fraction of error is the ceaseless effort of those charged with the administration of justice."

And it is only a few days after Whitmore's exoneration when, at our bureau meeting on the Madison Avenue shooting, Peter Koste alone joins me in voting to indict Crowe. In all fairness to my colleagues, notwithstanding their refusal to recommend a manslaughter indictment to the grand jury, the final instructions are that while we will not recommend an indictment, neither will we ask for a "no bill," but will simply present the case without any recommendation. We will let the chips fall where they may.

I make the presentation before the grand jury. As I begin to call witnesses, one of the senior ADAs in the bureau, James C. Mosley, enters and sits in the rear. It is clear to me that Al Herman has sent him in to monitor me and make sure I toe the line. Ironically, it is unnecessary To my surprise, the blue-ribbon grand jury has no interest in proceeding against the policeman. Instead, it votes misdemeanor information against the driver of the Peugeot, charging him with obstructing an officer in the exercise of his authority.

As I prepare the paperwork, I conclude that I should be moving on. However, I have a four-year commitment to the office until February 2, 1966, almost a year away. I know that Hogan often relaxes that pledge if the ADA leaves for public service elsewhere, and that is where I want to go anyway. So I make my decision. I will look for another law enforcement position. By February 19, 1965, the information against the driver of the Peugeot is ready to be filed, and my decks are clear enough for me to start looking. But two days later I abandon my plan. Malcolm X is assassinated.

Chapter Ten

The Murder of Malcolm X
February 21, 1965

February 21, Sunday

I have the duty again. Usually nothing happens on a Sunday. Particularly in the afternoon. And Sunday afternoons are almost as good as Wednesday and Friday nights for single people like me to do a little barhopping.

That's exactly what I'm doing. I'm dancing in a spot called Ondine's, a hot club on 59th Street, right across from the 59th Street Bridge. It is wildly popular. The dance floor is so crowded you could not fall down, even though couples are leaping up and down, sometimes with their hands straight up in the air. The music is throbbing and I am jumping around in what I hope passes as dancing, trying to impress my blonde partner whom I just met. As I approach exhaustion, she mercifully suggests a drink, and I gratefully lead her by the hand through the mob to the bar. As I get there, I hear a man whose back is to me say to another, "Yeah, Malcolm X was shot." I can't believe my ears.

I put my arm on his shoulder to get his attention, and when he turns, I say, "But he's not dead, right?"

"Yes, he's dead."

"But they didn't catch anybody, right?"

"Yes," he says, "they caught a guy."

"But it's not Manhattan, right?" I say, thinking that Malcolm X's home is in Queens or Brooklyn. I don't remember which, but I do recall it had been firebombed just a few days before. Anyway, it's my last hope.

"Yeah, Manhattan. The Audubon Ball Room in Harlem."

That did it. Without another word I abandon the blonde and all hope for the evening and start moving for the only telephone I can see in the place. It's in a booth, and I can see through the pane in the door that there's a guy in there on the phone. I don't care if he is talking to his mother or his bookmaker. I need that phone. So, for only the second time in my career, I pull out my shield and grab the door and open it. With badge in hand, I yank him out of the booth—gentler than with the pickpocket a couple of years before, but not much. He looks like he's about to hit me.

"Police business," I tell the guy as I brush past him and dial Manhattan North homicide as fast as I can.

"Mr. Stern, where've you been?" These are words coming out of the telephone that I will never forget. "We got the entire brass up at the 34th. They are waiting for YOU!"

So I'm out on the street as quick as I can get there and in a very few minutes I am in a police car speeding up to the 34th Precinct. A few minutes more, and I am fighting through a mob of reporters to get into the cop house and then up the stairs. There is more police hierarchy milling around than I have ever seen in one place before. They need me because they have a man in custody that they want to book. I'm told his name is Thomas Hagan. It turns out that's not his name. His real name is Talmadge Hayer. We learn that later in the day through an FBI check on his fingerprints.

Hagan won't talk. No chance for a Q&A. He's in the hospital, shot in the thigh by one of Malcolm X's bodyguards as he fled into the street. Other than giving cops an alias, he won't talk at all. There is no doubt that he is one of the shooters. And even this early we know that there are at least two, probably three shooters, and it looks like at least one and maybe more aiders and abettors who were in the room where Malcolm X was murdered. It is shaping up as a four- or five-man hit squad.

Before the end of the long evening, we have a preliminary but clear outline of what occurred in the Audubon Ballroom that afternoon.

Malcolm got up to speak in front of 300 to 400 of his followers. As soon as he greeted the crowd, two men caused a disturbance. One yelled, "Get your hand out of my pocket!" Someone threw a smoke bomb in the rear of the ballroom. While people turned away from the stage to see the disturbance, a man in the front blasted away at Malcolm X with a sawed-off shotgun. As Malcolm fell, two men rushed the stage, each shooting with a handgun. The three shooters fled, one out through a side restroom, the other two bolting from the stage, through the folding chairs of the audience to exit from the front entrance. The audience itself turned into a mob, boiling out the front entrance and into the street.

We have the shotgun. It was found at the scene wrapped in a coat. We do not have the two handguns. But we do have Hagan. As he ran to leave the ballroom, one of Malcolm's bodyguards, Reuben Francis, shot Hagan in the thigh. Although wounded, Hagan hobbled to the street where he was mobbed and beaten. A policeman and a sergeant reached him, but the mob continued the assault. The sergeant, Alvin Aronoff, pulled his gun and fired a warning shot in the air. The mob pulled back long enough for the two officers to save Hagan.

The scene, including the shot in the air, was captured on film by a TV camera crew. When Hagan was searched, in his pocket he had a clip for a .45 automatic with four live shells in it. Since we do not have the handguns, we cannot be certain that a .45 was used in the assassination, but we will find out for sure when the slugs in Malcolm's body are analyzed. Likely we will find he was shot with at least one .45, in addition to the shotgun.

I am satisfied with what we have so far. I order Hagan to be booked for homicide, and Reuben Francis to be arrested for feloniously assaulting Hagan and for illegal possession of a handgun.

By the time I leave the precinct there are other things that are clear to me. First, I will have no time to sit as a full-time second chair in the Donohue trial. Second, I will have to postpone any thought of leaving the office until the investigation is completed. Third, whatever we do, the investigation will be closely watched by different groups and factions and indeed by the general public. Fourth, and finally, whatever we do, and no matter how well we do it, we will be judged to be wrong in one venue or another. Maybe even in all of them.

Chapter Eleven

The Murderers
February–April 1965

FEW MURDERS ARE committed in a stadium setting with hundreds of onlookers, all disciples of the victim, all anxious to apprehend the killers, but virtually all suspicious of and antagonistic to the authorities. That is exactly what we are facing as I leave the 34th Precinct at the end of the very long first day.

We have to get the shooters. To do that we have to persuade the people in the ballroom, many of whom regard us as "white devils," not only to speak to, but also confide in us. They have to be persuaded not merely to name the perpetrators, but to testify and help us white cops and DAs put the black perpetrators in jail. Unless and until we get the shooters there is no hope of bringing the ones who ordered the assassination to justice. Yet even on this first night we believe we know who ordered the killing and why it was done. So do Malcolm's followers, who within twenty-four hours of the assassination burn down Mosque No. 7 of the Nation of Islam in Harlem. But we will have no ability to make a legal case against the higher-ups in the Black Muslims unless we can get the shooters to talk. To do that, we first have to identify and then find them.

Over the next few days we learn more about the two competing Muslim organizations in Harlem: the Nation of Islam (NOI), headed by Elijah Muhammad, known as the Black Muslims; and the recently-formed Organization of Afro-American Unity, the OAAU, established by Malcolm X after his expulsion from the NOI. They compete for membership and for money. And until he was shot, Malcolm was clearly winning. We know we must learn the history of this struggle to have any chance of apprehending the men who sent the shooters. Even as we begin to reconstruct the events of the twenty-first by locating the people in the ballroom who witnessed them, we steep ourselves in the history of the competing organizations.

The Black Muslims are under the absolute control of their founder Elijah Muhammad, whose birth name is Poole. It is a faith, religion, movement—whatever term one chooses. It is also a very substantial business, generating a river of cash that flows to Elijah Muhammad in Chicago. That flow maintains him and his family in an opulent lifestyle.

From our interviews we learn that each member of the church is expected to pay $13.50 per week, not an inconsiderable sum under the circumstances. Additionally, each member must pay $200 on Saviours' Day, which is the birthday of Elijah Muhammad. And then there are the *Muhammad Speaks* newspaper sales.

Long before the shooting, I had seen young men, always neat and well turned out, hawking these papers all over the city. I knew that they were Black Muslims. I had thought they collected the money from the sales and then turned it in to their organization. After the shooting, I learn that is not correct. These young men are required to buy the papers with their own money. They pay $44 for each edition. They recoup their money only if they can sell the papers allotted to them. It is their money that goes to Chicago. What they do not sell, they have to eat. Enormous funds flow to the elderly leader from this one source alone, with its claimed circulation of 60,000 copies.

There are NOI mosques in several major cities: New York, Mosque No. 7; Chicago, which is headquarters; Boston; and so forth. Each mosque has a minister and a captain. They share responsibility, although the minister seems first among equals. The captain heads the FOI, the Fruit of Islam, a quasi-military organization. It is the FOI that takes and gives karate classes. It is the FOI that is the strong arm of the Nation of Islam. It is the FOI that sells *Muhammad Speaks* on the street corners of the cities.

Malcolm had been the minister of Mosque No. 7 in Harlem, but he was far more than that. He was the charismatic voice of the Nation. As his eloquence grew, so did his reputation and his standing in black communities, until it eventually threatened to eclipse that of Elijah Muhammad himself. Then, too, there were Mr. Muhammad's sons. It was becoming clear that it would be Malcolm, not they, who would inherit the Nation once the elderly Muhammad was no more. What then would become of the 16-room mansion in Chicago and the recently built lavish home in Arizona, where Muhammad and his family reside? There is no doubt that the higher Malcolm climbed, the more the Chicago headquarters desired to cut him down, and if that was not possible, to cut him out.

A few days after the assassination of John F. Kennedy on November 22, 1963, Malcolm's comment that the president's assassination was "chickens coming home to roost" provided the old man with his opportunity. He ordered Malcolm silenced for ninety days. Malcolm meekly and obediently complied, fully expecting to resume his national barnstorming after the ninety days. But the old man had no intention of allowing Malcolm to keep his position. It took Malcolm time to comprehend that he was out of the Nation, but eventually he did. Then it became open war.

By March of 1964 the Nation demanded that Malcolm vacate the home in Queens, which had been provided to him in his position as minister. In April, when he refused to leave, the Nation sued to evict him. That month Malcolm made his pilgrimage to Mecca, traveled throughout Africa, and returned to the United States with a proclaimed changed attitude toward white America. He said he had come to believe that the races *could* work together. By June he had publicly attacked Elijah Muhammad for having fathered six illegitimate children. Malcolm claimed that he broke with the Nation because of these moral lapses.

On June 28, 1964, Malcolm announced the formation of OAAU, the Organization of Afro-American Unity, and launched a drive for members in competition with the Nation of Islam. Over the next six months, he drew members and funds from the Nation, as well as numerous threats from Black Muslims. He met with two of the women suing Elijah Muhammad for paternity, and offered them his support.

The fight between the two organizations became open and notorious, and violent. On February 14, 1965, Malcolm's home in East Elmhurst, Queens, was firebombed at two in the morning. His wife and four daughters were asleep inside at the time, fortunately unhurt. Finally, on February 21 he was assassinated.

So we know the likely motive for the killing, and the likely source of the order to kill. But this is worthless if we can't identify the shooters, and then climb the ladder of their information to reach the higher-ups.

Before the end of the first Sunday we have a team and a plan in place. Some thirty detectives, under the overall command of Assistant Chief Inspector Joseph L. Coyle, and led on the ground by Homicide North detectives John Kelly and Bill Confrey, plus Ferdinand "Rocky" Cavallaro of the 34th Precinct, begin to interview every person who was in the ballroom.

We create a funnel. The detectives are the large end of the funnel. They interview everyone they can find who was in the ballroom. What did he or she see and hear? Equally important, who were they sitting next to? Who did they recognize, whether seated next to them or distantly. In hour after hour of painstaking interviews, the team begins to reassemble the ballroom and to fill in as many seats as possible with names and addresses attached to them.

I am at the narrow end of the funnel. The detectives pass on to me persons with significant knowledge. I determine if these people should go before the grand jury. But there is one witness I never get to see: Brother Gene—Gene Roberts—an undercover cop who was in the audience. I never even hear his name. Chief Coyle finds a moment to casually mention to me that, "We had an undercover cop in the room." Then he laughs derisively, "but when the shooting started, he threw himself on the ground and saw nothing."

Within three days of intensive interviewing the detectives have several witnesses who identify Norman 3X Butler as the second shooter with the handgun. He is described as a diehard Black Muslim, a karate expert, and a member of the FOI, the Fruit of Islam. He is out on bail, accused of shooting a correction officer by the name of Benjamin Brown, another defector from the Black Muslims, who had opened a storefront church competing with the NOI.

I believe we have enough to authorize the detectives to bring Butler in to the 34th Precinct. I want a lineup so our witnesses will have a chance to identify him in person. On the evening of February 25 I wait at the station while the police bring in Butler. They are told not to arrest him but to invite him in. I want to see if the identifications will hold up before I authorize the arrest and booking.

They bring him in close to midnight on the twenty-fifth. His appearance is formidable. Tall, over six feet, looking fit. He matches the physical description of a karate instructor as described by our witnesses.

He goes into a room to stand with other black men who are similar in appearance. The witnesses are able to observe him through one-way glass. Two people identify him as one of the two pistol-shooters. I conclude it was the Luger, which we have not recovered, although it's been identified as a murder weapon by ballistics. The other handgun, the .45, has been turned over to the FBI, which turned it over to us. That gun matches the clip of bullets found in Hagan-Hayer's pocket when he was arrested. So Hayer used the .45, which leaves Butler with the other handgun, the Luger.

After the identifications are made, the detectives bring Butler back to me. I give him his rights, and he is more than willing to talk to me. He is self-confident, even loquacious. He proclaims his innocence and protests that, as a good Muslim, he is not capable of violence. After we speak at 3:00 a.m., I authorize booking him for the first-degree murder of Malcolm X. It is now the early morning hours of February 26, less than five days after the assassination, and we have two of the three shooters.

March 1

We convene the grand jury and I begin presenting evidence of the background of the conflict between Malcolm and his former colleagues, and also feed in eyewitnesses as they are discovered.

March 3

We have enough evidence and eyewitness identifications to get the third shooter, the man who wielded the shotgun, Thomas 15X Johnson. He is the other Black Muslim enforcer implicated with Butler in the shooting of the correctional officer, Benjamin Brown.

March 5

I instruct the team to pick up Johnson. I am at the stationhouse when he arrives. We have enough eyewitnesses identifying him to book him. But first I try to talk to him. He is less militant than Butler. He, too, denies any role in the shooting. I order him booked for the murder of Malcolm X. We now have all three shooters under arrest.

But the presentation before the grand jury must continue. We must put people under oath who were in the ballroom. They have to either ID the three men, or say they are unsure as to any one of them or, if it is the case, deny Butler or Johnson were the men who fired at Malcolm. Given the hostility of Malcolm's followers, many of whom are former Black Muslims, it is a difficult assignment for us.

Mrs. Betty Shabazz, the widow of Malcolm X, is a prime example. She has been interviewed by the detectives. Although she knows that we are trying to bring her husband's killers to justice, she is hostile to us. Inasmuch as she sat close to the stage at the time her husband was shot, she may be in a position to identify one or more of the three shooters. As it happens, she cannot. This is because, understandably, when the shooting started, she immediately got her four children under cover on the floor. She threw herself on top of them, protecting them with her own body as her husband, their father, was murdered a few feet away. Still, we must record what she saw and establish under oath what she has already told the detectives. That is, even though she cannot implicate Hayer, Butler and Johnson, she does not exculpate them.

Although she refuses to share it with the detectives, Mrs. Shabazz does have one important piece of information. She and her children had been driven to the Audubon Ballroom and escorted to their seats by a man who then sat somewhere in the ballroom. He, too, may have seen the shooting but she has refused to tell the team his name. We need to interview him, so I subpoena her before the grand jury.

She arrives with her lawyer, Oliver Sutton, who is one of the leading black attorneys in the city, and who is also the brother of Percy Sutton, an even more prominent lawyer and political figure. Mr. Sutton has to remain in the waiting room as I escort her in because only the witness, the DA, the stenographer, and of course, the grand jurors, may be present.

"Mrs. Shabazz, you were married to Malcolm X, is that correct?"

"Yes."

"And Mrs. Shabazz, on Sunday, February 21, 1965, did there come a time that you went to the Audubon Ballroom located here in New York County?"

"Yes."

I decide to see if she will give the name that she had withheld from my team. "And who were you with?"

"I'd rather not say."

My hope that once under oath she would reveal the name has been frustrated. I must get the information before she leaves, but I decide to postpone a possible confrontation until I have dealt with the identification of the shooters. "Well, in any case were you with your children?"

"Yes, the four of them."

"Where did you seat yourself?"

"It was in the front, in a booth."

I decide to bring her quickly to the event that ends her husband's life. "Did your husband walk up to the rostrum?"

"Yes."

"And did he say anything that you recall?"

"Yes, I don't recall the exact words, but it was the usual greeting."

"And after that what if anything happened?"

"Well, a few minutes later someone on the left-hand side, not too far back stood up and in a very loud and demanding voice said, 'take your hands out of my pocket,' or 'don't go in my pocket,' or something like that."

"When you heard that sound, or those words, did you turn around and look?"

"Yes, I turned around and looked."

"And what did you see?"

"I saw a man standing. I could see his back, sandy jacket on, more rust color."

"And then what happened?"

"I heard my husband say, 'Everything's right, everything's all right.' The guards that were in front went to see what the commotion was."

"After they moved in that direction, what if anything happened next?"

"I heard several shots in succession."

"And what did you see then?"

"Well, I thought it was the men that were, organizing you know, in the middle, so everybody was on the floor. So I got on the floor and I pushed my children under the seat and protected them with my body."

"Now, when you finally did raise up and begin to look again, was there any more shooting going on?"

"No."

It is time to move to the issue of identification of the shooters. The first question is whether or not she saw their faces. "Now, did you actually see the face of the man in this brown or rust colored jacket who you saw standing?"

"No, I only saw the back profile."

I place the photographs of Hayer, Butler, and Johnson on the witness table. "I ask you to look at the three photographs on the table before you, which have been marked grand jury exhibits number one, two, and three and I ask you whether or not you can say whether any of those men were or were not the man who stood?"

"I can't say if it was."

She cannot identify the defendants as shooters. But she does not exonerate them. She just doesn't know.

"Do you know any of the men portrayed in grand jury exhibits number one, number two, and number three before you?"

"Not by name, but I have seen them. I have seen this one."

She identifies Thomas 15X Johnson. And she goes on to explain where she has seen him before the day of the shooting. "I have seen him at the . . . when I was a Black Muslim, but I haven't been a Black Muslim since the last two years."

"And where did you see him, was that in Mosque #7?"

"Yeah."

I have now finished almost all that I have to cover, including the identifications, or the lack of them. I intend to obtain the name of the additional potential witness, even if it means a confrontation with her.

"Mrs. Shabazz, whom did you go to the Audubon Ballroom with that day?"

"I said earlier that I'd rather not say."

"Well, I can understand that, but on the other hand I believe you are required to answer that question. I understand that your attorney is outside, would you like to speak with him before you—before the question is put to you again?"

"No."

I can't believe my ears. "You do not wish to?"

"No," she says emphatically.

"Well," I say, shaking my head in disbelief, "do I understand that you refuse to answer that question?"

"I said I'd rather not say," she says, and then lets me have it. "You can put it in whatever language you'd like."

Now I am getting mad. "Mrs. Shabazz, I am asking you directly, who did you go to the Audubon Ballroom with on February 21, 1965? And I have to inform you that legally you are required to answer the question, and if you doubt what I say on the law, your attorney Mr. Oliver Sutton is right outside in the waiting room, and you can speak to him about it."

Things are getting very hot. And that is not what anyone wants. I look over to the foreman of the grand jury for help.

"Mrs. Shabazz," he says, "the purpose of the grand jury is to see that justice is done in this case or any other case. Please think very carefully about it before you decide not to answer it. Every question that the district attorney is asking is for that same purpose."

The foreman is black, but that does not help. She still does not answer. I am desperate to get her lawyer involved. I am sure he will tell her to answer. "Now, if you'd like to, your attorney is outside, and you can consult with him about it," I say, in my most conciliatory tone.

But she sits like stone. Not moving. Not speaking. I am unhappy. I don't want to bring her before a judge, but I will if I have to. I begin to make my record for the judge. "Mrs. Shabazz," I say, with my cuff pulled back as I look at my watch, "I think the record should reflect that there has been a silence on your part for at least a minute or a minute and a half," and with emphasis on each word delivered, slowly, "Do you wish to consult with your attorney?"

"Yes," she finally concedes, "I'll consult with him, but," she glares at me, "I still say I'd rather not answer the question."

Her body language tells me the issue is still in doubt. So I virtually beg her. "You understand that it becomes important and material to this investigation to determine the names of every person that we can who was in the ballroom on that day as a possible witness of the murder involving your husband. You understand that it is the purpose of this question? Do you understand what I am saying, Mrs. Shabazz?"

"I heard you, yes."

"Suppose you consult with Mr. Sutton now, would you do that?"

She leaves, returns, glares at me, and gives the name to the grand jury. I later give it to the detectives and they interview the witness who, as it happens, has nothing of value.

This exchange is typical of the entire investigation. Some attendees who were present at the scene of the murder help, some don't, until at last we reach the point that it is time to indict.

March 10

Exactly seventeen days after the shooting, we recommend, and the grand jury returns, an indictment against Hayer, Butler, and Johnson for murder in the first degree.

Of course the case is not closed. We desperately want to get to the person or persons who ordered the killing. No one in any community, black, white, or other can possibly believe that these three militant members, soldiers if you will, of the Black Muslims did this on their own authority. But we are stumped. We do follow rumors of sightings of higher-up Muslims who were in town shortly before the murder, but there is nothing concrete. We have no case against anyone other than these three shooters, but we keep trying.

Chapter Twelve

"The Kid Had the Key"
April–August 1965

April 8

Donohue is convicted of murder in the second degree. Keenan has done an outstanding job with a tough case. The jury has almost certainly reached the right verdict in rejecting Murder I and instead finding Murder II, unpremeditated murder. It would be tough to find the premeditation necessary for Murder I when the driver of a car shoots his passenger while turning a corner.

When the news reaches me, I celebrate. But I am not in the courtroom. The night before I had the duty and I got the call. It was Manhattan North homicide. An older lady, Mrs. George Georgious, the wife of a Harlem grocer, was found dead in her apartment. She had been bound with three different cords, one electrical. The seventy-year-old woman was apparently stabbed to death, after being sexually molested. According to the detective on the telephone, a TV was found missing.

"Who do you have?" I ask the cop on the phone.

"A kid, he worked for Georgious as a delivery boy. He admits the whole thing."

"How old is he?" I ask.

"Sixteen," is the answer.

"Why did he do it?"

"He says he entered the apartment to steal a TV set, and she caught him in the act."

"Did you recover the TV set?"

"No. We looked for it where the kid said he put it, but it wasn't there."

I don't like it. It is a sixteen-year old Harlem kid alone in a police station. I am thinking about George Whitmore. We need more, at least I need more than this. I ask the detective if he has any corroboration.

"Yes," he says, "the kid had the key in his pocket that fits the old lady's apartment."

Now I feel a whole lot better. "I'll be right there," I tell him, and pull on clothes.

When I get to the precinct, the kid is there. He is young. Alone. Scared. He has been in the stationhouse a long time. The cops get fuzzy when I try to find out how long.

I give the warnings and start questioning him even before putting him on the machine with the stenographer. Immediately, I do not like it. He is talking like a zombie. He knows the details of the three cords used to strangle the woman, but his voice is flat, and the language does not seem right to my ear. It sounds rehearsed. The longer I listen, the less I like it. After he is halfway through it, I stop him and say, "I am sorry. I missed part of that. Would you tell me again, from the beginning?"

He does. But the language is almost exactly the same, as though the lines have been memorized. I am getting more and more concerned. I let him go a little longer, and then I stop him and ask him to do it again. And he does, in almost identical language. Two more times I do this at different points of his story, and each time I get the same feeling of memorization.

Then I start pressing for more details, and suddenly the kid stops talking. The next thing he says is that he didn't do it, and he begins crying. That's great, I think to myself. I just talked this kid out of a confession. What if he did it? After all, he did have a key to the old lady's apartment. How can he explain that?

"What about the key?" I ask him. "The key to Mr. and Mrs. Georgious's apartment?" The kid tells me that it is a key to his friend's apartment. I ask for the name and address of this friend. He gives it to me.

I am angry. I take the precinct detective out of earshot of the kid. "Take the key and see it if works in the door," I tell him. He leaves and I wait, trying to figure out what to do if the key works in the friend's door. I know what to do if it doesn't.

The detective returns and I pull myself out of my chair and hurry to meet him. "Well?" I say. The detective shrugs. "The key works in his friend's door," he mumbles.

Can you believe it, I say to myself. One key and two different apartments? What are the odds of that? I have a confession to rape and murder, with absolutely no corroboration, except the key that obviously turned the cops onto the kid. But that key is more than useless as corroboration; it can create its own reasonable doubt. To top it off, the stolen TV is not where the kid told the cops he put it. All I have is a retracted confession from an impressionable and, from what I can see, a rather slow, under-aged kid.

I can't turn him loose. Not until we at least try to get to the bottom of it. After all, he did admit to murder. But I know that I am not going to prosecute him if this is all we are ever going to have against him. I will not simply throw it all in front of a jury and see if it says, "Guilty." I remember the words all too well, "*Mr. Stern, if you did not want us to convict him, why did you prosecute him?*" I do not want this kid convicted on his uncorroborated, retracted confession. We have to see if there is more. He is not going to face the chair or even life imprisonment on what we have. One George Whitmore is enough.

I tell the cops to book him, but I also tell them that there will be no prosecution if they do not find corroboration.

Chapter Thirteen

A New Beginning
April–September 1965

DONOHUE IS SENTENCED. He gets thirty-five years to life. Hayer, Butler, and Johnson are indicted. The investigation goes on, but we have no way to get above the shooters.

There is no more evidence to implicate the kid in the grocer's wife's killing. After the bureau votes not to indict, the grand jury votes to no-bill the arrest. Vincent Dermody will try the Malcolm X case, but that is months away and when the trial does come he will handle all of the witnesses.

I feel that I can depart without leaving a mess, and I do want to go. What really bothers me is the whole scene. I don't care for it anymore. Funny thing is I would have killed to get the job three years earlier. I loved it for most of those three years, but now I have had it with run-down police stations in the dead of night and even with the city itself. And things have not been the same between the bureau and me since the Crowe case.

I do want to stay in law enforcement, but at a different level and in a different place. My father wants me to stay, at least in the city. I have no siblings, and he has no wife since my mother died a dozen years ago. Our dinners every week or ten days are all the family get-togethers either of us has. When I go, it will be tough for him and me too. He is all that I care about in the city. I promise myself I will keep in close touch with him, but now it is time for me to go.

I apply to the United States Department of Justice, to its Criminal Division, to the Organized Crime and Racketeering Section. They say yes, as long as I pass a full field background check by the FBI. I know what that means. They will be checking with neighbors and with schools, past employers, and Hogan's office, for sure. I therefore figure I had better go see the boss before the FBI goes tapping on Executive ADA Worgan's door.

I have an appointment. You generally do not walk right in without one. I had to say why I wanted to see the boss. So Hogan knows what is coming, and I suspect that this is not going to be a good conversation. And it's not. As I enter the sacred precincts, he points to a chair. He is cold as he looks at me. I do not get to speak. There are no warm-up words, and certainly no words of thanks for three and a half years of service. Just "I will speak to Dermody. If he tells me that he needs you for the Malcolm X trial, I will call the attorney general in Washington and ask him to delay your appointment." He nods at me. I get the message to leave his office, so out I go.

But I am not worried. I figure the Homicide Bureau has had enough of me, as I have had enough of them. I reckon I will be leaving on schedule. I am not even mad at Hogan. After all, he did give me the job in the first place, and I am shaving four months off of the four-year commitment. The differences between us are philosophical, not personal. I would do some things he would not: I would go after cops who abuse people and I would not do what he tries to do as a policeman of morals, like obscenity crusades. But he is the boss, and I am not likely to be one.

September 25

My last day as an ADA. There are brief goodbyes in the homicide wing of the office. The guys give me the traditional desk/pen set with my badge mounted on the base of it. For me it's a nice memento, and it is their guarantee that I won't be pulling it on anyone in the future. With that, I leave 155 Leonard Street for the last time.

I have an apartment waiting for me in Southeast Washington, not far from the Capitol. It is in a project called The Capital Park. This apartment is a lot bigger than what I have been living in. I can afford more because the feds pay better. I am to get $12,000 a year with them, and to top it off, D.C. is cheaper than New York City. I am feeling flush.

I go back to 76th Street to meet the movers. But they don't come.

It's getting dark. I'm supposed to be out of the place. I am crazy mad with waiting, but eventually I have no alternative. I go into the street and stop small trucks and start conversations with drivers. Eventually, I find a truck with a man in it who is willing to make a deal. Some cash changes hands, and the two of us go up and down lugging my furniture the three flights of the four-story walk-up. In a few hours, we have it all loaded. I jump into the cab of the truck, which now smells like a gym, and off we go to Washington, D.C. I get there long after midnight, literally on top of everything I own in the world, ready for my new career. But first we have to unload the truck.

BOOK II

FOR THE UNITED
STATES

Chapter One

The Department of Justice
November 1, 1965

November 1

After a month off between jobs I report for duty to the Organized Crime and Racketeering section of the Criminal Division in the United States Department of Justice at 9th and Pennsylvania Avenue. It's a five-story building with the FBI occupying the fifth floor and the Department holding the rest. J. Edgar Hoover himself is on the fifth floor.

I am excited. I feel I have taken a step up, that is, until I am assigned to the Labor Unit to sit in a big room with two other guys. No more private office. I am one of three. The other two are young. Larry Lippe and Jonathan L. Goldstein are fresh out of law school. My new boss, Phil Willens, is a longtime department attorney who heads the Labor Unit within the Organized Crime Section. My job in the Labor Unit is to review labor racketeering investigations conducted by United States Attorneys around the country to make sure they are doing okay.

The country is divided into judicial districts, over ninety of them. Some states have as many as three or even four districts. Some have just one. For example, New York has four: the Southern, Eastern, Western and Northern Districts; New Jersey has just one; Pennsylvania has three; Massachusetts just one; and so forth. The number of districts per state is often a product of ancient local, political, and territorial wars for patronage within each state, most long forgotten. Each district has its own United States Attorney's office, its own federal marshal, and its own coterie of United States District Judges. The district judges and United States Attorney (USA) for each district are appointed by the president and confirmed by the Senate. The United States Attorney is the chief federal law enforcement officer for his district, and he appoints his own Assistant United States Attorneys (AUSAs) provided the candidates pass the full field security check of the FBI.

There are underlying tensions in this set-up. The USAs are "recommended" by the senators of their states on the basis of local relationships and/or political contacts. The recommendations go through the Justice Department to the White House, which makes the formal nomination to the Senate for confirmation. Unless the prospect is demonstrably objectionable, the recommendation of the home state senator is often tantamount to appointment, because the Senate will not confirm any presidential nomination for USA or district judge unless both home state senators approve by sending in a blue slip to the Judiciary Committee of the Senate. Through senatorial courtesy the members of the Senate, who have relatively little patronage to dispense—compared to governors or \—transform their power to confirm presidential appointments into the dominant voice in the appointing process.

That is only one of many tensions. While the rank and file of the department, particularly the supervisors, are career types, not unlike the DA's office I just left, the highest echelons are political appointees. There are younger department lawyers who come and go, just as in Hogan's office. The supervisory core of the department stays on— administration in, administration out. The top jobs, on the other hand, the bosses of the supervisors, are usually politically connected to the administration, often without experience in the department, sometimes without even a law enforcement background. That tension is usually well-managed by the professionals, who are aided by the fact that the top jobs of attorney general, deputy attorney general, and assistant attorneys general, who head the divisions like criminal, civil, lands and antitrust, are usually short-timers, often unfamiliar with the department, and these short-timers rely on the "professionals" to run things.

A particular frustration to department attorneys are the United States Attorneys. The department attorneys regard many of the USAs as political appointees and amateurs. The USAs, as independent presidential appointees, tend not to take kindly to direction from the department attorneys who head the sections or the various desks, such as the Labor Unit of the Organized Crime and Racketeering Section to which I am assigned. So there tends to be constant jockeying for control between the "seat of government" and the "field" as we refer to them, in mock imitation of the terminology used by the FBI, where the bureau's agents in the field were instructed to refer to Director Hoover's office as the SOG, the seat of government.

The Organized Crime and Racketeering Section attempts to solve the problem of control by sending area men into certain districts, men whose purported mission is to forge into one team the IRS, FBI, and postal inspectors, who are in different departments of the government. While that is the stated reason, it is only part of the reason. The larger goal is to put attorneys into the field who remain under the direct supervision of the professionals in the department.

The FBI presents a different problem. Although subordinate to and physically housed within the department, the bureau does not act as though it is a part of the Department of Justice. Under FBI Director J. Edgar Hoover, the FBI is a virtual law unto itself, except for the attorney-generalship of Bobby Kennedy between 1961 and 1964. That was a moment when the AG was not only professionally adept, having been chief counsel to Senator McClellan's select committee on labor racketeering, but also one of the few hands-on AGs. Kennedy, unlike predecessors and successors, would constantly reach down through supervisory levels and peer into ongoing investigations. To top it off, since Kennedy was the brother of the president, Hoover could not go around or over him. Except for that one brief period, Hoover's FBI functions as though it were an independent agency. It will cooperate with the department, but only when it wishes to. Unfortunately for me, I arrive after Kennedy left to run for the Senate.

This gulf between the FBI and the Department of Justice in Washington is replicated, even heightened, in dealings in the districts between the United States Attorneys and the FBI's special agents in charge (SACs) of the field offices. Each USA and each SAC has a separate chain of command, which, theoretically, meets, only at the attorney general-director level. The SACs report to various FBI desks in

Washington, depending on the category of investigation, even as the typical USA will report to the department. The supervision within the bureau is much tighter than the department's. The bureau is, after all, a quasi-military organization.

There is surface similarity in the relationship of USAs to SACs and in the relationship of the Manhattan DA's office to the New York City Police Department. But there is one big difference. In Manhattan we had our own DA's office squad, which, while administratively reporting to a higher police command, took direct and daily direction from the ADAs who ran the cases. The FBI in the field takes directions *only* from the FBI in Washington. They will work with the USAs, of course, and relationships create coordination. But the AUSAs can only make requests of agents, and USAs can only make appeals to SACs. The response can be and often is "no."

As I sit in my three-man office, reviewing files from districts around the country, learning more and more about this set-up, I wonder if I have made a good move. But I put aside such thoughts. There is no going back. But I need to get out of this building and into a place where I can develop and try cases. I want an assignment in the field.

Chapter Two

Peter Weber
November 1–December 31, 1965

WHEN I AM interviewed and hired, William G. Hundley is the chief of the Organized Crime and Racketeering Section. By the time I arrive in D.C. I am just in time for his retirement dinner, which I chip in for, although I don't see why I should attend for a boss I never had. But I do, just to get off on the right foot.

Henry E. Petersen, the man who actually interviewed and hired me, has stepped up from deputy chief to chief of the Organized Crime Section. He is the boss I have to persuade to put me on the road. After a few weeks I go up to see him. Everyone calls him Pete, but I started calling him Henry before I knew that and never stopped.

Henry has devoted his whole career to the department. A Marine who served in World War II. There he stayed. He began as a file clerk in the FBI while attending law school at night, then became a departmental lawyer in the Internal Security Division. When Attorney General Brownell created the Organized Crime Section in the early 1950s in response to the Kefauver Committee's exposé of the mafia, Henry transferred from the Internal Security Division, where he chased domestic communists, to the Organized Crime Section. The section had been small and weak under Brownell. Under Bobby Kennedy, the section had quadrupled. Now Kennedy is gone. Hundley is gone. But the apparatus that Kennedy created remains, and Henry is the man in charge.

As I sit in his office, I am impressed. Slim, fit looking, with a weather-beaten, craggy countenance and straight dark hair falling over his forehead, he exudes no-nonsense professionalism. My concerns prove groundless. I have no trouble with him. He understands what I want, and he is willing to give it to me.

He has a target for me: Peter Weber, a labor leader who presides in New Jersey. Weber is the president of Local 825 of the Operating Engineers, which controls all the heavy construction in the entire state of New Jersey and five counties in New York State. Nothing major can be built without his men. They run the bulldozers, the backhoes, the cranes, even the compressors that run the jackhammers.

"Compressors?" I ask. "I thought they ran by themselves."

"They do, once you start them. But someone pushes a button four times a day. Once to start in the morning; once for lunch break; once to start again. And the last push shuts it off for the evening."

"Is that legal?"

"Yes—and no. Take a look at the law after you take a look at this file." With that he points to a mound of folders on his desk.

The "file" he gives me is entitled "Weber—Colonial Pipeline." It's more than a file, it's volumes of material: investigations going back to the 1950s; reports; witness interviews; financial records; bank accounts; credit cards; interviews with employers suspected of payoffs. There are thousands of pages of summaries and exhibits. It tells the story of Weber going back many years.

I work the whole month of November on the material by reading, outlining, cataloging exhibits, and matching interviews going back ten years. I come in on Thanksgiving Day. I am all alone on the fourth floor, but then I am all alone in Washington, so it is no burden. I have no family here. No friends here yet. By the end of the month I have my arms around the whole thing.

First, the man. Weber is a giant, physically. Six foot two, 235 pounds, a prizefighter in his early years, later a professional union head-buster in struggles with employers, and bodyguard for the infamous Joey Fay, then head of the Local. In 1945 Fay was convicted by the Manhattan DA's office of extorting $420,000 from employers. After Fay went to jail, Weber took over the union. He also took over Fay's extortions and even Fay's practice of owning interests in construction companies. He became both employer and representative of his union members.

In 1960, a year before he became attorney general, Bobby Kennedy wrote *The Enemy Within*, an account of his time as chief counsel to the

McClellan Committee's investigation of labor racketeering. Weber was called to testify before that committee, whose members included then-senators John F. Kennedy and Barry Goldwater. Bobby did the questioning. He summarized Weber's testimony as follows:

> Peter Weber . . . took over where Fay left off. Weber, who appeared before the committee with a patch over his eye, ran the Union with the ruthlessness characteristic of Fay's day. Weber went into four separate businesses, each one with contracts with his Union. His business partner told us that whenever there were labor problems he simply called one of Weber's underlings in the Union 'who of course were mindful that Weber had an interest in the company.' In 1950, Weber's stock in one of these companies was worth $671. Today it is worth $108,000.
>
> We found that the evils that prevailed in the Fay-Weber regime of the Operating Engineers stretched from coast to coast.

After his 1957 testimony before the committee, Weber immediately transferred all of his holdings to a Mitzi Rocha. This lady also had a position on the union's payroll as Weber's private secretary.

Next, I study the project, the Colonial Pipeline. The nine major oil companies own the Colonial Pipeline Company jointly. Headquartered in Atlanta, Georgia, it was created to build the largest pipeline in history at the time. Called the Big Inch, it is a three-foot wide conduit carrying oil 1,600 miles from Houston, Texas, to Linden, New Jersey. Its construction was bid in roughly fifteen 100-mile segments as it made its way across the country. The oil of the nine companies is commingled all the way. The final resting place is the Colonial Tank Farm in Linden, New Jersey. There the common product is drawn down by each of the companies.

The last ninety miles of the pipeline, the New Jersey segment, was bid, won, and constructed by the Bechtel Corporation, then the largest engineering firm in the world.

According to the file, Weber wanted the New Jersey segment to go to H.C. Price Company of Bartlesville, Oklahoma, not to Bechtel. Even before bids were due, Weber, from New Jersey, telephoned Colonial in Atlanta demanding the project go to Price. Then Weber, certain that Colonial would obey his command, announced to his men that

Price had the job, even before the bidding. When the Bechtel bid was $3,000,000 less than Price's, Colonial felt it had to award the contract to Bechtel. Then the games began.

The day Bechtel was to start, Weber shut them down. The Operating Engineers would not work. No cranes, no bulldozers, no backhoes, no construction of any kind. With a ninety-day schedule for completion, and winter just beyond that, Bechtel and Colonial were desperate.

After a week Weber opened up the job. Then he piled on stationary engineers, whose jobs were to start and stop compressors. To this he added to the Bechtel payroll non-working shop stewards for twenty-one hours a day, six days a week, at double and triple time. The executives at Bechtel and Colonial got his message.

From that point the two mammoth corporations danced to Weber's tune. Not that anyone in either company would admit that they had been pressured, either to the Labor Department, who compiled the file, or in early interviews by FBI agents. But funny things started happening with the subcontracts. Colonial had given a small contract to the Osage Construction Company of Tulsa, Oklahoma. That was suddenly taken away and given to Napp-Grecco Company of New Jersey, whose bid was nearly double that of Osage's. Bechtel, which had planned to construct the pipeline river crossing from Delaware to New Jersey itself, instead gave a contract to Joyce Construction Company of Andover in upstate New York for the project. In the preliminary interviews, the Bechtel people said they did it because the Joyce people said Weber wanted it, but denied any illegal pressure.

After the review I am struck by the turmoil this man Weber visited upon just one pipeline project. I can only imagine what is going on in the scores, even hundreds, of other construction sites throughout New Jersey and into New York. The man is a colossus astride an entire industry. The worst of it is that the officers of every company deny any wrongdoing by Weber. Every one of them denies making payoffs, and Weber's lawyers speak of his legitimate interest in companies that will provide good working conditions for his men.

I am sure that the Price people paid Weber off. They deny it. I am sure James Joyce, the owner of Joyce Construction Company, paid off. He denies it. I am sure Colonial and Bechtel were extorted. They deny it. I have plenty of suspicions, and no evidence. I know what I have to do. I am ready to report to my boss, Henry Petersen.

Chapter Three

New Jersey
January 1966

PETERSEN LISTENS TO my recapitulation. He already knows Weber's background; the department has been after him for years. What he needs to hear is the Colonial Pipeline story. This I gave him in half an hour. It's a jungle of facts with Colonial, Price, Bechtel, Osage, Napp-Grecco, Joyce, and the players in the companies. When I finish, he asks the right question.

"What do you propose to do about it?"

I know that is coming, and I am ready. "I want to convene a grand jury."

"Where?" he asks.

"I'm not sure, either in Atlanta, where Colonial is, or New Jersey where Weber is operating, but I prefer Atlanta." The truth is I have no intention of going back to the New York area. But I want to sound like I am giving due consideration before recommending Atlanta.

"Okay," he says. "I'll get you two letters from the Deputy." He means Deputy Attorney General Ramsey Clark, the son of Supreme Court Justice Tom Clark, "One for grand jury authorization in Atlanta and one for Newark. What else?"

"I need to go on the road before we set up shop. I want to go to Tulsa to see the Osage people; to Bartlesville to see the Price people; to San Francisco to see Bechtel; and to upstate New York to see Joyce; and then to Atlanta to see Colonial. We have to bust through the wall of silence."

"Okay," he says. "I'll have Administration issue you a book of GTRs."

GTRs are government travel requests. They allow us to write our own airline tickets with the bills going back to government.

"Two books," I say.

"Okay, two books. What else?"

"Agents. I want a team of FBI agents to travel with me. Preferably agents with accounting backgrounds because I am going to—"

His laugh interrupts me, "No way. The bureau does not travel. And if they did, which they don't, they wouldn't travel with you."

Henry explains that they send out "leads" via teletype. The leads are the questions to be asked by other agents in field offices. The answers come back the same way.

"That is crazy," I say. "No wonder they get nowhere with investigations like this." Henry shrugs. He doesn't stop me, and I get bolder.

"I want to hear that from them myself. I want to hear the FBI tell me, personally, that they run sophisticated financial criminal cases by teletype." I am a little embarrassed by my own boldness. But Henry says, "Okay" and to my surprise, reaches for the telephone.

In fifteen minutes we are on the fifth floor, which is FBI-land, in the office of "Red" Adams, who runs the bureau's labor desk.

He is just what I expect, given my experience with the bureau in Boston in the Donohue meeting: dark suit, white shirt and conservative tie, picture of family on the desk and an autographed picture of J. Edgar Hoover at a suitable height on the wall. I'm a department lawyer now, not the outsider local ADA, and my boss heads the Organized Crime Section of the Department of Justice. That should get cooperation. But it doesn't.

He listens patiently while I outline the Colonial-Price-Bechtel-Osage-Napp-Grecco-Joyce tangle, much of which he already knows because the reports from the field agents investigating labor go to his desk for review. I tell him that I need accounting-type agents because I want to trace the cash I believe came out of some of these companies and into Weber's pockets. And, I tell him, I want agents specially assigned to travel with me.

"The bureau does not function that way." He turns me down flat. No discussion. I simply can't believe he doesn't understand that sophisticated investigations cannot be run by airtels. You have to look people in the eye. And how about follow-up questions? I am so angry that I lose it.

"You have gotten nowhere with these firms that way. What are you going to do, stick all your people around the country in front of teletype machines? How are agents in Georgia going to know when Bechtel people in San Francisco are giving misinformation about Colonial, or Price or—"

I stop because I can see there is no point. Adams will let me prattle on, but nothing is going to change. Henry spends a moment smoothing over our exit, and then back down we go to his office. Wearing an I-told-you-so grin, he tells me not to worry. He is going to take care of it. From what I have seen of the man, I believe it, even though I don't see how.

****

Three days later, Henry asks me into his office. He tells me he has called the Assistant Secretary of Labor in charge of compliance. They have concurrent jurisdiction with the bureau over labor leaders like Weber. The good news is that the Labor Department has agreed to assign as many as fifteen compliance officers, many of them accountants. Henry tells me he has also called the Treasury Department and they have agreed to donate two IRS special agents—special agents when it's a criminal investigation, revenue agents if civil—in Newark to work with me. Henry tells me that there will be revenue agents as well. I am going to have a small army. But Newark?

"Newark?" I say, with a wrinkled note in distaste.

"Yes," he says. "Newark. And there are some things you ought to know about northern New Jersey. Other places have mobs and some have corrupt politicians. But New Jersey is unique in that the mob controls the political bosses."

By the time he is finished talking, I am appalled. For all the years I spent in New York City within sight of New Jersey, I really had no idea of what he lays out. The place is a snake pit. The big cities, Newark and Jersey City, are totally corrupt. Newark, under Mayor Hugh Addonizio, is in the hands of the mafia. Leaders like Richie "the Boot" Boiardo and his son "Tony Boy," who are captains in the Luchese family; and Angelo "Gyp" DeCarlo, a captain of the Genovese family, these men control Addonizio and therefore the city. Richie the Boot has an incinerator in the rear of his palatial estate in Livingston, New Jersey, where he burns bodies after mob hits. The front of the home is adorned with statues of Boiardo family members, with an enormous figure of the Boot himself astride a plaster horse dominating the display. Petersen tells me that Gyp DeCarlo and Tony Boy sit around DeCarlo's headquarters in Mountainside bragging about the men they have murdered and the bodies they have burned at the Boot's. Now how does Henry know that? I wonder.

A little to the south, Henry goes on, you have Simone Rizzo DeCavalcante, "Sam the Plumber." He controls his own independent family. Anthony "Little Pussy" Russo and his brother, John "Big Pussy" Russo, control the Jersey shore.

The Irish politicians rule Hudson County, which includes Jersey City, Hoboken, Bayonne, Weehawken, and West New York. Former Jersey City Mayor, "Boss" John V. Kenny, the direct successor to Frank "I am the Law" Hague, rules supreme. The mob is there as well, of course. "Bayonne Joe" Zicarelli is the mafia man in charge in Hudson.

The difference between the cities is that while the mob controls the Italian pols in Newark, the Irish politicians in Hudson control the mob. No man in New Jersey has more power than Boss Kenny, although "Bayonne Joe" Zicarelli does control U.S. Congressman Cornelius E. Gallagher, a member of the House Foreign Affairs Committee. This is helpful to Zicarelli, who has a gunrunning business in Latin America, with the greatest emphasis right now on the Dominican Republic.

There are three dominant Democratic political bosses in the north, and a Republican in the south. Kenny in Hudson is first among them all. His close ally, David T. Wilentz, is the boss of Middlesex County, which happens to be where the Colonial Pipeline terminates. Dennis Carey controls Essex County, but since Newark is in Essex County, his voice is less. Frank "Hap" Farley, who took over from boss Enoch "Nucky" Johnson controls the Republican south.

I didn't want to go to New Jersey before this lecture. Nothing I just heard is a mind-changer. But my concern is not the mob. It's Weber. I ask Petersen if Weber is part of the mob. The answer is "no, and then again yes." Weber is his own man. He has 7,500 union men who follow his orders. No one tells him anything. But if there are favors to be done in either direction, they will be done, not as a matter of force or fear but rather out of the respect that rulers accord each other.

"For example," Petersen says, "the mob is paying off the superintendent of the state police, Dominick Capello, to protect gambling at the New Jersey shore, $1,000 per month for gambling in Long Branch and another $1,000 per month for Asbury Park."

Again I wonder how he knows that. And if he knows it, why is it still going on, but what I ask is, "What has that to do with Weber?"

"Weber? Oh, he and Local 825 are organizing the state police."

Chapter Four

Operation Pipeline
January 1966

I AM SURE THAT the Price Company in Bartlesville paid Weber off. Why else would he have called Colonial to demand that Price get the New Jersey segment? Why else did he shut down Bechtel the minute they stepped foot into the state, why else proclaim that if Price had the work there would have been no strike? There is no doubt in my mind. Price paid him off. Now I have to prove it. And I now have a team of investigators to help me, even if they are not FBI agents.

The Department of Labor investigators assigned to me are home-based in Detroit. They will be the nucleus of my team. They are under the command of Anthony Cosolo, deputy area director for Labor in Detroit. His men are not called agents. They are compliance officers. The Labor Department has termed the task force, "Operation Pipeline." The men are on call when I need them. My plan is to make an initial reconnaissance sweep. First Osage, then Price, both in Oklahoma; then Bechtel in San Francisco; finishing with Colonial in Atlanta.

I fly into the Tulsa airport. Cosolo is already there to meet me with a car. We have never seen each other, but I am not hard to spot in Tulsa. A hair under six feet, a pound or so under 160, with dark hair and a blue-striped shirt, initials at the chest, solid blue tie, I look more like an East Coast Jew, which I am, or even an Italian mobster, than a southwesterner from Oklahoma. The incongruities are highlighted by the government-issued briefcase in my hand. Cosolo has no trouble picking me out.

Our first call is on the Osage executives in Tulsa. They welcome the interview, but tell us that they had no direct contact with Weber. All they did was send in a bid from Tulsa to Atlanta for work in New Jersey and get a small contract from Colonial. Next thing they know, Glen Giles, the vice president of Colonial, called and told them Colonial is yanking the contract. "Because," says Giles, "there is going to be labor trouble if not." Colonial writes Osage a check for their "inconvenience." Osage goes quietly into the night. Napp-Grecco of Newark, New Jersey, replaces them.

Their story is interesting, and possibly useful as corroboration if Colonial decides to become a complainant, or if we find payments from Napp-Grecco to Weber. On its own, their testimony would not do it.

The next visit will be the Price people who could help. But I know they won't, because of their stonewalling of investigators from Labor and the FBI in prior interviews. We climb into Cosolo's rental and drive out to the Price Company in Bartlesville, Oklahoma.

Bartlesville is one of the wealthiest small cities in the country. It is the home headquarters of Cities Service and Phillips Petroleum. Those two, with Price are Bartlesville's three largest employers. The town is thriving. I can't believe there is any unemployment here.

The Price Tower looms before us as we approach. It is a Frank Lloyd Wright building, and in my uninformed opinion one of the ugliest office buildings that I have ever seen. Its nineteen stories dominate the Bartlesville skyline. With its peculiar angles and green coloration, to me it looks like a towering insect.

Cosolo and I have an appointment with Harold Price, Jr., the CEO of the privately held company, which had been started by his father, Price, Sr., now deceased. It is a large-sized business, doing pipeline construction all over the world. This is a very wealthy family. Harold lives in a Frank Lloyd Wright designed residence; his mother lives in a Frank Lloyd Wright designed residence; and his brother, Joe, lives in a famous Japanese-style house. All three are located in an enormous family compound.

Now here I come, in my New York City outfit with my Italian sidekick from Detroit, and we are supposed to persuade these people to put their economic lives in our hands by volunteering to be witnesses against one of the most powerful labor leaders in the country. As a government lawyer, I had no trouble setting the appointment. But I expect Price will tell me to go back to Washington as soon as I get upstairs. Cosolo and I get past the receptionist in the lobby and struggle into a weirdly shaped elevator, which expresses us up to the top floor, where Price awaits us.

We find him to be small man, dark, with close-cropped hair, and eyes peering back at us through spectacles. He reminds me of Mr. Peepers. He is modest, friendly, and genuine, not merely playing the rich man doing the gracious-host routine. All in all, he seems a decent, unassuming guy, for one as rich as he is. My trouble with him is his lies to investigators.

This is not his first visit from the feds. The FBI and Labor Department have each been there. He has consistently denied making any illegal payment to Weber. Ten minutes into our conversation, it is plain that he isn't going to change his story.

"Look," I say, "We know Weber called Colonial to get you the job. We know he had to have a reason, and you must have given him one. How much did you pay him?"

He sticks to his story, which is that he promised Weber to open a local office in New Jersey to give his men "year-round" work. That, he explains, accounts for Weber's enthusiasm for his company. That I know is bullshit. The contractors don't provide the sources of the work. New projects provide work to contractors after competitive bidding. No matter which contractor gets a project, Price, Bechtel, Osage, Napp-Grecco, they all have to use Local 825 Operating Engineers on the projects.

I get mad. I tell him that I represent his country; that I speak for the United States. I tell Price that Weber is hurting his country and mine and that we have to stop this racketeer. He listens patiently, polite man that he is. But I can see it won't work.

"If I had something to say—which I don't," he adds, "what are you and what is my government going to do if he sends thugs to break my people's heads? What are you going to do if other labor leaders around the country start slowing my jobs, or loading me up with non-working stewards and featherbedders? What will you do then?"

The trouble is that he is right. There won't be much we can do.

"By the way," he adds, "I hear that Weber is organizing the New Jersey State Police."

"Yes," I say, in defeat, "I heard that, too." That seals it. He is not going to talk. I am going to have to dig for it.

As the three of us stand there, I tell Cosolo that I am leaving. I am going on to San Francisco to see Bechtel, as we planned. But I am going alone. After Cosolo drops me off at the airport, he is to come back to this office and hand Price a Labor Department subpoena. I tell him I want him to go over every financial record in the company, starting a couple months before the Colonial bidding. I want him to turn every check. I want him to find the cash coming out, "because, Tony, I am positive that these people paid Weber." I talk loud, because I want Price to hear it, and I am sure that he does.

Turning to Price, I say, "We are leaving now, but Mr. Cosolo will be back. And once he has found the cash, I will return. And when I do there will be no more offers of immunity or help. We will prosecute you for bribing a labor leader." As I leave for the airport, I am much less confident than I hope I sounded.

As the plane lands in San Francisco, I contemplate the next day's problems, when I'll go to Bush Street in the morning to meet with Bechtel's executives, who will be represented by an outside law firm. The file shows that during interviews by the FBI, and also with the Labor Department, all of the Bechtel employees, from job superintendents in New Jersey to executives in San Francisco, have "chosen" the same lawyers to sit with them. In my opinion, this tends to keep a tight lid on information, which I'm sure is what Bechtel wants, but which is not so good for my client, the United States. I raised this issue when I called for an appointment, and I will do so again tomorrow. I expect that this will cause a flare-up.

I check into my hotel, ready to call it a day when the phone in my room rings. It is Tony Cosolo. He says two words, "they broke" and I go wild. While I am jumping around the room, he fills me in. Within hours after he returned to the building, Price decided to come clean. He took Cosolo aside and confessed. They did pay Weber.

"How much?" I yell into the phone.

"Fourteen thousand dollars," Cosolo replies. Fourteen thousand dollars is not an insignificant sum. It's more than my salary, $12,000 per year at the Justice Department.

"Price is prepared to lay it all out, instruct his people to cooperate, but they have to get immunity," Cosolo continues. I can understand why. An employer who pays off a labor leader is as guilty as the man he pays. No exceptions. I don't have the authority to make the promise. It has to go up the ladder. I tell Cosolo I will handle it.

It's late in Washington, but I call the Justice Department switchboard, and they patch me in to Henry Petersen at home. I'm still jumping up and down, yelling that we have Weber on the first try. Henry is happy, too, but in his quiet way. He immediately authorizes me to promise immunity to any Price employee involved in the payoff.

The next morning, I'm heading back to Bartlesville. The Bechtel meeting will have to be rescheduled.

Chapter Five

Price Tower
January 1966

SIT IN AN office in Price Tower interviewing employees. Harold Price's resistance has collapsed. The entire company is at the government's disposal. Every employee who knows anything about the payoffs has been told by management to cooperate. Men with any information are pulled off pipeline jobs around the world and told to report back to headquarters. No exceptions, no reservations. All Price asks is that his people not be prosecuted for bowing to Weber's pressure and agreeing to pay him off. We have no choice. We can't make the case without their testimony, so I make the deal.

It is a sordid tale. In 1961 Price Company did a pipeline job in New Jersey. Weber turned all the screws, and they lost their shirts under the crushing load of featherbedders, slowdowns, and stoppages. They saw that local firms, like Napp-Grecco, were working jobs without any trouble. Price's chief of construction, Roy Burgess, decided Weber favored them because they were local. At least that's what Weber said. The big Colonial job was coming up in New Jersey, and Price wanted it. Under the circumstances, they were afraid to bid.

So in 1963 Price bid and got two other jobs. Price was going to open up a local office. Burgess went to New Jersey and tried to get close to Weber, to convince him that Price was now local. No good. Nothing doing. Burgess's attempts to socialize, entertain, ingratiate himself with Weber came to nothing. The argument that Price would provide more work for the men of Local 825 was ineffective. Price Company began to lose twice as much money on the new jobs, and balked at the upcoming Colonial job. Disaster loomed. Finally, Burgess approached Weber directly. They met in The Roost restaurant in Newark. Burgess was desperate. His company was on the line for millions. What was it that Weber wanted?

Weber laughed as he leaned forward. With his face inches from Burgess, he whispered, "Tax free cash."

Burgess carried the message back to Bartlesville. The top executives met. Round and round they went. They didn't want to do it, or so they say, but now they were stuck in New Jersey quicksand, sinking under Weber's pressure. They had two ongoing jobs heading for disaster. They decided to pay.

"How did you decide on $14,000?" I ask Price.

"That's kind of an odd number," Cosolo observes.

"We paid $3,500.00 a shot. Every so often another payment was made. We tried to spread it out to cover the jobs we were doing. By the time we finished the work, we had made four payments, $14,000.00."

"What about the Colonial job?" I ask.

Price laughs. "This is the crazy part. Once we started paying him, he not only let up on us, he decided to help us, although we had not requested help. One day my telephone rings here in this office. It's Weber. I nearly fell off my chair. He told me he had just called Colonial in Atlanta, Georgia, and instructed them to give us the work in New Jersey. I couldn't believe it!"

"But you didn't get it?"

Price shakes his head no. "We were much too high on the bid. They gave it to Bechtel of San Francisco."

"Who handled the payments to Weber for you?"

"Roy, Roy Burgess. He made them all."

"We'd like to see him."

"Of course," Price gives us a long, long pause. "Look, gentlemen, he's scared to death. I mean literally afraid for his life," Price is pleading. "Please take it easy with him. And," Price ducks his head, "I'm sorry about all those lies . . . before . . . you know."

****

The days are long. But so are the nights. I have nothing to do in the evenings. I am not ready to socialize with Harold and his wife. Tony

Cosolo and I are living in a fleabag motel. You can't even go out for a drink in Oklahoma. It is against the law. You can get a drink in private clubs, and for convenience there just happens to be a club connected to our motel. With nothing else to do on our first night, we go in. A little celebration is in order.

It's dimly lit, with booths all around a dance floor adorned by a jukebox. I am in my New York costume, shirt-tie-suit, which is all that I have. I had planned for a two-day trip. I'm sure I look out of place. And I am.

I draw the attention of a fairly attractive young lady. Cosolo excuses himself, and she and I talk alone. Then we have a dance. Things are looking promising. When we return to our table she seems interested in where I am from. She learns that I am from New York City. I make polite inquiries about her. She says she is married, but separated. This is not insurmountable, but then she does something that is. Perhaps it's my clothes or my accent; for whatever reason, she comes to the conclusion that I am a New York City mobster. I tell her no, but she is not buying it, particularly when she asks me what I do, why I am in Bartlesville, and I duck her questions, which only confirms her conclusion. Sitting there, she tells me she is willing to pay $10,000 to have her husband whacked. She doesn't say it quite that way, but that is what she means.

I can't believe it. I'm a Department of Justice attorney in the Organized Crime Section, and she wants me to kill her husband! Of course she doesn't know what I do and, to protect the Price people, I have not disclosed what I do around Bartlesville. I am not going to pop up and tell her that now, either. One thing I know. I have enough cases in Oklahoma. I have to get out of there. I tell her I know she's kidding. Then I flee the place. I hope she was kidding, but this is nothing I care to pursue. The remaining days I devote to the case and stay in the hotel at night. I make sure I never see the lady again.

******

Roy Burgess and I sit alone in a room in the Price Tower for five days. Burgess is a wreck. He knows he paid Weber off. He remembers it was $14,000, in four payments. But he does not remember a single date or place. Only one thing saves the situation; Burgess is a meticulous record-keeper. His expense account records his every movement, not only back and forth to Oklahoma, but every activity and meeting while he is in New Jersey.

Cosolo collects every record relating to the two jobs. He goes over the financial records of the Price Company, identifying the checks that were used to generate the four cash payments. The dates of the checks are used in conjunction with Burgess's expense records to pinpoint his location when each cash installment is delivered to him. Then Burgess and I trace his route after he has the cash until his expense account reflects his next meeting with Weber. In this way, we lay out every cash delivery to Burgess and every rendezvous of Burgess with Weber after Burgess has the cash. We interview the Price employees who delivered the cash to Burgess, so we can ascertain the place in New Jersey when he first had the cash for each payment.

Price himself made one delivery. Admirably, he tells me he did not think he should sit back with clean hands and no personal risk while his employees stuck out their necks for his company. I like that a lot. And I figure a jury would like it, too.

I know that to convict Weber, Burgess must testify in court with precision as to each payment: dates, times, and places. He will have to stand up under withering cross examination. Details will be his protective armor. It is during these five days of laborious work that I use the technique I learned by watching senior men in Hogan's office. Their cases were different, but their techniques work on all cases. At the end of five days, the date, time, and place of every payoff is nailed down. Burgess even recalls the details of the last payment.

"I gave Weber the last $3,500 in Atlantic City. He had gone down to meet the Bechtel people getting ready to start the Colonial job. I gave him the cash on the boardwalk. After I slipped him the money, we passed a leather goods store. Weber wanted to go in. He bought some stuff, and then he saw a big leather bag. He asked me if I liked it. I said it was okay. He whipped out the roll of cash, paid a hundred dollars for it. As we stood there, he had them put my initials on it. Then he gave it to me."

"Do you still have it?"

"Yes. It's still in the original wrapping," Burgess looks away from me. "I could never bear to use it."

I have what I came for. It's time to go home.

Chapter Six

The Special Grand Jury
January–May 1966

THE FIRST WORKING day back from Bartlesville, I am in Henry's office with a shopping list. In just a little over two months on the job, my team has gotten enough to bag Weber, so I am pretty sure I will get what I ask for.

I need lawyer help. There is too much for me to do alone. There will be traveling to and from Bartlesville to continue debriefing witnesses at Price. Then there are at least four additional companies ripe for financial investigation: Bechtel in San Francisco, Colonial in Atlanta, Joyce in upstate New York, and Napp-Grecco in Newark, New Jersey.

Henry asks whom I want. I tell him Jon Goldstein, one of the two kids I share an office with. He is fresh out of law school, in the Justice Honors Program, and smart. He works hard. He is also idealistic. I get the feeling that he worries about targeting people like I did with Weber. That doesn't bother me even a little. For example, I didn't mind targeting Crazy Joey Donohue back in the day. I figure the kid will get over it. Not that it matters. We already hit the target with Mr. Weber. Now it's just a matter of more. I have no intention of going to trial on just Price unless I absolutely have to. With the kid's help, I expect to push the other companies until I get the truth.

I reluctantly give up on running the project out of Atlanta. A defendant has a constitutional right to trial—and with Weber there will be a trial—in the district where the crime is committed. That means New

Jersey. I need a grand jury in Newark to issue subpoenas for the records of the other companies. I also need an office in Newark, in the United States Attorney's office, to work out of.

Henry has called David Satz, United States Attorney for the District of New Jersey, and asked him to impanel a special grand jury just for us. Henry has also gotten a commitment from Satz to provide office space to us.

Before Jon Goldstein and I leave for Newark, Henry gives us a final briefing and instructions. He wants us to stay clear of the United States Attorney and to report directly to him. It's not that Henry doesn't trust Satz, he says, it's just that Satz is heavily connected to the Democratic Party in New Jersey, particularly David T. Wilentz, the boss of Middlesex County.

****

By the end of January we have established our office. Satz, to whom I delivered my "New Jersey" Ramsey Clark letter of authority, has impaneled our own special grand jury and we have started issuing grand jury subpoenas. The first recipient is the Bechtel Corporation of San Francisco. We subpoena every record that they have that refers to the ninety miles of pipeline work they did for Colonial in New Jersey. While we wait for the return date, Jon and I pay a visit to Ralph Bochman, the SAC, Special Agent in Charge, of the FBI in Newark. For departmental political reasons, we cannot run this investigation while excluding the bureau.

Bochman receives us in his office on the fifth floor of the United States Post Office Courthouse. They have the entire fifth floor. The USA has most, but not all, of the fourth floor. The similarity to the logistics of the department and the bureau in Washington, with the fourth and fifth floors, is entirely coincidental. As expected, Bochman is stiff, formal, and not particularly enthusiastic, which is an understatement, but he knows about the Price-Weber breakthrough. So does his boss Red Adams in Washington, who has become more enthusiastic since Price broke. He assigns two agents. Our staff is complete.

****

By the end of February we are ready and waiting for the Bechtel records. Then we get a call from Frederick B. Lacey, the New Jersey attorney Bechtel hired to handle the document production and to represent every Bechtel employee that we intend to place before the grand jury. That is the *very* practice I had signaled the California lawyers that I did not like. Lacey wants an appointment to discuss procedures and timing of production. We agree on a date.

Lacey, a former Assistant United States Attorney, now a leading New Jersey trial lawyer, comes striding into the small office Satz has given us. He is a towering figure, about six feet five inches with plenty of bulk, although clearly fit. The minute he enters, he goes right after me with a deep bass voice that rumbles like it is rolling down from Sinai, "Who are you to be telling lawyers who they can and can't represent?" his big hand with its big fingers thrusting at me in cadence with his big voice. "Where," he goes on, "did you learn to practice law? The Municipal Court of the City of New York?"

Well, he has it almost right. It was the magistrate court, not municipal court, but I don't correct him. I don't say anything. I just listen as he verbally works me over. There is no point to confronting him now. But I hang this moment up in my locker room until there is a time when I have my opportunity to deal with him. I'm sure it will come. The world is round.

By the end of the visit, things have settled down enough to work on the details of the document production. Within a few weeks, the documents begin to arrive, and the bureau agents and labor compliance officers go to work on the financial records. That is when Special Agent Leffler finds "the check."

****

I have developed two theories. First, in today's credit society, no one walks into a bank and cashes a check for five thousand, much less ten or twenty thousand dollars for a legitimate purpose. We don't make our large purchases that way. Theory two is that corrupt officials do not take checks; they take cash. The conclusion is obvious. Look for large cash out, and you will find a wrongdoer.

Now there may be isolated exceptions. Perhaps there is someone somewhere who pays all greenbacks for big-ticket items. But nearly one hundred percent of the time you find large checks negotiated for cash, you have a rotten transaction. It was the threat of that kind of examination by Cosolo that broke Price, and it is precisely that examination that my accountants are doing on Bechtel's financial records relating to the Colonial job when they find the check in early May.

It is a $20,000 check. Basil Licklider, of Bechtel, cashed it and walked out of the bank with a bundle of greenbacks on October 4, 1964. I'm looking at the check and I'm smiling. I know I've got them now. Goldstein and I are laughing together. "It's dirty, Jon," I say when we calm down. "I am going to enjoy our next meeting with Frederick B. Lacey." Jon just smiles. Unlike me, he is not out for blood. But then, Lacey did not bang him around.

We know just what to do. Jon immediately issues a grand jury subpoena for Licklider. I want him in on short, short notice. I have a pretty good idea of what this will do to the Bechtel folk. I can't wait for my rendezvous with their lawyer. The real treat will be watching him represent Licklider, and Bechtel, and whoever else at Bechtel told Licklider to get the money. Mr. Lacey is going to be in an interesting position.

The best news, of course, is that this should also be the next and hopefully last milestone in my quest for Peter Weber. Twenty thousand dollars from Bechtel has a nice ring to it, especially on top of Price's fourteen thousand.

As I expect, in two days my telephone rings. It's Lacey. He wants an appointment. I am delighted to give him one. He would like extra time to see about producing the man who cashed the check. Regretfully, I tell him that's impossible. So we make it a quick appointment. I can't wait.

When Lacey comes he brings Bechtel's California lawyers with him, which is a surprise. They file in. They don't look happy. I, however, am at my most cordial. I turn the meeting over to Goldstein. I plan to sit back and enjoy the event. Jon welcomes them and asks what they want. They say that they are prepared to cooperate. What they want is immunity for the Bechtel employees. They don't say what they are cooperating on, but of course I assume that it's Weber. Goldstein tells them it is possible, depending on what the lawyers tell us their clients will say.

They make what we call in the trade a "proffer." A proffer is when an attorney outlines what his client would say to a prosecutor and testify to in court, if the client receives immunity, a lighter plea, or some other consideration. Because the proffer itself is not evidence, the prosecutor can only use it if the deal is agreed upon.

The proffer they make is stunning. The money did not go to Weber. The money went to the mayor and to the president of the city council of Woodbridge, New Jersey, the sixth largest city in New Jersey. And it wasn't just $20,000. That was just the first installment. The total of three payments was $60,000. Jon and I sit in stunned silence as Bechtel's lawyers make the revelation. This is now too serious for childish games. I get into the conversation, "Why did they pay?"

"To get permits for a right of way to finish connecting the pipeline to the storage tanks," the California lawyer explains.

As Goldstein and I listen, we learn that Walter Zirpolo, the mayor of Woodbridge, and Robert Jacks, the city council president, put the arm on Colonial for $100,000, but Colonial bargained it down to $60,000. Colonial did not pay the public officials directly. Instead, the Colonial executives asked Bechtel, the contractor on the job, to make the payment in three $20,000 installments, and then to bill it back to Colonial concealing them as job costs. The Bechtel check on the table in front of us was used to generate the cash for the first payment, which Bechtel delivered to Jacks.

"When was payment number two?" I ask.

There wasn't a payment two, at least not by Bechtel directly, Jon and I are told.

"Why not?" Jon jumps in.

The explanation we get is that when the president of Bechtel, Stephen Bechtel, Jr., found out about the payment, he ordered his people to stop. So they stopped paying. That is, they stopped paying hand to hand. Instead, they persuaded one of their subcontractors on the Colonial job, Bob Gates of the Gates Construction Company, to take over the last two $20,000 payments. The money still went from Colonial to Bechtel, but it traveled through Bob Gates who made delivery to the public officials.

I'm sitting there and I can't believe these figures, in 1964 dollars. But that's not the worst of it. They tell us that because Gates had no way to expense the money, Gates told Bechtel that he would have to declare the $40,000 that Bechtel was giving him as income to his company and pay tax on the $40,000 at a fifty-two percent corporate rate. So to make the $40,000 in payments, Gates billed Bechtel $84,000, $40,000 for Zirpolo and Jacks, and $44,000 for the Internal Revenue Service. Bechtel, of course, billed the $84,000 right back to Colonial.

"What about the first $20,000? Did Colonial have to pay Bechtel's taxes on that?" I ask.

The answer is no. The California lawyers explain that Fallow of Bechtel falsely charged the first $20,000 to right-of-way expenses. It was deducted. No tax was paid.

"Let me get this straight," I summarize. "To pay this Zirpolo and Jacks $60,000, Colonial funneled $104,000 through Bechtel, in 1964?"

The answer from a glum group of lawyers is "yes."

As they leave, I am also told that Colonial is represented by the law firm headed by David T. Wilentz. That is a name I remember from the briefing by Henry Petersen. He is the boss of Middlesex County. Woodbridge is in Middlesex County, and both Council President Jacks and Mayor Zirpolo are political acolytes of Wilentz. The California lawyers tell us that they have met with Wilentz, who wants the Bechtel people to volunteer nothing and to take the Fifth Amendment if called before the grand jury.

I am amused. I know that while Wilentz is a Democratic leader, the Bechtel people are conservative Republicans. I'm thinking that the San Francisco crowd is not taking the Fifth for anyone, much less the Middlesex County Democratic organization. As soon as Lacey and his colleagues are out the door, Goldstein and I are on the telephone to Henry Petersen.

"Henry," I say, "we panned for silver and we struck gold."

Then Goldstein and I interrupt each other as we rush to tell Henry the story we just heard. His end of the phone is quiet for a long time as we go through it. When Petersen at last gets a chance to talk, I hear as happy a man as I have ever heard.

****

Now it is Colonial's turn. We know that they know that Bechtel has just turned them in. They must be expecting our knock on their door. The question is, should we knock soft, or hard? Should I call Wilentz and ask for a meeting, or tell the FBI to start interviewing in Atlanta? In the end I decide on a more subtle, lethal approach.

The next day Jon Goldstein has an agent serve our special grand jury subpoenas on Colonial, calling for records "that reflect any payment, directly or indirectly, to the mayor or president of the City Council of Woodbridge." Because corporations have no Fifth Amendment rights, Colonial—which knows we know—will have to make disclosures. Colonial will have to turn over each and every memo or check or financial record in regard to any such payments to Zirpolo and Jacks.

"Let them do the work," I tell Jon, "Let them figure out what records are responsive. We just sit back and wait. Let's see how they solve their problem."

Chapter Seven

The Visits
June 1966

I**T DOESN'T TAKE** long. I never thought it would. David Satz, the United States Attorney, comes for a visit.

David Wilentz has called him. Wilentz, according to Satz, wants to meet with Jon and me in Satz's office. I ask Satz what it's about, although I'm sure I know. It's the grand jury subpoena, Satz confirms. Wilentz has suggested a date for the meeting that Goldstein and I quickly agree to. I am anxious to meet this man Wilentz.

David T. Wilentz, now heading one of New Jersey's largest law firms, Wilentz, Goldman & Spitzer, in addition to being Middlesex Democratic county chairman, and the state's Democratic national committeeman, is also the father-in-law of Leon Hess, the principal of Hess Oil. But his real fame stems from the 1930s when he was the attorney general of New Jersey at the moment the Lindbergh baby was kidnapped. Wilentz took the case away from the local prosecutor and personally tried the accused, Bruno Hauptmann. His antics in front of the press photographers were so inflammatory that for decades thereafter photographers had been banned in courtrooms throughout the United States.

****

I'm sure I know what is going to happen at the meeting. Wilentz is going to blast me because I have been questioning people about him and his relationship to Jacks and Zirpolo. He is going to do what Lacey did in his first meeting. All things considered, I don't need to hear that from him. With some help from Goldstein, I think I can shut him up. "Jon," I tell him, "this guy is going to rant and rave. I want you to go into the meeting with me, and I want you to have a yellow legal pad. And I want you to write lots and lots of notes. I don't care if it's a letter to your mother. Just keep writing."

We go to Satz's spacious office when he calls for us. Wilentz is already there. He is fairly short, white-haired, looks to be in his early seventies. As we enter, Satz pulls out a chair and holds it until Wilentz seats himself. I do not regard this as a good portent. And it isn't.

Wilentz starts in strong. "Who do you think you are, Mr. Stern? What right do you have to ask questions about me? Just because I am in politics doesn't mean that I am corrupt."

He is blowing real well. He is now out of his chair, striding around the room. His performance is so magnetic that I suspect Goldstein has stopped writing, and I am right. I look over and Jon is staring at Wilentz, transfixed. Not good. So I kick Jon's chair. He gets the message and starts writing furiously.

Wilentz sees Jon making notes like crazy, and after a couple glances he starts spluttering to a stop. I use the quiet moment to say, "Okay, Mr. Wilentz. That was great. If you feel better, perhaps you'd like to tell me if Colonial is going to cooperate?" I say it with a knowing smile, not angry. Just kind of amused.

I see he is amused in return. This man is an adult. Whatever else he turns out to be, he is not a stuffed shirt. He says, "yes," with a laugh, "we will cooperate." And then he lays the news on us. Colonial, his client, not only paid Jacks and Zirpolo $60,000 in 1964, Colonial gave them a prior $50,000 in 1963.

I can't believe it. "You mean they paid a total of $110,000 to these men?
"Yes."

"What was the first $50,000 for?"

Wilentz mumbles something about a tank farm at the end of the pipeline.

"These were two separate transactions?" I ask.

He says, "Yes," but he is vague on the details.

"Did they use Bechtel on this one?"

"No."

"Who?"

"A firm called Rowland Tompkins, which was involved in building the tank farm."

"How many payments?"

"Three, totaling $50,000."

He has no details. No names. Not even the address of Rowland Tompkins. Not that it matters. Jon and I can get that easily.

There is only one thing I really need to know. Are the Colonial people going to agree to be interviewed and testify? He says that they are, because they were the victims of extortion, a shakedown as he calls it. They were forced to pay under threats of delay to their project. He says his clients have committed no crime. They are *victims* of a crime. He keeps repeating that claim. It's even funny. The political boss accusing two of his followers of extortion.

I figure he has no choice. Bechtel already turned his people in, and our subpoena would force Colonial to come in with the checks used to raise the prior $50,000, even though we had no idea about any of that when we issued the subpoena. I am making no deals with Colonial.

"Well, if they did nothing wrong, they have nothing to fear," I say, although I believe everyone in the room has to know you can't legally slip public officials a total of $110,000 in six payments after two separate negotiations. But if the Colonial executives want to say they are innocent victims of the rapacious New Jersey politicians, then good luck to them.

At the end of the meeting the three of us leave Satz's office together. As we walk the halls, we encounter a display of Wilentz's charm. And his humor. Wilentz asks about our backgrounds and families. He asks about me, and learns I am 29 and single. Jon tells him that he just got engaged, which he did, to Ellen Lowenthal, an aide on New York Senator Jacob Javits's staff in Washington. Jon, Ellen, and I were together in a Georgetown restaurant when Jon gave her the ring. While I am mindful of Henry's briefing that Wilentz in Middlesex and Kenny in Hudson together control the Democratic Party in New Jersey, it is difficult to resist his charm.

David—we are on a first-name basis now—says to Jon that when either he or Ellen are ready, David's firm does divorce work. We all have a laugh. We part company and that is the last I see of David T. Wilentz, although I know there will be plenty of lawyers from his firm coming in to see me with the Colonial "victims."

Our last pleasant task of the day is our ritualistic call to Henry in Washington. In the past six months I have called him once from Oklahoma and now twice from New Jersey. I hope he isn't getting too used to it. I'm not sure that Jon and I can keep up the pace. But today he is going to hear about another $50,000 payoff.

****

Jon and I are going to have our hands full. Colonial, in Atlanta, is our potential victim in the Weber case and our potential defendant in the Woodbridge case; their officers are potential witnesses in Weber and targets in Woodbridge. Bechtel, in San Francisco, and its employees are in exactly the same boat.

Then we have Rowland Tompkins in New York, which made the first $50,000 payment, and Gates in New Jersey, which made the last two installments (totaling $40,000) of the $60,000 payment. These companies cannot be charged in one conspiracy with each other because the two payoffs were unrelated transactions.

This is not to mention the complexities of the Colonial/Price/Bechtel story, the Colonial/Osage/Napp-Grecco story, and the Bechtel/Joyce story, ranging from Atlanta to Oklahoma to San Francisco to Andover, New York, with the shadow of Weber as the brooding omnipresence over all of them as they struggled either to obtain or to finish the Colonial Pipeline work in New Jersey.

Nothing I ever saw in the DA's office was anything like this. This is no Donohue or Crowe case. What Jon and I have to deal with here is beyond anything we have encountered before. And yet, while feeling overwhelmed, I do not feel totally unprepared. I have watched men like Dermody and Keenan put their cases together. The principles are the same, and we will apply them on a broad front as best we can.

One thing is clear. New Jersey must be a cesspool of corruption. In just one ninety-mile pipeline project, there were multiple payoffs to public officials totaling enormous sums. That doesn't even take into account the activities of Mr. Weber.

If I wanted to fish for thieves, all I would need to do is drop a line into these polluted waters and I would hook some oily creature every time. That is, if my hook was a United States grand jury. But I don't want to fish here. I don't want to be here. I want to continue to live in Washington.

Chapter Eight

The Best Lawyers in America
July 1966–February 1967

For MONTHS, JON Goldstein and I juggle balls between the Colonial case and the Weber case.

The three top officers of Colonial: Ben Leuty, president; Karl Feldman, executive vice president; and Glenn Giles, vice president, each go before the grand jury, along with the financial records and billings of the six payments. The Wilentz firm represents them all. They tell an orchestrated tale of extortion and shakedown, which led them to surrender and authorize the payments. The firms that delivered the payments also testified.

Rowland Tompkins of New York, the firm that built the tank farm, made the first $50,000 payment, in three installments of $20,000, $15,000, and $15,000. Their story is that they had no intent to bribe. They were simply delivering ransom to the criminals who held Colonial's baby hostage. Their position gives me a private laugh.

The total cost of this scheme is staggering. To make the $110,000 payoff to Zirpolo and Jacks, Colonial paid Bechtel and its subcontractor $104,000 to cover taxes, and paid Rowland Tompkins $150,000, for a grand total of $254,000, every penny of which is built into the cost of a project that the petroleum-consuming American public will pay for, one way or the other, and much of which escaped income taxes all along the path of the payments. As far as Jon and I can see, the only victims in this scenario are the American consumer and taxpaying public.

"They must think we are farmers," Jon says.

"What do you mean?" I respond.

"Do they really think we are going to let these businessmen get away with paying all this money, on the ground that they were scared into it?"

February 23

We will attempt something not usually done. We will seek indictments not merely against Zirpolo and Jacks, and not merely against the corporations that paid; we will indict the corporate officers who authorized the payment. That means, along with the public officials, Colonial, and President Leuty, Executive Vice President Feldman, and Vice President Giles, will all be charged, all in the same indictment; as well as Bechtel, Rowland Tompkins and Gates. Except for the Bechtel and Rowland Tompkins and Gates employees who are needed to testify to the delivery of the cash, we will prosecute all givers and all takers together in one trial. The grand jury indicts just that way.

There will be a trial, but first an arraignment, and then motions, plenty of motions by all the defendants in regard to all of the transactions. And I will lose Jon, at least for a while. He is a lieutenant in the Army Reserve, and has been called to duty in Thailand. He will be gone for twenty-four months. I will be alone facing the platoons of lawyers, many of whom are among the greatest in the country.

****

On the day of the arraignment, they troop into federal court. They are a regiment. Colonial has hired former federal judge Simon H. Rifkind to represent its president, Ben Leuty. Rifkind will quarterback the entire defense team for all the Colonial players. He has a dozen lawyers with him.

Rifkind heads the mighty New York City law firm Paul, Weiss, Rifkind, Wharton & Garrison. He is the undisputed "Dean of the New York Bar." Appointed United States District Judge for the Southern

District of New York by President Roosevelt in 1940, he served ten years before resigning to become a law partner of Adlai Stevenson in the firm of Stevenson, Rifkind & Wirtz in Chicago, while simultaneously joining and leading Paul Weiss in New York City. Jacqueline Kennedy is but one of his many famous clients. Even United States Supreme Court Justice William O. Douglas, when threatened with impeachment, hired Rifkind. His junior partners are former United States Supreme Court Justice Arthur Goldberg, and Theodore Sorensen, former counsel to President Kennedy.

As we wait for the judge to take the bench, I look across at Rifkind from where I sit in the well of the court, and I remember five years ago. Then, too, I sat in a courtroom in New York when he entered. I was still in military uniform, on leave, just one of the new classes of attorneys to be sworn in to the bar. By sheer chance, Rifkind's son, Robert, was sitting in my row. My father was in the audience to witness my induction, among family members of other candidates. When Judge Rifkind entered the courtroom, there was a buzz. Many heads turned. Now, five years later, he and a half dozen Paul Weiss lawyers are to be my adversaries for just one defendant—Ben Leuty.

The other three Colonial defendants, Executive Vice President Karl Feldman, Vice President Glen Giles, and Colonial itself are represented by the heads of three of New Jersey's largest law firms. Adrian Foley, former president of the New Jersey bar, for Feldman, and Matthew Boylan for Giles. Warren Wilentz, just-defeated Democratic candidate for United States senator and son of David T. Wilentz, represents Colonial itself. Each of these three firms had its own platoon of lawyers committed to the war.

Then we have the three conduits for the Colonial money: Rowland Tompkins, represented by the prominent New York white-collar defender, Joe Brill; Bechtel, represented by Lacey; and Gates, represented by former New Jersey Attorney General, Walter D. Van Riper. That completes the army for the givers. Then we have the warriors for the takers—Jacks and Zirpolo. From the standpoint of a freshman lawyer, they are the most imposing of all.

Jacks has former state senator John E. Toolan as his attorney. Tall, distinguished, white-haired, well into his seventies, but very fit. He has the eloquence of his Gaelic tradition. Imposing as he is, he is not my main concern. It's Zirpolo's lawyer, Edward Bennett Williams. He is without question the greatest trial lawyer of our time. Still in his forties, at the height of his power, he has represented Jimmy Hoffa, Frank Costello, Senator Joseph McCarthy, and Governor, then Secretary of Treasury, John Connally of Texas. Williams is tall, about six feet, conservatively dressed and trim of figure, as well he should be, for he is president of the Washington Redskins and works out with his football team. He is also the owner of the Baltimore Orioles.

Entering a federal courtroom for the first time in my life—a courtroom so crowded with adversaries that there is barely room for Jon and me—I get to say, "Herbert J. Stern for the United States." But too soon there will be no Jon next to me. I know that he is going into real danger, but for all that he looks a lot less scared than I feel.

It's a long, long way from Hogan's office to this arena, or should I say coliseum, stocked with hostile gladiators. They say that the trouble with the things that you want is sometimes you get them. Right now, the magistrate court of five years ago, with my judicial protectors Quinn and O'Brien, looks better than it ever did when I was in it.

Chapter Nine

Motions and Riots
February 1967–November 1968

COMPLICATED FEDERAL WHITE-COLLAR criminal cases come to trial slowly. And that's an understatement. It takes time to brief, to argue, and then to decide motions addressing a federal indictment alleging two separate conspiracies with some identical and some separate role players. Then, too, the federal rules provide far more opportunities for the parties to raise issues than anything I ever saw in New York, even for a homicide prosecution as elaborate as the Malcolm X case. For the next year and a half, the army against me buries me in motions. Forty of them. Jon has gone, and I must deal with this alone.

Every defendant wants to be severed from everyone else. The various deliverers of the two separate series of payments want severance from each other on the ground that the $50,000 and $60,000 transactions were unrelated and should not be tried together. All of the businessmen want severance from the public officials, claiming that the money they paid was extorted by Jacks and Zirpolo, who threatened to impede construction unless they were paid. They claim to be victims of extortion, not co-conspirators in bribery.

Jacks will not deny receiving the $110,000 because he can't. A host of employees of various companies will testify to handing him cash in half a dozen installments. No one would believe he did not get the money. His only claim is that the government has prejudiced him by joining all the defendants in the same case. "While the government is telling the jury that

I am guilty of bribery," he says, "my codefendants will be busy telling the jury I am guilty of extortion!" And so Jacks and, to this extent, Zirpolo as well, conceive a strategy and constantly implement it by moving to preclude Rifkind and company from mentioning extortion and, failing that, to repeatedly demand a severance from the codefendants.

The Colonial group, on the other hand, constantly demands the right to call the public officials harsher and harsher names. Actually, behind the scenes all of the defendants are working together closely to create serious appellate issues if they are convicted. I often see them with their heads together, although they are careful to keep such conferences out of the judge's view.

The third leg of the defense belongs to Edward Bennett Williams alone. No one saw or heard his client, Mayor Walter Zirpolo, do anything wrong! Zirpolo took no money personally, nor did he directly ask for it. It is true that, on two occasions, he sent Colonial representatives over to see Jacks, who did the asking and the taking, but Zirpolo was not physically present either time. The most the government has is that Fred Stewart, the Colonial employee who was negotiating the permit with Zirpolo, was eventually sent by Zirpolo to see Jacks, who promptly solicited him for the first $50,000. The second solicitation was many months later, when Stewart, on Zirpolo's instructions, reported to Zirpolo's private business office. There Stewart found Jacks, but no Zirpolo. Jacks then demanded the next $100,000. Stewart testified in the grand jury that he *thought* he heard Zirpolo's voice through an open door in an adjoining room. And that, basically, is the case against Zirpolo. Zirpolo's defense, obviously, would be that whatever Jacks did, Jacks did for Jacks alone.

****

Before the motions roll in, Jon and I use the time we have left together to put the finishing touch to the Weber investigation.

We go to Buffalo, New York. We know James Joyce of Joyce Construction received a contract from Bechtel after Weber demanded that he receive it. When Joyce refuses to cooperate, we obtain an obstruction-of-justice indictment against him in Buffalo. He reconsiders and admits that he agreed to pay Weber $30,000, which is ten percent of the contract Weber forced Bechtel to give him. He provides us with the financial records.

July 25

The grand jury indicts Weber twice: The Price payments and Colonial extortion in one indictment; the Joyce payments and Bechtel extortion in the other. Just after the indictments, Jon goes to Southeast Asia. There is an outside chance that he can return by the time Colonial goes to trial, but I know I can't count on it.

****

I have had to change my lifestyle. It is not possible to manage these cases while commuting to an apartment in Washington, D.C. I have no choice. I move back to Manhattan. It's not what I planned, but it turns out I get lucky. I want to live in or near Greenwich Village, so I can be near the PATH tubes for an easy commute to Newark. On a wild chance, I walk the streets on lower Fifth Avenue, asking supers about available apartments, when lightning strikes. I find a small one-bedroom at 45 Fifth Avenue, between 11th and 12th Streets. It looks right onto Fifth Avenue, and it is rent-controlled. I pay $170 a month, and they can't raise the rent!

Every day I go back and forth, daytime in Newark, nighttime in Manhattan when a cataclysmic event occurs that devastates Newark and will ultimately change my life.

July 14

Newark explodes into riots. It becomes a weird commute from home to work. The world is at peace when I enter the PATH train in Manhattan and at war a few miles west when I exit in Newark. Before the riots are over, 26 are dead, over 1,000 injured, and more than 1,000 are under arrest. National Guardsmen stand on the street corners with bayonet-tipped rifles. Armored personnel carriers roam the streets. Occasionally, there is the sound of automatic weapons firing at buildings, and a constant pall and smell of smoke. Pedestrians are few, and those few cluster by race. Whites walk together and cross the street to avoid black pedestrians. It is a war zone. In the evening I return to a place of peace, just a subway ride away.

The rioting eventually subsides, but much of the city has been gutted by fire and vandalism. Businesses are shuttered. Restaurants are closing. Professionals have begun to leave the city for the suburbs. We are in the first stages of "white flight." Newark is plainly on a downhill spiral, and there is no perceptible bottom. Six months after the rioting is quelled, a committee appointed by Governor Hughes finds that one cause of the riots was the open corruption of Mayor Hugh J. Addonizio's administration. It recommends the convening of a special grand jury. To this I pay no attention. I do not dwell on Newark's future. I have no intention of stepping foot in New Jersey once the Colonial and Weber trials are finished.

****

Once the grand jury hands down indictments against Colonial and Weber, the Labor Department pulls out of the team. Bribery of public officials is so far outside their mandate that I can no longer find a reason to justify their presence, particularly as the Colonial case will be tried months before Weber. With reluctance, I have to say farewell to Tony Cosolo.

"I'll be back," he tells me.

"Sure you will," I respond.

But we both know that is not true. He and his boys have made the cases, but now the bureau takes over responsibility. I am sure that I will see Tony no more. With Jon gone to Southeast Asia, all I will have is a senior man from the Organized Crime Section, Phil White, a friend of Henry Petersen, who will "supervise" me from Washington, with an occasional trip to New Jersey. As the supervisor of the "Pipeline Project," he has already gained a promotion in his GS level.

The good news is that his supervision does not include grand jury appearances, handling motions, or dealing with witnesses in or out of trial. As the Russians once said, "Heaven is high and the Tsar is far away." So is Washington. I go there as infrequently as I can. As the months pass, I am less and less a part of the section in Washington, and more and more head of my own operation. Henry doesn't care much for the arrangements, but of course I do. No more Washington for me. I have become a New Yorker, again.

****

All of the indictments, Colonial and Weber, have been assigned to Judge Reynier J. Wortendyke, a towering figure of a man, with close-cropped grey hair. The judge, over seventy years old, strides four miles every morning from the train station to the courthouse and back again at night. He presents a formidable figure on the bench. A captain in World War I, fond of quoting from the *Handbook for Infantry Officers*, he is a descendant of a long line of prominent Dutchmen in New Jersey.

Judge Wortendyke's manner is gruff, particularly to me, but he has a heart of gold. He constantly chides me from the height of the bench's perch, and the distance of the forty-plus years between us. And yet, I notice that for all of the "abuse," while not openly, he is as benign as Quinn and O'Brian in the magistrate court. During one of the arguments on motions, as I stand to make a statement, he barks, "You rise like an apparition." I immediately sit down. With that, I hear explosive laughter from the rear of the courtroom. It is a sound I recognize.

Turning quickly, I see my father sitting in a rear spectator row bent over in laughter. He has surprised me by sneaking over to Newark for a visit to court. I guess he wants to see Rifkind, Williams, and company, too. They are the great men of our profession. Now my father has the delight of watching the judge do to me what I am sure he would love to do himself. At the end of the day, I bring him up to the bench to meet the judge, which proves a mistake. When the two start chortling together, I flee the courtroom.

******

So it goes. Motions upon motions. I never saw more than a five-page motion as an ADA. Now I can't see over the top of my desk as they continue to roll in.

After numerous arguments I win all the motions, at least all the ones that matter. The case will not be severed or cut up in any way. All I have to do is promise that I will make it clear to the jurors at trial that the indictment does not charge all of the defendants with all of the crimes.

It is apparent that Judge Wortendyke has taken a dislike to poor Joe Brill. I think it is Joe's bushy beard and shaven head—he looks like bandleader Mitch Miller. Joe resoundingly loses all his motions. On the other hand, Rifkind is deeply respected by the judge, who invariably refers to him as "Judge." Toolan is always "Senator." So it is "Judge" this for Rifkind, and "Senator" that for Toolan. Rifkind, six years younger than Wortendyke, had been a federal judge in the country's most prestigious district fifteen years before Wortendyke even took the bench. Judge Wortendyke, then, is always deferential to Judge Rifkind. Nonetheless, Rifkind loses most of the motions that he has shotgunned at the indictment.

But it is Edward Bennett Williams who is my chief problem. He is the dominant voice in the courtroom, not by virtue of time or past position, but because of his eloquence, which is all the more lethal in its simplicity. In his pretrial motions, Williams constantly hammers for a severance. He repeatedly campaigns that the Colonial defendants are accusing his client of extortion, a worse crime than the bribery charged by the government. But no judge willingly makes two cases out of one. Williams fails to get his severance.

****

But it is a new day now. The case has been called for trial. We are about to pick a jury. Before we can complete that task, Williams is again on his feet. If he can't get a severance, then he wants the judge to preclude Rifkind and company from claiming that they paid the $110,000 under duress. As far as their defense, he doesn't "take any position as to whether or not that is a good defense or not. The government," he nods at my table, "will probably contend it is not, and counsel for the other defendants," he now nods at the Rifkind group, "will probably contend that it is."

"May I interrupt you for a moment?" says the solicitous judge in a tone he never uses with me.

"Yes, please do," says Williams.

"Would it be your contention that they would have no right to offer proof in support of the contention that it was an extortion and not bribery?"

"Exactly," says Williams, "so long as Zirpolo and Jacks are codefendants in this case."

Brilliant, I say to myself. He is rearguing the motion to sever, without saying so. Judge Wortendyke gets it, too. "You are in effect renewing the motion to sever Zirpolo which was previously fully argued and ruled upon by the court, is that right?"

"Oh no, never," claims Williams, "I was not optimistic enough to renew the motion, so I took the only course open to me, really, and I ask Your Honor to obviate the reason for which I asked for the severance."

To my amazement, the judge grants Williams's motion, not for severance, but to preclude the defense that the payments were extorted. "I'm going to, in the vernacular, stick my neck out in granting Mr. Williams's motion and thereby preclude the defendants who seek to rely upon the theory of extortion defense from so stating to the jury by way of opening."

Chapter Ten

Voir Dire
November 13–14, 1968

WORTENDYKE'S COURTROOM IS the largest, most elaborately decorated in the district, with inlaid ceilings and sconces on the walls. An enormous female statue of Justice is on a podium behind the bench. It is the ceremonial courtroom used for inductions of new United States Attorneys and federal judges. But spacious as it is, it is not large enough for this occasion.

As we wait for an oversized panel of prospective jurors to enter the courtroom, there are so many defense lawyers in the well of the court that some of the defendants are sitting in the spectator benches right where prospective jurors will sit while waiting to be called to the jury box. Not good.

"If Your Honor pleases," I address the court, "it might be more proper if the defendants were not seated in and among the prospective jurors. I would ask that additional chairs be brought in."

"All right," the judge crustily responds. And then to give me more agita, he adds, "I don't know where we are going to find them." But, chairs are found and we are finally ready for trial.

The moment the panel enters the courtroom they cease being ordinary citizens, people who would draw no attention passing on the street. As they file in, they are transformed into the most important people in the room, more important even than the judge, for they alone will have the power to condemn or to exonerate. The actors in the drama—defendants, their lawyers, and the prosecutors—search the faces of the prospective jurors. It is a useless exercise. All the countenances are deliberately kept expressionless. There is nothing to read.

In a few minutes, the box is filled with prospects. When it is time for me to begin my voir dire, the judge tells me, "Whether it is due to age or dissipation, the court has difficulty in hearing, and usually blames it upon the poor acoustics of the courtroom. Stand here in front of the lectern." The judge's difficulty in hearing has plagued us all from time to time. I see it hasn't improved. I move as directed. Facing the twelve in the box, I begin.

"Does any member of the panel know any of the defendants or any of the attorneys for the government or any of the attorneys for the defendants?"

Juror Number Seven pipes up, "Is there any reason why Mr. Williams' face might be familiar to me? Is he a public figure; I might have seen his face in the newspapers?"

I don't know if I am allowed to respond, so I spin around to face the judge, a mute appeal upon my face. "You may respond to the juror's question," he tells me.

The judge has put Williams right into my hands! All I have to say is, "Well, Edward Bennett Williams is probably the foremost trial lawyer in the country today, and certainly the leading lawyer defending white-collar criminal cases." That would have been enough to sink him and his client in the eyes of the jury. It would not even have been necessary to add the names of Jimmy Hoffa, Frank Costello, and Senator Joseph McCarthy as his former clients. And yet, I simply can't do such a thing. Of course I want to win. But not that way! "Mr. Williams, I believe, has been in the press from time to time. Do you know him personally?"

"No, I don't," he replies.

We call this process *voir dire*, which is French for "to see" and "to speak." It is my view that of the two purposes of voir dire—to find out information from prospective jurors, and to put information into them—only the latter has any value. You simply can't ask enough of the right kinds of questions to find emotional biases in prospective jurors. As for putting information into them, it must be subtle or you will be stopped.

Notwithstanding the judge's ruling, I know that sooner or later Colonial will claim that the payments were extorted. I want the jury to see the enormous economic power of the corporate defendants.

I name all of the nine major companies that own Colonial and ask, "Do any of you now own any shares of stock in any of these firms?" No response. Interesting. Not even one prospective juror owns even one share in any of the major oil companies. Clearly these are not people of means.

I eventually question jurors individually, but I really have no idea what to ask, and so I am soon done.

When I finish, I reserve my challenges. I have to husband them. The defendants have been granted two each, for a total of twelve to my six.

Williams, representing the first named defendant, gets to go next. He questions each of the twelve and without notes addresses each by name. He has memorized all those names and positions in the box in the fifteen minutes of my questioning. It is astounding. It hits me hard. I certainly could never perform such a feat of memory.

After a few questions about individual backgrounds, Williams zeros in on the heart of his defense. Whatever was wrong here—if anything—was not Zirpolo's responsibility. Williams will eventually claim that Jacks was operating without Zirpolo's participation. He asks only one question. And it's right on the nose of his theory of defense.

"Is there any member of the panel who believes that the mayor of a town or a city or a municipality of any kind should be held personally responsible for any act of misconduct by members of his administration, by other officials of the city government, or by other members of his political party in the city government?"

"You are specifically excluding the mayor's conduct himself?" Juror Number Seven, the one who seems to know Williams, volunteers.

"Yes," says Williams, "I am talking about the conduct of persons other than the Mayor."

"No."

Way to go, Number Seven! I say to myself. But I would bet my life that good old Number 7 does not survive. I am just as sure Williams will not do the challenging himself. That would be too obvious. He will get Toolan to exercise the strike. Williams's first challenge is to Number Nine. And now, as I see it, he makes his first mistake. Before he challenges, he leans over and consults with Toolan, Jacks' lawyer, right in front of the jury. If they were not in it together, why are they trying to get out of it together?

The amazing aspect of Williams's voir dire is that he did not even once mention the burden of proof beyond a reasonable doubt on the government, the presumption of innocence the defendant enjoys, or the lack of evidentiary value in the indictment. This is virtually unique in the annals of the defense bar as I know it from my DA days.

Now, with a new Juror Number Nine in the box, it is Toolan's turn to question on behalf of Jacks. Given the number of witnesses who will say they paid Jacks, Toolan knows that the jury will find that Jacks got the $110,000. So Toolan tries to implant the idea that it may have been legal for Jacks to take the money.

"My question is not directed to your personal political contributions," he tells the prospective jurors. "My question, rather, is directed to the whole area of raising money for a political party or for a particular candidate who is running for public office. Anybody who has had any experience in that area?" They all shake "no."

Then Toolan goes into the usual defense lawyer cant. The kind of stuff Williams did not touch. "Is there anyone on this jury who feels that if they have a reasonable doubt based upon the evidence, that they would not be able to give the benefit of that doubt to the accused person and acquit him?" No one volunteers to answer.

"Is there anyone in this jury box or in this courtroom who feels that they could not or would not give the accused person, accused defendant, the presumption of innocence unless that presumption is destroyed by the evidence?" Again no answers.

None of this bothers me. I believe that when jurors hear defense lawyers talk like that, they hear "guilty, but perhaps not provable." When Toolan finishes the usual defense script, he does Williams's work for him by excusing good old Number Seven. I watch him go with regret, although I know it had to happen. As Toolan strikes Williams's Juror Number Seven, the day draws to an end.

****

When court reconvenes, it is Rifkin standing at the podium.

"My name is Rifkind and I represent Mr. Leuty in this case." He selects new Juror No. 9 to be his platform. "And are you married?" he asks him.

"Yes."

"Do you have any children?"

"Yes, boy, one boy."

Rikfind is solicitous, "How old is he?"

"Twelve."

"Well, I see the smile on your face. I suppose you are proud of him."

"That's right," Number Nine beams. I make a note to be sure to get rid of Juror Number Nine.

Rifkind goes on to introduce the concept of the heavy burden of proof on the prosecution in a criminal case. He goes through the usual defense lawyer routine about reasonable doubt, presumption of innocence, the indictment not being evidence, and all the prospective jurors indicate that they will have no difficulty following a jury instruction on all of this. I have my doubts that their promises are of any value.

When it is Joe Brill's turn for Rowland Tompkins my doubts are realized. As he stands at the podium, with his shaven head and bushy beard Brill starts the usual cant.

"Does any member of this prospective panel have any views as to the necessity for anyone accused of a crime to prove the innocence with respect to that crime of that defendant?" Brill begins.

Juror Number Six, "I don't quite understand your statement."

And, I think, who can blame the good Mrs. Wallack.

"All right, Mrs. Wallack," says Brill, "I will try to explain myself a little bit better. I want to know whether any of you believe that there is a burden or a duty upon a defendant to prove his or its innocence and, if you do, will you please raise your hand?"

"Do you understand it now, Mrs. Wallack?"

"No."

Her "no" is a shot heard round the room, ricocheting around the defense tables. Poor Brill, standing at the podium, his shaven head beginning to show the gleam of perspiration, feels forced to press on.

"Do you think that a person who is brought into court and charged with a crime must go forward to prove his innocence?"

"Yes."

"You do?" Brill's beard is quivering. His "you do?" is more a plea of bewilderment than a question. While Brill is pondering this problem, another juror leans out of the box.

"So do I," Juror Number Nine volunteers. That's Rifkind's friend, the proud father of the twelve-year old. I reevaluate the merits of this good citizen, as I watch poor Brill deal with the rebellion in the jury box. It is as though the voir dires of Toolan and Rifkind had never happened.

Brill, in deep trouble, spins on his heel, away from the jury, seeking help from the judge. He stretches out his arms in an appeal to the bench. I can see Judge Wortendyke is of a mind to save him. That is, until he sees me shaking my head violently "no."

"Will Your Honor entertain challenges at this time?" says Brill.

I become the lawyer for Jurors Six and Nine. "I'd like an opportunity to be heard on that, Your Honor." I tell the judge that while the jurors are wrong on the law, they are not disqualified.

Brill needs that speech like he needs polio. He had almost reached salvation. The judge was about to get rid of Numbers Six and Nine without him having to use up his only two peremptory challenges. Brill, desperate to exclude the two potential jurors, calls them "biased."

Time to hit him again. "If Your Honor pleases," I jump in, "I don't think either one of these prospective jurors said that they had a *bias*. By their answers they displayed no bias; they displayed only the fact that they don't know the law."

That last one is too much for the judge, whose eyes are laughing while he keeps a stern countenance. "I am going to grant your motion for a challenge for cause of Juror Number Six and Juror Number Nine," he tells Brill. "They may step down."

Brill is still at the podium. He has been rescued. Now he gets into trouble again, as he tries to build rapport for his corporate client, Rowland Tompkins, which had delivered the first $50,000 for Colonial. "There are some corporations, as you know, that are family corporations." Brill goes on, "Have any of you ladies and gentlemen had any experience with a family corporation?"

"Yes," says Juror Number Twelve, "my son-in-law and daughter have a hotel in Lavalette, New Jersey."

"And that is a family corporation?"

"Yes, sir."

Brill is obviously delighted. Rowland Tompkins Corporation, his client, is also a family corporation. Sensing that he has at last found a kindred soul, Brill presses on. He wants to immunize the corporation from the acts of its owner-employees.

"And they have employees?"

"Yes, sir."

"And those employees perform acts, some on behalf of the corporation?"

"Yes, sir."

"And," Brill says, to separate the acts of the individuals from those of the corporation, "is it, to your knowledge, true that some of them perform acts which are not the acts of the corporation?"

"I wouldn't know, sir, because I am here and they are down there," the juror shakes her head "no." "I couldn't answer that."

Not so good. But Brill does not lose heart. He is confident that he can make this juror—who is now a witness for him—defend her own family corporation.

"Do you believe that all acts performed by all employees of a family corporation are necessarily the acts of the corporation itself?" I am rising to object when the juror stops me with her answer.

"Well, I'm not sure I understand you. You see they have a cocktail lounge now. If you mean if the bartender serves minors is the corporation liable, is that what you mean?"

I lose any concern. I sit back contentedly in my chair. I know exactly what is coming next. I know bars are liable for serving minors who happen to look like grandfathers. Apparently Brill doesn't, for with the cocked gun to his own head he asks Number Twelve to pull the trigger.

"Well, that's a good illustration of what we are trying to find out," he smiles at her to proceed.

"According to the Alcohol Beverage Control law, he would lose his license regardless, whether he knew or not," the juror explains.

"I am going to intrude here," the judge steps in to save Brill and the other corporate defendants, "we're not going into the field of the Alcoholic Beverage Control law. I will ask you to refrain from pursuing that particular inquiry."

****

Hour after hour of endless, sometimes mindless questioning has reached the point that the judge has supplanted the attorneys and is doing the questioning himself. Then a new Juror Number Two takes her seat. In just a few minutes I can see that the lady does not speak English well enough to serve. Unfortunately, when the hard-of-hearing Judge Wortendyke doesn't pick it up, it is my turn to go down in flames.

The inappropriateness of her responses to the judge coupled with her heavy accent persuades me that the woman should be excused. So I lean over from the end of the government's table to where Rifkind sits at the end of the Colonial table and whisper that the juror does not speak English. "I know," he whispers back. I suggest that we should both move to excuse her. He shakes his head no, with a twinkle in his eye, and says, "You do it." So I do.

"On behalf of the government, I would request, Your Honor, to ask Number Two juror whether or not she has any difficulty in understanding anything that's said in the courtroom?"

"Yes, I do," she volunteers.

The lady thus confirms her difficulty with English. I fully expect the judge to excuse her. The trouble is that the hearing impaired judge has not heard her. But he does hear what she says next.

"Also," says Juror Number Two, "I can't hear too good on one of my ears."

"I beg your pardon?" says the judge.

"I can't hear too good on one of my ears."

"I am in the same boat," the judge says as he turns to me, "what about it?"

"Under the circumstances, Your Honor," I begin, "the juror having said under oath that she doesn't speak English very well," I am virtually shouting this last, so the judge gets it. "She ought to be excused for cause."

"I might have to disqualify myself. I don't hear too good," the judge responds.

It takes awhile, but the judge eventually figures out that the lady does not understand English well enough to serve.

Then the judge himself gets in trouble. "If you are selected to sit as a juror in this case," he addresses Juror Number One, the presumptive foreman, "do you think that you can decide the case with complete impartiality between the government on the one hand and each and all of the defendants on the other?"

"Yes sir, I think I have always tried to be a good citizen."

"I am sure you have."

"I did work for President-elect Nixon, too," the man proudly proclaims.

"We have had enough about politics," Wortendyke says curtly.

****

By the end of the second day we have a jury of twelve and six alternates. That includes the Nixonite, Juror Number One, who by tradition will be the foreman. As far as I can see, we might as well have taken the first 18 in the jury box. All of the "voiring" and "diring," so to speak, was useless in predicting votes or even educating jurors. The only benefit these two days bring me is to dispel my awe of my adversaries. I see that they, too, are capable of error. This is what I have been waiting for since law school—a major trial against great lawyers. Well, now I have it. I hope to give as good as I get.

Chapter Eleven

The Opening Argument
November 19, 1968

I **SPEND THE WEEKEND** working on my opening argument to the jury—for that is what it is—an argument, even though you are not supposed to call it that. It's an opening statement, according to the books. Older lawyers tell me, "you are not allowed to argue, just state facts. Tell only what witnesses will say, not the inferences to be drawn from their testimony." Young as I am, I know that makes no sense.

I have a problem. Almost every witness I have is represented by the same lawyers that are defending the corporate defendants. I will not be allowed to speak to them before they testify and will have to painfully extract their testimony on the stand. That means I have to fill in the gaps of what they are unwilling to say directly by arguing what their testimony proves from their words.

This notion that an attorney is limited in opening to actual testimony, not its implications, is not a written law. It is a tradition. But judges enforce that tradition. Argument is for summation, at the end of the trial, they say, but no two judges will agree on what is an "offer to prove" facts versus an argument about what the facts prove. It is a silly rule, and I intend to overcome it by casting my argument as an "offer of proof."

To top it all off, while I know that Rifkind will say that Colonial was extorted, the law does not permit me to mention his defense, and then refute it before he speaks. I must find a way to answer what he will say without saying what he will say. I will not be permitted to even use the word "extortion" in contradicting it.

******

When the judge takes the bench on Monday I have the podium set up in front of the jury box. My notes are already on it, ready to begin once the jury enters. But the judge points me back to my table. He has given further thought to Williams's motion. He reports, "Something awakened me at five this morning and it came to me that I had been wrong to preclude Colonial's defense of extortion," the judge announces. "So I revoke what I said to the effect that I would preclude the defendants who seek to rely upon the theory of extortion defense from so stating to the jury by way of opening . . ." With that, he orders the marshal to bring the jury into the courtroom.

I return to the podium as the twelve jurors and six alternates file into the box. I watch as each settles in. Then, eighteen pairs of eyes stare at me. Waiting.

I make a personal accusation by pointing my finger at each one of the defendants. "The first count in this indictment charges the defendant Colonial Pipeline Company, its president, its president at the time of the events described in the indictment, the defendant Ben Leuty." I turn to Rifkind's side of the table and point directly at Leuty, sitting by his side, "its executive vice president, Mr. Karl Feldman," and he gets a finger pointed at him, "and the Rowland Tompkins Corporation." All I have is Brill. No point to pointing, "and the defendant Walter Zirpolo and the defendant Robert Jacks," each in turn gets the attention of my index finger, "with a conspiracy to violate the laws of the United States."

I stand before the eighteen jurors and outline the history of the Colonial Pipeline as it crawled up from Houston, Texas, to New Jersey, reaching for a terminus into which to pour the petroleum. For that, it needed a tank farm of twenty-two huge petroleum tanks. And it required permits from the town to authorize the construction. The company sent its permits lawyer, Fred Stewart, to town hall to see Mayor Zirpolo to find out if they could build the storage tanks.

Zirpolo informed Stewart that an ordinance required a permit for construction which could only be granted by the planning board after a public hearing. And it could be denied if the public protested.

"He told Mr. Stewart that the residents within the Third Ward of Woodbridge Township were very much opposed to any increase in the petroleum facilities, and he advised Mr. Stewart that he was running on a platform, promising the residents of the Third Ward that there would be no more petroleum tanks located within that area."

Stewart, this time with his boss, went to see Zirpolo yet again.

"We shall prove to you that Mayor Zirpolo's suggested possible method to overcome the objections of the residents in the Third Ward was to design the tank farm in the style of Colonial architecture. But the defendant Colonial Pipeline Company didn't want to make Colonial-style architecture because it would be just too expensive and they already had prefabricated dwellings or buildings on order."

I tell them that Leuty and Feldman sent Stewart back to see Zirpolo yet again. At this third meeting "the defendant Zirpolo told Mr. Stewart, 'All right, you don't have to put in Colonial-style architecture.' But then Mayor Zirpolo said to him, 'I want you now to see Mr. Jacks,' and that the defendant Zirpolo told Stewart that Jacks would be waiting for him."

Zirpolo wrote Jacks's address on a card, and Stewart went right off to Metro Motors, Jacks's used car lot. Jacks was waiting. I tell the jurors that Jacks "made it very clear to Stewart that if Colonial would pay $50,000, after the election Colonial would get its permit over the objections of the residents of the Third Ward of Woodbridge Township."

I tell the jurors how Leuty and Feldman, along with Glenn Giles, sat around in Atlanta and discussed the $50,000 "campaign contribution" to overcome the residents' objections, and that they decided to ship the $50,000 in interstate commerce from Atlanta to New Jersey, "but because these men knew that what they were planning to do was wrong, and that it was illegal, they wouldn't use any Colonial people to make the payments."

I outline the method of payment: a "dummy" contract between Colonial and Rowland Tompkins to get the "bribe money" to Zirpolo and Jacks. $20,000, then another $15,000, and then the final $15,000, each sent by Colonial to Rowland Tompkins and each delivered to Jacks acting as collector for himself and Zirpolo.

"We shall prove to you, ladies and gentlemen, that the defendant Jacks and the defendant Zirpolo fulfilled their part of the bargain, too. They kept knowledge of the Colonial Pipeline Company application from the public until after the election and that after the general election defendant Zirpolo and the defendant Jacks obtained a building permit for the erection of these twenty-two gasoline tanks without any public hearing and without any notice given to the residents of the Third Ward." Now let the boys from Atlanta claim "extortion."

I have been speaking for nearly one and one-half hours. And next I have to introduce a whole new conspiracy and some new conspirators. Both the jury and I need a break. So I ask for one.

"Well, I assume that since you have been talking now since half past ten or thereabouts, that you may be fatigued," the judge notes. "All right, we will take a brief recess."

Chapter Twelve

"That Was Very Good"
November 19, 1968

A S THE JURY files out of the room, I remain standing at my podium, rearranging my notes. This is valuable time, and I have no intention of squandering it on a smoke, although I am dying for one.

Just then Edward Bennett Williams, who had been quietly sitting at his table throughout my opening, rises and walks by me as he makes his way to the rear of the courtroom and into the hall. As he reaches me, he softly says, "That was very good. And," he emphasizes, "I mean it." In a second he is gone. It happens so fast that for the moment I do not think that it had. But it did. And I shall never forget it.

There he stood, the best and the most famous trial lawyer in America—and the fiercest competitor that I have ever seen—locked in combat in a case that he desperately wants to win, yet pausing to pat the back and to encourage a young adversary.

****

"All right, you may proceed Mr. Stern," the judge intones, as the jurors reenter their box.

I introduce the new conspiracy. The $100,000 solicitation, which Colonial bargained down to $60,000, for the right-of-way permits Colonial needed to cross city properties to connect the pipeline to the tank farm.

So the dance begins again. Fred Stewart, Colonial's right-of-way man, calls Zirpolo for a meeting to discuss the new easements, and

Zirpolo tells him to come, not to his mayor's office, but to Zirpolo's private business office, across town from city hall.

And now for the key part: When Stewart arrives at Zirpolo's business office, Jacks is there instead of Zirpolo. But Stewart does hear the mayor's voice in an adjoining room.

"In spite of the fact that he had no prior contact with Jacks, Jacks knew exactly what Stewart was there for, knew exactly the five city lots which Colonial wanted an easement through. We shall prove to you that Jacks, acting on his own behalf and on behalf of the defendant Zirpolo, requested and solicited a hundred thousand from the Colonial Pipeline Company as a condition of granting that easement through the publicly-owned property in Woodbridge."

> No witness will appear in the courtroom who will say that Jacks acted on behalf of Zirpolo. But if I don't say it to the jurors now, at the beginning of the case, they may not say it to me at the end. So I transform the inference that Jacks acted for Zirpolo into a statement of fact.

I tell the jurors that Colonial bargained the $100,000 down to $60,000. How, I never learned so have to skip over it. "We shall prove to you that in spite of the knowledge on their individual parts, that it was wrong and illegal for them to make these payments, they nonetheless refrained for months from informing any law enforcement officer or agency about it. Indeed, we shall prove to you that they took the deliberate and premeditated steps to conceal their activities from anybody who might stumble across them."

Now it is Bechtel's turn to be the conduit. Bechtel agrees to make the $60,000 payments to the city officials, and Colonial ups Bechtel's fixed-cost contract. When Bechtel became queasy after the first $20,000 payment, Bechtel gave the next two installments to their subcontractor.

I have been speaking for several hours. It is time to roll up the rest of the story. "Thank you for your patience with me. I know that you will be patient with the other counsel when they speak as well. Thank you very much."

As I return to my seat the judge announces, "We will take our luncheon recess, ladies and gentlemen," the judge glances at the clock, "until 2:00 p.m." Then it will be Rifkind's turn.

Chapter Thirteen

Simon Hirsch Rifkind
November 1968

WHEN WE RECONVENE, Rifkind has an enormous map, over six feet high, set up before the jury box. It shows the path of the 1,600 miles of pipeline, as it travels from Houston, Texas, to Woodbridge. Next to it he has three gigantic steel rings. Each so large a person could crawl through.

"May it please Your Honor, Mr. Foreman, ladies and gentlemen of the jury. Just a word of personal privilege, if you will allow me: During the voir dire when the jury was being selected Mr. Stern was very courteous and gallant in introducing me to you as Judge Rifkind. I should like you to know that there is only one Judge in this courtroom, and that is the presiding judge, Judge Wortendyke." The man has charm, and an old-world air about him.

"Now, you have heard Mr. Stern address you. Those of you who sometimes go to the opera know that you like to read the program notes in advance so you can follow the story. I must confess there were times during the opening that it read more like a libretto than a program guide, giving you the details of what he thought he could prove."

As I look at the jurors, none of whom own even one share of stock in any oil company, I wonder how many opera-goers we have in the box.

"From the witnesses you will get a certain picture of events. Upon looking at the picture, you will be asked to determine whether Mr. Leuty should be identified as a criminal or as a victim of a crime."

Rifkind, who has been reading and flipping pages from a yellow legal pad, takes the jurors from the halls of the opera to the walls of an art gallery. "I don't know whether any of you have ever visited an art gallery and seen a picture and you can't tell by looking at it at first whether it is a picture of a sunrise or a sunset because they look so very much alike. You will be asked to look at Mr. Leuty and to identify him in that picture, and in that ensemble, and ask yourself if he is a criminal or a victim of a crime."

I suspect that these jurors are no more regular patrons of the arts than opera goers, but the analogy to the picture of a sun either rising or setting I see has their interest.

I see Rifkind look over at Leuty, and I guess he is about to introduce his client to the jury. Rifkind calls upon Leuty to stand.

"That," he smiles at Leuty as he points to him, "is the man I have the honor to stand here and represent, to champion. Who is he? He is today about 66 years of age. He is by profession an engineer, what we have learned to call a pipeliner. At what stage of his career is he? He is now in retirement. He's approaching the end of his career in his profession," Rifkind nods, silently telling Leuty to reseat.

"At the time that we speak of, he had reached a stage in his career when he held the most important job in the pipeline industry. He was the commander-in-chief of the greatest pipeline ever built anywhere in the whole wide world."

Rifkind stands with a pointer in one hand confronting the six-foot-tall map displaying the length of the pipeline from Texas to New Jersey, and then some. He wields the head of the pointer to rest on the Texas coast, where a red line begins, and the pointer starts its journey across the southern part of the country as he speaks.

"Down here on the Gulf of Mexico near the city of Houston, that is where the pipeline has its beginning, its point of origin. It moves across the state of Texas, into Louisiana, up into Mississippi, straight across Alabama, all the way across the states of Georgia, South Carolina, North Carolina, into Virginia, Maryland, Pennsylvania, into New Jersey and up through New Jersey, into the area commonly known as the New York harbor area, with the terminal point of the main line at Linden, New Jersey."

Rifkind leans his pointer against the mammoth exhibit, and walks over to the end of the jury box where he has collected pieces of pipelines, cut into samples in the form of rings.

"Now I would like you to get an impression of the magnitude of this pipe, and for that reason I brought these three rings here. The big ring is a yard high, thirty-six inches. As you can see, you can crawl through it. It is a tunnel. What is lying across the eastern portion of the United States is a 1,600-mile steel tunnel. That is what the pipeline is."

I can see that Rifkind has captured the jury with his story of the massive project, the wonder of the North American world that the jurors know is about to be troubled by two minor officials in Woodbridge.

He tells the jury of the strategic need of the country for this pipeline. He reminds them of World War II, of the Cuban Missile Crisis, and promises they will hear of the "tremendous interest in the United States Department of Defense for the establishment of the pipeline as a safe route for the transportation of the life's blood of American industry."

As I observe the jury, I see that Rifkind has caught them up in his spiel, and I am going to have my hands full if he trots in admirals and generals to tell the jury how vital the pipeline is to America.

"Now, it has been suggested to you that in the township of Woodbridge, a crime was committed, and," Rifkind nods, "maybe it was. The prosecutor tells you that officials of Woodbridge were bribed. Bribed for what?" he asks. "In order for Colonial Pipeline to obtain a building permit; and in order for Colonial Pipeline to obtain some easements across which to lay their pipeline," Rifkind tells them. "Is it possible that Mr. Stern is not seeing the picture correctly?"

Rifkind tells them, that in spite of the fact that Colonial had a right to the permit, "one day there is a new note. Leuty receives a different kind of a message. The message is, 'Mr. Leuty, your whole operation will be brought to a grinding halt unless you pay ransom.' That is the message that he receives. 'Unless you'll pay off.'"

Rifkind puts down his notes. He has been largely reading, a Niagara of yellow pages flowing from his pad over the podium. But now he steps from behind the stand and walks up to the jury rail, holding his pad, but no longer looking at it, staring straight, eye to eye, at the jurors.

"The demand communicated in this message is for $50,000. That's when Leuty has one of the gravest decisions to make in his whole life. What do you do under those circumstances?" He waits to let the jurors consider. They are all Leuty now, or so Rifkind hopes, each one considering his options as CEO of the great enterprise.

"Mr. Stern said to you by implication that you complain to somebody. To whom do you complain? Who will believe your story? Certainly the officials concerned will deny it and that will result in an investigation. What happens to the investigation? It takes time. What is the cost of time? If the investigation is successful, you go to the courts. What do courts mean? Time. Delay."

I am watching the jurors closely now. This is the big one. Everything Rifkind has done is aimed at the moment. Rifkind raises his arms and opens them wide. "He is a man caught in an alley who has a gun pointed at him and pays out the money in his pocket in order to escape with his life."

He turns away from the box, puts down his yellow pad, and then faces the jurors again. "It is my judgment that you will conclude that Ben Leuty was an honest man; that he committed no wrong for which the United States government should pursue him; and that he's entitled to an acquittal at your hands as an honorable man, as a worthy citizen."

"He was the victim of a crime, and it is not compatible with common sense or with common decency or with the requirements of law that the victim of a crime should be punished."

He is "arguing" now, and I can object. But I figure the jury would not like it—to say the least—and I can see that he is done. Almost.

"When I was younger and was raising young children," Rifkind's voice has mellowed, "I kept a little farm up in Massachusetts just so my children might learn what nature is all about. One day, as I was returning from the village of Great Barrington, my little four-year-old came out running and said, 'Daddy, the sheep is chasing the dog.' We had a few sheep in a little enclosure," he explains. "I said, 'No son, the sheep aren't chasing the dog.' 'Well, look Daddy, you'll see there is the sheep and there is the dog.' Sure enough I looked," Rifkind peers out, "and in this ring there was the dog running and there was the sheep running." His hands are circling around depicting the chase. "I said, 'No, Sonny, the sheep is not chasing the dog. It's the dog that is chasing the sheep.'"

"'How can you tell?' he said."

"I said, 'Because, I know sheep and I know dogs. The sheep is running from the dog, and if that dog catches him he'll take a piece out of his side.' Don't you in this case punish the sheep because he bribed the dog to leave him alone."

I see the jurors got his point, although they try to keep their faces stony. Rifkind takes his yellow pad from the podium and returns to his seat. Funny, I think to myself, a contradiction. His opening was in many ways great. It was brilliant and persuasive and, yet, he began with librettos, took a tour of an art gallery, and finished up buying a farm just to teach nature to his son, Bob, who happened to be the kid who sat next to me on our induction to the bar.

I never cease to marvel at Simon Rifkind. You get to know a man pretty well when you are his adversary. Rifkind is one of the wealthiest and most important lawyers in the country. Yet he takes pains to dress with the utmost simplicity. Indeed, he appears to wear the same drab grey suit every day in court. It isn't the same suit, of course. He has a great many such suits, all cut of similar but not exactly identical cloth, appearing to be a one- or two-suit man. I have no doubt that he does this to give himself the common touch before the court. And yet each of those suits had little cuffs sewn onto the ends of the sleeves, much like cuffs on the end of trousers. Not obvious. Indeed subtle. But once noticed, those little cuffs are like hernias, a sticking-out in a desire to be noticed for custom-made suits.

Outside the courtroom is something else. Each day Rifkind arrives in a stretch limousine, accompanied by an entourage. I think that, too, is a mistake. I simply cannot believe that this daily armada is not observed by at least one juror. And one would be quite enough.

****

The other lawyers for the Colonial defendants make similar openings, claiming extortion. When they are done, and the jury is excused, Williams goes on the attack.

He holds a single page in his hand, and lifts it towards the judge as he continues, "Your Honor, I marked on a tally sheet here that five times this afternoon the defendants Zirpolo and Jacks were called

145

extortioners. The other counsel referred to their clients as the victims of a crime. The logical extension of that, of course, is that Zirpolo and Jacks extorted the money from them."

Looking up from his tally sheet, Williams continues, "Four times it was said that they perpetrated a shakedown under the threat, in the case of Colonial and Leuty, of being stalled, delayed, harassed every inch of the way on the 2,500-mile pipeline, stopped in their tracks," Williams counts. "And twice this afternoon it was said that they had pointed a gun at the heads of the other defendants."

"And finally, Your Honor," William concludes, "I enjoyed the opening this morning by the prosecution a great deal more than I enjoyed the openings this afternoon with respect to the defendants Zirpolo and Jacks, because finally, as I got the literal allusion, the defendants Zirpolo and Jacks were compared to dogs chasing sheep on a farm, trying to get a piece of the sheep." He again moves for a severance for Zirpolo.

Judge Wortendyke is unhappy having permitted the extortion defense. In his discomfort, his eyes fall upon me. "I must say that as I listened to the openings of the defendants I thought I was listening to summation, and I thought *someone* would pop up and object." There is no doubt who he thinks should have done the popping, as he stares frostily at me. "I didn't hear much of what they expected to prove. I heard more of a summation in each case."

But I am not deceived by his speech. I know that any objection I might have made would have been summarily overruled and I would have been told to sit down. In any event, I did not want to object. The defendants had let me have my inning, and I felt that they were entitled to theirs.

Jacks's lawyer John Toolan, is now on his feet. But the judge is tired. He wants to leave. "All right. I will decide it on the record tomorrow morning." He rises to go. But Toolan clamors to be heard. "I hope," Toolan cries out as Wortendyke leaves the bench, "that the same angel of light that visited you at five o'clock this morning will visit you again."

"It was not an angel," Wortendyke replies over his shoulder. "It was an aircraft."

Chapter Fourteen

"The Dirty Bastards are Shaking us Down" November–December 1968

IN THE MORNING the judge again denies severance. Now I am at bat. I had planned a simple case. Leuty, Feldman, and Giles each had testified before the grand jury, as part of David Wilentz's strategy of making Colonial's case for extortion. I figured, all I have to do is read their grand jury testimony at trial to prove each participated in the decision to pay Jacks and Zirpolo.

But just before the trial, the United States Supreme Court threw me a curve. In the *Bruton* case, it ruled that prosecutors can no longer read to the trial jury a defendant's grand jury testimony if it implicates a codefendant at trial. Inasmuch as Giles, Leuty, and Feldman had testified to joint discussions authorizing payments, with minor variations, it became too dangerous to put the transcripts into evidence. Without their grand jury testimony, there is no evidence that they instructed Giles to make the payments. One of the three will have to be immunized and forced to testify against the other two.

That choice is simple. Giles was low man on the totem pole of authority. If we are going to demonstrate that the top men in corporate America will be held personally accountable for their decisions in executive suites, Giles must be the immunized witness against Leuty, the president, and Feldman, the executive vice president of Colonial. Sounds simple enough. And so, before the trial started I severed and immunized Giles. As my first witness, he makes a mess of my case.

He refuses to speak to me before testifying. His counsel paid by Colonial and working hand in hand with the defense, forbids me to interview Giles. Then, the defense attorneys persuade Judge Wortendyke that, notwithstanding that Giles is a vice president of the defendant Colonial, he is *my* witness and that I cannot ask him leading questions on direct examination. To top it off, they even persuade the judge that as he is my witness, I am bound by everything Giles says, and cannot impeach him. So I have to put him on cold, and my questions of him are frequently interrupted by a chorus of objections for leading. It feels like I am flying through ack-ack over Berlin in 1944.

Nonetheless, I stumble through enough of a direct examination so the jury hears that both Leuty and Feldman authorized the payments. That is all that I have to do. But to achieve it I have to pay a price. Under the guise of cross-examination, Rifkind has a field day with Giles that goes on for days.

****

At the outset, Rifkind asks "my" witness, "Do you remember being in the court after the indictment was returned?"

"Yes, sir."

"And how did you plead?"

"Not guilty."

"Did you commit any of the crimes which are alleged in the indictment?"

"No, sir."

I am sitting at my table, stewing. It gets worse from there. Rifkind says anything he wants to, and "my" witness gives the desired and anticipated "yes." First, Rifkind describes the magnificent project and its importance to the nation. Then he comes to news of the first $50,000 solicitation. Rifkind and Giles make music together. It's a duet.

"The message delivered to you was that somebody in Woodbridge was demanding $50,000?"

"That's right, yes."

"Now, did he use the word 'demand,' 'holdup,' 'shakedown'; what word did he use?" Rifkind offers him a choice.

"Shakedown, as I recall," Giles makes his selection from Rifkind's buffet.

"And to whom did he attribute the shakedown?" Rifkind inquires.

"To Mr. Jacks."

"What did you do?"

"I went immediately and reported to Mr. Feldman and Mr. Leuty."

"Well," Rifkind suggests, "did you come in and say, 'We are the vic tims of a shakedown?'"

"Words to that effect, yes sir," says the dutiful Giles.

"Did you refer in any colorful language, colorful or salty language to the persons to whom you attributed this illegitimate demand?" Rifkind pushes Giles' memory.

"I am sure that I used one of my favorite expressions when I said 'the dirty bastards are shaking us down for $50,000.'"

"What was the reaction that you generated in Mr. Leuty as you visibly saw it?"

"Mr. Leuty, of course, was agitated. However, he's a mild-mannered man and he doesn't use the type of language I guess that I do sometimes."

"Did anybody pound the table?" Rifkind hints.

I am watching this waltz, betting that someone did, but which one? Let me guess. I bet on Feldman.

"Mr. Feldman raised up and pounded the table and said, 'They can't do this to us.'"

Rifkind shakes his head in sympathy. "Now, was that the very first time that, Mr. Giles, you had exchanged any words with Mr. Leuty and Mr. Feldman with respect to the danger of being subject to a shakedown in Woodbridge Township?"

"Yes."

I am constantly objecting. This is no real cross. This is Rifkind's witness. But my objections to the nearly two days of "cross-examination" are universally overruled. The judge has given Rifkind his head.

After suggesting that Colonial had helped the government document the crime, and that Giles had voluntarily testified to the grand jury, Rifkind attempts to draw the sting of Giles's grand jury testimony, which was quite different from his trial testimony. Rifkind, concerned that I will use that transcript, tells the jury, through his questions, that I led poor Giles into error in the grand jury. He concludes with, "at that time, when you were in the grand jury room, did you have a lawyer in the grand jury room?"

"No, sir."

Rifkind is now ready for his wrap-up. "You have already told us, I believe, that you, yourself, did not conspire with anyone to travel in interstate commerce or to use facilities of interstate commerce with the intention of getting either permits or easements by the bribery of officials of the township of Woodbridge?"

"I did not."

"I have no further questions," Rifkind beams at the judge. Maintaining his broad smile, he turns from the podium and takes his seat while his colleagues at his table openly congratulate him.

Rifkind's two full days of cross are just for openers. Foley for Feldman and Wilentz for Colonial beat the same tattoo. Even Lacey for Bechtel gets into the act, pointing out that Giles "wanted to testify" in the grand jury that "Colonial had in fact been victimized."

Even good old Toolan steps up to question on behalf of Jacks. What, I say to myself, can he do for Jacks with Giles? But the peppery lawyer surprises me.

"Count number one and count number six in this indictment charge that you conspired with Mr. Jacks to use the facilities of interstate commerce as a means to aid and assist in the payment of a bribe in the state of New Jersey. I ask you now, did you ever have such a conspiracy with my client, Mr. Jacks?"

"No, sir."

"And did you make any arrangement with Mr. Jacks to use the facilities of interstate commerce to violate the bribery law of the state of New Jersey?"

"No."

Of course not. In Giles' mind there was no bribe. He was extorted. "Do you know how the investigation got started?" he asked Giles.

"Yes," says Giles, "labor investigation."

"And in the course of that investigation, government investigators found somebody had drawn $20,000 to cash?"

"That is the way I understood it," Giles confirms.

****

After four days of cross by all the defense attorneys, except Williams, who asks nothing, I have had enough. I intend to redirect Giles by cross-examining him. Before the jury returns to the box, I make my motion to the judge.

But of course all of my adversaries vehemently object. After hearing six lawyers object, the judge rules that I cannot use leading questions.

I have to swallow my outrage at the ruling. But the judge has left me a little, very little, wiggle room. I will peg my redirect to the questions asked by my adversaries on their cross. I know that I am going to violate at least the spirit of the ruling, and I am going to take some wounds, but I am not going quietly into the night and let the government's case go down the drain.

I decide to show the jury how Rifkind had been misleading them by claiming that Leuty and Feldman had voluntarily reported the crime to the grand jury. "In reply to certain questions by Judge Rifkind, you said that you brought down certain documents to the grand jury with the permission of the defendant Leuty and the defendant Feldman, is that correct?"

"Yes."

"Did you have their permission, Mr. Giles?"

"Well," Giles says squirming a little, "permission in the sense that we had to put the articles and the material together and bring it down there, yes."

"You had been commanded by the grand jury by means of the sub-poena duces tecum to bring those documents down, hadn't you?"

"Yes," he admits.

"So you mean, then, that the defendant Leuty and the defendant Feldman gave you permission to assemble the documents which the grand jury had already commanded that you produce; is that correct?"

"Yes," he says reluctantly.

"Did you," I demand, "in any one of 80 pages of grand jury testimony, mention the word 'extortion' or 'shakedown' even once?"

"Not that I recall."

"But, of course, as Judge Rifkind pointed out, you had no lawyer with you in the grand jury room, did you?"

"No."

"You were there with me alone; isn't that correct?"

"Yes."

"But there did come a time, didn't there, when I turned the entire record over to you and told you that you could say anything you wanted to, didn't I?"

"Yes."

"Did you say this to the grand jury," I say with the transcript in my hand as I begin to read, "'Well, I think that we have covered the situation pretty well. The only thing that I would like to put before this grand jury, realizing that what we did and how we did it, perhaps, was not right, not good, not ethical, but it would seem right to the benefit of you all to know certain harassments and difficulties that we ran into during the course of this job in the northern part of New Jersey.'"

I put the transcript down. "Did you say that to the grand jury, sir?" I insist.

"Yes," Giles softly replies.

Most of my questions are objected to as leading, and almost all objections are sustained. The lawyers accuse me of undermining the judge's rulings—as indeed I am—but I also see that Wortendyke knows what I am doing, and while he continually rules against me, I can sense that he does not want to completely stop me, until Williams steps in.

"Your Honor," Williams interjects, "we covered this exhaustively on direct examination. We are back where we were a week ago."

"I will sustain the objection. It is leading."

"It has been leading throughout, Your Honor." Williams closes in for the kill, "I have tried not to clutter the record with technical objections. I submit, Your Honor, that he is flaunting your order that he should not engage in cross-examination of this witness . . ."

"That's my ruling," Wortendyke breaks in. "And he will be limited to the appropriate scope of redirect," Wortendyke looks very serious.

"I will, of course, abide by Your Honor's ruling," I say. And add, "I am merely limiting myself to the questions that were answered."

"I know what you are doing," Wortendyke says. "I can hear you."

Well, I would be happy if this time Judge Wortendyke did not hear me. I come to the conclusion that I have pushed the envelope as far as I can. Time to sit down and shut up. But I make one solemn oath to myself. If I get out of this alive and try another case, I will *never* put a weak, cross-examinable witness on as my first witness. So help me God.

Chapter Fifteen

"The Meat of the Coconut"
December 1968

A S THE JUDGE takes the bench in the morning, Williams rises and announces that he was awakened in the night to learn that Zirpolo had suffered a massive heart attack. I am suspicious, of course, but Williams not only offers to permit any physician of my choice to examine Zirpolo, but also to waive Zirpolo's presence in the courtroom so that trial can continue while we determine if Zirpolo can return. It is an offer that appears to favor the government, but it doesn't. If we go forward, Williams gets a free shot at every witness. If things go well for Williams, Zirpolo can continue to waive. If not, Zirpolo stops waiving his presence and Williams can go back home, having previewed my case. But until I determine whether Zirpolo's heart attack is genuine, I feel there is nothing I can do but proceed.

My next witness is Fred Stewart, a Mobil employee on loan to Colonial who obtained permits and rights of way. This is the man whom Zirpolo twice sent to see Jacks, and who was twice solicited for money. He is my big gun. Although a permanent employee of Mobil Oil, he alone has been willing to meet with me pretrial.

As he enters the witness box, remaining standing to take the oath, the jurors are presented with a pleasant, ordinary looking man in his early sixties. He puts on no airs. He is pure middle America. There are still traces of his Missouri accent as he softly answers my questions. I introduce him to the jury as a pipeliner who has worked for Mobil for many years before going on loan to Colonial.

He tells the jury that his job was to find the site for twenty-two huge storage tanks in the Woodbridge area that would terminate the 1,600 mile pipeline. Stewart recounts his effort to interest Zirpolo in the project and Zirpolo's reluctance, telling Stewart that "the people on the north side of the Township were very much aroused, that they don't want any more tankage up there, and he says, 'I have promised the people that there will be no more tankage up there.' He says, 'This is election year, and we just can't entertain this thing until at least after the election. Do you realize you have to go through a public hearing?' he said. I said, 'No, I didn't know that.'"

Zirpolo told him to get the ordinance and check it out. So Stewart did and reported to Atlanta. They sent him back again, this time with his immediate boss, Lou Humann. Zirpolo reiterated to Stewart and Humann that no application for a permit should be made until after the election. Then, as Stewart and Humann were leaving, Zirpolo "suggested to Mr. Humann perhaps another thing to quiet the people down would be to make the buildings with Colonial architecture so it would be in keeping with the company name, and it would be a kind of a thing of beauty. It wouldn't be such an eyesore."

But Atlanta refused. It already had prefabricated buildings on hand. Stewart's boss sent him back to Zirpolo yet a third time. Zirpolo relented. "He said, 'All right, we'll forget the Colonial architecture, but,' he says, 'things haven't quieted down a bit. Do not file any application yet.' I said, 'Is there any way in the world to avoid a public hearing?' He said, 'I'll tell you what. I think it's time that you ought to see Mr. Jacks. He is the president of the council. He is expecting you.'"

The moment has arrived. I can see that the jurors are transfixed, as Stewart explains that Jacks ran a used car lot called Metro Motors.

"I got in my car and drove over to Metro Motors. I went into the office and there was one man present in the office. I told him I was looking for Mr. Jacks. He said, 'I am Mr. Jacks.' I said—well, I told him my name, my business, that I was with Colonial Pipeline and that Mayor Zirpolo had directed me to come over to talk to him about a building permit. He says, 'Yes, I know all about it.'"

Now some of the jurors are leaning forward, as Stewart explains Jacks's response to the Colonial request for a prompt permit. "'Well,' he said, 'we've got to have a campaign contribution.' 'Well,' I said, 'we don't make campaign contributions.' 'Well,' he said, 'you are going to have to in this instance if you want to get anywhere with your permit.'" He tells Stewart that he wants $50,000 from Colonial.

The way the testimony is coming in, I grow concerned that jurors might believe that Stewart is quoting verbatim. "Are you relating the substance of what you said to each other?" Stewart shakes his head, "It is the substance of the conversations. That's the meat of the coconut."

Now for a little drama. Placing both my hands on the back of my chair—Dermody style—and speaking very slowly for emphasis, I say, "Do you see Mr. Jacks in court, the man that you spoke to?"

"Yes, sir." Stewart nods, "I think I recognize Mr. Jacks."

A personal accusation is always a moment of both drama, and demonstration of confidence for the identifier. I intend to make the most of it.

"Will you point him out, please?" I say.

Stewart begins to rise from the stand, simultaneously raising his arm to point.

"The gentleman sitting . . ."

Toolan does not want Jacks to look like he is avoiding the identification. "Stand up," Toolan sharply directs Jacks, who bounds up on his feet before Stewart can finish.

"Right there," Stewart points his finger like it was a gun. I am not going to let the moment pass as quickly as Toolan would like. With Jacks still standing facing Stewart, I ask, "Is this the man you spoke to?"

"That's the man I spoke to."

"That is the man that asked you for $50,000?"

"Yes, sir."

By the time Jacks reseats himself, Toolan's face is flushed.

The time has come to introduce the second conspiracy, the $60,000 payment.

"Directing your attention to February of 1964, did there come a time when you knew that you needed easements through five city-owned lots?"

"Yes sir, yes sir," Stewart replies.

"What did you do after you found that you needed easements through five city-owned lots?"

"I wrote a letter of application to Mr. Zirpolo as mayor."

In response, Zirpolo called Stewart and directed him to Zirpolo's private business office in a shopping center. Stewart went to the office, asked for Zirpolo, and a secretary told him to wait.

When she opened the door to the interior office, Stewart could hear Zirpolo's voice. "When she returned, she said, 'Just be seated. He is busy. He will see you in a few minutes.' With that I sat down and picked up a paper or something."

"What happened next?"

"In a few minutes she got a buzz or a telephone call, I am not sure, and I was escorted into his office. When I walked in the office, the mayor wasn't there, but Mr. Jacks was sitting there behind a desk."

"The Mayor was not in the room? Did you have a conversation with Mr. Jacks?"

"I told him I was there on this application for our easement to go across the city-owned lots. He said, 'I know all about it,' or words to that effect. 'This is all well and good,' but he says, 'we have got to have some money in this thing.'"

"I said, 'What are you talking about?' He said, 'I am talking about a hundred thousand dollars. That's what I'm talking about.' I said, 'We just got through paying you $50,000.' He says, 'Yes, but we have got to have more this time.' I said, 'That sounds like extortion to me.' He says, 'I don't care what you call it. We got to have it before you will ever get your permit.' That was it."

"Are those the exact words that were used?"

"As I said this morning, that is the meat of the coconut."

Stewart has nothing more to give me. But then I don't need anything more, at least not from him. There will be evidence of raising money and of payments. But as far as Colonial and its people are concerned, my case that they committed bribery is in, except for one thing. For my case to survive, Stewart will have to survive cross-examination.

Chapter Sixteen

"I Swear Before My God"
December 1968

THE SCARIEST MOMENT for a trial lawyer is turning his main witness over for cross-examination. With the words "no more questions," he becomes a spectator to whatever his adversaries are about to do to his largely defenseless witness. To be sure, a witness can be prepared for the cross, and the lawyer may object to questions posed. But not everything can be anticipated. And too many objections to questions betoken fear of answers.

With heart in mouth, I say, "no more questions," and turn poor Stewart over. They will all question, of course. But the two I fear are Rifkind and Williams. Stewart has put a big hole into Rifkind's extortion defense, assuming that legally there is such a defense.

Williams is another matter. Stewart is the one and only witness that can implicate Zirpolo. And that only by inference. A strong one, but still only an inference. On one occasion Zirpolo referred Stewart to Jacks; and on the other Jacks showed up instead of Zirpolo at Zirpolo's office, with Zirpolo's voice coming from the next room; and that is it. Still, it will be enough as long as Stewart holds up under the best cross-examiner in the country.

As Rifkind rises to interrogate Stewart, he is all old world charm. He knows he must deal with the allegation about the payment to avoid a public hearing, and so he goes right after it. "You said that Mr. Zirpolo referred to the possibility of a public hearing, is that right?"

"That is true."

"Were you fearful of a public hearing?"

"Well, I will put it this way. I have gone through a number of public hearings with applications of this type and it always delays you."

"But," Rifkind emphasizes, "you believe that in such a public hearing, Colonial Pipeline Company could make out a case for itself in favor of its permit?"

"I felt we could," Stewart is happy to agree.

"Did you intend to convey the notion that you would do anything illegitimate to avoid a public hearing?" Rifkind knows the man will say no, and he does.

"No, sir. I asked him if there was another ordinance, some way we could lawfully avoid a public hearing."

Stewart has gone right where Rifkind knew he must go. Rifkind can safely close the point. "You did not invite a suggestion for a bribe?"

"It was not my intention."

Rifkind, satisfied that he has dispelled the aroma of bribery, swings into his extortion defense. Turning to the final conversation when Jacks demanded $100,000, Rifkind asks, "He said, 'You will pay or else.' Did he say those words?"

"He said those words."

Rifkind has decided to conclude on his theme that Colonial, the victim of the crime, was a cooperative complainant to the government.

"Mr. Stewart, from the very beginning of the inquiry into this matter instituted by the government, you have been willing and eager to report to the authorities the whole story as you knew it?"

"I was. I wanted to tell the truth about everything I know about it, that's all."

Satisfied that he has established that Stewart, and by implication Stewart's employer, Colonial, had volunteered to help the government, Rifkind contentedly sits down.

The lawyers for the three corporations briefly examine. Like Rifkind, they are not hostile. It would not fit in with their "victim" defense to attack the man.

The next cross-examiner is Edward Bennett Williams. This is my dreaded moment. Stewart had been interrogated by numerous oil company lawyers, Colonial in-house lawyers, and Wilentz lawyers before he had been brought to see the grand jury and me. Many of them had made notes, which were erroneous. Some had taken signed statements from poor Stewart, who, in the rush, had adopted their mistakes. Williams has all of this material and I am sure he intends to bludgeon Stewart with it.

As Williams rises and takes his place at the lawyer's podium, there is an air of anticipation in the unusually packed courtroom. When the trial first started, there was a crowd for the opening. As the days passed, it thinned. Now, there isn't a vacant seat. Lawyers from the community have crowded in the spectator benches to hear Williams.

"Mr. Stewart, my name is Williams. I represent Mr. Zirpolo. You and I have never talked before this moment, have we?"

"No, sir."

Williams brings out that beginning on June 1, 1966, Stewart was interviewed by lawyers on June 1, 26, 27, 28, and 29, culminating in his grand jury testimony on July 1, which contained numerous errors. Since I knew what was coming, I had made sure that Stewart testified on direct examination that his memory on the stand was better than his memory at the time he testified before the grand jury on July 1.

"Now yesterday under examination you testified, did you not, that your recollection is more vivid today than it was when you testified before the grand jury?"

"That is true."

"Now, is that because, Mr. Stewart, you have had further interrogations by Mr. Stern since the grand jury returned the indictment in this case?"

"No, that isn't the reason. The reason is because I have had the opportunity to see numerous documents, letters, memorandums, and my old files when I was with Colonial. It has all jelled in my mind from referring to these memoranda."

Williams knows that these answers are the product of the preparation of Stewart that has anticipated Williams' cross. So he goes after that preparation.

"Excuse me, have you in fact been interrogated a number of times by Mr. Stern?"

"Yes, sir."

"Give us an estimate. Was it as many as twenty-five?"

"I don't think I'd go that far, because there were times when I would call Mr. Stern and ask him if I could come over and look at certain documents."

"Mr. Stewart, did you not in fact go through a rehearsal of your direct examination since this trial began?"

"I wouldn't call it a rehearsal, no sir."

"So was the only reason that he went over this, as far as you know, so that he would know the answer to your questions? Or was it that you would answer the questions confidently and after having repeated your answers many times?"

"No. The only assurance Mr. Stern has ever given me, he just wanted me to tell the truth and that's all."

Williams having gotten nowhere with that, goes right to the issue at trial, commencing with Zirpolo's suggestion that Stewart see Jacks about the tank farm.

"Mayor Zirpolo suggested that you see Mr. Jacks, the president of the city council, is that right?"

"Yes, that is right."

"You were told, were you not, Mr. Stewart, that Mr. Jacks, in addition to being president of the city council, was the committeeman for the Third Ward, were you not?"

"He may have mentioned it. I wouldn't say he didn't."

"Well, did you discuss the possibility of opposition from the residents in the area?"

"Oh yes, that was paramount in our discussion."

"It was in that context that he said, 'You'd better see Jacks,' right, at that meeting?"

"Well, he told me at that meeting he thought now was the time to go see Mr. Jacks."

"You wouldn't deny, would you, Mr. Stewart, that he told you that Jacks was the committeeman from that very ward?"

"No, I wouldn't deny that . . ."

"And the last thing that Mayor Zirpolo said to you, the last time you ever saw him on August 16, 1963, just before he suggested that you see Mr. Jacks, was 'File your application and let the chips fall where they may,' isn't that so?"

"He said, 'File it after the election,' yes sir."

"And let the chips fall where they may?"

"Words to that effect."

"He said that, didn't he?"

"Yes."

Williams has subtly suggested that as far as Zirpolo was concerned, there was a legitimate reason for the referral to Jacks. That done, Williams also knows that he must deal with the second meeting with Jacks, the one in Zirpolo's private office.

"You are not prepared to swear that Mayor Zirpolo was in that Menlo Park Shopping Center in March of '64 when you had the conversation with Mr. Jacks, are you?"

"I am prepared to say, Mr. Williams, I thought he was in there. I could have sworn, and I still feel today that I heard his voice in there before I ever went in, but I did not see him."

"Well, could you be mistaken . . . could you have been mistaken about that, Mr. Stewart, as you had been mistaken about other things here?"

"I don't think I was mistaken in all honesty. I do not think I was mistaken."

"You are not prepared, are you, Mr. Stewart, to *swear* under *oath* to this jury that you heard Mayor Zirpolo's voice or that he was present in that office?"

Williams has pushed him too far. "I am swearing under oath to this jury, to this court and," with his hand raised in the air, "*before my God, that I thought I heard his voice in there that day and I still think I did.*" Stewart delivers "before my God" like a blow.

In a few moments Williams is done. When I hear "no more questions," a weight comes off my chest. Williams was superb, but Stewart was firm and even hit back hard enough so that I think we came out just fine.

The judge declares a brief recess, and I walk over to Williams, who is putting his table in order. I remember how kind he had been during my opening, and I say to him, "Great job, Ed." But he shakes his head, and he and I know that he will stop waiving Zirpolo's presence at trial. Williams may wait a day or so, but he will pull the plug.

Chapter Seventeen

Final Argument
January 1969

I T TAKES SIX weeks to get from the end of Stewart to the start of summations. Of course, Thanksgiving, Christmas, and New Year's in between don't help. And flu season costs us more than a week when Judge Wortendyke becomes ill.

The contractors testify to the payments and identify all of the back-up documents. The records of the planning board are introduced to show that the permit for the tanks was obtained without a public hearing, and without any notice that it was on the docket. And throughout, Rifkind and company make endless speeches and motions and cross-examinations.

But not Williams. Shortly after Stewart leaves, Zirpolo, who is genuinely sick, withdraws his waiver of his constitutional right to be present. I am forced to consent to Williams's motion for a mistrial for Zirpolo. As Williams leaves the court, we shake hands cordially. I tell him that I will be seeing him again, when Zirpolo has recovered. He laughs, and then he is gone.

Trial is an ordeal. I remember my father's words, "harder than shoveling coal." I no longer commute. I can't afford the time. During the week I check into a fleabag hotel in Newark. I pick up daily transcripts after dinner. Every night I prepare for the next day. I get up at 4:00 a.m. to excerpt the previous day's testimony, and then to the office by 7. My secretary retypes the excerpts onto pages in a three-hole notebook. In this way, I am building my summation. I intend to read the witnesses' words to the jurors, rather than a speech by me.

****

Throughout November, December, and into January, there is a world around me in which I am sure a lot is happening. But I am an island of indifference, except when Jon Goldstein completes his time in Southeast Asia and rejoins the team.

As the government's case winds down, Jon and I begin to contemplate our futures. We have the Weber case to deal with next, of course, but after that, what? Neither of us has any desire to return to Washington. Each of us will probably wind up back in New York. During one of the breaks in the trial, we receive a call that appears to decide the future for us. It's Tony Cosolo, my Labor Department investigator, on the other end. He sounds grim.

"Tony, what's wrong?" I ask.

"It's Roy Burgess," he says and then stops.

I don't know what to say, so I wait.

"Herb, he's dead."

"What?" I can't believe it—Burgess, the H.C. Price man that paid Weber off. The first thing that comes to my mind is that Weber had him killed. Cosolo knows what I am thinking.

"No, nothing weird. He had a heart attack. That's it. He went out at once."

"Tony, without Burgess we don't have a case. He paid Weber four times, hand to hand. He was the only one in the room each time he paid Weber."

"You still have the Joyce payments."

"Tony, we had to indict Joyce to get him to talk. Joyce won't hold up without the Price payments. And without the Price payments, we won't be able to show why Weber called Giles to pressure Colonial to give the contract to Price instead of Bechtel. Face it, it's over."

"Herb, you'll come up with something."

But I don't see how. Anyway, as Scarlett O'Hara said, "Tomorrow is another day." Today, the Colonial defendants begin their summations.

****

After all their bluster during their opening arguments to the jury, once I rested my case, all of the defendants rested theirs without calling a witness. In spite of my fears, no generals or admirals came to tell jurors of the desperate need for the pipeline and its terminal, and no defendant took the stand. I am both sorry and relieved. I would love to take a crack at Leuty and Feldman on the stand but, after handling every witness and argument for the government, I am nearly exhausted.

****

Summation is the moment of high drama in movies, novels, and public imagination. But I conclude it can't much influence our jurors, who have sat listening to our case for two months. I can't believe the jurors have been waiting for our last words to make up their minds.

I suspect that, generally, summations are more influential in short rather than long trials, precisely because they come closer to the beginning. No one sits through weeks of an adversarial contest with an open mind. In the long trial we just concluded, I am sure that the summation's purpose is not so much to persuade, as rather to arm friends on the jury with ammunition to deal with hostiles in the battle that will shortly take place in the jury room. That argument in the jury room will be the true final argument in the case. I intend to read testimony, lots of testimony, from my daily excerpting, to equip my friends. That is, if I have any friends among the jurors. I do know that I have at least one enemy, one non-believer as to Karl Feldman, executive vice president of Colonial. Jon Goldstein has been studying the jurors from the back benches. He tells me that a lady juror in the front row keeps looking over at Mrs. Feldman in the audience. And that is not a good sign.

****

For three days I listen and make notes while the defense hammer at the jurors. First Brill. Then Lacey. Their guilt or innocence depends on Colonial's defense. And that rests on the slim shoulders of Simon Hirsch Rifkind.

The diminutive Rifkind rises and begins by deprecating himself:

"Mr. Foreman, ladies and gentlemen of the jury, when it happens to be my turn to rise to speak after these giant, tall lawyers, like Mr. Lacey and Mr. Brill, I sort of shrink a little bit and I am overawed. But I will confess to you right at this moment I feel nine feet tall. I feel nine feet tall because at this stage of my life it is my privilege and my opportunity to stand here before an American jury and champion Ben D. Leuty."

He does not intend to fool the jurors with false modesty. Only to charm them. And by their welcoming smiles I see that he has succeeded. Do they know that he is a rogue? At least some must, for it is hard to conceal who you are from people who have you under close scrutiny for nearly ten weeks. But I suspect that even those who have figured him out don't care if he is a rogue. Even I don't. He has been admirable in his fierce competitive spirit that neither gives nor asks for quarter.

At the very outset of his summation, he continues to mislead the jurors as to the origin of the investigation, characterizing Colonial and its officers as complainants, implying that they blew the whistle on the faithless public servants. "Colonial," says Rifkind, "cooperated fully in this matter. It brought the entire story of this situation to the prosecution attorneys and to the grand jury."

Listening to this, Arthur Barger, my FBI agent next to me at the table, pulls my sleeve to get my attention. Turning, I find him leaning over to whisper, "That's a bunch of crap. Can't you do something?" I shake my head and turn back to Rifkind.

"You have seen how many times from that witness stand," pointing to the empty chair and then to me, "Mr. Stern said to a witness, 'Isn't that a paper that came out of the files of Colonial Pipeline Company?' That happened time after time because the officials of Colonial Pipeline Company were eager to give this information to the government. They were complaining they had been shaken down."

The man is irrepressible, in some ways like a mischievous boy hidden within an old man's body. It's all false, of course, and I could have tried to object. But I would have surely lost. In spite of the realities, Wortendyke would have allowed Rifkind to argue the "inferences" from the testimony, irrespective of the out-of-court "truth." As to the moral question, if it were I, knowing the truth as I do, I would not make such an argument. No matter what anyone says, winning is really not the only thing. I sit quiet because I have no choice. But I intend to deal with him when it's my turn.

As he warms to his subject, he finds a way to mention Martin Luther King, Jr., without looking directly at the black juror in the last row. Then seamlessly, he finds a way to mention that the nine oil companies that own Colonial are all "constantly" looking for real estate. As he does so, I watch Mr. Bucino, Juror Number Two, who is a real estate agent from Hoboken. As Rifkind touches the subject, Bucino, wearing his usual bowtie, begins to lean out of the jury box, listening intently.

"Each of these big oil companies that I have mentioned, each of these companies, has a real estate division for obvious reasons," Rifkind explains, "They have tremendous organizations. They are constantly having to buy offices, sites, stations, plants, and so on," Rifkind points out, "So they all have real estate divisions and each of those companies assigned its real estate division to help Colonial find a site for this tank farm."

I am watching Bucino closely as he leans even further, head tilted, as though seeking to capture every word. I wonder if his bowtie is going to go into a spin and elevate him from his seat as he contemplates the image of the nation's nine major oil companies flocking to Hoboken in their eternal quest for ever-increasing real estate purchases. But then I see Bucino shake his head, just once, but vigorously, as a man does when he shakes off a misperception, or a blow. I feel like doing it as well. Anyway, watching Bucino, I feel better about the effectiveness of Rifkind's arguments. But I look at Rifkind in wonderment, finding myself caught between outrage and, believe it or not, amusement.

Rifkind continues reading his summation from his usual yellow legal pads. As he finishes one pad, he draws another from a pile of folders stacked before him. Rifkind recounts Giles's testimony. He tells the jurors, "Giles made it perfectly plain that Mr. Leuty had no intention to commit bribery but, on the contrary, that he was the victim of a shakedown and that he responded to the fear of mammoth injury to the corporation whose fortunes were entrusted to his care."

For nearly two days Rifkind pounds at the jurors, selectively reading from transcripts. I am making notes like crazy, but it is hard to keep up with him as he goes through his yellow pads and folders. It is with relief that I see him enter his finale. He again speaks of pictures of sunsets and sunrises in art galleries and sheep chased by dogs around a ring.

"Are you not prepared to agree with me that in looking at the picture of Ben Leuty you saw not a criminal but a victim of the crime? I recall to you a simile that I used in the concluding remarks of my opening, not a predatory dog but a sheep that yielded a piece of its hide in order to escape with its fleece."

Now Rifkind adds "the golden rule," which is not allowed. He asks the jurors to treat Leuty as they would wish to be treated. The law does not permit attorneys to ask the jurors to imagine themselves to be the defendants. If jurors did that, no one would be convicted.

"Can you," Rifkind asks the jurors, "visualize a situation where *your* house is on fire? You ring the fire alarm. The fire company pulls up to *your* house and the fire chief comes in and says, 'Well, I don't think this house is worth saving. Oh, you disagree with me? We will have a hearing about that. However, for a hundred dollars I will turn on the water.' Are *you* going to stand there and argue with him, or are *you* going to pay him the hundred dollars, and if *you* do, do *you* think that *you* ought to be convicted of bribery?"

I turn to the back of the room and glance at Jon Goldstein, who shakes his head, then shrugs. I agree. Nothing to be done. I turn back quickly as Rifkind goes after me personally.

"The jury is the bulwark between the accused citizen and the prosecutor. You might say to me, 'Why does a citizen need a bulwark? Is it not the prosecutor's sworn duty to do right?'" Agent Barger pulls on my sleeve again and whispers, "Watch out."

"I call it the hunting syndrome. You know when you go hunting you like to get the deer with the biggest spread of antlers. When you go fishing you like to catch the biggest one in the pond, so it is with prosecutors," he glances at me, "some prosecutors. It is so much more exciting to go after a captain of industry than it is to go after a couple of politicians in a small community."

It's plain that "some prosecutors" means me. And I don't even hunt or fish. Don't care to, either. Besides, I'm too busy hunting "captains of industry" to be bothered shooting mere animals.

Rifkind swings into his ending, telling the jurors to "wipe the tear" off Mrs. Leuty's cheek with their acquittal of her husband. He puts the last of his yellow pads away and resumes his seat, to the open admiration of his colleagues, who pat his back, or nod from places at the table too far to reach him.

"We will take a ten-minute recess, ladies and gentlemen of the jury," says Judge Wortendyke, "It will give you a chance to get a little fresh air. You may retire, please."

Chapter Eighteen

"Political Money Is Cash Money" January 1969

WHEN THE JURY returns, there are three summations yet to go. Foley gets up for Feldman, and does the extortion routine. He also insists that Feldman only participated in the first $50,000 payment and played no role in the second $60,000. This summation, like Brill and Lacey's, is useful to me. If there is no wrongdoing, why the big desire to create separation between Feldman and the second payment?

Then on comes Wilentz for Colonial itself. Wilentz goes even further than Rifkind in his claims that Colonial reported the payments to the government.

"We gave him," pointing to me, "practically every document because we didn't believe that we were guilty of any crime. This is the most ironic case that I have ever had or been involved in in my life. Because in this case all of a sudden the victims become the defendants." He finishes quickly enough and now there is just one more to go. Toolan, on behalf of Jacks.

"Now, don't misunderstand me," Toolan stands without a note in his hand, and in his raspy voice tells the jurors, "I am not asking you to put any medals on Jacks or decorate him with any crown, but I am going to ask you to bring in a verdict of not guilty against him. Now, that may sound a little bit peculiar to you lay people who have heard testimony here that Mr. Jacks received in one instance $50,000, another instance $60,000, and that a man who received that money should go scot free."

Toolan, standing ramrod straight, delivers a devastating commentary on the American political system. "I am going to talk for a minute about campaign contributions and cash, and maybe it will be a shock to some of you folks. How do you think political campaigns are run? Did you ever try to hire a poll worker or a car or get a babysitter for somebody to go out to vote, and think you can pay them with a check on Election Day?"

Every soul in the courtroom has his jaw open as Toolan, chin thrust out, proclaims, "Members of the jury, elections in this nation are run with cash in every municipality, in every county, and everywhere along the line. Do you think all that money came in checks? Do you think they paid all their bills in checks? Members of the jury, you just have to realize that political money is cash money."

And then, turning towards his client, he says, "Every political party must have somebody in it that has the capacity to raise money. Bob Jacks was that person in the Woodbridge political organization. Now, this is an oil company coming through. He has to raise money either by going around and sandbagging local people, or you get it on a one-shot deal with some big asset that is coming through, and you take advantage of it."

****

The defendants have summed up for three days. It is now 4:00 p.m., and I am scheduled to begin my summation at 10:00 a.m. I do not see how I can possibly deal with all that they have said in over three days with just a few hours to prepare. In most federal and state courts the prosecution sums up first, then briefly rebuts. But not in New York and New Jersey. Here the prosecution sums up last and it is his only chance to speak.

The corporate defendants have proclaimed that it is okay to pay off if there is enough economic pressure, and Jacks suggests that political donations from favor-seekers are commonplace. It's a mess that I have to clean up, and I don't have the time to put it all together.

I tell the judge that after three days of defense summation I need a day off to prepare my response. It now being ten minutes to four on a Thursday, it is going to be impossible for me to make a full reply by ten o'clock tomorrow morning.

If I expect sympathy, I sure don't get it. "I have an accumulation of court matters, and indeed I think that the government is going to bring another prosecution before me before too long," says Wortendyke. He is obliquely referring to the Weber case. I can't tell him, of course, that Burgess, my star witness against Weber, just died, so he can give me a day without worrying about the next case.

"I am going to deny your request," he adds, "I have been fighting a cold." As I stand wondering what his next trial or his potential cold has to do with anything, he rules, "I must *insist* that you present your summations to the jury tomorrow morning." With that, he sweeps from the courtroom, leaving me crestfallen.

As I go back to my place, Jon Goldstein leaves the spectator benches and joins me at my table where I am cleaning up. "Herb, I think the old man is trying to help you."

"Help me? He is killing me!"

"I don't think so, and neither does he. You don't need any more time. And tomorrow is Friday. If he gives you time off, the jury will have to wait nearly four days before they hear a word from you in response to the pounding our case took. Not good. Why don't you go along now and get to work. I'll take care of all this stuff."

Chapter Nineteen

The Thing We Have to Fear
January 1969

CAN'T PUT A summation together in our tiny offices with agents all around and others popping in. I can't do it in a hotel room either. By the time I get home with two bags full of exhibits, my extracts of testimony, and a slice of pizza it is after 6:00 p.m. I have sixteen hours to eat, prepare, sleep and get back into the courtroom and answer three days of summations. I don't see how it is possible.

I work almost all night. By the morning I am in a state. I am certain the government would be better served if I waived a summation rather than bollix it up. Part of me knows that is crazy. But the part of me that is terrified, what with lack of sleep and self-doubt, has me narcotized. I am determined to waive final argument and instead rely on the jury's recollection.

I ride the PATH train to Newark and walk into the courthouse. I head directly to Wortendyke's chambers. His clerk, Al DeCotiis, is in the antechamber. He is surprised to see me.

"Al, I need to see the judge."

"What is it about?"

"It's personal."

He tells me to wait a minute and goes inside. In a minute, he waves me in.

The judge is seated behind his enormous partner's desk. He looks different without a robe and on ground level rather than perched up on the bench. Still, the old man is a formidable figure. I quickly blurt out to him that I want to waive my summation. He just looks at me for a long moment. Then he says, "All right, if that's what you want."

I don't know what I expected. Maybe I wanted a pep talk or some sympathy. But I don't get anything more than "all right." So, I walk out of his chambers and go over to the courtroom. It's still empty. I sit down at my table. In a few minutes, the lawyers start drifting in. As they do, I get up, take my materials from my bag, and put my notes on the lectern. It is almost a mechanical act. I know I have no choice. I can't waive. I guess Wortendyke knew it, too. I figure I may make a fool of myself, but I can't run away from my adversaries or from myself. So here goes nothing.

When the judge takes the bench, he sees me standing, with my lectern full of pages of testimony and a pile of exhibits on the table next to me. He doesn't say anything, doesn't smile, just nods knowingly and sends for the jury.

"Good morning, ladies and gentlemen," says Wortendyke as the jury files in. Turning to me "the government may present its closing argument to the jury."

Before I can even open my mouth, Juror Number Two, our Hoboken realtor, says, "Not past four o'clock." He rasps it softly. I don't know if anyone else in the well of the court heard. But I sure did. I give him a quick nod, and begin.

"If it please this honorable court, gentlemen for the defendants, Mr. Foreman, and ladies and gentlemen of the jury, as you all know a criminal trial is supposed to be nothing more than a search for the truth. At least, that is the way we all understand it. It is not supposed to be some sort of a contest of skill between attorneys to see which one can outsmart the other. What we have been doing for the past several months now is by means of testimony and documents and exhibits trying to strive for the truth, because I know that is what you are interested in."

I say it because I mean it. Anyway, I don't know how else to begin because I still feel inferior to my adversaries. And then, because I have nothing really planned, I just let it out—the years of digging, of preparing, the struggling in court just to get the basic facts out. I take a deep breath and just let go.

"Ladies and gentlemen, rarely if ever has the United States been able to pull back the curtain and to display before you or any jury the kind of naked corruption that we have displayed in this case, the intimate details of corrupt public officials met and joined, furthered, and promoted by big businessmen who were equally corrupt for their own reasons. Ladies and gentlemen, I suggest to you that rarely if ever has the United States been able to prove such a deliberate, knowing, intentional, and willful flouting of the laws of the United States. Ladies and gentlemen, I suggest to you that rarely if ever has any case been proven, before any jury, any time or any place as completely as this case has been proved here in this courtroom."

I do not know where the words come from. They are not written out. But I do know that it will be all right. I am no longer afraid. Now it is *their* turn to be afraid.

"Ladies and gentlemen, these cases are rare indeed, and they are not easy to come by. Let me suggest to you the reason that these cases are so rare is because the men don't often get caught. The reason they don't get caught is because generally they hide it too well, and if you doubt it, ladies and gentlemen, look how well it was hidden in this case."

I am just fed up with the gamesmanship, the false innuendo, the cute manicuring of the trial record and indifference to the truth. As to fear—what fear? I am having the time of my life.

"Ladies and gentlemen, there has been a suggestion made to you in the argument of counsel that Colonial and its officers came down and revealed this matter to the United States, but if I can recall to your mind the actual testimony which you heard, do you remember, when Giles was on the stand, Senator Toolan brought out that we, the United States government, found this case by accident. Do you remember that? That during a grand jury investigation of some other matter, the grand jury stumbled across a $20,000 check, the Bechtel check. Do you remember the first $20,000 that Licklider cashed from Morgan Guaranty Bank?" I take the exhibit from a pile and flourish it. "That is the check."

I am smiling at the jurors now, "Ladies and gentlemen, based not on my arguments to you or," I turn to look at Rifkind and make brush strokes, "by painting sunsets into sunrises, but on the cold facts, isn't it clear that this case came to the government not because anybody ran and told us about it, but because quite by accident a grand jury stumbled across a check, started asking questions, started subpoenaing documents and then and only then did Giles, Leuty, and Feldman come on to tell a story to the grand jury?" I tap my finger on the podium. "They had no choice. If the grand jury hadn't found that check, if the grand jury hadn't issued those subpoenas for documents, none of us would be here now."

It is time to meet this extortion defense head on. After a pause for a little water, I say, "Ladies and gentlemen, you are going to be in for a big surprise. You are going to find out from the judge that the law of bribery is just what you always thought it was after all."

I nod in Toolan's direction, "The judge is also going to tell you, ladies and gentlemen, that it is no defense to a public official charged with bribery that he received such money as a political contribution. Isn't that what you always knew in the conduct of your affairs?" I ask them, knowing that they cannot respond, at least not now. And with that I swing around to face the defense table.

"Just as you knew it, so did they." I start to point at the defense table. "The gentlemen who worked for the Colonial Pipeline Company,"—so much for Leuty and Feldman. "The Rowland Tompkins Corporation," my finger indicates Brill. "The Bechtel Corporation," Fred Lacey is at the point of the finger. "The 'captains of industry,'" a bow back at Rifkind, "they knew it, too. I am going to suggest to you that it was because they knew that what they were doing was criminal that they hid it and they concealed it, and, as I told you in my opening, that I would prove to you that they were ashamed of it and that they wouldn't use their own people to do it."

I turn to Jacks. I point my finger at him, "There are no muggers in this courtroom, just a faithless public official. There certainly aren't any sheep in this courtroom, not in this courtroom there aren't," I turn to look directly at Leuty and at Feldman. "They are just highly-placed executives who have misused their positions and their affluence to alienate public officials from their duty."

"If there are any sheep in this case," I shake my head, "they are not in the courtroom. They never had a chance to be here at all." Everyone in the courtroom knows that I mean the people of the Third Ward who never got a hearing before the permit was issued.

I start to read from my excerpts of testimony. Giles, Stewart, other witnesses' voices speak through my lips. "I am taking your time now to read transcript to you so that," I nod to Rifkind, "if anybody tries to tell you that a sunset is a sunrise, remember the testimony and decide for yourself."

For an hour I read testimony, flourish exhibits, and demonstrate that the ordinance required a public hearing before a permit for a tank farm could be granted. Thus far there have been no objections to interrupt me. But when I go after Rifkind yet again, he objects.

"Judge Rifkind asked you to examine the intent of the men who acted. Ladies and gentlemen, these are the documents in this case," and I point to the pile of false bills used to generate the cash, "documents that you are going to have in the jury room. Have you ever known such conduct to be so violative of all the known rules of honesty and integrity?"

"I must protest, Your Honor," Rifkind cries out, "against this distortion of what I said."

"The protest will be noted," says Wortendyke, "The jury will rely upon its own recollection as to what was said by numerous counsel in their respective summations. Go ahead," he tells me as he thrusts his chin up, in a giddy-up gesture.

"Ladies and gentlemen, I submit to you that it is quite clear that these men were hiding this transaction, and the reason they were hiding it was because they knew what they were doing was *criminal*, yes, *criminal* in spite of the fact that they were men of position, *criminal* in spite of the fact they were men of responsibility, *criminal* in spite of the fact that they were, if you will, 'captains of industry' who," I turn to Rifkind, "if I understand counsel's argument, should never be reached for by a prosecutor."

I turn to the judge, "I would just suggest for the convenience of the jury, it might be a convenient place to break for lunch."

"I know you've been talking quite a while. According to my watch it is now twenty-five minutes of one. We will take our luncheon recess until two o'clock. Is that going to give you enough time to finish today?"

"I will finish today no matter what," with a glance over at Bucino.

But we do not reconvene at two, at least not with the jury present. At 2:00 p.m. the defense attorneys begin making motions, objecting to what I had said in the morning sessions. They are obviously chewing up my clock. I stand quietly by the podium, watching, smiling, and then, with arms crossed, actually laughing out loud at them. I had been so terrified that I had wanted to run and hide rather than speak, and now here they are desperately burning up my time to shut me up. I feel elated. As for the time, I do not care. I have largely said what I had to say and am certain I can finish in less than an hour. I have just one more job to do. I have to do something about the juror who keeps looking over at Mrs. Feldman.

Wortendyke also sees what they are doing and quickly disposes of their motions. When the barrage is over, the jurors are ushered back in.

I use the last of my time on Feldman. Foley, his lawyer, had made much of a change in Giles's grand jury testimony about Feldman and the second payments. Foley claimed that Feldman was not involved in those. I show the jurors the document that Feldman signed approving the bill that was used for the last payments. And now I speak to my problem juror. It is time to use the "in all fairness" approach that I learned from Jack Keenan in my assistant DA days.

"I cannot pretend to you, or suggest to you, that this evidence against Mr. Feldman on the last series of transactions is as strong and as overpowering as the evidence against the other defendants on all the other counts or even against Mr. Feldman on the first five counts. It would be wrong for me to suggest that to you." I see she nods her head in agreement.

"I do suggest that there is sufficient evidence to show that Feldman was aware of the transaction and approved the payments." Well, I can see that the one juror does not want to hear that, but I hope the others do and will use it on her in the jury room.

It is 3:00 p.m. and it is time to be done. I cannot do much more even if I had a whole other day to do it. And Mr. Bucino is very clear that he wants out early. I close my book of notes and extracts, and speak to the jurors for the last time.

"Ladies and gentlemen, it has been a long time since we found the first check and the road has been, as you can imagine, a long and difficult one to reach this point. But, on behalf of the United States, I give this case and the responsibility for it to you without the slightest fear that you will fail to do your duty to all parties.

"Thank you very much."

Chapter Twenty

Verdict
January 23, 1969

VERDICT. THE WORD is derived from Latin. When translated, it means to speak the truth. Is a verdict "the truth?" In terms of objective reality, sometimes; in terms of our legal system, always. Unless set aside, the verdict becomes the binding truth for the parties and for society.

Before the jury gets to speak, Judge Wortendyke must charge them on the law, which they must apply to the truth that they find. The judge, reading endlessly, instructs the jury on nearly as many legal points as a law student hears from a professor in the course of a semester. That's the way it always is, in every case. Maybe that has something to do with divergences between verdicts and reality.

As the jury leaves to deliberate, there is more to struggle over, as the lawyers object to portions of the charge. Not that the resolution of most of the controversies could possibly matter to the jurors, who leave the courtroom numb from the legal bombardment they just experienced. But the fine legal points will indeed matter if there is a conviction. Then, the appellate judges will carefully weigh each of the disputed instructions. The reviewing court will be more attentive to any deviation from legal principle than to discretionary rulings of the trial court concerning the conduct of the trial, such as time to address the jury, order of witness, rulings on leading and non-leading questions, and the like—although these are the decisions that directly impact the outcome far more than the instructions intoned at the end of the case.

After all the squabbling is done, Wortendyke rises. "The court will remain in recess pending the return of the jury." With that he starts to leave. But Rifkind stops him.

"May I say just one thing on the record, Your Honor? It has been my good fortune to try cases in many jurisdictions from New York to Portland to Los Angeles and back. In no court have I ever received more considerate attention, more courteous treatment, than I received at your hands, and I express to you my deep gratitude."

"Thank you, Judge Rifkind," he nods to him, "The court will stand in recess."

* * * * * * *

The jurors are deliberating, sequestered in their room. Now all the lawyers are totally helpless. There is something that I have wanted to do for months. Now that we are all prisoners in the empty courtroom, I ask Rifkind if he will step out and chat with me alone. He nods, and together we walk the halls of the courthouse, past empty courtrooms, alone in a marble palace with our shoes clicking and resonating as we walk.

And as we walk, we talk. This is my precious moment. Here is a man who came to the bar in the 1920s, who served as law secretary to the original Senator Robert F. Wagner, who tried cases with the all-time great lawyers of that era, such as Max Steuer and Emory Buckner, and who argued cases before and even sat with legendary judges such as Learned Hand. With great kindness, he answers my questions and opens the window on two prior generations of practitioners.

* * * * * * *

The second day. The jurors send out a note. "Please, request for interpretation of bribery and extortion as read from his Honor's charges. If possible, the complete charge for our use in the jury room to clearly understand the law. Thank you."

Judge Wortendyke reads the note to all of us assembled. He says he will not send his whole charge in, but he would be willing to reread the requested portion. All my adversaries object. So Wortendyke brings the jury in and tells them, "No." The jury goes back into their room, doing the mysterious things that jurors do and we just sit and wait. And wait. The remainder of the day passes and the jurors are sent to a hotel.

****

The third day. The jurors are back in their room. No word. Just silence. All of us sit spread out around the courtroom reading newspaper and books. I find myself next to Fred Lacey, sitting in the jury box. We have become friends, the way boxing and football adversaries do.

"Fred," I say during a light moment, "you are a rock-ribbed Republican, right?"

He laughs and nods.

"Why don't you become United States Attorney in the new Nixon administration?" I say, half kidding. He just looks back at me with a quizzical expression, like I hit on something.

At the end of the day, the marshal informs us that the jurors have finished deliberating and are on their way to their hotel. We shrug into our overcoats and file out. No one is happy.

They have been out two and one half days. What does it mean? Whom does it portend well for, prosecution or defense? Most would say defense if for no other reason than there is no conviction yet.

****

On the morning of the fourth day we are all in court again. Everyone is miserable.

At two thirty the judge reenters the courtroom. The wait has become intolerable for him, too. "Good afternoon," he says to us, "It is a long while since I have had the pleasure of looking into your smiling faces." If he means to be funny, he isn't. Not a one of us is smiling.

The judge tells us he is going to call the jurors into court and see if they are having a problem.

All of us are so sick of waiting that no one objects. We all put on our suit jackets and scramble back to our places at our trial tables. When the jurors file in, they see the usual scene, the one they have seen for months.

Wortendyke addresses them. "I am aware earlier this week you sent a written request. I refused. However, in view of the length of time that has transpired, I inquire what difficulties you are having. First, I ask, through the Foreman, whether any unanimous verdict has been reached with respect to any one defendant under a particular count."

Juror Number One, "Yes, sir. We have reached a conclusion on . . ."

"Pardon?" says Wortendyke, who did not hear.

"We have reached a conclusion on most of the defendants."

"You have reached a decision on most of the defendants?" Wortendyke repeats.

"Yes," Juror Number One repeats. "Most of the defendants, on most of the charges so far."

"On most of the counts?" The judge is driving me nuts with anticipation.

"On most of the counts," Juror Number One repeats. Then adds, "Up to the point where we are now, we have one question," he says, and Juror Number One looks to his left at my problem juror near the end of the first row.

We all turn in her direction. She, we see, is shaking her head no, silently telling him to go no further. "If that were resolved," Juror Number One turns back, "if that were resolved, we may be able to clear up this point. I think," he continues, "we can get it done by four or four thirty."

"Thank you," says the judge, "you may return to your labors."

****

For the next hour we all remain in trial positions at our respective tables. At precisely 4:00 p.m., the jury reenters the courtroom. Once they are seated, the clerk of the court says, "Ladies and gentlemen, have you agreed upon your verdict? Who shall speak for you?"

We are all transfixed on Juror Number One, but it is Juror Number Two, Mr. Bucino, the Hoboken real estate man, who is the one who stands. The jurors have elected him to speak. Now, I ask myself, what does that portend? What does he have in store for us? As Bucino stands, holding the verdict sheet, I recall Rifkind's summation about real estate and Bucino's demand that I stop my summation by 4:00 p.m.

The clerk calls out the names. Colonial Pipeline. Wilentz is on his feet, while the clerk lists the nine counts. Bucino says "Guilty," nine times.

"Rowland Tompkins?" says the clerk and lists the five counts against the company while Joe Brill stands facing the jury. Bucino says "Guilty," five times.

"Bechtel," calls the clerk, and lists two counts against as Bechtel, as Lacey rises. "Guilty," says Bucino, twice.

"Jacks," calls the clerk. Toolan and Jacks rise together as the clerk lists nine counts. "Guilty," says Bucino, but he just says it three times. The jury has found Jacks guilty of both conspiracies and one substantive payment. The other six counts are "Not guilty." But that's okay with me. You don't have to kill a man more than three times, or even more than one time.

"Leuty," calls the clerk and lists nine counts. Rifkind and Leuty are on their feet. "Guilty," says Bucino, but only twice. The jury has convicted Leuty of both conspiracy counts.

"Feldman," calls the clerk and lists nine counts. Feldman and his lawyer rise, I look over at my problem juror. I see she is crying. "Guilty," says Bucino, twice. The jury has treated Feldman exactly the same as Leuty.

My attention turns to Rifkind, who is still standing. I am right next to him, and I see a tear in his eye. I know it's odd, but at this, the greatest moment in my professional life, I feel a wave of sympathy for him.

"Before Your Honor proceeds," Rifkind says, "may I ask whether the jury could be polled?"

"All right," says the judge.

And the clerk calls each juror by name, and reads each verdict as to each defendant. Each says, "Yes." When he gets to Feldman's name and to the lady in the front row my heart stops. But, tears and all, she says, "Yes."

It's over. In one sense. In another, for me it is a beginning. These past two months have helped to forge me as a lawyer. Pounded by masters of the courtroom upon an anvil of unremitting work, I have become more than I was. Not all I will become, I hope. But more than I was.

Chapter Twenty-One

Dead Man's Testimony
January 23–April 15, 1969

A S SOON AS the verdict comes in, Jon and I telephone Henry Petersen in Washington. There is jubilation at his end. When the noise subsides, Henry asks me about the Weber case. He knows Burgess is dead. "Can you still prosecute?" he asks.

"I don't know. I've been working on a few ideas, but I've had my hands full. Right now I am on my way to sun and R & R in the Virgin Islands. Okay?"

"Okay," he says. No "bon voyage." Henry and I just aren't the pals we used to be.

****

By the end of the week I am on a plane, out of the cold, and on a beach in St. Thomas. For the first few nights, I go nowhere. Just bed. The days are passed dozing on the beach. I am exhausted. I am spending virtually my whole vacation sleeping. By the time I am ready to party, it's almost time to go home.

Sitting on the beach, I'm thinking about Weber. I have two indictments. The first case is—or was—the good one. The four Price payments and Weber's call to Giles at Colonial to get the big job for Price instead of Bechtel, coupled with Weber's call to Giles to knock out Osage of Oklahoma in favor of Napp-Grecco of Newark, was a real case. That is, until the only witness to the Price payments died, not to mention Giles himself getting indicted. In the second case, Weber extorted Bechtel to give Joyce Construction Company a $300,000 contract because Joyce promised to pay Weber $30,000. That case is not so good, because we had to indict Joyce before he confessed—and he is a lousy witness anyway. That case is not triable alone. Without the Price and Colonial stuff to show the overall way Weber operated, Joyce alone would be too vulnerable to go to trial with.

I have nothing much to do but think. By the time I leave I have developed a plan. In order for it to work, I have to join the two cases together in one trial. This I can do if Judge Wortendyke grants a motion to consolidate. I'm pretty sure he will. Second, I need the active help of Colonial and Bechtel. Their people have to take the stand. And I have to be allowed to prepare them. I figure they ought to be pretty good at testifying to extortion by now. That doesn't solve my main problem, the fact that Burgess is dead. But I'm working on that one, too.

★★★★★★★

It is right at the beginning of February when I'm back and make my appointment with Rifkind.

Rifkind's office is plush, even by New York City standards. He may not have as many plaques on his wall as Hogan, but the signed photographs, including Eisenhower's, in uniform as Supreme Commander in Europe are even more impressive.

Rifkind sees me alone. We each know what the other wants, so we get right down to it. "Judge," I begin, "I want to use your exhibits for the Weber case. You know, the great big map showing the route, with all the tributaries and the pumping stations. And I want the samples of the pipeline itself."

He nods. Not in agreement, but in recognition. "Call me Si," he says.

I regard that as a good sign, so I continue, "And I want something more."

He nods again, expectantly.

"I want the Colonial people as witnesses, not like last time," I say quickly. "I need to be able to interview and prepare them."

"You mean Giles?"

"Yes. He's the man Weber called to knock out Osage and put in Napp-Grecco. And Weber called Giles to push Price ahead of Bechtel."

"I see," he says gravely. Then, with a small smile, "You know, our motions for a new trial are due soon and will be argued in March."

I nod back.

"And while I certainly expect to be victorious," he smiles and pauses, as I frown and shake my head, "it is, of course, possible that I may not prevail. Then there would be the matter of the sentencing of Leuty and Feldman."

"Si, I understand."

"Of course you do," he says, "The oil companies don't care about the fines. The money," he waves his hand, "is just like garbage. But it's the men . . ."

"Si, if Colonial helps, and by that I mean makes its employees available to tell the truth . . ."

"Of course," he interrupts.

"That assistance will be brought to the attention of the court."

"Very satisfactory," he says.

****

The next week the exhibits are delivered to the FBI for safekeeping. There is no room for those monsters in our little office.

We have moved to consolidate the two Weber cases. But we must prove that four $3,500 payments were made to Weber by Burgess on the specific dates of the indictment. "All right," Jon says to me in our one-room office, "Let's have it. How are we going to prove the payments to Weber without Burgess testifying?"

"We will use two hearsay exceptions," I explain, "First, we will use the co-conspirator exception to the hearsay rule to make admissible in evidence Burgess's reports back to Harold Price as to each conversation with, and each payment to Weber."

"Co-conspirator? But we haven't charged a conspiracy between the Price people and Weber in the indictment."

"We don't have to. As long as there was a conspiracy in fact—and there was because an employer can't agree to pay a union leader—all the conversations among the Price people and with Weber, come in as an exception to the hearsay rule. I have a case on it."

"Okay," Jon says, "But, even if we get the conversations between Burgess and Weber into court, based on Burgess's reports back to Price, how do we prove the dates, times, places, not only of the meetings, but of each payment?"

"Oh, that. Well, we'll use the books and records exception to the hearsay rule to introduce Burgess's expense accounts, which are detailed and mention each meeting with Weber, plus the dates that each check used to generate cash was itself cashed."

"Great. And who is going to tie this all into testimony on the stand?"

"Harold C. Price."

"You mean," Jon laughs, "you are going to have him narrate conversations with Burgess in telling Price about paying Weber, all the while having Price read Burgess's expense account entries to the jury, tying it all to the dates of the checks used to raise the cash?"

"You bet."

"Great!" he says, "In the first case, Colonial says that they were extorted by Jacks and Zirpolo, but we say, 'No, you bribed them,' right?"

"Right."

"In the Weber case, we say Colonial was a victim of extortion in acceding to Weber, right?"

"Right."

"Now we have Price, right?"

"Right."

"But they are not the victim of extortion by Weber, they are his coconspirators, right?"

"Right."

"Well," he says, "tell me one more thing. If Price and Weber were in a conspiracy together, and you say the company was as guilty in paying as Weber was in taking, how come we didn't indict the H.C. Price Company as well as Weber, just like we did with Colonial and Jacks?"

"I can see that might be a problem. But let me tell you about my Uncle Benny, who owned a barbershop right across from a police station. . . ."

Chapter Twenty-Two

Mugs, Jurors, and Openings
April 15–18, 1969

April 15

Eleven weeks after the Colonial verdict, Jon and I walk into Wortendyke's courtroom to try Weber. We have been in and out of the courtroom on motions—the Colonial defendants' motions for new trials, our motions to consolidate the Weber indictments, Weber's motions on discovery. And in between we have prepared witnesses, organized documents, marked exhibits, and attended to countless pre-trial tasks. But now we are ready. We hope.

But we are not ready for the scene in Wortendyke's courtroom. Weber has packed the room with Local 825 members. They fill the spectator seats. They are even lined up against the walls, among them the largest men I have ever seen. Big as Weber is, some dwarf even him. We have to elbow our way past scowls and glares to get to our table.

"Look at that," Jon says, nodding toward one of the giants as we pass.

"I see him. I can't miss him."

"Should we do something about this?"

"Not on your life," I respond, "I want the jurors to see these characters. Weber is doing us a favor. He is demonstrating that he is a hoodlum even before the trial starts." For all that, I am not as happy as I try to sound. These guys are scary.

For two days we pick a jury. Weber's lawyer, Joseph A. Hayden, is a veteran of scores of trials. I can see he knows what he is doing. I also see that his questions are implanting the idea in prospective jurors' heads that the big oil companies behind Colonial and construction giants like Bechtel are out to get Weber because he is effectively improving wages and benefits for his men.

During the two days of jury selection, I am, as usual, racing for the hall during each recess for a cigarette. With the crowd and the small walking space in the aisle, it's not easy to get in and out. It is a lousy addiction, I know, but I am hooked. On the first break of the second morning, I am struggling through the aisle to reach the hall, when I encounter the largest of Weber's giants, taking up the entire aisle space. He has obviously been waiting for me. He stands, arms like tree trunks crossed, looking down at me, glaring intently at me, as he totally blocks my way. I go up to him until we are almost touching. Standing on my tiptoes, I lift my head as far as possible to get my face as close to his as I can, and then I give him an enormous wink. With that he dissolves into laughter and steps aside. I figured he would, in court. But if he and I were alone in a dark alley, I would run like hell.

After two days we have our jury. We are to open to the jury tomorrow, but first we need to know whether Wortendyke will let us use Roy Burgess's out of court statements about paying off Weber. If not, we will have no case and we will discharge the jurors the next morning. I argue round and round but, in the end, Wortendyke goes for the principle and rules for us. The case will go on.

"You know, Jon," I say, as we pack up for the night, feeling a little bit of buyer's remorse, "it may be tough to get this past the Court of Appeals—four unwitnessed payments on the report of a dead man . . ."

"I suggest we win the case first, and worry about the appeal later."

****

The next morning, I deliver the government's opening. And it is almost as long as the one in Colonial. In Colonial I had to speak for witnesses who refused to speak to me. Now I have to speak for only one witness, my main witness, who can't because he is dead. The one great piece of corroboration of the Price payments to Weber that I have is Weber's attempts to force Colonial to give the work to Price rather than to Bechtel. I intend to harp on it.

I outline the four payments Burgess made to Weber, pointing at the large man as I rattle off the dates and places. I can see that Weber's boys don't like the pointing stuff, but Weber himself, bulging over his chair, merely looks amused as I outline the facts underlying each charge.

"Ladies and gentlemen," I say from the podium, as I turn back to face the jurors, "we are going to prove to you that, because Price was making these payments to Weber, the defendant Weber picked up the telephone and called up Giles in Atlanta, and Giles will testify in this case, and Giles will tell you that the defendant Weber instructed him to give the award to the Price Company. We will prove to you, ladies and gentlemen, that after instructing Mr. Giles to give the award to the H.C. Price Company, Mr. Weber picked up the phone and called Oklahoma, and he spoke with Harold Price, the president, and reported that he had just called Mr. Giles and instructed him to give the award to Price." I tell the jurors that Giles immediately reported this to Leuty and Feldman, "who instructed Mr. Giles that, in spite of what Mr. Weber wanted, they were going to run their own business and that they were going to use competitive bidding and they were going to award this ninety-mile job to whichever firm was low bidder."

Ironic, I say to myself, the boys in Atlanta knew how to say no when they thought it was in their interests. They awarded the job to Bechtel, which bid three million less than Price, and ignored Weber's pressure.

"Ladies and gentlemen, you will recall that I told you that we would substantiate by evidence independent of Mr. Burgess's reports that Mr. Weber was in fact receiving the money. We are going to prove to you, ladies and gentlemen, that this defendant," and now I turn to face Weber directly, "was so confident that Giles would follow his instructions that when Colonial was opening up the bids, this defendant," now I point straight at him, "appeared before the members of his union and announced that the Colonial Pipeline Company had just awarded the 90.8-mile project to H.C. Price Company. We are going to prove to you that the defendant became enraged because the award did not go to Price, a firm which he knew would continue to pay him if it got the work, and he shut the job down for ten days. Thereafter, he controlled the project, forcing Colonial to contract with Napp-Grecco instead of Osage, and Bechtel with Joyce, who in turn paid him off."

When it comes time to conclude, I say, "I speak for myself and my colleagues in thanking you for your attention. I trust if Mr. Hayden chooses to address you, you will give him the same attention as you have given me."

"You may present the defendant's opening to the jury," Wortendyke nods to Hayden.

Hayden can't wait to begin. He bounds to his feet, eager to hit back. Tall, solidly built, I judge him to be in his late fifties, he speaks without a note. And there is nothing quiet about what he has to say or the way he says it.

"Members of the jury, in the brief time that I will take, I ask you from this second to please remember that we will meet every single so-called issue raised in the government's opening. We will meet and we will defeat it," Hayden booms. "At the end of this case, may I assure you that you will agree with me that the issue is: Could Colonial Pipeline Company, could H.C. Price Company, could Bechtel Company, could any other out-of-state company in this business come into this state and impose on the working man under these union contracts its will? This is the issue in this case."

I don't have to make any notes. This is what I expected, a raw appeal to emotions, to class struggle. This is going to be a tougher case than Colonial. There are no "captains of industry" in the dock in this case. Weber is a for-real, hands-on labor leader who started in the rank and file, and this jury is comprised of working men and women. We are not going to be strolling through art galleries or pleasant country retreats. Weber is a tough, old-fashioned labor leader and a very effective one for his men.

Unlike my practice, which is to stand still behind the podium, Hayden is striding back and forth. His voice is powerful and emotional. Unfortunately, I see he has captured the attention of the jury. Hayden plays his trump card. His voice ringing in the courtroom, he promises to put Weber on the stand.

"I tell you now in my opening that Mr. Weber will take the stand in this case at the earliest possible opportunity, and Mr. Weber will start with the inception of the trouble that befell this union at the hands of these companies, and he will detail it. We will support it with corroborative evidence and again we will come back to the issue which I most respectfully beg your pardon for repeating all the time, but I will repeat it and repeat it." Hayden has stopped striding. Standing totally still, he roars, "The issue in this case is could the petroleum giants come into New Jersey and run roughshod over these labor contracts or were these labor contracts to be honored?"

His voice rising in indignation, Hayden tells the jury what Weber will tell them from the stand. "He will tell you what he has been put through, all going back to taking on these giants and beating them, and he beat them. He will testify that every single time that he took an action it was only after a meeting of his local when there were a thousand or more men present. A thousand so when the government stands in front of you and they tell you that Weber sold them out for $14,000, this is a disgrace."

"I close now," he tells the jurors, "and apologize for my excitement, but I close with the same question: You tell me if he sold out his birthright in the men's room in the Roost. If you think he did, he is guilty. You will not be able to find that from the evidence. But you will say by your verdict at the end of the case, 'I think the issue that Mr. Weber's counsel suggested at the beginning was the issue in this case. He backs up his men. We find him NOT GUILTY.'"

With Hayden's words still ringing in the courtroom, Wortendyke sends the jurors home for the night.

****

"What do you think?" Jon asks me, when we are back in our office.

"I think we got trouble. There are people on the jury who belong to unions and others with relatives in unions. There was no way to keep all of them off."

"But the guy took money. Union workers don't like their leaders feathering their own nests."

"So who says Weber took the four payments, including one in a restaurant men's room, a dead man? The next thing we'll hear is that Burgess glommed the cash after telling Price a tale that the money was for Weber."

"Well, when they hear Price . . ."

"They are not going to hear Price until they first hear Giles."

"But Giles comes after Price. Weber called Giles *after* he got Price money."

"Yes," I respond, "that is true. Chronologically, Price comes before Giles. Price was paying Weber on another job, before the Colonial bid came up. But, look, we could call Price first and then, after he gets beat up, call Giles in an effort to resuscitate Price. Or, we could call Giles first, prove the Weber call to Giles on behalf of Price, and make it harder to cross-examine Price when he takes the stand and says his company paid Weber. What do you say?"

Chapter Twenty-Three

"Déjà Vu All Over Again"
April 17–18, 1969

GILES IS BACK on the stand. As Yogi Berra says, it's "déjà vu all over again." I see it that way. But, the jurors don't. It's their first time with him. Except this time Rifkind and company have allowed us to prepare him to testify. Standing in front of him, with the jury on my right, the story of Weber's pressure is easily presented.

"Weber called me at our headquarters in Atlanta and wanted me to give H.C. Price Company of Bartlesville, Oklahoma, the prime contract for building the pipeline in New Jersey."

"Did you obey his demand?" I ask.

Giles shakes his head, "No. I talked it over with our president, Ben D. Leuty, and our executive vice president, Karl T. Feldman, and they were adamant about giving the work to the lowest bidder."

As I glance over to the jurors, I almost expect them to react to the familiar names of Leuty and Feldman. But those particular jurors left three months ago. I have to remember that these folks see it as an entirely new event.

Under questioning, Giles tells the jurors, "Before Bechtel, the low bidder, could begin, Local 825 men walked off the job and shut down the entire project."

I then bring out from Giles that Weber told the Colonial people that "when we crossed the Delaware into New Jersey, we were in his territory and that he reserved the right to approve contracts."

Giles explains that thereafter, contracts were awarded only after checking with Weber. Except one. While Giles was out of town, unbeknownst to him Colonial awarded a small contract to the Osage Construction Company of Tulsa, Oklahoma. When Giles got back, he called Weber. "He told me I would be in trouble if Osage received the contract." So Giles took it away, paid off Osage, and gave the contract to the firm mentioned by Weber as desirable—Napp-Grecco of Newark.

On Friday afternoon, Joe Hayden takes Giles on cross. But, by now, Giles is a ring-wise witness. Hayden has to settle for getting Giles to admit that, Weber or no Weber, Giles had been able to get Napp-Grecco to substantially reduce their bid, by $120,000, before giving them the contract.

Giles's testimony completed, the first week of trial comes to an end. Our next witness would have been Roy Burgess. But now it will be Harold C. Price, who will have to be Burgess's voice from the witness stand.

Chapter Twenty-Four

A Dead Man Testifies
April 18–May 28, 1969

I SPEND THE ENTIRE weekend with Price in a suite in the St. Regis Hotel in Manhattan. Very fancy digs. Lots of furniture that looks like it belonged to some Louis with a number instead of a name. The good news is that Price is in a panic. He is afraid he will be unable to master the enormous detail: the dates of checks used to raise cash; the Burgess expense account entries showing Burgess's comings and goings between New Jersey and Oklahoma; Burgess's entries of his meetings with Weber; and the verbal reports by Burgess to Price of payments to Weber each time Burgess returned. Because Price is terrified of making a fool of himself in public, for the first time I've known him he loses his flippant manner and demands to work. We go eighteen hours a day.

When court convenes Monday morning, he is ready, I hope. As we enter the courtroom, I see that there have been two changes. First, the goons are gone, which I regret. Second, Hayden has added a fine trial lawyer to his team—Dino Bliablias, which I regret even more. Hayden is tall, and fiery. Bliablias is short in stature and fiery. I am sure the two of them will give me all the trouble I can handle. My problem is that I can't seem to say the man's name correctly. I don't want to offend him, so Jon and I practice. But I still can't get it right.

When the jurors enter, they find Price on the stand, ready to be sworn.

"What is your business or occupation?" I ask him.

"I am Chairman of the Board of H.C. Price which is a pipeline construction firm."

"Mr. Price, are you a union or non-union firm?"

"We are a union firm."

"Mr. Price, did there come a time when you began to consider whether or not you were going to enter a bid on Segment 15 of the Colonial work?"

"We had a problem. We had problems in bidding in New Jersey. We had done work before in New Jersey and lost money."

Bliablias is on his feet. He is steaming mad. "If the court please, I object to the answer." He walks forward as he repeats himself, "I object to the question and I object to the answer."

Unfortunately, Wortendyke sustains Bliablias. But I really do need to show that Price was willing to pay Weber only because of past pressure. So I take another shot at it.

"Mr. Price, were those prior projects successful or unsuccessful?"

Bliablias is on his feet again, "Objection, if the court please. What the terms 'successful' or 'unsuccessful' are . . ."

"What?" says Wortendyke, leaning over the bench. I see the good judge still has his hearing problems.

"I object to the question," Bliablias shouts, then repeats it to be sure the judge heard the initial question. "Were they successful or unsuccessful."

"Sustain the objection," Wortendyke deadpans, "they might have been unsuccessful because somebody didn't have the proper equipment. I don't know."

I am at a loss. I have to do something to explain why Price felt compelled to pay. I give it another push. "Did you have any particular reluctance in bidding on the Colonial job?"

"Yes."

"I object to that," says my tormentor, the pit bull.

"Yes," says Wortendyke, "sustain the objection to the form of the question. I am going to ask a question and each of you may object," Wortendyke looks first to Bliablias, then to me, then to Price, "Did you submit a bid on a New Jersey section of the Colonial project?"

"Yes, sir."

"And what did you do in the course of determining to submit the bid?" Wortendyke asks.

"I instructed Roy Burgess to come back to New Jersey and meet with Mr. Weber and see what we needed to do to improve our relations with his union in this area," answers Price, who is no fool. But neither is Bliablias, who objects to Wortendyke's question. "If the court please, I am going to object on the ground . . ."

"I have your objection," Wortendyke acknowledges, "and it is over-ruled." The umpire has taken a turn at bat and also called the pitch. Bliablias shrugs in resignation and sits back down.

"Mr. Price," I resume questioning, "is Mr. Burgess living or dead?"

"No, he died several months ago."

"Was that after or before the indictment was returned?"

"After the indictment was returned."

I introduce Burgess's expense account to document his meeting with Weber and ask, "What instructions did you give Mr. Burgess?"

"I told Mr. Burgess to meet with Mr. Weber, and ask if he would put us on the same working conditions as other contractors in New Jersey."

I establish through Burgess's expense account that he went to New Jersey on May 2, and returned to Bartlesville on June 7. "Did you have a conversation with him in Bartlesville?"

"Yes," Price acknowledges. "Mr. Burgess told me that he had met with Mr. Weber and explained to Mr. Weber that the H.C. Price Company was considering opening an office in New Jersey. Mr. Weber replied to him that while this was all right, it would have no particular effect on our operating condition. That what Mr. Weber needed was TAX-FREE CASH."

In spite of Price's virtually yelling the last three words, the hearing-impaired Wortendyke swings into action.

"Was what?" he leans forward.

"Tax-free cash," repeats Price to my delight. Out of the corner of my eye, I see Bliablias shake his head in disgust. Having been there myself, it's hard not to grin.

Price testified that his people could not come to a conclusion as to how much, or how to pay. "I couldn't decide how to conceal the payments, and we didn't know how much payment was needed," Price says.

"So what did you do?"

"I told Mr. Burgess to come back to New Jersey to meet with Pete Weber and find out how much money he wanted."

"Using that Burgess expense account, can you fix the time that Burgess left Oklahoma and returned to New Jersey?"

"Yes, he left on June 11, 1963."

"Mr. Price, did there come a time when you received a report back from Mr. Burgess?"

"Yes sir, there did."

Bliablias is on his feet again. His objections are emphatic, and strident. "It is hearsay," he argues over and over. Indeed it is. If I were him, I would be yelling too. But it is legal and the judge overrules his objection.

"Yes, Pete Weber wanted $10,000," says Price.

"Did you ascertain what system you were going to use to pay Weber?"

"Yes, sir. I decided to have Roy Burgess draw an expense . . . draw an expense check, a travel advance for the amount of the first payment. But they had taken so long that the four $2,500 monthly payments had to be done in three months. So they increased each installment to $3,500."

Wielding the checks used to raise cash and the Burgess expense accounts, I take Price through each payment, including the one that took place in the Roost restroom.

When it's time for the payment, back goes Burgess to New Jersey. His expense account pinpoints the date he arrived and the date he met Weber. The checks document the procurement of the cash. Price and I are flipping through documents, while Bliablias is peppering us with objections, but Wortendyke holds firm, so I keep going. We establish that Burgess returned on July 26 and told Price that, while in the Roost Restaurant in Newark, he took Weber into the men's room and gave him the next payment.

I bring Price to the invitation he received to the Colonial bid. It arrived just after the Roost payment. "I told Roy Burgess to come on back to New Jersey to meet with Pete Weber and ask him how much money we should put in our bid for him in the event we were successful."

"Did there come a time after Mr. Burgess left that you had a report from him?"

"The report that we had was that Mr. Weber would not tell how much money he wanted. If we were successful in our bid, he would let us know."

So Price decided to bid anyway. But without knowing what to put in for Weber, Price bid very high. The job went to Bechtel, who wound up with the big headache.

That bit of testimony concludes the day. As we leave the courtroom, heading for the train to Manhattan, I say to Jon, "Price is lucky he did not get the job—we would have indicted him instead of Bechtel for paying Jacks."

We both laugh. But we stop laughing when we notice that we are being followed by cars, two union cars, both with "825" on their New Jersey plates. They trail us all the way to the train. It gets even less funny when another set of cars with 825 plates start tailing us when we get off the train in New York City.

Jon starts to go his way to his and Ellen's apartment, and I back to the St. Regis. After a little more direct next morning, Price will be on cross. He and I have a lot of work to do. As we separate, the two cars also separate. One goes after Jon. The other starts after me.

"Don't say a word to Ellen," Jon calls out over his shoulder.

"Okay," I call back, knowing he's talking about the cars.

Chapter Twenty-Five

"You Were Out with a Blonde"
April 22–May 28, 1969

AFTER QUESTIONS ON direct, first yesterday and then this morning, Price is relaxed when I turn him over to Bliablias, but my heart is in my throat. It is not as bad as it was with Fred Stewart and Edward Bennett Williams, but bad enough.

Bliablias has his problems, too. He has no one to cross-examine on Burgess's reports of his claimed conversations and meetings with Weber. Price got the reports, but Price wasn't there. "You were not present when Burgess made the alleged payment to Weber?" Bliablias demands.

"No," Price admits. "But I know that he gave him the money," he adds with a glance at my table, "because Weber called Glen Giles, and he would not do that if Roy didn't give him money."

Bliablias immediately objects to Price's "gratuitous remarks." He turns to the judge, "Outside the scope of the question."

Wortendyke looks to me, but I can only shrug. "Sustained," Wortendyke rules. But I am content. Calling Giles before Price has given Price the protection I anticipated. However, Bliablias has a surprise for me.

"Did you know," Bliablias strides forward and confronts Price, "did you know that Burgess was attempting to raise a stake in New Jersey so he could go into business for himself?"

What? I say to myself, should I object to the question as merely a suggestion of counsel without a good faith basis? Half out of my seat, I decide to sit back. It's a good thing I do because Price reluctantly concedes, "I knew he was unhappy but," he adds meekly, "I had no information that he wanted to go into business for himself." I never heard that before. I try to keep my head down, making notes, to protect my expression of concern. Bliablias suggested that Burgess had a motive to keep the money, and Price has confirmed it.

Bliablias confronts Price with the statement he had made to Tony Cosolo of the Labor Department in October 1965, flatly denying any payments to Weber. Price has to admit that, too. He struggles to add that he stopped lying a few weeks later, when I came to Bartlesville. "I didn't know if it was a casual pass over by the government . . . I just couldn't incriminate myself and my employees," he explains about his lies to Cosolo. "Later," he adds, "I started to feel they wanted to clean up the mess in New Jersey, and I agreed to cooperate."

Right, I say to myself, but only after I told Cosolo to go over his financial records. I am happy enough when Price leaves the stand.

****

For the next several weeks, we present the other Price employees who cashed checks to generate the cash for Burgess. They, too, confirm the Burgess reports of payments to Weber. I also read the union's minutes to the jury quoting Weber's announcement to the rank and file that Colonial had awarded the job to Price.

We then go on to present Bechtel employees. Some testify as to Weber's fury at the award of the contract to Bechtel instead of Price. Some testify to Weber's demand that Bechtel give a subcontract to the Joyce Construction Company. On cross-examination, almost all admit to lying to investigators led by Tony Cosolo. Bliablias and Hayden tear them apart. Not a witness leaves the stand unmarked.

I'm still racing for the hall for a cigarette during breaks, and Weber has started to wait for me. Sometimes he manages to collar me. "Hey, kid," he says, "Hogan tried to get me. Bobby Kennedy tried to get me. They didn't, and you're not going to either." And the Local 825 cars are still following me every night. Weber, who wants to be sure that

I know all about it, tells me in the hall what I did the night before. "The boys tell me you were out with a blonde last night," Weber says to me, "But," he nods his okay, "I told them it's nothing wrong, because you're single." With that he laughs and walks away. Well, there is one date I know I have, and it's with Weber. I know, and he knows, that he will take the stand. When he does, it will be just him and me. And the whole case will turn on it.

May 28

Six weeks after we picked the jury, Bliablias announces that Weber will take the stand.

Chapter Twenty-Six

The Most Important Witness
May 28, 1969

THE MOST IMPORTANT witness in every criminal case is the defendant. There are no exceptions.

The testimony of the defendant, if believed, will compel acquittal. If disbelieved, a conviction is certain. Defendants do not take the stand to agree that they are guilty. Whenever the defendant is on the stand, there will be a credibility contest between the prosecutor's assertions in his "questions" and the defendant's denials. The prosecutor must cross-examine the defendant as a liar. One of the two—but only one—will be believed by the jurors. The outcome of the case is on the line.

I have learned a lesson from my ADA days. When a cross-examiner puts forth an assertion, and the witness denies it, each juror votes internally, then and there, on the assertion and the denial. The jurors will not tarry until the summations to pick between past exchanges. And when the votes go too often against the cross-examiner and in favor of the defendant, that defendant will almost certainly be acquitted. The prosecutor must pick the subjects of his examination of the defendant with great care, for they will become battlefields of the credibility war between them.

I have been struggling with the cross of Weber even before Hayden's opening. It was easy to predict that Weber would take the stand. In his case, I must do more than prevent the jurors believing him. I must not permit the jurors to like him. A defendant who is believed will be acquitted—but a defendant who is liked, believed or not, may escape conviction. And I have come to realize that Weber is a likeable man.

I've watched him for a month now. There are no airs to the man. He is simple and direct. Yes, he is a mug. Yes, he takes money. But what you see is what you get. And he is a real-life labor guy who fought his way up from the ranks. He takes good care of his men and they really do love him. I started out this enterprise to corral him. And I will, if I can, because he is out of bounds and an obstruction to interstate commerce. But what was the silhouette of a target has been fleshed out by the substance of the man. I find myself kind of liking him, the way you might a polar bear, if you don't get too close. The business between him and me in the hall has come to amuse me. All in all, I have to figure out how to deal with him on the stand.

I do have the transcript from the Senate hearings, when he was questioned by Bobby Kennedy, about his secret and unlawful ownership of business interests employing his own men. As much as I would love the jury to hear the questions posed by the slain Bobby, and Weber's answers, under the rules of evidence I will probably not be able to use it. As we sit in our little office on the third floor of the Post Office Courthouse, Jon and I go over it yet again.

"You say I can't use his illegal ownership of public contractors, Oscar Leasing, Jersey Equipment, and United Engine?"

"That's right, those are unrelated other crimes," Jon repeats, "There's nothing in the indictment about those transactions, not to mention they took place years ago."

"And the jury is not to hear about Weber putting the stock into his girlfriend Mitzi's name?"

"That's right. Same reason."

"And the two yachts are out, too?"

"Unless he puts his character at issue, unrelated crimes are out," Jon insists. "Even if you get by Wortendyke, we'll get bounced back when the Third Circuit hears the appeal."

"Great. That's just great. But if I have nothing to question him on except the word of a dead man, we won't have to worry about an appeal. There will be no conviction to appeal from."

"Don't worry," Jon laughs, "he will give you an opening. Just be ready."

The next day Weber takes the stand.

Chapter Twenty-Seven

A Union Man
May 29, 1969

"**M**R. WEBER, HOW old are you?" Bliablias begins.
"Fifty-nine."

"Mr. Weber, how many of those fifty-nine years have you spent engaged in one phase or another of the labor movement with relation to the Operating Engineers?"

"About forty-seven years."

"That would take us down to the time when you were approximately twelve years old?"

"Thirteen years old," Weber corrects him.

"Were you engaged at the age of thirteen in work which is related to the Operating Engineers?"

"Practically all phases of equipment," Weber proudly says, "very few pieces of equipment today that I can't run."

I glance at the jury. They are listening intently. The large man filling the witness box is making an impression.

"You have always been a union organizer and are up to the present time?"

"All my life," Weber says proudly.

"Despite the fact that you became the local organizer," Bliablias emphasizes, "were you still working out in the field on various equipment on various jobs?"

"I was running a steam shovel."

"What method did you use to go about seeking work for the members of your union as a business representative?" Bliablias reaches for more clarity, "What did you do?"

"Whenever a contractor had a piece of equipment, I tried to convince him that we had men that are qualified and had the ability to do the work and run that type of equipment."

Bliablias establishes that Weber was promoted to international organizer. "Does that mean you traveled throughout the entire United States?" he asks.

"I did."

"Mr. Weber, as an international organizer plus a business representative from 825, how many hours a day did you work and how many days a week did you work?"

"Well," Weber proclaims, "I worked seven days a week. I have averaged about 18 hours a day."

"Bingo." Jon Goldstein was right. Weber has given me my opening. He is now in my hands.

Bliablias brings out that Weber ultimately assumed command of the union. I know it was because his predecessor, Joey Fay, went to jail. But I won't be able to tell that to the jury. Bliablias tells the jury, through Weber, that it was Weber who set up a welfare and pension plan for his men. "Did you play an active role or were you instrumental in bringing these programs about?"

"Every part of them," Weber emphasizes.

"Prior to these welfare programs or funds, was there any protection for the employee from the point of view of health, welfare or otherwise?"

"No, there was not," Weber proudly proclaims.

"How many years did it take to get the employers to agree to these programs?" Bliablias inquires.

"Maybe fifty barrels of whiskey," Weber laughs, "and some food."

I glance at the jurors and see some of them smiling—others nodding.

To my delight, Bliablias returns to Weber's devotions. "And were you, as the business manager of Local 825, actively engaged in these projects?"

"Every major one."

"And did that almost necessitate your every waking hour seven days a week?"

"It does," Weber answers solemnly, "I averaged about eighteen hours a day."

"Do you still average about eighteen hours a day?"

"It's more than that," Weber adds, "sometimes we work continuously in negotiations. I don't believe in strikes and I have no strikes in negotiations."

Bliablias, good lawyer that he is, spends most of his time on Weber the man. He well understands that this is what the jurors really want to evaluate. He does get around to denying the charges, to denying receipt of payment of money from Burgess and from Joyce. But only after he has established his bona fides as a self-effacing union man.

Weber has helped himself, a lot. But I sit back in my swivel chair, rocking, quite content. For hours I sit, without making any objections. I have seen my chance and I intend to take it. So I let him go on and on. He claims that Price himself offered him $50,000, which he refused. He claims that the Price Company did not want him to send black operating engineers to the job because Price's full-time employees were from Oklahoma and refused to work with black men. This, I figure, is aimed at the three black jurors. It's ludicrous. Harold Price is the Chairman of the American Civil Liberties Union of Oklahoma. But I say nothing. I wait patiently for my turn.

Chapter Twenty-Eight

The Miss Mitzi
May 30–June 5, 1969

WHEN I WAS a young ADA, Harold Rothwax, an equally young public defender, was fond of telling the story of his Jewish mother who criticized him for representing a man accused of bank robbery. "Harold," she said, in a heavy Jewish accent, "how can you do such a thing? The man went to a bank, hit a woman teller on the head, and while she was bleeding on the floor, stole the money."

"Mamma," Harold explained, "You don't understand. He says he did not do it. He says he is innocent. He says he is not guilty."

"Harold," his mother replied, "It's *you* that doesn't understand. A man who will steal, will lie!"

It seems to me that the converse is also true. A man who will lie, will steal. I must show the jury that Weber is a liar. The very first question must set the tone. And I have come up with a doozy. I know it will sound innocuous, but Weber will recognize it as lethal.

The first question I decide to ask violates all theories of cross. It is not leading. I do not know what the answer will be. And the question seems unconnected to the case. But any answer Weber makes will ultimately show him to be both a liar and a thief.

After Weber was summoned before the McClellan Senate Committee and grilled by Bobby Kennedy about his ownership of businesses that employed his own men, he "divested" himself of his ownership. But to whom? Why, to his secretary, Mitzi. But, who is Mitzi—a girlfriend or a wife? Either way, he will be cooked.

"You may cross-examine," Wortendyke nods to me. I nod back and get on my feet. After I settle in behind the podium and place my exhibits by my side on the table, I look at Weber for a long moment.

"Mr. Weber," I ask, "Are you married or single?"

He looks at me, and I at him, and he knows it is the beginning of the end. "Single," he mumbles, head down.

"I object, if the court please," Bliablias sees the distress. But he does not yet know why. "What difference, what is the materiality or relevancy of that?"

"I don't know," Wortendyke shrugs, affording no help.

Bliablias turns to Weber, "Have you answered?"

"Yes."

Bliablias raises his hands in surrender, "Withdraw the objection," he says and reseats himself.

The first step taken, the next questions will cash in on the gift Weber gave to me on his direct—it must be repeated early in the cross, to remind Judge Wortendyke of what Weber said. "Now if I understand your testimony of yesterday, you have told us that you have devoted yourself eighteen hours a day, seven days a week solely and exclusively to the betterment of the wages, hours, and working conditions of the men of 825. Is that right?"

"Yes," he is eager to agree.

"Now then, that hasn't left you much time for other interests in other business, is that a fact?"

"Like what?" he says suspiciously.

"Like a brewery interest," I prompt him.

"A brewery interest?" he repeats, as though perplexed.

"Isn't it a fact that you yourself did own at one time a brewery distributorship?"

"I did," he reluctantly agrees.

"Was it your distributorship?"

"I did not own any of it. My name was on the title. My name was on the basic permit, and that's all there was to it."

"You took title in your name, is that correct?"

"I did."

"Did you receive any funds at all from that?" I demand.

"Your Honor," Bliablias appeals to Wortendyke, "this is all very interesting. What has it to do with this case?"

"It goes to the issue of credibility and relates to the direct testimony," Wortendyke rules. "If I recall, he worked eighteen hours a day, seven days a week as an officer and/or member of the union," Wortendyke gets it. It is my open sesame. "Read the question," he directs the court reporter.

"Did you receive any funds?" the court reporter repeats my last question.

"Not anything for myself," Weber states. But then he qualifies his answer, "with the exception of the moneys that I put in. That is how I was drawing it out."

"What money did you put in?"

"$22,000."

"Is it a fact, Mr. Weber, that in 1958 your annual salary from the union was $14,500?"

"I do not know."

This gives me the second opening. I can use the transcript of his testimony when Weber was examined by the martyred Bobby Kennedy.

"Do you recall being questioned by Mr. Kennedy on January 29, 1958, and being asked this question: 'What salary did you receive as business manager?' 'MR. WEBER: $14,500.'" I put the transcript down and address Weber.

"Do you recall making that answer to that question?" I demand.

Weber turns away, "I could have said it."

"Now then, sir, you have already told us that you were working eighteen hours a day, seven days a week for the betterment of the working men of New Jersey, is that right?"

"That's right," Weber reluctantly agrees, as though he would like to forget about having said that.

"Did you have any other business or financial interest during that period of time?"

"I had investments maybe in contracting," Weber mumbles. He and I both know we are going to Public Constructors, a contracting company he partly owned, which employed Local 825 men. As an owner, he had a company credit card. And when Kennedy brought the heat, Weber transferred his stock to Mitzi, which, he and I both know, will bring us back to my first question, "Mr. Weber, are you married or are you single?"

"Investments in what?" I repeat.

"In a contracting company," he reluctantly responds.

"After assuming the office of business manager of Local Union 825, isn't it a fact that you thereafter established a business known as United Engine Company?"

"Yes," he mumbles.

It is now time to introduce the omnipresent Mitzi. "I show you Government's Exhibit 80 for identification," I say as I walk up to him, "Is that your signature, sir?"

He looks, and then looks away, "That's it."

"Isn't it a fact that you own twenty-five shares of Public Contracting Corporation?"

"No."

"Didn't you by that document give it to Mitzi Rocha?"

"I signed it as I approved the transfer."

"You gave your stock in Public Constructors and Jersey Equipment to Mrs. Rocha?" I insist.

"Yes, she received the paper."

"In other words, you put it in her name, is that right?"

"That's right."

"Now Mrs. Rocha is your secretary, is that right, sir?"

"That's right."

"Last year she was paid a salary of $9,000 a year by the union, is that right?"

"What difference does that make," Bliablias leaps to his feet, "how much money she received last year as his secretary?"

Unfortunately, I can see that the judge has had enough. "I don't know what my secretary receives," he dryly observes. "I agree," he looks at Bliablias, "on the grounds of improper cross-examination, I sustain the objection," Wortendyke frowns at me.

"Is Mrs. Rocha the president of Oscar Leasing Corporation?" I ask to get the judge back in the groove.

"I object," Bliablias is on his feet again. "What Mrs. Rocha's interests are, what difference does it make in this case?"

"That's a horse of a different color," the judge observes, "I overrule your objection to that."

"The Judge said you may answer," I say.

"I don't know if the company is still in business."

It is time to launch Weber's maritime career; that is, his two yachts. "Did you buy a boat known as the *Co-Pilot*?"

"Yes."

"On May 6, 1963, your boat sank, didn't it?" I press on.

Weber answers, "Yes, it did."

"Isn't it a fact, Mr. Weber, that while the fifty-two foot *Co-Pilot* was laid up, and you paid $22,000 to restore her, you bought another boat, a thirty-six-foot Viking cruiser, for which you paid $18,000?"

"I did, with a check."

"Yes, sir," I agree, walking right up to him. "And this is the check that you used, a cashier's check?"

"That's right."

"Now, then, Mr. Weber, as of August 1, 1963, you owned two boats?"

"No, I did not," Weber protests.

"You owned the *Co-Pilot* in Georgia?"

"That's right, it was mine."

"You bought, using your money, the Viking on August 1, 1963, the 36-foot Viking?"

"As a loan."

"Who did you loan the money to, sir?"

"Mrs. Rocha."

"Is that your secretary again?"

"That is right."

"What was the name of that boat?"

"*Co-Pilot II*," he shoots back and adds, "I guess."

"How about the *Miss Mitzi*? Isn't it a fact it was named the *Miss Mitzi*?"

"I don't think so. I think it was the *Co-Pilot II*," then looking away because he knows I have the registration, he mumbles, "I could be wrong."

I move on to the house in Florida that James Joyce testified he went to pay Weber off for getting Joyce a subcontract from Bechtel.

"Is that your house?"

"No."

"Whose house is it?"

"Mrs. Mitzi Rocha's house."

"Is she also the one to whom you conveyed all your stock?"

"I object," Bliablias cries out, "What difference does it make?"

"I am not going to spell out the purposes," Wortendyke rejoins, "I can see that it is proper cross-examination in view of the direct."

In closing, I confront Weber with the call he made to Giles of Colonial to get the job for Price and his certainty that Giles would obey, which led Weber to announce to the union that Price got the work.

Weber, true to form, denies making the announcement. I confront him with the union minutes the very day he made the announcement. After I read the excerpt aloud, Weber responds, "That's a typographical error. Our regular secretary was off that day."

Chapter Twenty-Nine

Verdict
June 5–7, 1969

June 5

The summations begin. Hayden goes first, for the defense. I am to follow for the prosecution.

It is class warfare, again. "There will be a big celebration in Priceville tonight if Weber is convicted," striding back and forth before the jurors, Hayden booms out. "Harold Price and his boys will be celebrating with champagne and confetti—the confetti will be a torn-up contract between Price and Local 825."

I watch the jurors closely, looking for trouble. But I see nothing, either good or bad.

"Harold Price should have been indicted, the Price Company should have been indicted for the same things—why are there double standards?" Hayden asks in the form of an accusation. Well, he has a point. But I intend to leave that alone.

When it's my turn, I stand unmoving before the jury. I read the transcript that I have been excerpting daily. In the end it comes down to a simple point. The defendant "used his position as a labor leader to pressure companies to use contractors who would pay him . . . any other explanation of his conduct is completely nuts!" The summation is only a few hours. There is no need to belabor anything. This case has been won or lost on Weber's cross-examination.

Wortendyke, anxious to get the case over, charges the jury Thursday night. They get the case at 6:00 p.m. Soon thereafter they are sent to a hotel. And the long wait begins.

All day Friday the jurors deliberate. No verdict. Wortendyke holds them late. No verdict. He decides we will sit on Saturday, so we all go home for the night. The Local 825 cars have ceased following us. Since Weber left the stand, that nonsense has stopped. No more banter in the hallway either. Weber goes out of his way to avoid me, as we wait for the jurors.

It's not until Saturday afternoon that the jury comes back. I study their faces as they file in. They are like stone. They do not look at anyone. The air is heavy. It probably means a conviction. But a conviction of what?

Under the law, if Weber is convicted of just the first four counts, the Burgess payments, he could be sent to jail, but would not have to forfeit his union office. If Weber is not convicted of either the Colonial or Bechtel extortions, counts five and six, he can continue to dominate the construction industry. The jury does not know that, of course. But the spectators do. .

And the courtroom is filled with spectators. All Weber supporters. The mugs and goons are back, and tons of others. The benches are all filled. The overflow lines the walls.

Wortendyke surveys the scene and nods to the courtroom deputy clerk. The final ceremony begins.

"Have you reached a verdict?" the clerk inquires, "And who shall speak for you?"

"We have, Your Honor," Juror Number One rises, addressing the judge.

"The defendant will please rise," commands the courtroom deputy.

Weber rises and faces the jury, his lawyers standing with him.

"Count one," says the clerk, "guilty or not guilty?"

"Guilty," Juror Number One replies.

"Count two?"

"Guilty."

"Count three?"

"Guilty."

"Count four?" which is the fourth Price payment.

"Not guilty," the foreman reads from his sheet.

"Count five," the clerk demands.

"Not guilty," the foreman replies.

There is a cheer in the courtroom. The Colonial extortion count, one of those that will disqualify Weber, has been dismissed.

I lean over to Jon, "Weber's on a roll. If the rest of the counts go down, we lose."

Wortendyke silences the room with a tap of his gavel.

"Count six?" the clerk resumes questioning.

"Guilty," replies the foreman. Weber has been convicted of extorting Bechtel.

The remaining two guilty verdicts are superfluous. Weber is finished. There will be an appeal, of course. But Weber must surrender his control over the Operating Engineers.

Surrounded by hostiles, Jon and I get out of the courthouse as quickly as we can. The mood is too ugly to stick around.

Chapter Thirty

"No One May Pay a Public Official"—Simon Hirsch Rifkind
June 9–27, 1969

MY **FIRST CALL** Monday morning is to Judge Rifkind. "I heard," Rifkind says, "but why did it take the jury so long?"

I know he is ribbing me, but I can't resist answering, "Judge, there were eight counts, involving four companies, and the jury only got the case on Thursday night and . . ."

His laughter interrupts me, "Are we ready for the sentencing of Leuty now?" turning serious.

"Not quite yet," I respond, "but we will be in a few weeks."

The Colonial sentencings had been put off from the January verdict until after the Weber conviction in mid-June. Prosecutors don't permit cooperators to be sentenced until they have finished cooperating. The reasons are obvious. Now the sentences can proceed. And I have to honor my deal with Rifkind.

It is true that I lost the Colonial count, but that does not matter. Without the Giles testimony, I could not have gotten the three Price counts. In the end, Rifkind performed and, whether successful or not, the rules are that I must too. I have one more call to make.

"Al," I am on the telephone to DeCotiis, the judge's law clerk, "I need to see the judge." In a few minutes I am in his chambers.

Dealing with the old jurist is never as simple as it looks. It's like when he denied my request to put off my summation because he was "fighting a cold" and had a busy schedule. He is a plainspoken man, without artifice, in an old-world way. But his simplicity can be misleading. His waters run deep.

"The presentence reports on Leuty, Feldman, and Jacks are ready," I tell him.

He nods expectantly. I note it is time to schedule sentencing. Nodding again, knowing that I did not come to tell him that, he waits. I finally bite the bullet and tell him of Colonial's help on the Weber case and that I would not regret any leniency he showed to Leuty and Feldman. He nods. Nothing more.

* * * * * * *

June 27

Sentencing day. The old gang is together again, one last stop before our journey to the United States Court of Appeals for the Third Circuit.

"The government moves the sentencing of Roland Tompkins Corporation," I say.

Joe Brill stands at the podium to plead for Roland Tompkins Corporation. He knows Wortendyke is not fond of him and that the judge believes that some germs entered the courtroom in Brill's beard, giving him the flu during trial.

"With Your Honor's permission, first on a personal note."

"I don't follow what you said," Wortendyke interrupts, "your voice bounced off that lectern over my head."

"I said with Your Honor's permission," Brill shouts, "I wanted to address the court on a personal note in as much as rumor credited me with the responsibility for being the carrier of the virus which felled Your Honor. I want to express my regret."

"Oh well," the judge begrudgingly says, "I don't blame you." But then he continues. "Of course, I know I didn't get it in church, because I didn't go to church," thus eliminating that source. "I know I didn't get it in a movie house because I haven't seen a moving picture in thirty years. So I didn't get it in any theater." Wortendyke eliminates that as well. "But," he concludes, in a charitable moment, "I am not blaming you." However, for everyone else in the courtroom the evidence is conclusive. Joe Brill was the disease carrier.

That settled, Roland Tompkins is fined $50,000, which is the maximum available. The other two corporations, Colonial and Bechtel, get the maximum fines as well.

Before sentencing Leuty, Feldman, and Jacks, the judge looks around the courtroom at each group of lawyers. Pausing a moment, he begins, "I have something to say about this entire case."

"It was a liberal education to me of the amorality of business, politics, and human relations in this democracy of ours. I may be a little old-fashioned and a bit narrow in my views, but I was astounded when I looked into the faces of the individual defendants and heard about what the corporate defendants in this case did. I cannot yet understand why a corporation such as the Colonial Pipeline Company would pay any money. I must say that their conduct, and the conduct of the other corporations that participated in it, shakes my faith in business in this country."

Rifkind, with Leuty standing beside him, agrees, "No one may pay money to a public official and nobody acknowledges that more readily than I do and my client," Rifkind concedes, "even if the object is not to corrupt people officially but to persuade him to remove illegitimate obstacles, it is still wrong."

"Great," I whisper to Jon. "Where was this Rifkind when the other Rifkind was hitting me in court?" Jon cannot respond, for Rifkind is continuing.

"Leuty committed a grave error when he failed to discern where the true path of responsibility lay," Rifkind goes on, "and because he made this mistake he stands before you today labeled a felon and none of his virtues, neither his loyalty nor his fidelity, nor his frugality, nor his patriotism, are capable of erasing that smirch from his otherwise shining record. Because he made a mistake, his life has been one of grinding anxiety, of sickening jeopardy, distraught by fear of shame and contrition. Ben Leuty, by the judgment of his peers, knows how grave a mistake he made. If only time were reversible, the past were somehow made retrievable, he would have chosen a different course."

Rifkind, worried that the judge might make Leuty an example for other corporate CEOs, makes his final plea. "You might say, what about others similarly situated? The story of his trial and tribulations and of his tragic conviction has been circulated the length and breadth of this land. Its lesson has been studied, Your Honor, and learned in many executive suites . . . and all the computers have been clacking out the answer in capital letters, don't do as Leuty did if ever you are confronted by the same dilemma."

Rifkind is soon done. Now we all wait for the judge, for the final word on Leuty. "I don't hold myself out as a righteous person," Wortendyke begins, "but I wouldn't intentionally do wrong to anybody. As far as reputation is concerned," the judge pauses as he considers Rifkind's argument, "that is an evanescent temporary thing. The only way by which, in my humble opinion, a man should conduct himself, the only objective towards which a man's conduct should be aimed, is the satisfaction of his conscience. I can tell you I have a conscience, and it is a darn nuisance sometimes. But you can talk about all the religious creeds in the world, my Bible is my own conscience." As Wortendyke pauses, everyone in the room knows that what the judge has declared is true of him, and a great truth of life.

"I cannot understand why you and your company ever paid this money." Wortendyke shakes his head. "Mr. Ben Leuty, I impose a fine upon you in the sum of $10,000 on each of counts one and six for an aggregate fine of $20,000. I commit you to the custody of the Attorney General of the United States for the term of one year and one day, but," he pauses, "I suspend the execution of that sentence and place you on probation without supervision for a period of five years."

"Thank you, Your Honor," Rifkind says quietly, relieved that Leuty has escaped jail.

Karl Feldman gets a suspended sentence as well. But, of course, this is a foregone conclusion in light of Leuty's sentence.

Jacks is next. Toolan, standing side by side with his client, makes an impassioned plea for leniency.

"If Your Honor please, Mr. Jacks is forty-five years of age, married and has two children, two boys. One is twenty and the other is fourteen. He has a rather unusual war record. He was a student in a prep school when war broke out December 1941. He immediately stopped school, came down and sat up all night at a recruiting office so that he could enlist in the Marines the next morning. He was then only seventeen years of age. His father wouldn't permit him to go into the service. As a result, and with a boy-like reaction, he quit school and went off and got a job in the defense industry. But as soon as he approached the area of his eighteenth year, he went back to his father and his father finally consented. He enlisted in the Marines. He spent approximately thirty-three months in the Pacific arena during World War II. In that period of time, he was in six major military campaigns. He was at Guadalcanal, he was at Rendova. He was at Lavella, and he was at Guam, he was at Bougainville, and he was at Iwo Jima.

"In each and every one of these campaigns, he went in with the first wave of Marines. He received the Presidential Citation for Bougainville and a Bronze Star Medal for Iwo Jima. He was honorably discharged as a platoon sergeant, although he was only about twenty-one years of age. During the Iwo Jima campaign, he was acting platoon leader on three different occasions because three of his leaders successively had been killed in action."

When Toolan finishes, the judge imposes sentence, "I am not going to send you to the penitentiary, although if anyone should go to the penitentiary out of the group of individual defendants, probably you should, because you received the money. It may very well be that after all the publicity respecting the trial of this case, there may be further publicity with respect to my decision not to send you to the penitentiary."

At the conclusion of the proceedings, the old judge looks over at Jon and me. "I want to compliment the dedicated counsel for the government, because I know that holidays and hours meant nothing as far as the performance of your duties were concerned." The comment means everything to me. I have come not only to admire, but to love the old gentleman. As we leave the courtroom, Jon says to me, "What was all that about? Jacks not going to jail—because he was a war hero?"

"Jonathan, it's not what it seems."

"What do you mean?"

"I mean I went to him and asked him to give Leuty and Feldman a break."

"You did?" says Jon, who sometimes does not approve of my conduct.

"Yes," I tell him. "And I guess Wortendyke felt he couldn't send Jacks off to jail if he was going to walk the businessmen. At least that's my guess. And you know, Wortendyke figures the press is going to excoriate him for letting Jacks go. He referred to that, but still he let him go."

As we reach the hall and separate, I find Fred Lacey waiting for me. "Can I call you at home tonight?" he asks.

BOOK III

BATMAN AND ROBIN—
The Fulcrum

Chapter One

Jersey Boys
June 27–August 14, 1969

WHEN MY HOME phone rings, it's in my apartment in New York. I have no intention of returning to Washington. During the past several weeks I have been putting feelers out to New York law firms. Small firms that specialize in criminal law. Big firms don't interest me, and I would not interest them. I have never even seen a civil case. Jon Goldstein feels differently. He is looking around New York, too, but he has no concern about big firms. Perhaps because Ellen's father, Dan Lowenthal, heads one of the prominent Philadelphia law firms.

As I expect, it's Lacey on the phone. "Herb," he says, "I am about to be nominated by the president to be U.S. Attorney."

"Great, Fred!" I am not surprised. There have been rumors and the appointment also makes sense.

"I want you on my team."

"Fred, I am not admitted to practice in New Jersey."

"You don't have to be. Not representing the government. But," he adds, "you do have to be a resident of New Jersey."

"But I'm not."

"I know," he says, "but you can move."

"I don't want to move."

"Let's meet for coffee tomorrow," he says.

In the morning, Fred Lacey makes his position clear. The United States Attorney's office is in disarray. Dave Satz, the United States

Attorney, has submitted his resignation to the new Nixon administration, as has Ed Stier, chief of the Criminal Division. The office is totally understaffed. There are eighteen assistants allocated by Justice for the entire state, including the Newark, Trenton, and Camden offices. That is one less than when Lacey was an AUSA fifteen years ago. He intends to double the assistants.

Some of the present AUSAs will have to leave. Particularly the ones who owe their appointments to leaders of the Democratic Party, such as David T. Wilentz, in Middlesex County; Dennis Carey, in Essex County, which includes Newark; and, worst of all, John V. Kenny, "the Boss" of Hudson County, which controls Jersey City, Hoboken, and Bayonne. And there will be no Republican political appointments replacing them, Lacey emphasizes.

He tells me he has already called the heads of major law firms in New Jersey and requested that each send him one of their best young lawyers.

"You haven't wasted any time," I tell him.

"I haven't any time to waste," he responds, "and I want you to be my first assistant."

"Fred, I don't know anything about New Jersey. These two cases, Weber and Colonial, were just out of the blue. Except during the trials, I've not slept a night here. I don't know anybody, or about anybody here."

"I'll educate you," he insists.

"Who would be chief of Criminal?" I ask.

"Jon Goldstein. That's what you want, isn't it?"

"Wait a minute," I say, "I was just asking, not joining up. Besides, I don't think he will take it. He's not admitted here either."

"Let me take care of that," Lacey responds.

"What about John Barry?" I ask Lacey, referring to the youngest member of Rifkind's team at his firm in New York. He had impressed me with his briefs in Colonial.

"I see no problem there," Fred replies. "Is he admitted to New Jersey?"

"No."

"Well, we can do it, but we may have to wait a little."

"Fred, it's not 'we.'"

"It will be," he says, in his big bass rumbling voice.

We agree to talk again in a few days. In the meantime, he says he wants to send me some materials to read. I want to ask what they are, but I am afraid to get sucked in further. When I don't ask, he tells me anyway.

"Have you read the DeCavalcante tapes?"

I know he means the transcripts of the conversations of Simone Rizzo DeCavalcante, popularly known as "Sam the Plumber," who heads his own crime family in New Jersey. The FBI broke into his office and bugged it for a solid year.

"No," I respond, "I know that Peter Richards of the Organized Crime section and U.S. Attorney Satz's office indicted DeCavalcante last year, and that they filed a bunch of transcripts. But I was busy getting ready for trial."

Lacey tells me he is going to send over three things. First, the report of the Lilley Commission, a body empanelled by the Governor to inquire into the Newark riots of July 1967; second, two *Life* magazine articles that appeared in the September 1967 issue, exposing the mob in New Jersey; and finally, the excerpts of transcribed conversations by the FBI.

The package comes hand delivered at the end of the day. I spend the weekend reviewing the materials.

****

It comes down to this: After the black population of Newark rioted in the summer of 1967, Governor Richard Hughes appointed a special committee headed by Robert D. Lilley, president of the New Jersey Telephone Company, to "inquire into the causes of the riot." In February 1968 that Committee found that the one cause was "a widespread belief that Newark's government is corrupt . . . everything at city hall is for sale." The report recommended the convening of a special grand jury to ferret out the corruption.

Two months after the July riots, but five months before the 1968 Lilley Commission Report, in September 1967, *Life* magazine published its blazing two-part report on the mafia. The article claims "informants" as sources. But it is apparent that the true sources are FBI bugs of mobsters that had been installed in 1961, when Bobby Kennedy became Attorney General. The bugs remained in place after Kennedy was replaced by Nick Katzenbach, until 1965, when Ramsey Clark became Deputy Attorney General and the Johnson administration ordered the electronic monitoring discontinued. Any doubt about the source of the articles is resolved by the third package containing 2,200 pages of transcripts derived from a bug planted in Sam the Plumber's office from August 1964, until it was turned off on July 12, 1965.

The *Life* articles led with a full-page photograph of the entrance to Richie "the Boot" Boiardo's house in Livingston, New Jersey. The driveway has statuary depicting members of the Boot's family, dominated by a large statue of the Boot himself, astride a horse, and another statue of his son and heir, Tony Boy.

> A lot of Mr. Boiardo's fellow gangsters are mortally afraid of going up that driveway alone. Some who did never returned. . . . Ruggiero Boiardo—or Richie the Boot, as he is called—is a significant figure in organized U.S. crime and his estate, literally, is one of its monuments.
>
> Deep in the rackets since Prohibition days, with a reputation for unabashed savagery, Boiardo gets paid $4,000 a month out of the Mob's Las Vegas "skimming" profits.
>
> Two other New Jersey gangsters, Angelo "Gyp" DeCarlo and Anthony "Little Pussy" Russo, once babbled like schoolboys about the foul deeds that have been committed beyond these colorful gates. Russo, 48, is the gambling and rackets boss of Monmouth County, New Jersey, and also has interests in Florida. Gyp DeCarlo, sixty-five, an obese character who detests his nickname, like Boiardo is a Capo in the Genovese Family. He grows fat off gambling and loan shark racketeers in Union County, New Jersey, and operates crap games that float from borough to borough in New York City. As an informant was to relate, the conversation went like this:
>
> "Stay away from there!" said Russo. "So many guys have been hit there. There's this furnace 'way up in back. That's where they burn 'em."
>
> DeCarlo, fascinated, asked for details. Russo cheerily ticked off victims by their first names. "Oliver . . . Willie . . . Little Harold . . . Tony . . ." He himself, Russo, bragged, had carried Little Harold to the furnace by a chain tied to the dead man's throat.

It is clear to me that the "informant"—giving a word-for-word account—is actually a microphone implanted in a room, not a phone tap. This type of bug is what the bureau calls a "black bag job." Agents break into a home or office and plant a bug. Then they sit in a secure location and listen; they record; and then they type up extracts of the conversation which they airtel to headquarters in Washington. A few years later, after the microphones were silenced, the frustrated FBI leaked the tapes to Sandy Smith of *Life* magazine.

The next portion of the article is even more revealing. It recounts a conversation in DeCarlo's headquarters, "The Barn."

> In February 1963 three men sat down in a ramshackle club called "The Barn" on Route 22 in Mountainside, N.J. to discuss the rising cost of fixing police officials. Two of them were gabby old friends who discussed Richie Boiardo's beckoning incinerator: Angelo DeCarlo and Tony Russo, the Genovese family's betting boss in Monmouth County. (Russo's sobriquet in the Mob is: "Little Pussy." His brother John—"Big Pussy"—did a stretch for murder.)

Some "third man," I say to myself. That man is a microphone with an FBI man on the other end.

> The specific complaint of the two gangsters was the forthright grabbiness of a top-level officer in the New Jersey State Police. Russo said the police official was collecting $250 a month for ignoring bookies around Monmouth Park race track, plus $1,000 a month in gambling payoffs in Long Branch and another $1,000 from Asbury Park. The irony of it all, DeCarlo added bitterly, was that he and Russo had only themselves to blame. They had personally picked their greedy policeman and arranged for a well-connected Hudson County politico to promote him to his high place on the force.

Based on Henry Petersen's briefing, I know the top-level police official was Dominick Capello, the then superintendent of the state police; and the "well-connected Hudson politico" was none other than the supremely powerful John V. Kenny. I now know where Henry got his information when he told me about official corruption in New Jersey, two years before the *Life* articles appeared. The transcripts derived from the bureau's black bag break-ins were obviously shared within the department—before being leaked to *Life*. The meeting described by the *Life* article concluded with a discussion of the Jersey shore.

> In Long Branch, a town of 26,000 on the Jersey shore, Russo told the informant that the Mob had taken charge. "What we got in Long Branch is everything," said Russo. "Police we got. Councilman we got, too. We're gonna make millions."

A third *Life* article entitled "The Congressman and the Hoodlum," obviously based on FBI-leaked bugs of "Bayonne Joe" Zicarelli, exposes the control that Zicarelli has over Congressman Cornelius "Neil" Gallagher, who had been the ranking member of the House Committee on Foreign Affairs.

The *Life* magazine articles, followed by the Lilley Commission Report, could not be ignored by New Jersey officialdom. In accordance with one of the Lilley Commission's recommendations, the Essex County prosecutor, Joseph P. Lordi, convened a special grand jury to investigate the Addonizio administration. Within months he indicted Dominick Spina, the mob's handpicked director of Newark's police department, for malfeasance in failing to enforce the gambling laws. Unfortunately, the case was dismissed on motion.

Nonetheless, Lordi and his two assistants, Donald Merkelbach and Michael Riccardelli, pressed an investigation into Mayor Addonizio's finances. Their emphasis was on whether a wealthy engineer, Paul Rigo, who did enormous city business, had paid for Addonizio's summer home in New Shrewsbury on the Jersey shore. Some of the prosecutor's subpoenas directed to the mayor were quashed. Nonetheless, they kept digging into Rigo.

The state government's response to the *Life* articles was something else again. A joint committee of the state legislature was empanelled to investigate. It heard testimony from Robert Blakely of Cornell Law School, one of the nation's leading experts on organized crime. He made a series of recommendations for legislation. A few were implemented. But, after New Jersey Attorney General Arthur Sills criticized the Blakely testimony as an exaggeration of the existence and influence of organized crime, the Blakely recommendation for creation of a division of criminal justice was put aside.

To buttress his claim that Blakely had exaggerated the problem, Sills appointed William J. Brennan, III, the son of a sitting supreme court justice, as a special assistant attorney general. Brennan was directed to empanel a grand jury and subpoena Blakely before it. Sills expected to establish that the professor did not know what he was talking about in his legislative testimony. But the strategy backfired.

By 1968 Dominick Capello was no longer superintendent of the state police. David Kelly had succeeded him. For the first time in years, the state had an honest man at the helm of the police. Kelly, nauseated by what he learned about his predecessor, and limited by Attorney General Sills, secretly started an organized unit reporting directly to him. To guarantee security, Kelly kept the files in the basement of his home. It was to Kelly that Brennan went to learn the extent of organized crime in New Jersey.

After reviewing the Kelly files, Brennan spoke before the journalist society, Sigma Delta Chi on December 11, 1968, and publicly charged that "three of the state legislators are too comfortable with organized crime." It was a bomb. The legislature then subpoenaed Brennan to support his allegations. Unfortunately for him, Governor Hughes ordered the state police files sealed, "to protect informants."

Brennan, unable to document his charges, testified, "I can't disclose, but there are actually six legislators" who are too close to the mob. The legislative committee found Brennan's testimony "of absolutely no value whatsoever." Brennan, branded a hothead and irresponsible, returned to private practice. Six months later, on June 10, 1969, United States Attorney Satz filed the DeCavalcante tapes in federal court in the DeCavalcante case.

The last of the packages Lacey sent me are the DeCavalcante tapes—2,000 pages of mafia conversations, detailing the overall corruption of the state, in particular, Tony Boy Boiardo's and Gyp DeCarlo's grip over Mayor Addonizio and his entire administration in Newark. Unfortunately for Brennan, these illegally obtained tapes had not yet been filed when he fell under attack as a "shoot from the hip" alarmist. One recorded conversation infuriates me. Tony Boy Boiardo, the Boot's son and heir; Sam the Plumber DeCavalcante;

and Angelo Gyp DeCarlo, whose pals called him "Ray," were recorded reminiscing.

"Ray," said DeCavalcante, "you told me years ago about the guy where you said, 'Let me hit you clean.'"

"That's right," DeCarlo replied, "So the guy went for it. There was me, Zip, and Johnny Russell. So we took the guy out in the woods and I said, 'Now listen. . . . You gotta go. Why not let me hit you right in the heart and you won't feel a thing?' He said, 'I'm innocent, Ray, but if you've got to do it . . .' So I hit him in the heart and it went right through him."

That stimulated a recollection of Tony Boy's. "How about the time we hit the little Jew?" Tony Boy reminisced.

"As little as they are, they struggle," said DeCarlo. "They're fighting for their life."

"The Boot," Tony Boy continued, referring to his father, "hit him with a hammer. The guy goes down and he comes up. So I got a crowbar this big, Ray. Eight shots in the head. What do you think he finally did to me? He spit at me and said, 'you obscenity!'" I have to smile at the straight-laced agent's reluctance to use the "F" word. I guess Hoover did not approve of profanity, but had no trouble authorizing burglaries.

That did it. The "little Jew" business gets to me. I am going to say yes to Lacey's offer. The other thing that strikes me is that the conversation about hitting the "little Jew" took place in DeCarlo's headquarters, The Barn, not DeCavalcante's. That means there were at least three bugs—one in DeCavalcante's place, one in Zicarelli's, and one in DeCarlo's. Only the bureau knows what is on those last two.

I come to the conclusion that New Jersey must surely be the most corrupt state in the nation. I figured it was bad when just one pipeline project yielded payments by two contractors to Weber totaling $44,000, as well as the massive $110,000 to Jacks and Zirpolo back in 1963 and 1964 dollars. And here I am in 1969 making $17,000 a year, and it's already five years of inflation later. The tapes go beyond what I could even imagine. This state is totally in the grip of corrupt labor leaders, venal politicians, and a violent criminal syndicate.

Chapter Two

Henry and Me
August 14–21, 1969

I N A FEW days Lacey and I sit down in my small office in the federal Post Office Courthouse. He wants an answer.

"If you get Jon Goldstein, you've got me."

"I'll handle that," his big voice rumbles then, laughing, "Anything else?"

"Yes," I say tentatively, because I don't like to talk about money. "I need a raise."

He asks and I say that I now make seventeen and want to get to twenty-two thousand dollars. Without a raise, I can't afford to set up a legal residence in Newark and still keep my place in New York.

"Okay," he nods. "The U.S. Attorney gets twenty-nine thousand, so there should be no trouble with twenty-two thousand dollars for the First Assistant."

****

Establishing a new office is exciting. Lacey, Goldstein and I cannot move in yet, because the president has only nominated Fred, and he has not yet been confirmed. But we don't wait for the formal takeover. We inspect the premises; it is, simply put, a dump. No reception area. No ceiling, wires hanging.

When we meet again with Lacey, we tell him that we have to move. "I know," he says, "it was a dump when I worked there fifteen years ago. I am sure it's worse now."

I tell him that there is a federal office building across the street, but that the GSA—General Services Administration—refuses to make space available.

"We'll take care of that," Lacey rumbles as his lips thin. "One other thing," he says. He fills us in on his telephone conversation with Henry Petersen, whom he called to inform that Jon and I were transferring in as First Assistant and Chief of Criminal.

"You," he says to Jon, "are okay. But as to you," he nods at me, "Petersen told me you would not be 'suitable.'"

"Well, maybe I'm not."

"I told him," Lacey ignores my comment, "that I saw you in the Colonial and Weber trials and that you are going to be with me."

Lacey wants to know what gives with Petersen, so I try to explain: Henry regards USAs with suspicion. I outline the efforts of Henry, and his bureaucrat allies in the "Seat of Government," to take control of the serious criminal cases in districts around the country. At first he used area men, shuttling back and forth to Washington; more recently, he established "strike forces" with temporary offices in selected cities.

"And we have one here, in the federal building across the street. The one we can't get into," I tell Lacey.

I explain that the purported purpose of a strike force is to coordinate the various agencies in the field. But the true reason is to shift authority from the USAs in their districts to the long-term bureaucrats in the Criminal Division in Washington.

"When I first came to work for Henry, the Organized Crime section would review, and even approve or disapprove, of the major cases in the USAs' offices. But there was only limited direct control of the bringing or running of a case. Now, first in Buffalo, then Detroit, now Newark, the section has their own offices, called strike forces, with personnel hired and fired by them and, most important, totally outside of the administrative control of the United States Attorney for those districts."

"We'll see about that, too," Lacey says.

"Funny thing, Fred," I say, "Henry used the success of Operation Pipeline to sell the idea of strike forces in the field. Once we broke Colonial and Weber in 1966, he used what we did to sell the idea of setting up similar efforts called strike forces."

"So why is he adverse to you?"

I explain how Henry worked his way up from being an FBI messenger, to deputy chief of the Organized Crime and Racketeering Section, which is what he was when I first got to Washington, then to chief of the section, and now first deputy assistant AG, supervising all federal criminal cases throughout the country. It was incremental. Step by step, carefully he mounted the ladder of bureaucracy, and as he went up he pulled his pals up the ladder with him, all the while expanding the authority of Washington over the United States Attorneys throughout the country. All except the Southern District of New York. Bob Morgenthau had been able to preserve the traditional independence of that district.

"And he and you?"

"I did not want to play on that team."

"Why?"

"It's a bureaucracy. Nine to five. Lots of worry about the next GS level promotion. They carpool a lot. You know what that means? It means the poolers have to arrive and leave at the same time. You can't work late even if you want to. Not without planning in advance. I don't believe it was that way under Bobby Kennedy. But that's the way it is now. Let me give you an example. Phil White, Henry's pal who he made my supervisor, and I were traveling around investigating Weber. One evening when I tried to talk to him on an airplane, he told me that I should talk shop during office hours and picked up a magazine."

"That's amazing."

"Right. So once I knew that I was never going back to D.C. and the department, Henry and I got more and more remote. He could not get rid of me, not with Colonial and Weber open, and with him having used us as the model for setting up his own offices in districts around the country. In just five months, from January to May of 1966, we made the Weber and Colonial cases out of a temporary office in New Jersey. Henry then sold the strike force idea. But instead of temporary offices, he began to set up permanent facilities. So we were both stuck. He wanted me out. And I wanted out. But we were stuck with each other until Weber and Colonial were done. Now he has no intention of having me inside the department but outside his tent."

"Okay," Fred says. "We'll just go around him. I know Harlington Wood, who is Deputy Attorney General Kleindienst's executive assistant."

Unfortunately for our desire for a fast start, Harrison Williams, the Democratic senator from New Jersey, holds up Fred's Senate confirmation. For the next six weeks all we can do is plan what we are going to do once we get into office. Fred will get additional bodies and undertake to get us moved out of the courthouse and into decent offices. Jon and I continue to work with the United States Attorney's office and prepare to take it over. The Senate does not confirm Fred until late August. His swearing-in is set for September 2, 1969.

Chapter Three

A Letter from the Grave
August 22–September 2, 1969

August 28

Satz's office has been sitting on an investigation of Angelo Gyp DeCarlo. They say nothing about it for two months. Then, five days before we take office, the grand jury indicts DeCarlo and three of his henchmen: Daniel "Red" Cecere, Pete Landusco, and Joe "the Italian" Polverino for the loan sharking of Louis B. Saperstein.

I begin reading the file. On November 21, 1968, Saperstein wrote two letters to the FBI. He did not mail them until November 25, the same day he entered a hospital with stomach pains. He died the next day. His death was diagnosed as "cardiac shock induced by acute gastro-enteritis." It would have stayed so, except the same day that Saperstein died the FBI received the two letters. The most significant one read as follows:

> Federal Bureau of Investigation
>   Newark, NJ
>   Gentlemen:
>   I am writing you, maybe others can be helped by my plight. To-date, I am indebted to Ray (Gyp) DeCarlo, Joe Polverino (known as Joe the Italian) and Daniel Cecere (known as Red Cecere), the total due these three is $115,000 on which I was

charged and paid 1 1/2% interest per week, amounting to $1725 per week; the amount of $1725 was delivered weekly to Red Cecere at the Berkeley Bar. On September 13, 1968 I was severely beaten at a place in the rear of Weiland's Restaurant, Route 22, DeCarlo's headquarters. I was then told and given 3 months until December 13, 1968 to pay the entire accumulated amount of $115,000—the interest was then raised to $2000 per week, which was delivered to Cecere every Thursday at the Berkeley Bar in Orange, NJ. This was delivered by Lenny Banks, my employee – on November 14, 1968 I cashed 2 checks totaling $31,000 at Essex County State Bank and personally delivered to Cecere $30,000—under the threat of death. Cecere, DeCarlo and Polverino, also stated many times my wife and son would be maimed or killed.

Last night from my home I called DeCarlo at the Harbor Island Spa in Florida, and pleaded for time but to no avail, over the phone DeCarlo stated unless further monies was paid the threats would be carried out. Today, Lenny Banks delivered to Cecere $2000 at 11:30 a.m. Cecere called by phone while I was in Staten Island—& I had to send this money to-day.

Louis B. Saperstein.

The second letter detailed another $250,000 that Saperstein owed to DeCarlo and Company, and begged the FBI to protect Saperstein's family.

When the agents received the letters, they ran to Satz's office. Edwin Stier, chief of the Criminal Division, obtained a court order to exhume Saperstein's body. When the body came out of the ground, the state medical examiner determined that it hosted "enough arsenic to kill a mule."

With no evidence other than the letters, which were inadmissible hearsay, and no witnesses, there seemed little chance of proceeding against DeCarlo. There was not even unanimity as to whether the death was suicide or homicide. Fortuitously, the case was assigned to a combination bloodhound-bulldog of an FBI agent by the name of Fred McMahon.

McMahon interviewed Saperstein's wife and friends, discovering a close associate of Saperstein's by the name of Gerald Martin Zelmanowitz. McMahon learned that Zelmanowitz had been arrested for passing stolen bonds in June of 1968, but had not yet been indicted. The investigation had been assigned to Edwin Stier, the chief of the Criminal Division. So McMahon went to see Stier, who checked and found that on December 17, 1968, less than one month after Saperstein's death, Zelmanowitz had been arrested in Miami, Florida, again for passing stolen bonds. Stier, scheduled to leave on January 20 for a new post in state law enforcement, had a warrant issued to bring Zelmanowitz to New Jersey. And then he did something that would hardly endear him to the ACLU.

Stier called in the chief deputy United States marshal, Carl Hirchman, and told him to bring Zelmanowitz to New Jersey from Florida, making "all the stops along the way." Hirchman knew that that meant.

From December 17 until January 11, 1969, Zelmanowitz was taken on a trip that included major cities, such as Washington, D.C., Atlanta, Georgia, and numerous tank towns along the meandering path to New Jersey. Frequently, he was held in county and even municipal jails, sometimes in solitary, sometimes with other prisoners in a crowded cell. Both had their disadvantages. When he finally arrived in Stier's office, Zelmanowitz was in the same silk suit he had been wearing when arrested the month before.

"It's a shame what happened to you," said Stier to Zelmanowitz. "I would just like to ask you a few questions about an old friend of yours."

"Who is that?" said the resigned Zelmanowitz.

"Louis B. Saperstein," said Stier.

Zelmanowitz immediately opened up. He outlined all the financial dealings between himself, Saperstein, and DeCarlo. He told of opening Swiss bank accounts for DeCarlo, and provided the records. He detailed the monies owed, Saperstein's flight when he could not repay. It was Zelmanowitz who found Saperstein in New York under the assumed name of Stone. It was Zelmanowitz who informed DeCarlo where Saperstein was, and aided in bringing Saperstein to DeCarlo's headquarters, The Barn. And, most important, Zelmanowitz was present when Saperstein was beaten until he was nearly dead.

Stier had made the case within six weeks of Saperstein's death. Then, on January 20, 1969, Stier left the office. Two months after Stier left, Zelmanowitz went before the Grand Jury as Mr. X, and his family went into hiding. Satz waited months to indict. Now, on August 28, just one week before Fred, Jon, and I are to take over, the indictment comes down. DeCarlo and three of his goons are charged with extortionate extension of credit—loan sharking. The victim is the deceased Saperstein.

For the sake of good relations I do not push into the reasons for the delay between the January 1969 confession and the indictment at the end of August seven months later. I have everything in the file I need, except the transcripts of the bug the bureau planted in The Barn, DeCarlo's headquarters. I know they must exist because both the Life article and the DeCavalcante tapes reported verbatim conversations inside DeCarlo's place. Satz's office had not obtained them from the bureau.

So we do.

Chapter Four

"Hughie Gave Us the City"
August 28–September 2, 1969

AGENT FRED MCMAHON brings the multi volumes over in a shopping cart. Hundreds of pages of excerpts from conversations in The Barn, commencing in the early 1960s until the microphones were silenced by the Johnson Administration, perhaps under the influence of the new deputy attorney general, Ramsey Clark. Like DeCavalcante's, the DeCarlo tapes are actually whatever excerpts of conversations the agents thought worthy enough to be transcribed. These were sent by airtel to bureau headquarters in Washington. By the time of the Saperstein beating in 1968 the microphones had been turned off for three years. Even if the beating had been recorded, the illegal recording could not have been used in court. The tapes were worthless as evidence under the Supreme Court's decision in *Mapp v. Ohio*. But the taped conversations were valuable raw intelligence on the mob. They document the existence of a mafia, and also DeCarlo and Tony Boy Boiardo's domination of Newark mayor Hugh Addonizio, and the mayor's entire administration of the largest city in the state.

To begin with, in 1962 the mob endorsed then Congressman Addonizio's run for mayor against the incumbent Irish mayor Leo Carlin. But the gangsters needed to make certain that no other Italian entered the race to split the Italian vote. When DeCarlo learned that Michael Bontempo, president of Newark's city council, intended to run, he complained to his men, "He's gonna split the Italian vote. Carlin got him to do it."

The soldiers of the mob brought Bontempo to The Barn, where he was recorded. "Well, Mickey," DeCarlo said, "let's get down to business. What is it you want from Addonizio to work together?"

"Motor Vehicle Director," said Bontempo.

It was doubtful that the mob could obtain that statewide appointment. So DeCarlo decided to be blunt. "Now, look, you're in this business to make money, ain't you?" De Carlo demanded.

"At my age I am," the city council president replied.

"You've got to be reasonable," said Joe DeBenedictis, the Democratic boss of Newark's North Ward, who was in attendance. "We want to win. You've got to sit down with Hughie."

After Bontempo departed The Barn, DeCarlo said to DeBenedictis, "We'll see if we can raise ten thousand for him. We'll get all the bookmakers. The Boot will pay up to five thousand."

Bontempo was paid and dropped out. Then another man of Italian descent, Nick Caputo, indicated he would file unless he was appointed Administrator of Newark after Hugh Addonizio's victory. He was persuaded to change his mind when DeCarlo announced if "we'll go and break his legs."

Hugh Addonizio won the 1962 election. The mob put Dominic Spina in as police director and the city was theirs. Two years later, the microphone heard DeCarlo proclaim, "Hughie helped us all along. He gave us the city." As for the state, the mob already had Dominick Capello, the superintendent of the state police. The mob was safe. And the public? Aside from the FBI's illegal leaks of a small portion of the DeCarlo tapes through the *Life* magazine articles in 1967, the curtain remained closed. But only as to details. The rotten stench of gangsterism and public corruption in the state became the dirty joke of the nation.

Chapter Five

"A Stench in the Nostrils"
September 2, 1969

September 2

Jon and I walk into the ceremonial courtroom, the same courtroom we appeared in against Lacey eight months before. Now we are back to attend his induction as the United States Attorney, and our new boss. It seems odd to sit on the spectator benches in this courtroom. Odder still to see Chief Judge Augelli presiding over the ceremony, with Judge Wortendyke lost among the other four judges on the bench.

The big courtroom is only half filled—or only half empty—depending on one's outlook on life. Some of the new members of our team of young lawyers are there. Aside from a token appearance by the state attorney general, Arthur Sills, there is no representation from the official world of New Jersey, except, of course, for United States senator Clifford P. Case, the man responsible for Lacey's appointment. He stands in the well of the court, the five federal judges on the bench behind him. First, he and Mrs. Lacey together hold the Bible as Fred takes the oath of office. I have never seen the senator before, but I will never forget what he says when he speaks to the audience. He makes no bones about why he insisted that President Nixon appoint Fred Lacey United States Attorney.

"I am tired of having New Jersey a stench in the nostrils and an offense to the vision of the world, and," he adds, "of ourselves."

There are gasps in the audience. The judges on the bench turn to each other. I cannot believe what the Senior United States senator of New Jersey has just said about his own state.

White-haired, tall, dignified, the son of a Presbyterian minister, he has been elected to his third six-year term in the Senate in 1966. Republican, he is viewed as too liberal by his own party. He had condemned the redbaiting senator Joseph McCarthy in the 1950s; he sponsored the Civil Rights Act of 1964; and, with his wife at his side, he listened to Martin Luther King's "I Have a Dream" speech at the Lincoln Memorial. Among the first of the Republican senators to oppose the war in Vietnam, Case tried to block the nomination of Nixon for president in 1968, failing when a young New Jersey lawyer named Nelson Gross led the New Jersey delegation away from Case and Nelson Rockefeller and put Nixon over the top at the convention.

Case, standing in the well of the court, declares his support for Lacey's crusade and his right to appoint his own staff. Case promises, "These people are going to be on the run." And everyone knows to whom the senator is referring. His speech, if one can call a declaration of war a speech, lasts less than five minutes. As he reseats himself, people are still looking at each other open-mouthed when Fred rises to address the audience.

His bass voice booming, Lacey delivers his address to a mesmerized courtroom. "There is a message I would like to get across to you to carry back to your neighbors, friends, and your community." He tells the assembly that he is going to rid the state of the "mafia, cosa nostra, or organized crime, whatever you want to call it." And to do it, he says, he intends to "step on toes."

If anyone does not understand whom he plans to attack, he tells them to read the *Life* magazine articles and, lest there be any doubt, to study the DeCavalcante tapes. He reads aloud portions of the transcripts, particularly the murders committed by Tony Boy and the Boot, "son and father with crowbar and hammer."

He tells us, "Tony Boy lives in a very nice community," and then names it, Essex Fells. Lacey reminds the audience that they are complicit when they give status to hoodlums. "You live in communities where organized crime members reside," he tells us. "They may even be in your country clubs . . . it is kind of the 'in' thing to talk about these fellows, to be nice to them and maybe even brag a little bit about having been in their company." He tells us, "I took this position with an objective of demonstrating to you and to your community that there are those of us willing to get involved." He demands that the nice people of his state get on board.

Then he gets to me. "The key to the kind of office I hope to have here is to be found in my appointment of Herbert J. Stern as my first assistant."

"Oh my God," I say to myself, "what next?"

Lacey tells the assembly that I beat him in court a few months ago. He goes on about my "high degree of diligence, of skill, of talent for investigating, of fearlessness."

"Great," I say to myself. Some fearlessness. All I want to do right now is get out of town, before what happened to Bill Brennan happens to me.

"Ladies and gentlemen of the bar," Lacey booms on, "I tell you this firsthand. He is thorough, he is tough, he is fair, and," he says, hitting the podium that has been turned to face the audience, "he is going to have my backing one hundred percent."

Well, that does it. I now know that I have just been signed up for the duration of the Jersey wars. It would help if I could figure out where on the map Boiardo's house actually is. Father or son! I know nothing of New Jersey, except Newark.

Jon Goldstein and I have been sitting in the front row of the spectators. I do not meet Senator Case, who exits with the judges through their door behind the bench. As we file out to the rear of the courtroom, we marvel at this Fred Lacey. It is a man we've never seen before. "Where has he been?" I say to Jon, who just shrugs. As we exit, I look over at a few of the faces of the kids who are about to join the office. At thirty-two, I will be the oldest assistant in the office. I can't help wondering if the others have the experience to appreciate what just happened.

I see Fred Lacey in the hall and go up to him. "Great speech," I tell him. "I can't believe what Senator Case said about New Jersey."

"Well," Lacey smiles, "you want to hear the real funny part?" I say yes. What else can I do? "Pete Weber is one of the senator's biggest supporters," he says.

I am shocked, "Weber, a Republican?" I say.

"No," Lacey says, "a Case man. For example, Local 825 supplies cars to the Senator's campaign on election day."

"My God."

"You've got to be local," Lacey grins. "I told Case about you, of course. He knows you prosecuted Weber. I told him I wanted you."

"What did he say?"

"Why, he just laughed and said, 'Of course.'"

I leave the courthouse to ride the PATH train to my New York apartment. I also now have a half-share in an apartment in Newark across the street from the post office-courthouse. So I have a legal residence in New Jersey. I just don't use it. Tomorrow I will return to Oz to become its First Assistant United States Attorney.

Chapter Six

Stepping on Toes
September 3–December 3, 1969

THERE IS MORE to running a U.S. Attorney's office than meets the eye, particularly one that covers the whole state and has three offices—Camden, Trenton, and Newark. And then there are the agencies: the FBI, IRS, Secret Service, Alcohol & Tobacco Tax, Postal Authority, and Customs. The USA is the lawyer handling the cases agencies bring to him. That is a fair amount to supervise. The USA is also the chief law enforcement officer in his district. That means, or should mean more than functioning as a courtroom lawyer prosecuting crimes brought by agencies. He should lead in uncovering sophisticated white-collar crimes of political and business corruption that are unlikely to be exposed without lawyers' conducting grand jury investigations, for example Operation Pipeline. But first you need a physical office to manage.

September 3

Fred personally swears me in as his chief assistant. Then, sitting at his conference table, Fred gives us all assignments. "You," Fred tells me, "are going to get the DeCarlo case ready. We have a January 5 trial date. There will be no adjournment."

Lacey swings his attention to Jon. "You will run the office. Make sure the court calendars run on time and supervise the new assistants," Jon nods in agreement. "And," Lacey continues, "you will run the investigation of Peter Moraites." Peter Moraites is the Speaker of the New Jersey Assembly. He is also a director of the Midland Bank. And it looks like he has personally taken money from shippers and in return had the Bank grant them loans based on fraudulent applications.

"As for me," he goes on, "I am going to try Judge Pollock."

Pollock is a sitting state court judge who has been charged with failure to file income tax returns. The trouble with the case is that he owed no tax. It had all been withheld on his W-2 forms. This is a case that could easily be lost.

"Fred," I say, "this one could be a loser. Send in someone else. We don't need the head of the office taking a loss in our first high-profile case."

"No," he replies emphatically. "I want the bar here to see we know what we are doing, and that we are not afraid to go to court."

He is not finished with his assignments. I am to supervise the interviewing of the new assistants who will be hired. What assistants, I ask him. He tells us that he has already spoken to Attorney General John Mitchell. There were nineteen AUSAs when Lacey left the office. Now, fifteen years later, there are eighteen—one less. Mitchell has committed to giving us six new spots immediately. But we have no place to put them.

Lacey has taken care of that, too. While waiting to be confirmed, he went to Chief Judge Augelli and got him to promise to issue a letter evicting us as executive branch interlopers in the "Post Office Courthouse."

"How did you do that?" I ask.

"You've got to be local," Lacey chortles. Since we are now homeless, he tells me to get the GSA to give us space in the federal office building across the street.

****

Over the next several weeks, Lacey gets even more local—and vocal. He goes on a speaking campaign all over New Jersey. From the DeCarlo tapes, he knows the details of the extent of mob dominance in New Jersey. The trouble is that he can't use them. They are secret, the result of unlawful break-ins. So he is forced to speak in generalities. It culminates in what we call "The Seton Hall Address."

Lacey goes before an audience assembled at Seton Hall University in Newark and flatly charges that the mafia has the state by the throat, and that state law enforcement has not done enough to combat it. That does it! The state authorities, led by Attorney General Sills, challenge Lacey to put up or shut up. What should the state be doing that it has not done? Coming as it does in our first few weeks, before we have had any achievements, the state's challenge sends us into crisis mode. We have to respond or lose all credibility.

Sills has been attorney general for the entire eight years of Governor Hughes's administration. And guess where he had come from? The prestigious law firm of Wilentz, Goldman & Spitzer, the firm of David T. Wilentz, the political boss of Jacks and Zirpolo, who not only represented the Colonial Pipeline Company, but tried to persuade the Bechtel people to take the Fifth Amendment rather than reveal the use of that first $20,000 check we had stumbled over. It is Wilentz who secured the AG job for his law partner, Sills, at the outset of the Hughes administration. No wonder Sills says the threat of political corruption and mafia influence is overstated. On a hunch, I check the DeCarlo tapes, and this is what I find: Sitting in The Barn, DeCarlo told a member of his mob how he went down to see Wilentz in order to save two minor thieves who were being prosecuted in Middlesex County.

According to DeCarlo, Wilentz asked, "Is this a favor for you?"

"I said, 'No, it ain't no favor. They're going to pay five thousand.'"

"He said, 'The hell with the money. I owe you a big favor. I want to do something for you. I don't want money for it.'"

Well, of course it could be bullshit. DeCarlo is hardly a man of sterling reputation for honesty.

****

Lacey assigns AUSA Jack Bissell to head a team to respond to Sills. Fortunately for us, our report and recommendations are largely outlined for us in the recommendations that Professor Blakely made to the Legislature a year before—the establishment of a department of criminal justice, independent of the State Attorney General, staffed by experienced professionals—which Sills has resisted.

The only good news is the efforts of Essex County prosecutor Joe Lordi, and his men, Merkelbach and Riccardelli, in their investigation of Mayor Addonizio and Paul Rigo. Prosecutor Lordi has now subpoenaed Rigo's financial records. And the Intelligence Division of the IRS has jumped in. Rigo is now in a squeeze between the local prosecutor and the Feds. But we are caught up with other things.

****

The preparation of the DeCarlo case is troubling. It is a one-witness case. And that one witness is Gerald Martin Zelmanowitz. The whole case turns on his word that Saperstein had borrowed money from DeCarlo; that Saperstein could not pay the "vigorish," or "vig" for short, which is the interest, much less repay the loan; and that DeCarlo had Saperstein beaten at The Barn and threatened his life. The trouble is Zelmanowitz himself is a total bum.

As far as I can tell, the man has never done an honest day's work. He lives by his wits. His principal source of income is from two criminal enterprises: selling huge amounts of stolen bonds, which the mafia provides; and from a totally illegal arbitrage scheme in which he simultaneously buys and sells millions of dollars of the same securities using Swiss and American banks. The buys and sells are immediate. Profits and losses are minimal. He makes his profit by using improper tax equalization forms to avoid the eighteen percent equalization tax due to the U.S. government, which is built into the difference between the market price in Europe and the United States for the identical security. This theft he splits with his mafia "investors."

And that is for openers. He pays no personal income taxes. Most often he does not even file returns. He lives in a magnificent home in an affluent neighborhood, which he has paid for in cash and has put in the name of his father-in-law. He and his wife drive new Cadillacs, and his home is exquisitely furnished. An original Marc Chagall painting hangs on his walls. Gerry—we are on a first name basis—is not only a brilliant con man, he is a man of taste, although he barely finished high school. All in all, his jury appeal is nil.

That is not even the worst of it. Zelmanowitz, when he can, steals from the hoods. He doesn't give even them an honest count when they invest in his arbitrage scam. Zelmanowitz helped Saperstein drain money that they had persuaded DeCarlo to invest. And at the end, when Saperstein was hiding out in New York under the name of

Stone, in fear for his life, Gerry helped DeCarlo's murderous lieutenant, Daniel "Red" Cecere, find Saperstein and take him to The Barn where Cecere beat Saperstein until he was nearly dead. It was then that DeCarlo gave Saperstein the ultimatum of repayment or death for him and maiming for his family.

Of course, none of these thefts from DeCarlo excuse the beating and the threats, if Zelmanowitz were to be believed by the jury. But the big question is, will the jury place any trust in the unsupported word of Zelmanowitz? There is only one solution. We have to let the jury hear the voice of Saperstein himself, confirming Zelmanowitz's story. We have to introduce the letters from the grave.

Lacey, Jon, and I meet. "How on earth will you get the letters into evidence?" Lacey inquires, "As a dying declaration?"

"No," I respond. "The doctrine can't be used in federal court because the letters were written six days before Saperstein's death."

"Well," Jon says, "we brought Burgess back from the grave to testify through Price, so I guess we have to find a way to use Zelmanowitz's voice to speak for Saperstein."

"That's part of it," I say, "We can use Saperstein's statements to Zelmanowitz expressing fear of DeCarlo under the state-of-mind exception to the hearsay rule. The charge is extortion, so Saperstein's state of mind can be proved by his statements to others about his fear. But that's not good enough because the whole point is to corroborate what Zelmanowitz says he saw and heard, and we can't do that by what Zelmanowitz says he saw or heard."

"What do you recommend?" Lacey wants to know.

"I want to introduce the Saperstein letters directly into evidence."

"You mean the ones that say, 'DeCarlo stated many times my wife and son would be maimed or killed. Please protect my family?'" Jon asks.

"That's right. If others can say what Saperstein said to them about his state of mind, why can't the FBI read what Saperstein wrote to them about his fear?"

Lacey shakes his head and laughs. "Good luck to us."

But I am sure I'm right. Now all I have to do is persuade Robert Shaw, the federal judge assigned to the DeCarlo case.

Judge Shaw is no old world gentleman like Judge Wortendyke. He is one of the toughest—no nonsense—judges in the nation. Short in stature, he is a junior replica of the prizefighter Jack Dempsy. His judicial colleagues have nicknamed him "Iron Balls." They even presented a set of them to him as a joke. Tough as he is, he is just as smart. A courtroom warrior, he built one of New Jersey's best firms. He is smart enough and tough enough to let the Saperstein letters into evidence. If he does, and the jurors hear them, any credibility issues with Zelmanowitz will be over.

****

By the beginning of December, ninety days into the job and just thirty days before trial, I am in full trial preparation mode. The lawyers for the defendants have demanded that the transcripts of the electronic surveillance of DeCarlo be given to them. They know transcripts exist because of the *Life* article and the DeCavalcante disclosures. But, unlike DeCavalcante's counsel, they demand that the tapes be given to them privately, and not filed publicly. We are cornered. Much as we would like citizens of New Jersey to read the material, we cannot simply file them, as Satz had done with DeCavalcante—not in the face of the limited motion.

The situation is worsened by the fact that Mayor Addonizio is running for reelection. One of his adversaries is a young black engineer, Ken Gibson, who, if elected, would become the first black mayor of a major northeastern American city. Gibson, we know, is clean. But he has little by way of organization and virtually no money. Addonizio, we know, is in the grip of the mafia, and has all the people and money he needs. As it is, the voting public must go to the polls without the information on the tapes. Gibson is a sure loser. Newark will remain in the grip of the mob. There is nothing we can do about it, except one thing.

In responding to DeCarlo's motion to see the transcripts, we attach copies of the volumes to our responsive pleading delivered to Judge Shaw. He can see what we have. And then we cross our fingers. It will be up to Iron Balls Shaw.

****

The first week of November, Republican William Cahill is elected governor. His campaign made much of his past as an FBI agent. It also promised to implement an independent department of criminal justice.

After his election, he designated George Kugler, a prominent South Jersey lawyer, to become the attorney general. But Kugler refuses to make the new "department" independent. It will be a "division" under his authority.

****

November 24

We argue the DeCarlo motions, including his demand to see the transcripts of electronic eavesdropping privately. As Michael Querques, DeCarlo's lawyer, argues in front of Judge Shaw, I watch the judge closely.

Querques, short and stocky, with dark balding hair, is among the most able of the criminal defense bar. Skilled in cross-examination, he does not indulge in histrionics. His clientele includes the Boot and the leading racketeers in New Jersey.

"If you order a filing of the transcript," Querques argues to Judge Shaw, "they should be provided to counsel with clear and explicit instructions that the material contained therein not be disclosed." I am not looking at Querques as he argues. All that matters is Judge Shaw.

"You don't want it to be a matter of public information?" Shaw asks. And Querques nods in agreement. "But," the judge adds, "I can't be sure until I see what we are talking about whether I can agree with you."

"I can't either," Querques responds.

I let out a deep breath. That concession was a mistake. If I know people, Judge Shaw is going to publicly file the transcripts. I don't see how Querques misses that last comment by Shaw. This stuff is going to be out there, and then when the public reads the secret conversation of the mafia, there will be an explosion.

I can't help asking myself, was it right or wrong to employ illegal electronic surveillance to monitor the mob and confirm its existence? Would I have authorized the break-ins? That's a tough one. No matter what the bureau or the department says, those "black bag" jobs were clearly illegal. What about a public filing? That, at least, is not illegal. In the end, I figure I'll leave that debate to the philosophers. The city is on fire. I am a fireman. I also have a case to prepare. And while I prepare for the DeCarlo trial, I also keep an eye on county prosecutor Joe Lordi's grand jury investigation of Addonizio and Rigo.

****

Between Lordi's subpoenas and the IRS pressure, it appears Rigo is about to crack. He called Lacey's office to arrange for an appointment in mid-November. But Rigo did not show up. Instead, he flew to Mexico for a "vacation."

December 3

Fred calls a council of war. "I got a call from Will Wilson," Lacey reports. Wilson is the assistant attorney general in Washington in charge of the Criminal Division. "He says that while in Mexico, Rigo called the president's special assistant Pete Flanagan at the White House. Then Flanagan called Attorney General Mitchell, who referred him to Deputy Attorney General Kleindienst, who set up an appointment for Rigo with Wilson, the assistant AG, Criminal."

Same old story, I say to myself. John Mitchell, the AG, a bond lawyer partner of Nixon, ran the Nixon campaign last year. Kleindienst was the defeated Republican candidate for governor of Arizona. And Wilson was the defeated Republican candidate for governor of Texas. The new top three in the Justice Department are hardly professional prosecutors. But the Democrats before them had been no better. Ramsey Clark's chief qualification was being the son of Supreme Court Justice Tom C. Clark; and Fred Vinson, Jr., assistant AG, Criminal, was the son of former Chief Justice Fred Vinson, Sr. Bobby Kennedy, of course, was appointed AG by his brother Jack, but that was okay by me. He turned out great.

I know what will happen when Rigo hits the Justice Department. "Fred," I tell Lacey, "Petersen will funnel Rigo over to Bartells at the strike force."

"I'd better get down there," Lacey says. And within half an hour he leaves for the Eastern Airlines shuttle at Newark Airport with nothing but the shirt on his back.

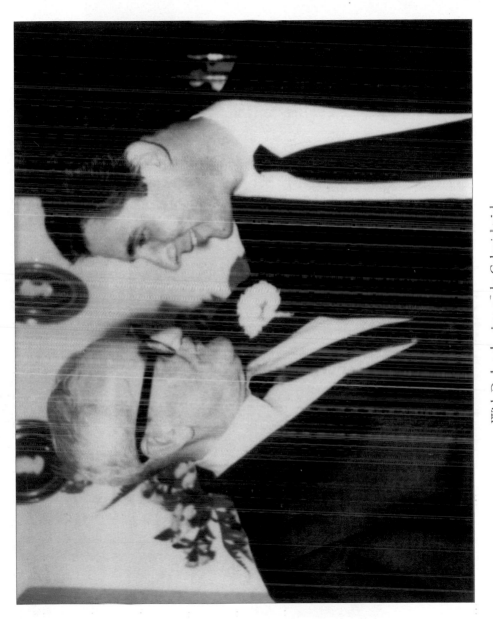

With Dad at the time of the Colonial trial.

Peter Weber at the time of his indictment.

Robert Jacks at the time of his indictment.

Batman and Robin

Mafia boss of Newark, Anthony "Tony Boy" Boiardo.
He and his group (including "Little Pussy" Russo)
were the models for the hit HBO show, *The Sopranos*.

Mayor Addonizio, in handcuffs, off to prison after sentencing.

The court appointing me United States Attorney:
(from left to right: Lawrence A. Whipple, Reynier J. Wortendyke, Chief Judge Anthony T. Augelli, Frederick B. Lacey, James A. Coolahan, Leonard I. Garth, Robert "Iron Balls" Shaw, Clarkson S. Fisher)

The team:
(from left to right: John Barry, Bruce L. Goldstein, Garret E. Brown, Jonathan L. Goldstein, John W. Bissell)

The boss of Hudson County, John V. Kenny.

Mayor of Jersey City, Thomas J. Whalen.

Chief of Police of Hudson County, Fred J. Kropke.

Former Democratic Chairman of Hudson County, John J. Kenny.

On the steps of the courthouse, after the Hudson County verdict, holding the cash that was put in evidence.

United States Senator Clifford P. Case and I in his office in Washington, D.C.

Roger DeLouette, an agent of the French CIA, after his arrest for smuggling 100 pounds of pure heroin into the United States.

Conference in New York regarding the President's program to have U.S. attorneys prosecute street-level narcotics cases (with President Nixon and Robert Morse, United States attorney, Eastern District of New York).

Announcing an indictment of New Jersey Secretary of State, Paul Sherwin.

Cartoon courtesy of Bil Canfield

Cartoon courtesy of Bil Canfield

I take the bench for the first time with my new colleagues.

Dad and me at the party after my induction as a United States District Judge.

Chapter Seven

"Let's Go"
December 4–5, 1969

LATE THE NEXT afternoon, Lacey calls in from D.C. "It's like a madhouse here. I finally got to see Rigo."

"What took so long?" I ask.

"You sure are right about this place," Lacey growls. "They tried to keep me away from Rigo."

"Who did?"

"Petersen, of course. He and Wilson told me that the investigation of Rigo and the Addonizio ring are assigned to the strike force. But it isn't anymore."

"How did you get around them?"

"Rigo told them that he had tried to see me, but got an anonymous call telling him to 'keep the hell away from the Federal Building.'"

"Well," I say, "that ought to do it."

"It helped. But," Lacey laughs, "it turns out I went to high school with Rigo's wife." More rumbling laughter comes over the phone. "Like I always tell you, 'You got to be local.'" Before hanging up, Lacey asks me to come down to Washington ASAP.

****

On Friday we rendezvous at the department. It is a scene I know well. Avoiding Petersen, Lacey gets us alone with Paul Rigo, and we get to work.

Rigo has paid hundreds of thousands of dollars to the public officials of Newark. Some payments were made directly, such as those to Anthony LaMorte, the director of Public Works; to Philip Gordon, the city's corporation counsel; and to various members of the city council. Some of the payments, such as ones made to Mayor Addonizio, Rigo paid through Tony Boy Boiardo. Hand to hand. Other payments were funneled through Mario Gallo, who is one of the largest contractors in New Jersey. Rigo is prepared to lay it out in detail, beginning with his first major project, Newark's Southside Interceptor Sewer System. Best of all, Rigo kept diaries beginning in 1965, in which he made coded entries for each payment on the day the payment was made.

He says that he has hidden the diaries in his house. Normally, we would send bureau agents to retrieve the diaries. But we have no agents. Lacey immediately calls John O'Hara, chief of intelligence of the IRS in Newark, who sends a squad of agents to Rigo's house. We wait with Rigo for word from them. If the diaries are not there, Rigo is making a fool of us. But, if they are, we are sitting on dynamite. We can prove that the mafia controls Newark.

While we wait, Lacey tells me he is going to call Phillip Gordon, the corporation counsel of Newark, and invite him to meet us at Washington National Airport. Still fresh from private practice, Lacey has Gordon's phone number.

"Phil," he tells him as I listen, "something serious has come up about you here in Washington. I need you to meet me here tonight at the Eastern Airlines gate."

Although Lacey refuses to tell Gordon the reason for the request, by the end of the conversation Gordon agrees to come. Just before we leave for the airport, the IRS chief calls. When I grab the phone he tells me, "We found them, the diaries."

"Did you look inside them?"

"Yes. There are coded entries for names, with dollar amounts next to them."

Shortly after we arrive at the airport, we see Gordon walking slowly from the Eastern gate to where we stand waiting. "Phil. Thanks for coming," Lacey says. "Let's get a cup of coffee." Gordon, a smallish man, a little portly and balding, in his mid-fifties, looks up at Lacey and nods.

As we stroll over to the coffee shop, I wonder if Gordon knows what's coming. And, if he does, why he agreed to immediately fly down and meet us. If it were me, I would have stayed home and gotten a lawyer. After the coffee comes, I give Gordon his Miranda rights. I don't have to, because he is not under arrest. But I figure it can't hurt because he did not fly down to clam up.

Lacey puts it right to him. "Phil, Paul Rigo has charged that illegal payments were made by him to the mayor and others, and to you personally," Lacey pauses and stares at Gordon. "What about it?"

Gordon hangs his head. Then nods. "It's true," he mumbles.

"He says he gave you money for yourself and also cash to pass along to Judge Guillano, when he and you were both councilmen."

Gordon nods again, "Unfortunately, that's true too," he sighs.

"Where did you keep the money?" I break in.

"In a closet. In a bag on the back top shelf." There are tears rolling down his cheeks. "Every so often I would reach in and take some out. And then, one day, it was all gone."

"Mr. Gordon," I tell him, "you are going before the grand jury next week. You better go home and get a lawyer."

Lacey looks over at me. I can see he feels bad for the guy. Probably because he knows him. To me he is just a grafter. The fact that he is a lawyer, and Newark's top lawyer, just makes it worse in my eyes. As we leave the terminal, I tell Lacey, "We got Rigo. We got his diaries. We got Gordon. Let's move."

"What do you mean?"

"Let's subpoena Mayor Addonizio and every one of the Council members before the grand jury."

"For when?"

"Tuesday."

"This is Friday."

"Yes."

"Okay," Lacey says, "Let's go."

We have one small difficulty. Rigo's diary is in code. We do not know which payments go with which official. We do not even know the names of all the Newark Councilmen. I call Jack Bissell in the office. "Jack, subpoena Addonizio and the entire council before the Tuesday grand jury."

"What are their names and addresses? It's rather late on Friday. We may have to serve them on the weekend." Jack, a graduate of Exeter, says "rah-ther" instead of the way I say it.

"Christ, Jack, I don't know. Get a municipal directory and figure it out. Then give the names to the United States marshals. Then let them figure it out. And by the way, Jack," I add, "get a subpoena out for Judge DelMauro, chief judge of the city."

"Why?"

"We've got a tax case on him, so we might as well bag the lot of them. And while you are at it, get grand jury invites for Richie the Boot and Tony Boy Boiardo."

I wish I could add Anthony Little Pussy Russo to the invited list. But we have nothing on him. Yet.

Chapter Eight

"The Biggest Secret"
December 5–7, 1969

BEFORE WE LEAVE Washington on Saturday, we arrange to meet assistant AG Will Wilson. We simply cannot visit a tornado of subpoenas on every official in Newark without at least advising someone in the department. We don't pick Petersen.

When Wilson arrives early Saturday morning we are already standing before his locked office in the deserted building. Finding us in the corridor, he says, "I am going to show you the biggest secret in the department." With that he moves aside a portrait in the hall and reveals the key to his office taped to the wall.

We rapidly clear the decision to subpoena the mayor and the entire City Council. Before we leave I notice that Wilson has a telephone number taped to his phone with one word written: "Home."

As we leave Saturday morning, the marshals are fanning out to serve the subpoenas. Rigo, at his request, is in protective custody, and Lacey and I are at the airport waiting for the shuttle to Newark. I am trying to look ahead. Once we start putting all the top Newark officials before the grand jury next Tuesday, there is going to be a circus. Then there is the election between Gibson and Addonizio. We can't sit quietly. We know that whatever we do, we will be accused of interfering. If we indict, we should do so quickly. The problem is that we are at the very beginning of an investigation that will surely yield evidence of more payoffs. According to Rigo, lots of contractors paid the mayor through Tony Boy and two of his boys, Joseph Biancone and Ralph Vicaro. But we don't have that evidence yet. If we indict now, we can indict only on the Rigo payments. What do we do with whatever we uncover after the indictment?

I'm sitting in the Eastern Airlines waiting area that Saturday stewing over the problem. Lacey is reading the *Washington Post*. Then it comes to me. I begin to laugh. Lacey looks up, "What's so funny?"

"I know how to indict now, and find the additional evidence later."

"How?"

"We will indict alleging a conspiracy to extort money from everyone doing business within the city. With that charge, everything we pick up after the indictment would be covered by the indictment itself and introducible at trial without having to use some funky rules like the admissibility of similar crimes, which are discretionary with the trial judge."

"But isn't that dangerous?" Lacey asks. "Suppose the defendants call people who testify that they did work on Newark projects and did not pay?"

"Well, I'm betting that they won't, because they can't. It's our theory that the Lilley Commission was right. *Everything* at city hall is for sale."

After we land Fred goes off to meet with the Essex County prosecutor Joe Lordi, who has agreed to turn over his grand jury information on Rigo and Addonizio to us. He has also agreed that both assistant prosecutors, Merkelbach and Riccardelli, can join our staff as special AUSAs. Joe Lordi is the best.

Chapter Nine

"An Efficient and Effective Government"
December 7–17, 1969

B Y MONDAY AFTERNOON all the public officials have been served. We haven't found the Boiardos yet, but that is not an immediate concern. They would just take the Fifth. Tomorrow is Public Official Day. These men must either testify or refuse, and then go back to their public offices with their Fifth Amendment claims in public view. The Supreme Court has prohibited firing people from public office just for invoking the Fifth about their public duties, but let's see what the public has to say.

We meet to decide which one we should put in first. "We won't have time to do them all tomorrow," Lacey observes.

"I want to put Gordon in first," I say. "We have to get him on record before he changes his mind. His confession is vital to corroborate Rigo."

"I agree," Jon adds. "But after him, I say we go with Addonizio, and then Judge DelMauro. They'll both take the Fifth. Let's get the chief executive and the chief judge of the city out there saying the answers to questions about their official conduct will incriminate them."

On Tuesday morning the mayor and the entire city council of Newark troop into the grand jury waiting room. One of them remarks, "This is the first time the council has met on time in many years." I tap Gordon on the shoulder. He separates from the group and shuffles into the grand jury.

I confine his testimony to what he personally did with Rigo, without mentioning anyone else. I have learned my lesson from Colonial. I want to use his grand jury testimony at a multi-defendant trial. Gordon admits taking the money. "It was wrong legally, morally, any way you want to put it," he says. "It was wrong."

With that in the bag, I beckon Mayor Addonizio in next. Average of height, but substantially overweight and nearly totally bald, Addonizio carries himself with dignity. His lawyer has told him to refuse to answer any questions, even whether he is the mayor of Newark. He continues to refuse when Lacey and I bring him down to open court to test his invocation of the Fifth. The application has been assigned to Judge Shaw. His courtroom is packed with newsmen.

In open court, Lacey has all the questions read and Addonizio's invocation of the Fifth read by the grand jury reporter.

"Do you know Ruggerio Boiardo?"

"Do you know Anthony Boiardo?"

"Did you receive any money from Paul Rigo?"

To each question, the grand jury stenographer reads the same answer by the mayor, "I refuse to answer on the ground that my answer might tend to incriminate me."

Judge Shaw reserves decision on the propriety of the invocation, and schedules briefs and a hearing next week, on December 17. Fred and I exchange glances. We know that hearing will not take place. As Addonizio leaves the court, he is mobbed by reporters in the hall and then by the broadcast media on the street. To all he gives "no comment." Having finished taking the Fifth, Addonizio goes back to his office to continue his campaign for reelection as Mayor of New Jersey's largest city.

The same afternoon I put Chief Judge DelMauro into the grand jury, and when he claims to remember nothing about his finances, I push him. He is reluctant to take the Fifth. He testifies "no recollection" to all questions. Down he goes into Judge Shaw's third-floor courtroom.

Again the courtroom is packed with press. Again the questions and the refusal to answer because of "no recollection" are read aloud. Shaw again reserves decision, and Chief Judge DelMauro exits into the welcoming arms of the press.

Back into the grand jury I go to present Mario Gallo, head of a gigantic family construction business. He is represented by none other than Dino Bliablias, our old adversary in the Weber case. Gallo, too, invokes the Fifth Amendment but, while in the grand jury room, he breaks down in tears. Attempting to choke back his sobs, Gallo is barely able to invoke his rights. It looks promising, so we do not bring him into open court. And that is all that can be done in just one day. The other public officials will have to be rescheduled.

****

The investigation itself is barely under way. It has been less than one week since we met Rigo. The most important first step is to organize ourselves and to coordinate with prosecutor Joe Lordi. Lacey and Lordi agree to hold a joint press conference on Thursday, two days after the grand jury extravaganza. They will announce that Lordi is turning over all the information he has, including grand jury transcripts, and his two assistants, to our office.

Unfortunately, I can't attend. My job is to entertain Will Wilson, the assistant AG of the Criminal Division, who has flown up to lend his "expertise" to the fight. Lacey greets him, then turns Wilson over to me while Lacey goes off to meet with Lordi. My job is to keep Wilson busy and out of trouble. That turns out to be easy. Wilson has lots of ideas, which he shares with Jon Goldstein and me.

Sitting at Lacey's conference table, Wilson, who has failed to master the various Italian names, like Boiardo, Addonizio, Rigo, Guillano, DelMauro and, a key figure, LaMorte, the director of public works in Newark, gives us advice.

"First thing," he instructs us, "you got to turn this guy Lordi." I think he means LaMorte, but he has named our colleague Joe Lordi instead. I say nothing. Just nod and make a note. I try not to look at Goldstein who has turned to look out the window.

"Next," says our Washington leader, "when you are in the grand jury with witnesses, always conclude your questioning by asking, 'Is there anything that I did not ask you that I should have asked.'"

"Brilliant," I say, and make a note on my pad, which is blossoming with his nonsense.

Well, anyway, Jon and I keep him out of the way while Fred and Joe Lordi make their announcements. By the end of the day, Wilson has flown back to Washington, and we are free to work on the indictment. We have decided to indict in exactly one week.

That's less than two weeks after we first met Rigo, but we have no choice. On January 5, we start the DeCarlo trial. I need time to prepare. I can't believe that we have been in office only two months!

* * * * * * *

Rigo, the diaries, and me. There are sixty-five separate payments listed over several years of diary entries. Each in code. For example, Mayor Addonizio is "The Pope." Each of the 65 payments becomes a count in the indictment, each naming a recipient. Mayor Addonizio, Corporation Counsel Gordon, Public Works Director LaMorte, and six present or former members of the council will be charged. Count I names them all in a conspiracy, along with Tony Boy, and two of his henchmen, Joseph Biancone and Ralph Vicaro. In plain English, the city administration is accused of delivering the largest city in the state into the hands of organized criminals with the intent to wring tribute from everyone seeking to do business with the city.

We cannot indict without prior clearance from Washington. I send a draft down to Petersen's office. A day later I am summoned to defend it. Henry Petersen grills me. He has Bea Rosenberg, the legendary head of the appellate section, to help with the grilling. I spend the day in a chair answering questions about a case that is less than one week old. Henry is not happy, but, since Wilson is on board, we get permission to file.

December 17

Exactly two weeks after Lacey departed for Washington, the grand jury hands down the sixty-six-count indictment. A dozen public officials and organized criminals are indicted together. The motions on the Fifth Amendment invocations have become moot. The mayor himself is arraigned and immediately released on bail. As he walks from the courthouse back to city hall across the street, the press besieges him in a trailing mob. "Will business go as usual?" one reporter shouts at him. "We will continue with an efficient and effective governing of Newark," Addonizio responds.

****

December 17 is memorable for another reason. Bob Morgenthau, the United States Attorney for the Southern District of New York, a Kennedy appointee from back in 1961, has been hanging on to his position. He refuses to leave even though the administration changed a year ago with the election of Nixon. Using the cover of the announcement of our indictment of the mayor of Newark and the mafia in one conspiracy, Attorney General Mitchell has a letter hand-delivered to Morgenthau firing him. It's too bad. Morgenthau has been a great U.S. Attorney. On the other hand, it is true that he did leave the office within months of his appointment in 1961 to run for governor against Nelson Rockefeller. The Kennedys kept it open for him, reappointing him after he lost.

****

Lacey and I agree that I must turn away from the Addonizio case. DeCarlo is scheduled for trial in less than three weeks, and that includes Christmas and New Year's. "You get the case ready for trial," Lacey tells me. "You will present the witnesses, and I will open to the jury. We'll put Jack Bissell and Gary Brown and Jack Nulty (a holdover from Satz's days) on the Addonizio case with Lordi's guy, Merkelbach, and get whatever more we can before that case goes to trial in June, right after the mayoral elections in May."

"Tell the boys to subpoena all the financial records from the city on the Southside Interceptor Sewer System," I ask Lacey. "According to Rigo, that was the first job he paid on."

"Okay," Lacey agrees. "The subpoenas will go out by Wednesday."

"One more thing," I say. "Rigo says that the mob used a guy named Irving Kantor to wash the money on the job and deliver it to Tony Boy."

"We'll put men on him, too," Lacey assures me.

Chapter Ten

Gerald Martin Zelmanowitz
December 17, 1969–January 5, 1970

WHILE I IMMERSE myself in the DeCarlo trial preparation, Jack Bissell and Don Merkelbach and their team dig into the Southside Interceptor Sewer System project. I have no time to help them. I am putting the case against DeCarlo together—not just preparing the witness, Zelmanowitz, but also collating the Swiss bank records of Zelmanowitz's arbitrage activities on behalf of his "investors."

The Swiss bank records document an ugly story. Saperstein, already in debt to DeCarlo and paying $800 a week in vigorish, brought Zelmanowitz to DeCarlo and to DeCarlo's chief hench-man, Red Cecere. Zelmanowitz and Saperstein persuaded DeCarlo to invest $50,000 in an arbitrage account in Switzerland. When DeCarlo authorized the payment, Saperstein promptly took half the money, $25,000. He told Zelmanowitz he needed it for his vig payments, and so only $25,000 was deposited into the Swiss account. Saperstein and Zelmanowitz then persuaded DeCarlo and Cecere to "invest" another $100,000 in the Swiss bank account, bringing the total investment, according to what they reported to DeCarlo, to $150,000. Trouble was, Saperstein diverted $30,000 of the new deposit and put only $70,000 of DeCarlo's additional $100,000 into the account. DeCarlo, of course, thought that he had $150,000 in the account. But actually there was only $95,000. Zelmanowitz claims that every penny diverted by

Saperstein was kept by Saperstein. According to Zelmanowitz, he personally got nothing.

Nonetheless, using a criminal technique involving false tax equalization forms—which I have no hope of explaining to the jurors—within a matter of days Zelmanowitz turned a profit of $85,000 on the $95,000 in the account. That brought the account to an actual total of $180,000, although DeCarlo was told there was $235,000 in the account.

The trouble was that Saperstein, according to Zelmanowitz, diverted $40,000 of the $85,000 in profits to his own pocket. Again, according to Zelmanowitz, Zelmanowitz took nothing for himself. He allowed Saperstein to take it all on his plea that he needed it to pay vigorish to DeCarlo on the old loans. So instead of the $235,000 DeCarlo had been told, the account held only slightly over $140,000. Saperstein had pocketed the other $95,000. According to Zelmanowitz. It is clear that these two were busy ripping off some of the most dangerous people in the world.

The mobsters, not being completely stupid, soon enough demanded $200,000: their $150,000 original investment and $50,000 of the $85,000 profits. That was the way they saw the proper division of partnership profits. But not even Saperstein and Zelmanowitz could get $200,000 out of an account with only $140,000. Nonetheless, when Zelmanowitz and Saperstein arrived in Switzerland with Red Cecere, Zelmanowitz was able to persuade Cecere to limit the withdrawal to $130,000. And so Saperstein, and Zelmanowitz, were saved. For the moment.

By August the situation had deteriorated. DeCarlo called in all the loans. A desperate Saperstein told Zelmanowitz that DeCarlo had demanded repayment of $350,000 in outstanding loans and vigorish. Saperstein then begged Zelmanowitz for $80,000 to make vig payments and to buy time. Zelmanowitz refused. Saperstein went into hiding. And then Red Cecere leaned on Zelmanowitz to find Saperstein.

In a few days Zelmanowitz received a telephone call from Saperstein, who was hiding under an assumed name in a New York City hotel. Saperstein begged Zelmanowitz to meet him and bring funds on September 13. Zelmanowitz agreed. But instead he called

Cecere, and led Cecere and another thug to Saperstein. Saperstein, surprised when he saw them in the hotel lobby, tried to run, but he was taken from the hotel and brought to DeCarlo's headquarters, The Barn where, in Zelmanowitz's presence, he was beaten and threatened, just as described in Saperstein's letters to the FBI. Quite an ugly tale, told by a very ugly witness.

All in all, I conclude that Zelmanowitz, who has at least three federal and one state indictment against him, as well as a $1.7 million IRS lien is, shall we say, highly vulnerable. And this is a one-witness case. I am more than ever determined to use the Saperstein letters. I do not want to go to the jury on Zelmanowitz alone.

Chapter Eleven

Trials and Tapes
January 5–6, 1970

January 5

In office just four months, we assemble in Judge Robert Shaw's courtroom. The configuration is different from Judge Wortendyke's. In Shaw's, the judge enters through red curtains draped behind the bench, which suddenly part, and there he is, standing behind his judge's chair. Small in stature anywhere else, he looks formidable on the bench. And he is.

He picks the jury in a matter of hours. He alone does the questioning. When he is done, he informs the jurors that they will be sequestered, kept in a hotel as guests of the government, for the duration of the trial.

Sitting at counsel table with Lacey, I whisper, "Fred, he did not sequester them for no reason."

"I know," Lacey grins. "It's the tapes."

The next morning Fred is to open to the jury for us. I am then to begin calling witnesses. If I had my way, the first witness would be the mail clerk for the FBI, and the second would be Louis Saperstein, speaking through his letters. I want to use them before Zelmanowitz is cross-examined. They would protect his credibility, rather than redeem it after cross has crucified him. It's the same principle as the decision to call Giles before Harold Price in the Weber case.

But the judge has forbidden any mention of the letters until he has decided their admissibility. And, he tells us, he is not yet prepared to decide. As Lacey rises to open to the jurors, the judge specifically limits him. "As far as the Saperstein letters are concerned, I don't want any reference in the opening to them." With Judge Shaw, there is no argument. Only compliance.

Fred opens to the jury on our behalf, laying out our case, and weaving in the diversion of DeCarlo's money as best he can. He tries to lay out Zelmanowitz's criminal record, to draw the sting. The opening is short. Less than fifteen minutes. It is the best that can be done under the circumstances.

There are four lawyers opposing us. Mike Querques has relinquished three of the defendants and represents only Red Cecere. Nonetheless, he is lead counsel. Mike Direnzo, from New York City, has DeCarlo. Samuel Bozza has Joseph Polverino, and Milton Diamond represents Peter Landosco, two of DeCarlo's hoods who had pressured Saperstein. Querques gives the main opening for the defense.

Querques, turning from the jury, faces Lacey at our table. "He," says Querques, pointing at Fred, "is going to produce people here, and one in particular that I was not aware would be a witness until he said so categorically, and this is Mr. Zelmanowitz. He has already opened your eyes to some, but I trust not all of the makeup, of the mentality, the personality . . ."

"Your Honor—" Lacey rises to object.

"And the behavior—" Querques ignores him.

"Your Honor!" Lacey calls to Judge Shaw.

"The objection is overruled," Judge Shaw says curtly.

"—The behavior of Mr. Zelmanowitz. With respect to him, I am going to ask you to closely scrutinize this individual. Is his testimony given in the hope of reward for himself? It has already been said that he is a forger and a manipulator, he was a mover or transporter of something like a million dollars' worth of securities, and the word 'forgery' was used. It would seem unusual that a government would use a person who has already been blackened by his own foul doings. I think we have heard that it was Mr. Zelmanowitz who had entry into banks in Switzerland. What kind of individual is this Mr. Zelmanowitz? This is the question."

After Querques finishes flaying Zelmanowitz, and the others have had their turn, it is time for our first witness. Since it cannot be the dead voice from Saperstein's letter, it is Gerald Martin Zelmanowitz.

"Mr. Stern," Judge Shaw looks down at me, "I don't know what the arrangements are between you and Mr. Lacey. Was it your intention to conduct the interrogation of the witness?"

"Yes sir," I respond. "I have been instructed by Mr. Lacey to present the witnesses to the court on behalf of the United States."

I do not get far with Zelmanowitz before it is time for the lunch recess. With the jury out of the room, Judge Shaw announces that he has ordered the DeCarlo tapes filed in the clerk's office. "They are public records," Shaw announces. With that, the press benches empty in a rush. The press is racing to the clerk's office.

Querques is steaming. "That is not the motion we made," he insists. "We asked that only counsel be permitted to see them. We insisted that they not be made a matter of public record!"

"If you did not want it," the judge rejoins, "you should not have asked for it."

"If necessary," Querques responds, "I will withdraw the application. I think I have been taken advantage of. I made one application, and Your Honor ended up ruling a different way."

Judge Shaw reminds Querques that, "at the time of your oral argument, I told you that I would make the decision as to the manner in which they are to be released." Then, leaning over the bench, the judge says, "I have made the decision," the judge pauses, "and the decision stands."

Now all of the defense attorneys are jumping in with objections. "All right," Shaw notes, "you all join?" When they do, he denies their motions to withdraw the application to see the tapes as well. To give counsel the opportunity to study the DeCarlo tapes, the court is adjourned until the next day.

Chapter Twelve

A Beating and a Stipulation
January 7, 1970

BY THE MORNING, the front pages of every newspaper in the metropolitan area are filled with the DeCarlo transcripts. No newspaper gives greater coverage than *The New York Times*. And the papers are far from done. There has not been enough time or space in just one day for what they want to print. But already the state is rocking. There are also the reactions of the various persons named in the conversations. Not the mobsters, of course. But state and local politicians are stridently denying the references to them. And condemning the release of the tapes.

In the courtroom the defense attorneys repeatedly move for Judge Shaw's disqualification. They constantly accuse him of malice. The judge repeatedly denies their motions. The sequestered jury is totally unaware of the earthquake in the community around them, and the turmoil in the courtroom during their absence. They, however, have a bizarre world of their own to contemplate.

Zelmanowitz is back on the stand, and I take him through his life of cheating and crime: the stolen securities that he fenced for the Boston and New York mobs; his illegal arbitrage business that Saperstein used to attract DeCarlo; his trips to Europe with Saperstein to set up the arbitrage account; the systematic looting of that account by Saperstein, claiming to use the funds to pay DeCarlo vigorish on outstanding loans; and Saperstein complaining that these sums were still insufficient to get the mobsters off his back, begging Zelmanowitz for money. Zelmanowitz testifies that he loaned Saperstein $5,000 from his own funds, but it was not enough. "A very frightened Saperstein approached me. He said he had fallen behind, and the loans had come due. He told me that he was in debt for almost a quarter of a million dollars, and he asked me to lend him $80,000. I refused. He left in despair."

Saperstein went into hiding. Red Cecere called Zelmanowitz, hunting Saperstein. "He told me if I heard from Saperstein to make sure I got in touch with him. There was a large sum of money due, and he wanted to work it out."

A few days later Saperstein did call Zelmanowitz. Zelmanowitz immediately called Cecere. Together with one of Cecere's goons, they proceeded to the Hilton Hotel in New York.

When Saperstein saw Cecere and the other thug in the lobby with Zelmanowitz, he tried to run. But it was too late. He was caught.

"He was frightened," Zelmanowitz recounts. "He was in great fear for his family. Saperstein made the statement that he would take out a $100,000 life insurance policy, 'make you my beneficiary, and jump out of the window if you don't hurt my family.'"

Cecere calmed Saperstein down. They "'just wanted to talk,'" he told him. They would work it out. They left the hotel in two cars. Zelmanowitz, trailing behind, arrived late at DeCarlo's headquarters in New Jersey.

"What happened when you arrived?" I ask.

"When I got there Mr. Saperstein was laying on the floor," Zelmanowitz pauses as he remembers. "He was purple. He was bloody. His tongue was hanging out of his mouth. There was spit all over him. I thought he was dead, and . . ."

"Was anybody doing anything to Mr. Saperstein?"

"Yes," Zelmanowitz responds. "He was being kicked and punched."

"By whom?"

"By Mr. Polverino and Mr. Cecere."

"What happened when you entered the room?"

"Saperstein seemed to come awake, and he started to say things. He said, 'Stop hitting me.' He pleaded. He pointed to me and said, 'He is the cause of this. Hit him.' He was trying to get them away from him and on to me."

"Did the defendant Cecere and the defendant Polverino continue to hit and beat him?" I ask.

Zelmanowitz nods. "He was lifted up off the floor and placed into a chair, and in the chair he was hit again."

"What happened after he was hit while he was in the chair?"

"He was knocked off the chair, Mr. Stern, and picked up again and hit again. Mr. DeCarlo arrived." Zelmanowitz continues to a hushed courtroom, "Mr. Saperstein saw Mr. DeCarlo standing outside the room, and Mr. Cecere and Mr. Polverino went over to Mr. DeCarlo and tried to explain that Mr. Saperstein had said that he had no money and that he used the money, and Mr. Saperstein was running to Mr. DeCarlo and pleading with him to have them stop, and please don't hit him anymore, he was going to die if he was beaten anymore. He couldn't breathe."

"Were Mr. Cecere and Mr. Polverino asking Mr. DeCarlo for anything?" I inquire.

"Yes," Zelmanowitz nods again. "They wanted to kill him."

DeCarlo stopped the beating. Calmly he told Saperstein, "You will pay $5,000 per week every Thursday and pay all the monies that are due by December 13, or you will be dead."

When Zelmanowitz is finished on direct, the jury hears that on November 25 a distraught Louis Saperstein was admitted to the hospital. On November 26 he was dead. His death is stipulated to by the defendants. And with that the stage is set for Querques's cross-examination.

Chapter Thirteen

Trial Within and Without
January 8–28, 1970

A S NEWSPAPERS CONTINUE to publish excerpts from the tapes, the reaction in the community is enormous.

David Wilentz, denying that he ever met DeCarlo, calls the release of the tapes outrageous, pointing out that they were merely "hearsay conversations between organized criminals." And Governor Richard Hughes, with only a few days left in office, criticizes the "dissemination of gossip and character assassination by braggers and name-droppers." The one that gets me is *The New York Times*, which condemns the release of the tapes in an editorial: "The activities and names of various people mentioned makes interesting reading, but the method of disclosure hardly makes for good law."

"Those holier than thou boys in New York printed more of the tapes than even the New Jersey papers!" I say to Fred on the way to court. "If they condemn the release, they were under no obligation to print the contents!"

But Lacey just laughs. "If you ask them, they'll tell you that the news department is separate from the editorial page. Different functions, don't you see?"

"No," I say. "I don't."

Congressman John Rarick, a white supremacist from Louisiana, denounces Lacey and the release of the tapes. On the floor of the House of Representatives, he says, "Many dedicated public servants, after years of devoted service, were publicly smeared for no apparent reason." Lacey shows me the Rarick release and, with a ferocious glint in his eyes, points to the rest of the Rarick statement. It's about Fred's son, Fred Jr., who had worked on a civil rights project in Louisiana. Fred Jr.'s name had once been mentioned in a report of the Louisiana State Legislative Committee on "UnAmerican activities." That "committee" had branded Fred Jr. a communist because of his civil rights work. Rarick introduced that material into the Congressional Record. Then he called for Fred's resignation as U.S. Attorney, concluding that "Lacey is unfit to discharge his duties." Within a day, Essex County Sheriff Ralph D'Ambola, assisted by his deputies, is circulating reprints of Rarick's congressional speech on the streets of Newark.

There is little we can do in response. Fred issues a statement about his son, "a boy, now twenty-five-years old, whose ideals have led him to go to Louisiana where he lived with and helped educate young black children." And a furious Senator Case weighs in. "Rarick and his bunch," the senator publicly states, "have a meanness of spirit exceeded only by their stupidity."

****

Meanwhile, Judge Shaw comes under increasing attack by the defense.

Standing before the packed court, attorney Milton Diamond speaks for the defense. He holds the New York Times editorial in his hand. "I would like this marked for identification. It is an editorial of *The New York Times* dated January 8, 1970," Diamond flourishes the page. "I make an application that you disqualify yourself from proceeding in this matter on the ground that by releasing the tapes to the public you have indicated malice toward these defendants, that your action in doing that, which is better described by this editorial in *The New York Times*, your action in doing that was not a judicial action but a political action. I came prepared to defend my client on the law and the facts. I cannot protect my client from your personal malice nor from any of the political actions that you have taken in this matter."

Judge Shaw denies that motion and similar ones shotgunned at him daily by all the defense attorneys. Whatever else those motions achieve outside the courtroom, they cannot injure our case before the sequestered jury, which knows nothing of any of this. Querques's cross of Zelmanowitz is another thing. That is where they can beat us.

Chapter Fourteen

Confrontation, In Court and at the Bar
January 1970

ZELMANOWITZ IS TOUGH, but Querques is skillful and has plenty of ammunition.

First, there is a $375,000 grand larceny from a federally insured bank. "So in the summer of 1966 is when you committed the grand larceny?" Querques prompts Zelmanowitz.

"Correct, sir."

"And it was in the summer of '66 that you committed the forgery?"

. "Yes, sir."

"And this is long before you met Mr. Saperstein?"

"Yes, sir."

"And how many thefts and forgeries did you commit up to this day that you didn't get arrested for?" Querques points his finger at the unhappy witness.

"None," Zelmanowitz responds. "I got caught on everything."

I try not to look at the jurors on that last answer which, on the odds, is clearly bullshit. I figure I am going to have to straighten that out on redirect. But then Querques does it for himself.

"I am asking you whether there were any other frauds practiced by you on anybody else?"

"Yes, sir."

"All right. Does that get involved with that so-called one million in bonds stolen from the Boston bank?"

"That is correct."

"You got them all from a person?"

"From people, yes."

I rise to my feet. "Can we know the names of the people?" I ask. Zelmanowitz has constantly refused to tell us, so this is my chance to make him. But Shaw sits me right down.

Querques moves on to Zelmanowitz's Swiss bank transactions, demonstrating the "arbitrage" scheme to the jurors. "Is it true that this arbitrage was also illegal, involving the element of fraud?"

"Correct."

"It involves, does it not, the element of deception?"

"True."

"It involves, does it not, the element of dishonesty?"

"True."

"And all of the chicanery, all of the dishonesty, all of the fraud, and all of the deception is with respect to depriving the United States government of money due it from the sale of the securities?"

"That is correct."

"To the tune of exactly eighteen percent of the ultimate sale price of the security?"

"Correct, sir."

"So if you sold $10,000 worth of securities, Uncle Sam got clipped out of $1,800?"

"That is correct."

"And if it is a million dollars, Uncle Sam got clipped out of $180,000?"

"That is correct."

"How many millions would you say, by the time you met Saperstein?"

"I would say around six or seven million dollars."

"Six or seven million dollars," Querques pauses. "My arithmetic isn't that good, but Uncle Sam, I take it, got clipped out of over a half a million dollars?"

"Approximately," Zelmanowitz quickly agrees. Querques's math is as poor as he says it is. Eighteen percent of seven million dollars is actually $1,260,000.

Querques, in devastating questions, demonstrates that DeCarlo's money was stolen by Saperstein and, probably Zelmanowitz, too. He goes through each of the diversions. First, $25,000. Then $30,000. Then $40,000.

"Which means," Querques confronts Zelmanowitz, "that Saperstein took $95,000 over a period of approximately eighty days?" Zelmanowitz is forced to agree.

"And then you say . . . you loaned him $5,000?"

"That is correct."

Then, in an effort to show that Zelmanowitz is lying in claiming that he personally took none of the arbitrage money, Querques drills Zelmanowitz on his living conditions. Zelmanowitz's house, paid for in cash, was put in his father-in-law's name. The furnishings. The cars. The furs. All paid for in cash. By his father-in-law.

"Now, you were not working at the time?"

"Correct, sir."

"Are you going to tell me that the furnishings were paid for by your father-in-law?"

"No. I gave my father-in-law the money to purchase the house, all of my furnishings, the cars, my wife's jewelry, and my wife's furs."

"And Mr. Zelmanowitz, did you file a tax return in 1965?"

"I did, sir. A false return and a false return in 1967, and no return in 1968 and no return in 1969."

So much for the man who has been caught for every crime he committed. All of my concerns about this one-witness case, with Zelmanowitz the one witness, have been realized. I am watching the jurors. Querques is scoring. I turn to Fred and whisper, "I sure hope that Shaw will allow us to use the Saperstein letters."

At every break in the proceedings, Diamond, Landusco's lawyer, seizes opportunities to attack Judge Shaw. "Your Honor, if it should develop after this trial that these defendants are convicted, I really do not believe Your Honor, in light of his undisguised malice toward these defendants, can properly sentence them, because it demands that the judge who is sentencing must temper justice with mercy, and I do not believe Your Honor can possibly do that under the circumstances."

"Well," Judge Shaw calmly replies, "I have indicated earlier, I think on several occasions in this trial where the subject came up, that I did not think it appropriate for me to engage in back-and-forth argument with counsel."

It reaches the point that Diamond claims that his client, Landusco, is so upset by the release of the tapes that the two of them can no longer communicate. "Do you wish to have a physical and mental examination?" Shaw asks Diamond. Diamond says that he does.

The trial grinds to a halt. The designations of doctors for the defense and for the government take a long time. Their examination of Landusco takes more time. And the court presentations of their findings take yet even more time. Meanwhile, the jury remains sequestered.

Then Polverino becomes ill. He is hospitalized. Landusco is found to have uncontrolled diabetes. He needs immediate medical attention. The trial has been hopelessly derailed while the medical condition of the two defendants becomes the center of attention. Judge Shaw cannot hold the jurors in sequestration unless he can restart the trial. And given the extraordinary publicity about the tapes, he cannot relax the sequestration and permit the jurors to return to their communities. Reluctantly, he grants a severance and a mistrial to Polverino and Landusco. "In light of the fact that I have a sequestered jury, I can't recess indefinitely, nor can I take a man out of the hospital and force him to sit in the courtroom." With that, the trial restarts against DeCarlo and Cecere, which is a lot better than dumping the whole case until the two minor defendants are well enough to stand trial.

****

Near the end of the government's case, Judge Shaw rules that a portion of one of Saperstein's letters can be read to the jurors. He has edited out the references to specific sums of money demanded by DeCarlo. The letter is to be used only to prove Saperstein's state of mind and his fear of DeCarlo. The judge hands out and marks as Court Exhibit Six the version he will permit. Querques and Direnzo are vociferous in objecting. They are overruled.

****

At the close of our case, I stand before the jurors. They know that they are about to hear the letter from Saperstein. They have been told the limitations in its use. Nonetheless, eighteen sets of unmoving eyes are on me as I stand at the jury rail and slowly read Saperstein's plea for help. There is absolute silence in the courtroom.

When I finish reading, after one long look at each juror, I quietly return to our table. I glance over at Lacey and he gives a slight nod. We both know this trial is over. "But," I whisper, "God help us on the appeal."

There is little by way of defense. However, when Mrs. Saperstein is called by us to describe her husband's appearance after the beating, the defense cross-examines her by bringing out that several days before entering the hospital, Saperstein had overindulged in food and drink in a restaurant. We consider that an attempt to suggest he died of natural causes caused by gluttony. In response, we call the medical examiner who testifies that Saperstein died of an overdose of arsenic large enough to kill a mule. It is our theory that in his terrified state of mind, Saperstein committed suicide. We do not say so. We let the jury come to their own conclusion from the facts of the case.

Direnzo is to sum up for DeCarlo. Querques for Cecere. There are no surprises. Direnzo, silver-haired and conservatively dressed, attacks Zelmanowitz, just as we expect him to. "They," he points to DeCarlo and Cecere, "they were the victims. They were cheated. They were taken by Zelmanowitz." His voice raspy and little more than a whisper from a bout of the flu, he tells the jurors, "You're lucky you were sequestered. If not, he'd be selling you something." There is, of course, much truth in what Direnzo says.

Then Querques goes even further. "If Saperstein stole fifty-five thousand dollars from you . . . would you give him a punch? . . . certainly you would. The law calls that justifiable."

"There is no such law," Lacey bounds to his feet. "Objection," his voice reverberates in the crowded courtroom. Judge Shaw, with a glare at Querques, instructs the jury to ignore the claim of justification. Still, I think to myself, that is a problem in the case. Maybe they will agree that Saperstein deserved a beating. But I figure the letter about the threats to his family should carry the day.

Fred sums up quickly. He wisely ignores the defense summations. The letter is clear, and he reads it to the jurors again. He returns to his seat in less than half an hour.

Chapter Fifteen

The Don January 1970

THE NEXT DAY Judge Shaw charges the jury on the law. He has a surprise for us. At the conclusion of his charge, he passes out a pledge for each juror to sign, promising that the juror will only use the letter as evidence of Saperstein's state of mind, and not as proof that a beating took place, or any other fact alleged in the letter. Each juror signs. Fred whispers, "That man is a genius. Who ever heard of such an exchange between a judge and jury?" My mouth is still open as the jury retires to deliberate.

Lacey and I decide to wait around the courtroom rather than going up to our office on the fourth floor. Jon Goldstein is with us. So is Fred McMahon, the bureau agent on the case. We go into the hall so I can have a cigarette. Standing there, Fred says, "If we get a verdict, let's go out to dinner together."

"Where?" Jon asks.

"How about Mayfair Farms?" Lacey says. Mayfair is a pretty posh restaurant. We agree. Jon Goldstein leaves us to make a reservation.

In less than four hours the jurors are back. As they file into the room, we search their faces. Grim looks and averted eyes mean conviction. Smiles and glances at defendants portend acquittals. These jurors look solemn.

"Have you reached your verdict?" the courtroom deputy intones. "And who will speak for you?"

It's Juror Number One. He reads from his verdict sheet. With DeCarlo and Cecere and their lawyers standing before him, the foreman announces the verdict of guilty on all charges. None of them appear surprised, just resigned. I quickly move for revocation of bail.

I want them "inside." But the judge denies my application. He says he wants to see the pre-sentence report before ruling.

As we leave the courtroom, a photographer stops us and asks to take a picture. We cannot do it on the third floor, which houses the courtrooms. So we take him up to our fourth floor offices. In the elevator he tells us, "You know what they call you two?"

"No," Fred says.

"Batman and Robin."

Fred laughs. I don't. I'm not sure I want to be Robin. Anyway, the photographer kind of sets up the picture that way, and promises to send us a copy in a few days.

Fred, Jon, and I pile into Agent McMahon's car, bound for Mayfair Farms. As we enter, Jon, McMahon and I turn right to the men's room. Lacey heads to the bar on the left. When I emerge, I can't believe my eyes. The mafia don Sam the Plumber DeCavalcante has Fred Lacey backed up against the bar. DeCavalcante, silver-haired, elegantly dressed, but built like a former heavyweight boxer, is thrusting his finger in Fred's face, animatedly making a point.

"Holy shit," I say to Jon and McMahon, as we all run to the bar area. By the time we get there, DeCavalcante has faded away. In a moment, we can't even find him in the building.

"What was that?" Jon asks.

Fred shakes his head, and indicates he wants to wait until the agent, who is moving to the public telephones, is out of earshot. "Where were you guys?" Fred begins.

"In the can. What happened?" I repeat.

"He was telling me about one of my sons. How I have to be careful because young people can get into drugs."

"Fred Jr.?" I ask.

"No. Another boy."

"Fred," Jon says. "This is a threat. We should arrest and prosecute."

"No," Fred says. "If we do, it will look personal. I'd have to bring the charge as a witness. The office might be disqualified. We'll leave it alone. But it goes up in the locker room."

"Fred," Jon says, "you know the strike force indicted him three weeks ago. It's an interstate gambling charge."

"I know," Fred responds. "It's all up there in the locker room."

"Locker room or not," I say, "you and your family are going to get protected."

Chapter Sixteen

"Even the Nice People"
January 29–February 10, 1970

"**H**OW IN THE world did the son of a bitch know we were going to be there?" I ask McMahon.

The agent, built like a fireplug, filling a chair in my office, has no answer. He is furious, too.

"Fred," I tell him, "we did not know ourselves where we were going to dinner until maybe three hours before we got there."

"I know," McMahon says, "I was there."

"How did he do it?"

"One of two possible ways," the agent replies. "Either someone overheard us in the hall outside the courtroom, or someone in the restaurant tipped him when the reservation came."

"What did you guys learn when you interviewed the staff?"

"Nothing, except for the car jockey. When DeCavalcante arrived, he was driving a big white Cadillac. As he gave it to the kid, he said, 'If you scratch this, I'll cut your fucking head off.'"

"Can't we . . ."

"No, we can't. The kid says the Plumber was smiling, and gave him a big tip."

****

The Addonizio case has been scheduled for June 2, which is three weeks after the May municipal elections. I cannot believe that Addonizio will still be the mayor once the trial starts, not with "Hughie gave us the city" on the DeCarlo tapes, or him taking the Fifth Amendment in open court, and finally our indictment charging him in a conspiracy with Tony Boy Boiardo. I am confident that when the trial starts young Ken Gibson will be in city hall.

The new AUSAs, Jack Bissell and Gary Brown, combined with Merkelbach from Lordi's office, and Satz's holdover, Jack Nulty have made amazing progress putting the Addonizio case together. By far, the most important find was Irving Kantor, the proprietor of Kantor Plumbing Supply.

While Lacey and I were preparing for DeCarlo's trial, our men subpoenaed Newark's financial records on the Southside Interceptor Sewer System job. They discovered that the city paid nearly ten million dollars to the prime contractor, C. Salvatore & Sons. Salvatore, using subcontractors, funneled $911,000 in checks to a company called "Kantor Supply." The largest contributors to Kantor Supply were companies controlled by Mario Gallo, the man who had sobbed in the grand jury. Under indictment with the others since December 17, Gallo had fought our subpoenas seeking his company records. He lost on December 23. By the time we opened in DeCarlo, our colleagues had Gallo's records and $911,000 in canceled checks to Kantor Supply.

Subpoenaing the bank records of Kantor Supply, our guys found that, after depositing $911,000 in checks, the $911,000 had been withdrawn in cash by a Mr. Irving Kantor. Check in. Cash out. These were staggering sums in 1964 for just one construction project. And these were in addition to direct payments on the same project made by Rigo in the amount of $253,000, without the use of the Kantor Supply account. Our men then quickly established that "Kantor Supply" was a fictitious company, nothing but a bank account opened by one Irving Kantor, whose real company was Kantor Plumbing Supply.

****

With the DeCarlo trial finished, Lacey brings the team together to catch up on the City of Newark case.

"Tell us about Irving Kantor," Lacey asks Jack Bissell.

"Unfortunately, he is dying. He has amyotrophic lateral sclerosis, 'Lou Gehrig's disease,'" Jack tells us.

"Where is he?" I ask.

"Veteran's Hospital in East Orange," Jack replies. "Nulty and I have been visiting with him several times a week."

"What stage is he at?" Lacey says softly.

"It is tough," Jack replies. "He is bedridden. He can't move his limbs. He is hooked up to machines for food and waste elimination. And," Jack says meaningfully, "his speech is bad. We have trouble understanding him sometimes. We often ask his wife Jane what he said. She is with him every day, all day. She understands him when we can't."

"What can he give us?" Jon asks.

"He can identify the checks that came in, the cash that came out, and," Bissell smiles, "he puts the money directly into Tony Boy's man, Joe Biancone."

Kantor, only fifty years old, knows that he is dying. There is nothing our office can threaten him with. Nor is there any need to. He is ashamed of what he did. Irving Kantor wants to make amends. Although he is helpless in his hospital bed, he is willing to testify. We have kept his identity secret, so far. Even so, we keep United States marshals outside his hospital room, twenty-four hours a day. I have no doubt that the mob would kill him if they knew he was cooperating.

****

As soon as I can, I have Bissell take me to the East Orange Veteran's Hospital to see Irving Kantor.

The sight of the bedridden man is pitiful. His body is shrunken, his face almost obscured by his heavy black horn-rimmed glasses. His wife Jane is seated next to his bed. The purpose of this first visit is simply to thank him.

"I want to help my country," he squeezes the words out of his throat. "I did a bad thing." Each word is an effort. "I took five percent to cash the checks."

"It's all right," I try to soothe him. "You are doing the right thing now."

"I am a veteran, you know," he rasps out. "World War II . . . I want to help my country . . ." I can see his eyes are wet, so I stop him. "I know you do, and you will."

I look over at Jane Kantor, an attractive woman, still in her forties. I think the woman must be a saint. Sitting there, ministering to him all day, day after day. It is a hard scene. I know I will have to be back to prepare Irving to testify. I am not looking forward to it. As I leave I ask Bissell to spend as much time as possible with Kantor, going over the checks that were deposited and the cash withdrawals. "He will have to identify the pieces of paper when he testifies, that is, if he lives to testify," I say. Jack knows that I am referring to the trial, which, close as it is, may be too far into the future for Kantor.

* * * * * * *

It is fine for Bissell to prepare Kantor initially, but I am the only one who is going to prepare Rigo. He has years of diaries to go over and scores of canceled checks used to raise cash to identify. I remember what I learned watching Vince Dermody and Jack Keenan in my DA days. This is a job I must do myself. These sessions with Rigo will have to begin very soon. The days are becoming crowded. We have the DeCarlo sentencing, the Addonizio pretrial motions, and the continuing efforts to find witnesses, all ahead of us. But all that is pushed aside when I get a call from Dino Bliablias, who needs to see me immediately, or so he says. I figure it must be about his new client, Mario Gallo, not Pete Weber, whose case is in the appellate process, after Judge Wortendyke pronounced a ten-year sentence. Jon and I are responding to Weber's brief on appeal. In our spare time.

I cancel an appearance at the induction of our newest district judge, Leonard I. Garth, scheduled for Friday afternoon, and see Dino instead. As with my adversaries in Colonial, my relations with Bliablias and Hayden are most cordial. We spend time reminiscing. Then he gets down to business. "My partner, Jerry Stein, and I want to meet with you and Lacey. Mario Gallo is interested in cooperating in return for immunity."

I want to jump up and down. With Gallo added to Rigo and Kantor, the City of Newark case is made. Whatever else we come up with will just be gravy. And that's the least of it. Gallo is one of the biggest construction suppliers in the state. He has enough information to lock up grafting politicians from North to South Jersey. "All right," I tell Dino, trying to sound calm. "We will need to meet Gallo and take a proffer from him personally, to see what he has."

He smiles, knowing full well what this means to us. We agree to meet in a suite in the Americana Hotel on the evening of February 9. It has to be New York, Dino tells me. Gallo is terrified to meet us in New Jersey. As soon as Dino Bliablias is out the door, I am walking through Lacey's. We can't believe our luck.

Early on the evening of the ninth, Lacey and I drive over to New York together. In spite of the sleet and snow, we are like kids on our way to a candy store. When we get to the suite, we find Bliablias, his partner Stein, and Mario Gallo. It has been just six weeks since I put Gallo into the grand jury. He has lost weight. His complexion is sallow. Only forty-four years old, he looks more than sixty.

The purpose of the meeting is for Lacey to set the ground rules. He tells Gallo that he expects him to come clean about pay-offs throughout the state, not just Newark. I can see this hits Gallo hard. Obviously, he had hoped to get out of the Newark indictment by being a witness in the Newark case, not opening new cases against people throughout New Jersey. Gallo blanches, but Lacey is insistent. It must be everyone.

"You mean even the nice people?" Gallo mumbles.

"Well," Fred says, "maybe not the nice people."

"But what if you and I don't agree as to who is nice?" Gallo asks.

A great question, I say to myself. How will Lacey get out of this? Lacey smiles at Gallo, "If you and I don't agree on who the nice people are," Lacey pauses, "you think of your kids."

What does that mean? I say to myself. It makes no sense. But apparently it does to Gallo, who nods his head and says, "Okay."

We agree to start meeting within a few days. In a half an hour, Gallo and his entourage leave. After we break, Lacey and I go downstairs and have a drink to celebrate. We are reluctant to leave each other; the moment is too delicious.

"The weather is lousy," Lacey says. "I think I'll stay at the New York Athletic Club rather than drive back to New Jersey. My membership still has a few months to go." I have no problem getting a cab to my apartment on lower Fifth Avenue.

****

On Tuesday morning I follow my routine. PATH train into Newark, then do my walk to the Post Office Courthouse and report to my office. As I walk in Jon Goldstein, the only other person aware of last night's meeting, grabs me. "Herb, did you hear? . . . Mario Gallo is dead."

"What!"

"Yes. He died in an automobile accident on the way home."

When Lacey walks in, he is almost in a depression. "I can't believe it," he says. "I woke up this morning on top of the world. But then I hit the train station and saw the headline on the newsstands. . . . I can't believe it." Shaking his head, he enters his office, leaving Jon and me standing, looking at each other.

"I've never seen him so down," Jon says.

"He has a right to be. With Gallo gone and Kantor maybe dead before trial, we may have nothing but Rigo. You know, Jon, if we lose this case, you and I will just saunter over to New York, where we were headed anyway. But what about him?" I nod over towards Lacey's closed door. "He is a leading member of the bar here. If we lose this case, they'll run him out of town, whether Addonizio wins or loses the election, maybe with tar and feathers if Addonizio beats Gibson *and* we lose in court."

Chapter Seventeen

"A Frame Up All the Way"
February 10–March 5, 1970

WHETHER OR NOT it was a good idea to release the tapes, there is no time for looking back. Lacey, Goldstein, and I hit the speaking circuit to defend Judge Shaw's decision. I get the invitations to speak to Jewish organizations. I am to be at the Hillside B'nai B'rith on February 16 and the North Valley Lodge Chapter on February 26. Or I will be if I can find these places. I don't know how many people will come out to hear me. But it doesn't matter. I have learned that the size of the audience is not as important as handing out a prepared text to the newspapers. A speech attended by twenty people reaches thousands, if the press reports it.

As I prepare my talks, the investigation into Gallo's death is completed. The autopsy of Gallo's body and the examination of his automobile satisfy the bureau that Gallo died in an accident. His car slid on the highway and hit an embankment so forcefully that his "heart was torn loose due to impact," the autopsy noted.

In my talks, I tell my audience that the criticisms of Judge Shaw are "entirely erroneous." I tell them that the tapes are not "idle boasting of mobsters who did nothing but gossip. . . . These were the actual business meetings of the mafia. . . . There may be some innocent people who were maligned, but the vast majority of the conversations is accurate." I quote Red Cecere and DeCarlo discussing how they beat up a Jewish debtor behind in his payments.

"DeCarlo says, 'I hit him a slap on the face. He cried like a baby.' Then DeCarlo added, 'The yellow Jew —they're all yellow!'" Then I tell the audience, "His buddy Cecere was quick to agree. 'All alike— all alike.' DeCarlo then summarized the discussion as follows, 'There's about three good Jews in the whole world.'"

All in all, my talks go over very well with these particular audiences, who don't seem at all upset by deprivations of DeCarlo's constitutional right to privacy. But there are others who are upset, such as the ACLU, for example. The executive director of the American Civil Libertics Union writes Lacey to demand that we prosecute the agents who broke into DeCarlo's premises and installed the illegal bugs.

Could they be prosecuted? It's an academic question. We have no such intention, just as I would not take the baby from the woman who, in the grand jury, admitted to buying it on the black market; or prosecute cops for failing to enforce blue laws against Uncle Benny; or prosecute a husband and a wife under criminal adultery statutes or sodomy laws. I'd like to think that, a hundred years ago, I would have refused to enforce the fugitive slave laws. I would and did report a lying cop in a penny ante narcotics case. I would, and tried to, indict a cop for a needless shooting. But I will not prosecute men who committed minor burglaries in the belief that they were protecting their country. What was it that Wortendyke said about a man satisfying his own conscience? Sure, there are inconsistencies in this; and sure, discretion in prosecutions threatens the "rule of law." But, as Mr. Justice Jackson noted, our law and our Constitution unleavened by "a little practical wisdom" becomes a "suicide pact." Anyone who expects prosecutors to act as automatons, is just not in this or any possible world. Am I happy with all this? No. But I'm doing the very best that I can.

****

Our new offices on the fifth floor of the federal office building across the street are nearing completion. They better be. We have half a dozen new AUSAs coming on, and they are already doubling up in the old offices.

****

Judge Shaw has called the DeCarlo sentencing for March 4. I have to get ready. After which, twelve days later the Addonizio pretrial motions are to be argued before Judge Barlow in Trenton. Gary Brown has been in charge of our briefs, with Jack Bissell assisting, when Jack can break away from Irving Kantor's hospital room. We have three days reserved for argument. Most important, we need to confirm an early trial date, while we still have Kantor available. The thing now is to get ready for DeCarlo's sentencing, just next week.

****

March 4

I have to push my way through the crowd of reporters to get to the well of the court. DeCarlo and Cecere are already there. They did not run. I aim to make sure they can't. I will make another attempt at revoking their bail after their sentencing.

We all rise as Judge Shaw steps through the red curtain behind his bench. Once seated, the judge calls for the sentencing.

"These men, for all of their mature lives, took part in an organized criminal conspiracy against their government and their fellow citizens," I tell Shaw. I ask for jail and revocation of bail. Then the judge speaks the last words. "I think it is clear that these defendants are engaged in an organized criminal conspiracy, whether you call it La Cosa Nostra, the mafia, or the Black Hand, it exists." He pronounces a twelve-year sentence on each defendant and then immediately revokes bail. The moment he finishes, the marshals quickly move in and handcuff both men. They lead them out of the courthouse, into the street. As DeCarlo is placed into a marshal's car, he shouts at the press, "It was a frame-up from the beginning. You know it was, and I know it was. It was a frame-up all the way!"

Chapter Eighteen

"We'll All Have to Stay Home"
March 4–May 12, 1970

As DeCarlo and Cecere begin their journey to federal prison, I leave the third floor courtroom to appear before the grand jury down the hall from our offices on the fourth floor.

Our deal with Zelmanowitz had been that he could confine his cooperating to the Saperstein extortion. He had refused to reveal the names of his co-conspirators in the fencing of securities stolen from Boston banks.

On the stand Zelmanowitz, cross-examined by Querques, had been forced to reveal the names of his confederates. I sat there rubbing my hands. A few weeks later, I put Zelmanowitz into the grand jury, and today I am asking the jurors to indict "Fat Tony" Salerno, a capo mobster in New York. He is even more important than either Boiardo, father or son, or even DeCarlo.

Zelmanowitz, however, is a problem. He has to be relocated and given a change of identity, and not just him, but his whole family, including wife, daughter, and in-laws. And nothing the department offers to do for him is good enough. Thankfully, Justice has set up an office to handle these relocations. I am not involved, or even allowed to know Zelmanowitz's new name. Unfortunately, whenever he is dissatisfied, he reaches out for me. It's like having to pay a big check at the end of a meal. It may be worth it, but it's not fun. And this check keeps coming.

****

I am consumed with preparing responses to the Addonizio pretrial motions. Thirteen defendants, represented by numerous attorneys, produce a lot of paper. Gary Brown and Jack Bissell have worked on our written responses. Now we are set for oral argument in Trenton. Judge Barlow has set aside four full days to hear us, March 16 through 19.

****

We have been interviewing and hiring new assistants. That's evening work. There is no time for administration during the day. One of the new ones, Donald J. Williamson, is no kid. He has been in the antitrust division in Washington and comes to us from a big New York law firm. Best of all, John Barry has come on board. Fred, Jon, and I regard him as the best lawyer in the place. We are up to almost twenty-five AUSAs once everyone clears their FBI background checks.

****

In the middle of my preparation for the Addonizio motions, Lacey wanders into my office. "Let's chat," he says, as he seats himself in the only guest chair I have. I don't want to, but I see he isn't taking any no's.

"Now that we are getting some people in, I want to talk about our next project."

I can't believe it. We just finished DeCarlo, we are about to try Addonizio and Tony Boy, and he wants to put more on our plates. We have only been on the job six months.

"Fred," I say, "please leave me alone. If I don't get the arguments prepared, Barlow may dismiss the case. Then we will be out of business, instead of new business." Because I can't resist, I add, "What do you have in mind?"

"Hudson County," he says. "Jersey City, Hoboken, West New York, Bayonne . . ."

"Fred," I say, "please get out of my office. I have work to do."

****

For four days we argue motions, including motions by Bernard Hellring, the mayor's lawyer, to move the trial from Trenton to Newark. He wants "the people of Newark" to judge the case, where "the bad publicity is at least coupled with the good the mayor has done." The three mafia hoods, Boiardo, Biancone, and Vicaro, are represented by three former partners of Edward Bennett Williams—Tom Wadden, Tom Dyson, and Pat Wall, respectively.

Motion after motion. Response after response. By the fourth day I feel, in all fairness, as we say, that I should let one of the younger men on our team handle one of the arguments. So I tell Bissell to argue against the defendants' motion to be severed from each other, and I tell him, "Jack, when you are up there, see if you can sow a little dissension in their ranks." And what do I get in return? The ever-proper Jack Bissell whispers back in my ear, "You're a horse's ass." The way he speaks it comes out "ah-ses."

Well, horse's ass or not, we win the motions. Judge Barlow confirms the trial date for June 2, after the May 12 elections, and the trial will be held in Trenton.

****

The mayoral election gathers steam and gets ugly. The Addonizio crowd is pulling out the race card at every opportunity. They are attempting to scare the white population. Dominick Spina, the mob's handpicked police director, issues statements fanning white voters' fear of the election of a black mayor. As the *Newark News* reports, "Spina predicts an increase in the crime rate if Gibson is elected."

The New York Times reports, "An elderly Italian shoe repairman remarked, 'With Addonizio, we can't go out at night. With Gibson, you won't be able to during the day. We'll all have to stay home.'" I am becoming concerned that this city could be pushed into another riot, this time by the white population.

Between monitoring the election, interviewing our new "victims," and preparing Rigo and Kantor, there is no time for anything else. But that does not impress Fred Lacey, who still wants to talk about opening an investigation into Hudson County.

****

As the election nears Fred calls Jon and me into his office. I know what he wants—Hudson County—so I try to divert him. "Did you see the press? The white areas of Newark are getting into a frenzy. This could get out of hand if Addonizio loses, and worse if he wins."

"It will be all right," Fred replies. "Gibson will be elected and things will calm down." Then, with a knowing smile, he asks, "Have you thought about Hudson County?" Yes, of course I had. Hudson County is almost certainly the most corrupt urban area in the entire country. And has been for over sixty years. Boss Frank "I am the Law" Hague ruled Hudson County as mayor of Jersey City from 1917 until 1949. No public employee worked in Jersey City, Bayonne, West New York, Weehawken, or Hoboken who did not pay tribute. The civil service was dominated by the "Democratic" machine. Public employees kicked back three percent of their salaries. Labor leaders were run out of town. Presidents, including Franklin Delano Roosevelt, paid homage to Hague. By the time of his death in 1956, Frank Hague, whose salary never exceeded $7,500 per year, left an estate of over $8,000,000.

The Hague machine ended when Boss John V. Kenny kicked out Hague in 1949. The Boss changed, but nothing else did. The payoffs and the kickbacks continued unabated.

Unlike Newark, where the mob controls the administration, in Hudson County the pols control the mob. They coined a phrase for it in Jersey City: "A way of life."

"Fred," I tell Lacey, "We don't know a thing about who pays who in that place. It's not like Newark, where at least we had a place to start with Rigo. We have nothing in Jersey City."

"What do you propose?" Lacey asks, as though I hadn't just said that we couldn't do it.

Here we go again, I say to myself. But I have thought of a plan.

"We can do what we did in Colonial. We start with a target. Jersey City. We know everybody pays, right? So we subpoena the records of everyone who did big work for the city or the county. Then we look for cash coming out of those businesses. Then we make the businessmen tell us what they did with the money. Simple."

"But," Jon says, "We don't know who did what work on which project."

"Right," says Lacey, as he slaps a big hand on the table. "So first we subpoena the records from the city and the county to see who got the jobs. Then we get the contractors' records, right?" says Lacey, looking at me.

"Right," I say, with a resigned shake of my head.

"Great," Lacey gets up. "We'll put Don Williamson and John Barry on it right away. The subpoenas go out this week."

Chapter Nineteen

"The Kind of Thing Americans Don't Like"
May 12–June 1, 1970

May 13

On the morning after the May 12 election, I go to Jon's office, still stunned by the result. Gibson got forty percent of the vote—no majority. The other half dozen candidates, all of whom are white, received the remaining sixty percent, with Addonizio the leader at twenty percent. That means there will be a runoff election between Gibson and Addonizio.

"Jon," I say, "you know what this means?"

"Yes, I do," Jon looks upset. "If all the votes against Gibson are added to Addonizio's, Addonizio wins."

"You think all the non-Gibson votes will go to Addonizio?"

"God only knows," says Jon.

****

The runoff election has been set for June 16. That will be smack in the middle of the trial, which is set to start June 2. Addonizio's lawyers immediately move to delay the trial to after the June 16 election. We will oppose.

"What will you argue?" Fred asks me.

"Irving Kantor," I respond. "A two-week delay before we even begin picking jurors may be too much for Irving. He seems to be barely hanging on as it is."

May 21

We are back before Judge Barlow. The quiet and composed jurist has a storm breaking before him. Bernard Hellring, short and round, with white hair and pink skin, attacks us with a vigor that belies his Santa Claus appearance. "This man," Hellring points to Addonizio sitting stoically beside him, the mayor, "is fighting for his life in this election as well as in this case." Turning to the press rows, Hellring continues, "Holding the trial before the election strikes a low blow. It's the kind of thing Americans don't like."

"Your Honor," I say when it is my turn, "a two-week delay might not only prejudice the government's case, but could very well decimate it." I ask for a private hearing to explain why, and Judge Barlow grants it. After hearing about Kantor in the sealed record, the judge denies Hellring's motion. "Even a short delay could have an extremely prejudicial effect on the prosecution," he rules.

****

Both sides of the case go into overdrive. Addonizio appeals for delay to the Third Circuit Court of Appeals. Denied. He seeks a stay before Mr. Justice Brennan of the Supreme Court. Denied. He appeals to the entire Supreme Court. Denied 7-0, with Justices Hugo Black and Thurgood Marshall not participating.

****

Our trial team moves lock, stock, and barrel, to our office in Trenton, and we get rooms at the Holiday Inn, a mile from the courthouse. We will live there until the case is done. From our offices and rooms, we follow the election campaign reported in the press and the media.

The Newark Patrolmen's Benevolent Association endorses Addonizio for his "high degree of dedication to the police and the citizens of Newark." On June 1, *The New York Times* reports:

> John P. Caufield, the white former Fire Director who ran fourth on May 12, is campaigning hard for Mr. Gibson, even though it caused him to be spat upon and manhandled by a gang of hostile white youths at a campaign stop with Mr. Gibson last Wednesday night.

June 1

The day before the start of the trial, fifty of Addonizio's supporters, mostly Newark patrolmen, demonstrate outside the federal courthouse in Newark. According to The *Star-Ledger* report of June 2, the demonstrators wanted "Chief Federal Judge Augelli to accept a petition for delay of the trial, which they said contained 15,000 signatures. The demonstration was led by the Women's Organization for Restoring Law and Decency (WORLD). Most of the marchers were men."

I call Jon Goldstein back in the Newark office. "What is going on back there?"

"It's crazy. The streets are getting tense. This white-black thing could blow. Oh, by the way, we sent out the first wave of subpoenas to Jersey City and Hudson County for all bidding records for the past five years."

"Wonderful," I say.

"We expect to start receiving documents in a few days. Then we will go after the records of the successful bidders."

"Great."

"We have a team of IRS agents all lined up to . . ."

"Wonderful," I stop him. "You, Williamson, and Barry handle it. I have my hands full right here."

Chapter Twenty

"A Reign of Terror—Like the French Revolution" June 2–9, 1970

KANTOR WILL BE our lead witness. It's not because of what we had told Barlow to defeat delay. We will call Kantor and a number of others who paid off before we call our main witness, Paul Rigo. It's the old lesson again. We must make it harder to cross-examine Rigo before he takes the stand, rather than bringing up reinforcements to resuscitate him. But first we have to get a jury.

The street outside the Trenton courthouse is mobbed with press that has been waiting for hours. We are down to seven defendants. Death, illness, and unavailability of counsel engaged in other trials have slimmed the field. Prosecutors, defendants, and defense attorneys struggle to get into the building. As he pushes his way through, Addonizio says to the encircling press, "It is unbelievable that they could not delay the trial for two weeks in fairness to me and the people of Newark."

Judge Barlow has assembled a large panel of prospective jurors. They know that they will be sequestered if selected, and that the trial will take weeks. Fred and I sit at the table as they are called into the box, and one by one questioned by the judge. As he did in DeCarlo, Fred will open to the jury and then sum up at the end of the case. I will put on all the witnesses and cross-examine defense witnesses, except for Addonizio himself, and I will select the jurors. It is my fourth major trial in eighteen months. I have gotten all the trial work I could wish for—and then some.

The defendants have fourteen challenges. We have six. They use all fourteen, seven of them to eliminate the only seven black potential jurors called into the box. We do not use a single challenge, up to the point that an accountant with an Italian-sounding name, Forcillo, is seated.

"Fred," I whisper, "I don't go for this ethnic crap. I want to keep him."

"Agreed," Lacey whispers back.

At the end of several days of jury picking, our six challenges remain unused.

****

Fred presents a powerful opening to the jurors. Looking down on the jury box from his imposing height, his bass voice reminiscent of a radio announcer, Lacey outlines the defendant's scheme to exact tribute from all who work on Newark's projects. He describes the phony Kantor bank account, set up by Joe Biancone on orders from his boss, Tony Boy Boiardo, to turn the contractors' checks into cash for the mob and the politicians. The use of Rigo on city projects not only to obtain kickbacks on his work, but also to collect kickbacks from any subcontractors, such as $100,000 from Verona Construction; Mario Gallo, who paid $300,000; Lock Joint, who kicked back $35,000 on the next project. Lacey identifies seven contractors who paid. The jurors do not know that we "broke" all seven after the indictment. In less than an hour Lacey presents a devastating picture of a graft-ridden city delivered by the mayor into the grip of organized crime. But he cannot ignore the major problem in our case. He knows he must prepare the jurors for Rigo's personal venality, his yacht and helicopter. "You may not approve of the way he lived, but we will show you he is telling the truth," he tells them.

When he finishes, Hellring addresses the jury. He tries to bring the riot by the black population into the courtroom. "The riot is the beginning of this case; the investigation was designed to find a scapegoat."

"I object," I speak from my table.

"Come to the sidebar," the judge summons us.

"Your Honor," I appeal to Judge Barlow, "Mr. Hellring's remarks are a blatant appeal to racial prejudice."

"The indictment was returned in the atmosphere of the DeCavalcante and DeCarlo tapes," Hellring responds. "There was a reign of terror in the federal building in Newark like the French Revolution."

"It is no defense to the charges," Barlow shakes his head. "Objection sustained." Hellring decides to reserve his opening and sits down. The moment has come to reveal our first witness, and where he is. Standing before the packed courtroom, I announce "Irving Kantor," and then ask to move the trial to Kantor's hospital to hear the testimony from the paralyzed witness. It is the first the defendants have heard that Kantor is our witness. Their lawyers explode.

Wadden, Boiardo's lawyer, with his large hands outstretched, shouts, "It's unfair to cross-examine a basket case." Phil Gordon's attorney adds, "If I have to shake the basket case, I'll do it. But it won't be nice."

"A United States marshal will be on hand to protect the witness," I shout back.

"Nobody is going to shake a witness in this court," Judge Barlow says calmly, granting my motion to move the trial. On that we adjourn for the weekend.

****

On Monday the trial will convene at the Veteran's Hospital in East Orange to hear Irving Kantor. Unfortunately, Kantor's degeneration has reached the point that he simply cannot be understood by the nearly forty people who comprise the well of the court—jurors, alternates, defendants, their counsel, and us.

"What are we going to do?" Lacey asks Bissell and me, after court.

"We can ask for the judge to swear Jane Kantor in as Irving's interpreter. She has been doing it for us for months."

"Have you ever heard of anything like that?" Lacey turns to Bissell.

"No. I can't say that I have."

"Fred," I say, "if the man spoke Greek, we could use a Greek interpreter. The man has his own communication system. That's all."

"Sounds wild."

"I know. But if we lose the motion, we lose Kantor. And if we lose Kantor, we maybe lose . . ."

"I know, I know," says Fred.

Chapter Twenty-One

Hero and Heroine
June 8–16, 1970

THE WEEKEND HAS been wild. On Saturday, the *New York Daily News*, referring to Lacey's blistering opening, has its whole front page in block letters: CALLS ADDONIZIO MAFIA BAGMAN.

The *Newark News* reports, "the campaign has been high-pitched, with obvious appeals to racial fears and prejudices." Addonizio, standing on street corners with a bullhorn, proclaims, "Gibson has rejected whites when he accepted the nomination of the Black and Puerto Rican Convention."

Michael "Mickey" Bontempo, the public servant caught on tape bargaining with DeCarlo for money from the mob not to run against Addonizio, speaks at a political rally. "The whites and the good blacks will elect Addonizio," he predicts.

****

On Monday morning, the auditorium of the Veteran's Hospital has become a makeshift courtroom. Green plastic chairs are to the left for the jurors. A small table raised up on a pedestal, with a covering cloth set in the middle of the room is the judge's bench. Beyond the jurors' chairs, tables are set left and right, facing the judge for lawyers and defendants. Beyond them are chairs set in rows for spectators. The room is filled with people when Kantor's hospital bed is wheeled in, with bottles and tubes connecting him to a rolling stand behind the bed.

A nurse cranks his bed up, so that he can see the judge. A court attendant has to lift Irving's hand and place it on the Bible to take the oath. When the attendant finishes reading the oath, Irving croaks "I do." His two words are barely discernable. There is no way the jury will be able to understand his testimony.

I make my motion to have Jane Kantor sworn in as an interpreter for her husband. It is vigorously opposed, of course. After inquiring and learning how Mrs. Kantor has been with her husband every day—frequently interpreting for us—Judge Barlow grants the motion and swears her in as an interpreter. We are saved.

Jane moves over next to Irving's bed, her hand holding his arm with her blonde head leaning over his emaciated face.

"You understand the questioning may be protracted and last for days," Judge Barlow addresses Kantor. "And that it may affect your health."

"It . . . doesn't . . . matter," Irving struggles to be heard.

Judge Barlow, overriding a host of objections, turns to me, "Proceed." As I rise, I can see that two of the women jurors can't even look at the wasted form lying in the bed before them.

Standing by Kantor's bed, we introduce the many checks that Biancone washed through "Kantor Supply."

"Where is Kantor Supply?" I ask.

Irving croaks and Jane answers. "No place. An empty lot."

Using Jane as the intermediary, we outline the scheme where by Irving cashed the checks for the mafia payoffs.

As I present each check to Irving, Jane removes his glasses so he can make identification, and then replaces them for the questioning.

"Did Mr. Biancone tell you why he was cashing the checks through you?"

"Contractors had to pay cash to his boss," Irving slowly delivers through Jane.

"Did he tell you the name of his boss?"

I see Irving take a deep breath, then slowly, painfully say, "Tony Boy Boiardo," between gasps, struggling to be clear enough so that Jane does not have to repeat.

"Mr. Biancone," I turn to the defense table, "will you please step forward so Mr. Kantor can see you?" Biancone glances at his attorney, Tom Dyson, who nods a yes. Then Biancone slowly rises and walks over to the foot of Irving's bed.

"Do you recognize this man?" I ask.

"Yes . . . that's . . . Bi . . . an . . . cone."

To spare the poor man, I try to conclude the direct as quickly as I can.

Then, I watch as the defense has the unpleasant duty of cross-examining a dying man, attempting to demonstrate that he is lying to avoid income taxes due as a result of his criminal activity—criminal activities with their clients. I could almost feel sorry for the cross-examiners. The jury, obviously, doesn't like what they are seeing.

****

June 12

After three days of Kantor's testimony, we return to the Trenton court-room. During the next three court days I put on two new victims of shakedowns by Tony Boy's man, Biancone. Hellring asks for two days off so Addonizio can campaign. Judge Barlow says, "No. Not even ten minutes."

When the court recesses on Tuesday, the balloting has been well underway in Newark. The polls will not close for several hours. After a quick dinner, I go to my room at the Holiday Inn to watch the returns. If the mayor is reelected, I expect several thousand people will ring the Trenton courthouse Wednesday morning. Just what we need. I call the US Marshall from my room. "Carl, I want every available man outside the courthouse tomorrow."

Chapter Twenty-Two

"The Spaghetti Is On"
June 16–July 1, 1970

June 16

The results are in by late evening. We have a new mayor! Unfortunately, when the outcome becomes clear, the streets of Newark erupt. "Kill the niggers!" whites are shouting. The cry is even coming over police radios. Television reporters are being chased through the streets. An NBC camera crew is beaten, their equipment smashed. TV reporter Gabe Pressman is forced to seek sanctuary in a residence from a mob at his heels. It is the riots of three years ago, in reverse.

I am stunned by Addonizio's totals. In spite of the DeCarlo tapes, in spite of the indictment by a federal grand jury, in spite of the testimony in court, Addonizio received 45 percent of the vote! What if, I ask myself, there had been no tapes, or no indictment, or no trial? Tony Boy and his band would still be in charge.

On Wednesday no supporters appear outside the courthouse. Inside, the stream of suppliers, engineers, and contractors continues. These are businessmen who had been hit on the head by Biancone or LaMorte—the director of public works—to make "contributions" to the administration in order to be paid. But these are just preliminaries, designed to set the stage for our main witness, Paul Rigo.

Fred Lacey has been shuttling to and from our Newark office, keeping track of the Hudson County investigation. We have taken over our small Trenton office for our trial team of Newark AUSAs. Now that we are about to call Rigo, we sit squeezed around our small conference table to evaluate where we are.

"I'm worried about Rigo," I announce.

"Why?" Fred asks. "Isn't he prepared?"

"He knows his stuff, all right. But he tends to get flip. Frankly, he's a bit of a wise guy."

"Hold him tight," Fred tells me, which is good advice, but not easy to follow.

****

June 22

When Rigo takes the stand, the jury is presented with a forty-five-year-old-man of average height, deeply tanned, with the marked puffiness of self-indulgence.

As he settles into his seat, a feeling of apprehension comes over me. The entire case will come down to his credibility. Every count in the indictment is pegged to a payoff entry in his diary. We simply did not have any of the other witnesses when we indicted on December 17. All the other witnesses have been offered under the catchall conspiracy charge we created for that purpose. Rigo alone must support the 60-plus counts keyed to each payoff. I must introduce the checks he used to collect the cash to make each diaried payment. Complicating that, I must show that he used none of that cash for himself by taking him through every trip he made—and there were many, all over the world, over many years—and demonstrating how he paid for each one, without touching the cash for the payoffs.

Five days of direct examination. I am running around the well of the court, as every time I offer a check into evidence, the defense attorneys demand to see the original. On one occasion, as I pass by the jury box, I think I hear an alternate say, "Don't let them get you down, kid." But maybe it is just my imagination.

On the first full day of his examination, Rigo gets me in trouble. LaMorte, according to Rigo, approached Rigo and said he is taking Rigo to "the most important meeting you will have in Newark, to the man who really runs this town." LaMorte drove to Valentine Electric, which was the front for Tony Boy Boiardo. There, Boiardo told Rigo, "This job you have down there on the South Side, that was set up by me. Johnny Sepede and I had an understanding, and that understanding is that you pay ten percent of what you get on that job."

The testimony is awful. It would read all right in the record, I know, but it sounded lousy, as if he memorized the whole thing word for word. Out of the corner of my eye, and through the soles of my shoes, I can see and feel that the jurors did not like it. So I try to fix it.

"Are you giving us the exact words that this man Tony Boiardo said to you?"

"No, sir."

"But do you remember the substance of the conversation?"

"Yes, sir."

"What else did he say?"

"Well," Rigo launches on, "he said ten percent I said, 'I can't pay you ten percent.' He said, 'You will pay ten percent and you will pay it in cash.' I said, 'What are we getting for paying you ten percent?' He said, 'There are lots of mouths to feed in City Hall,' he said, 'You pay me the ten percent.' He said, 'I take care of the mayor. I take care of the council. I take care of anybody else that has to be taken care of down there.'"

It is getting worse. He has become an advocate instead of a witness. I am desperate and again reach for a fire extinguisher.

"Once again, Mr. Rigo, are you giving us the exact words which this man Tony said to you?"

"No, sir."

Even these palliatives are of little value. There is nothing I can put my finger on directly, but I know it is no good. The atmosphere in the courtroom is all wrong. I can't seem to reverse it. Perhaps it would help to have a physical confrontation. I am willing to try anything.

"Mr. Rigo, before you go on with the conversation between yourself and this man whom you identified as Tony, I want to ask you whether or not you see this man in court."

"Yes, sir, I do."

"Will you point him out, please?"

Tony Boy stands up. A slender man, not above middle height, he is impeccably dressed in an expensive suit. He has a cold smile on his face as he slowly pirouettes, presenting himself arrogantly to everyone in the courtroom. But even this does not help, not with Rigo's next answer.

"What happened after you concluded the conversation with the defendant, Boiardo?"

"The telephone rang. It was for Boiardo. He hung up and he said, 'I have to get out of here. That was my wife. The spaghetti is on.'"

That did it! I don't dare look at the jurors, afraid I'll see noses wrinkled in disgust. As soon as I can, I get a recess. "What the hell is wrong with you?" I shout at Rigo in our office. "Are you a comedian? You think this is a night club act!" I want to strangle the bastard. "Will you just answer the goddamn questions!" I can see that Rigo just doesn't understand what he has done. He figures he has charmed the jurors. To placate me, he agrees to play it straight from now on. But that is not good enough. He has to repair his credibility.

"Paul," I calm down so as not to freak him out, "You later met Boiardo in his house, right?"

"Yes," Rigo says.

"How many times were you there?"

"Just once."

"If I ask you to do it, could you draw the inside of Boiardo's house?"

"Sure," he says, with a smirk, "I'm an engineer."

After the recess I quickly go through a series of payments, with Ralph Vicaro acting as collector for Boiardo. Rigo, who was having trouble meeting the payment schedule, asked to meet Boiardo. LaMorte arranged to pick him up and drove him to Boiardo's house.

"What community was that in?"

"In Essex Fells."

"Can you describe to us what you saw as you approached this house?"

"It was a very nice residential community, winding roads. We got down to the end of the road. The road curves around to the right and there is a winding driveway up to Mr. Boiardo's house. The house is situated on a rather steep slope."

"Did there come a time that you entered Mr. Boiardo's house?"

"Yes, sir."

"Do you think you could sketch for us the approach you took up to his house and so much of the inside of his house as you saw that evening?"

"Yes, sir, I think so."

Wadden, Boiardo's attorney, objects and goes to sidebar, states, "Mr. Stern wants him to draw the Boot sitting on his horse." Judge Barlow, who may not have read the mafia tapes, looks at me questioningly.

"You have the wrong house," I tell Wadden with a laugh. "That's daddy's house in Livingston. The one with the incinerator. The one where they burn the bodies."

"There is no need for this!" Wadden insists.

"If he can draw the inside of Boiardo's house," I appeal to Judge Barlow, "it means he was there . . ."

"Let him describe it," Wadden interrupts me. "You don't need theatrics." After more wrangling, Judge Barlow allows Rigo to diagram Boiardo's house.

Rigo, standing at an easel, does the drawing. As he does so he gives a running tour. When he finishes, I ask, "Is that your best recollection of what you saw that evening?"

"Yes, sir. By the way," he adds, pointing at the room in which he met Boiardo, "as an engineer I could do a better job on that room." I can't believe it! I have just wagered the whole case on this guy being able to accurately diagram a house he had been in only once. And this dummy is still making wisecracks. But when I glance at the jurors they are sitting back, relaxed, smiling and nodding at Rigo's joke. They now know he had been there and that his story is true. The curse has been lifted.

Chapter Twenty-Three

"You May Sit ... Mr. Guilty"
July 1–22, 1970

July 1

The first thing Ken Gibson does as mayor is order the dome of the municipal building painted gold. Good. The second is to fire Dominic Spina as police director. Very good. Let's hope Gibson remains straight. If not, as Jack Bissell would say, we will all be horses' "ah-ses."

****

Tony Boy is in jail with his bail revoked. We discovered that while the case was pending, Boiardo's goons tried to put a hit on Rigo.

In the middle of my direct of Rigo, Lacey called from Newark. "You won't believe this," he said. "A couple of months before trial, two of Boiardo's goons entered Joseph Stracco's barbershop and asked Stracco when Rigo is due in. Stracco refused to say. A few days later, Stracco's shop was burglarized and the fixtures destroyed."

"Incredible," I responded.

"Wait until you hear the rest," Lacey continued. "These goons then grabbed Stracco in a bar and asked him again when Rigo was due. He again refused to say. Three days later, a car full of men pulled up next to his, and one of the men fired a shot over Stracco's car, narrowly missing a school bus unloading down the street."

"How can we tie this to Boiardo?" I asked.

"Well," Fred says, "a couple of weeks later one of the thugs entered Stracco's shop and said to him, 'Forget about it. It's all a mistake. When we win, you are invited to Tony Boy's party.'"

"Will Stracco stand up?" I asked Fred.

"Jon Goldstein just put him under oath in the grand jury," Fred replied, "and I am coming down to Trenton with the grand jury stenographer. Tony Boy is going to have his bail revoked."

****

A few days after Tony Boy goes to jail, he suffers a massive heart attack in his holding cell. The trial cannot continue with him as a defendant. We must either wait for his recovery or sever him from the trial. All the doctors agree that the attack is real, and Boiardo's recovery could take weeks. Maybe months. That leaves us no choice. Boiardo and his lawyer, Wadden, are gone from the courtroom when the cross of Rigo begins. Before it does, I read Gordon's grand jury confession to the jurors. Between Irving Kantor, a half dozen contractors who paid, and now the jury hearing Gordon's testimony, I figure I have done all that I can to buttress Rigo's credibility before the defense falls upon him.

Which they do . . . for days. The defendants bring out Rigo's yachts and helicopters, and the excesses of his style of living are displayed for the jurors. It sounds great. On paper it reads great. But the defendants are only hurting themselves. In cross-examining Rigo, the defendants prove that Rigo received enormous sums of public money from the public officials to whom, he says, he paid kickbacks.

The only defendant to put in a personal defense is Addonizio. Hellring calls him as the first witness after the government's case closes. We are caught by surprise. Normally, defendants take the stand as their last, not first witness. I am glad Fred will cross-examine him. I would not have been prepared. Addonizio, of course, denies everything. He calls Rigo a liar. He admits knowing Boiardo, even attending his wedding twenty years earlier, but contends their contacts were usually at charitable events like St. Anthony's Orphanage and the Pope Pius XII Humanitarian Award Dinner.

On cross, Lacey nails him. Addonizio has to admit to numerous trips to Puerto Rican gambling casinos. "I find gambling very relaxing," he says. As to meeting Boiardo in the casinos, "I just kept running into him."

"Have you ever taken a vacation and written a check paying the hotel bill?" Lacey demands.

"Not to my knowledge," Addonizio replies, and then adds, "I have many good friends."

He cannot deny that his good friend, Paul Rigo, wrote $16,000 in checks to a contractor who built Addonizio's summerhouse. Addonizio can't deny that he repaid Rigo after the investigation started, using backdated checks that made it appear as if the repayment had been made before the investigation began. "You used backdated checks?" Lacey hammers him.

"I'm not sure what backdated means," Addonizio mumbles. "I suppose you could presume they were backdated." Then adds, "If that's what you want me to say."

****

The defense calls a few more witnesses, whom I cross-examine. When the defense rests, we call no additional witnesses, and after lengthy legal arguments, summations begin. Fred immediately sums up after the defense. It is all anti-climactic. The jury has been at this for well over six weeks.

July 23, 4:55 p.m.

Judge Barlow finishes his final instructions and sends the jury out to deliberate. Fred and I stay close by. We know we can get a quick verdict. We can feel it. I am in the hall, smoking like a chimney. At 9:40 p.m. the judge summons the jurors and announces that he is discharging them for the night. Fred and I run to the bench. "Why not ask them?" Fred says. "Maybe they want to deliberate longer?" The judge does. The jurors say they do. They go back in. At 10:20, they come back with their verdict sheet. There are sixty-four counts against the five remaining defendants. That means the jurors had to fill out 320 boxes on the verdict sheet while eating dinner in the jury room. They get it done in five hours.

Lyle G. Cook, an older man who is the foreman of the jury, rises to begin reading the verdict. Guilty. Guilty. Guilty. Once he has done eighty verdicts, naming each defendant as to each count, Judge Barlow says, "You may sit down if you wish, Mr. Guilty." But Mr. Cook continues to stand until he has read all the guilties on all the counts.

Chapter Twenty-Four

"For the Greater Good"
July 23–August 31, 1970

S EVEN WEEKS OF trial—particularly a trial like that one—leave you exhausted. Judge Barlow has set September 22 for the sentencing, which gives me some breathing space. I know the Hudson County investigation has been going like gangbusters. With Jon, Jack Barry, and Don Williamson, it is all in good hands. I intend to take some time off.

July 25

Saturday night. I am relaxing, doing some barbecuing, when the phone rings. It's Lacey.

"How are you feeling?" he asks.

"Great."

"Good," he says, "because I want you to know that Senator Case has just offered me a federal judgeship."

"What!" I just can't believe it. We haven't been in office even eleven months.

Fred laughs again, "I'm sure it will hit the press in a few weeks. So I wanted you to know."

"Thanks," I say. I'm happy for him, I guess. But I figure I'm on my way out.

"No," he says, reading my mind, "Senator Case is going to recommend you to replace me as U.S. Attorney."

"Fred, that's impossible. I'm only thirty-three. I don't know anyone in this state. I am not a member of the New Jersey bar."

"Well," he replies, "the senator is going to do it. You have a house here now, so that's okay. And I told him you will take the next bar exam."

"That's not until February."

"That's right. But I am going to stay around for a few months, for the Hudson County indictments."

"Indictments? When?"

"It depends on how soon you get back in harness."

****

As Fred predicted, the senator's recommendation leaks to the press. The immediate public reaction is dismay. On August 31, WNBC TV editorializes, "We do not think this is the proper time for Mr. Lacey to don federal robes . . . there still is much to be done in New Jersey . . . it is almost too hard to ask him to refuse. However, for the greater good, we think he should continue his present role as prosecutor." And to that I say, "Amen." I can't see how we can possibly get along without Fred Lacey.

Chapter Twenty-Five

"No Ordinary Crimes"
July 27–September 22, 1970

WE ARE IN our new digs. My office is directly across from Fred's, with each of our secretaries sitting between. I am buried in administrative matters and in catching up on the Hudson County investigation. Our intention is to indict, if possible, before Fred leaves.

We have some new people, but we are still understaffed. First getting more slots, then finding suitable candidates is tough enough; add the full field FBI check, which takes about two months, and we are far behind where we want to be. Still, we haven't been doing so bad considering we've been at it less than a year.

AUSA Donald Williamson, who joined us only at the end of April, is doing excellent work on Hudson County, along with Jack Barry. Our subpoenas went out in early May, and by June the two of them are inundated with records. While I was preparing Kantor and Rigo for the June 2 trial, Lacey was desperately seeking help from the department. The FBI, as usual, refused.

August 6

Lacey writes our appeal to Assistant Attorney General Will Wilson. "There are presently two Assistant United States Attorneys conducting this investigation without the benefit of a single agent, accountant, or investigator." He asks for the assignment of the IRS agents who worked the Newark case with us: Bob Wynne, Bill Miller, Dick Phillips, Bob Shore, and Asher Greenspun.

We get no help from Wilson. At the end of August, Fred, who knows the Commissioner of the IRS, Randolph Thrower, goes to see him in Washington. Presto. We have our own team of agents transferred from the Newark case over to the Hudson investigation. As the agents trace cash, they pass the information to Williamson and Barry, who immediately subpoena our potential "victims."

In they come, contractors, suppliers, and engineers. One after another they report cash to Bernard Murphy, Jersey City purchasing agent, and Frank Manning, the Hudson County Engineer. Our guys are doing a fabulous job. Business people are virtually standing in line in our office waiting their turn to make a good confession. In return, they get absolution—at least from federal prosecution. It is almost comical. Williamson and Barry sit in a conference room with a line of businessmen in the hall. They keep making reports of each new "break." I can't keep track of it all. I have my hands full on other matters.

****

First, there is the Weber appeal. Jon Goldstein has been writing the briefs while I have been on trial. The argument before a three-judge panel on the Third Circuit is scheduled for September 18. I have to get ready for it. And on the twenty-second, Addonizio is due to be sentenced. There is that to prepare for. Another distraction is Anthony Little Pussy Russo.

This is the man who controls the rackets on the Jersey shore; the man who had boasted on the tapes of dragging a victim by a chain around his neck into the Boot's furnace. This worthy has brought an action against the IRS to return the financial records of "Anthony Russo, Inc.," a construction company he heads in West Long Branch. He has submitted a personal affidavit claiming he needs the records to run his business. I can't believe my luck. A personal affidavit from a mobster! I can make him take the stand and cross-examine him on his sworn statement. His application has been assigned to Judge Shaw. Shaw, of course, has read the DeCarlo tapes.

The courtroom is crowded as Judge Shaw sweeps through his red drapes and seats himself. When everyone else is seated, I call Russo to the stand.

"What is your name?" I inquire.

"Anthony Russo."

"Do you have a nickname?" I smile at him.

He looks back. Pauses. Gets very red in the face, and says, "Yes."

"And what is that?" I gently ask.

He looks back and mumbles, almost inaudibly, "Little Pussy."

"I'm sorry, I can't hear you," I say.

He says it loudly, as the courtroom erupts in laughter. I can see even the dour Shaw fighting a grin. Russo himself is laughing, his face bright red.

When I ask him about the business described in his affidavit, the one he says he needs records for, the climate turns serious. He denies having read the affidavit before he signed it. He even denies knowing how to read. Twirling a pair of black-rimmed glasses, the balding mobster denies he even knows how to recognize numbers, "One-two-three-four, like that you mean?" Russo smiles at me.

"Do you count?"

"No," Russo responds with a laugh, "I don't count."

As he leaves the court, Russo gives a cheery wave to the press. All in all, a good time was had by all. But the IRS gets to keep the records, and we are well on our way to an income tax indictment of Russo. When we get it, we will have convicted or at least indicted all the major figures of the DeCarlo tapes.

****

September 18

I am on my feet in the Court of Appeals in Philadelphia. Because Lacey can't participate, having represented the Bechtel witnesses at trial, I am listed on the appeal as the acting United States Attorney. I am arguing the appeal against Weber's appellate counsel, Walter D. Van Riper. The words of the dead Roy Burgess, reported through Harold Price, again dominate the courtroom. I sense no trouble in the appeal.

"How did it go?" Lacey asks Jon and me when we return.

"Great," Jon says and looks over at me with a grin.

"What?" Lacey says.

"Well," I say, "Old Judge Biggs is half deaf and kept yelling at me to keep my voice up. I tried, but he couldn't hear me. 'I told you to keep your voice up,' he said. So I wound up yelling, which he didn't like either."

"Do you know who he is?" Lacey asks, then answers himself when he sees I don't care. "He was F. Scott Fitzgerald's roommate at Princeton, executor of his estate, and guardian of Fitzgerald's daughter, Scottie." Lacey pauses, expecting me to be impressed.

"He should still get a hearing aid."

September 22

Lacey and I are back in Judge Barlow's courtroom for the Addonizio sentencing. It is a glorious day for weather, sunny and warm. The street in front of the courthouse is thronged with press. The courtroom itself is standing room only.

The five defendants are each seated next to counsel. The two mobsters, Biancone and Vicaro, can expect nothing but major jail time. And they get it. Biancone gets a ten-year sentence and Vicaro, whose arrest record started with a conviction at the age of ten, gets twelve. I speculate that if Tony Boy had been there, he would have gotten more. But that is work for another day.

When it is the turn of the former politicians, Addonizio heads the list. Hellring, standing cherub-like beside his client, makes his plea. He speaks of Addonizio's war record and his service to his community in Newark, his popularity, the fact that Addonizio was able to get over 40 percent of the vote despite "public calumny in the press, culminating in an indictment that was tried in the press."

I lean over to Lacey. "That forty percent is not going to do him any good." Lacey smiles and nods in return. Then Judge Barlow makes an eloquent sentencing speech.

"These were no ordinary crimes; they were not the product of a moment of weakness." Barlow shakes his head. "The criminal acts of the defendants were as calculated as they were brazen . . . How can we calculate the cynicism engendered in our citizens, including our young people, or the erosion of confidence in our system of government, and the diminished respect for our laws, by these very men who, as governmental officials, inveighed against crime in the streets while they pursued their own criminal activities in the corridors of city hall?"

As he speaks, my mind turns to past scenes in the streets of Newark. The racial conflicts. The burnings when the frustrated black residents rose up in revolt. The white residents violently reacting to Gibson's election. The sheriff's deputies handing out literature about Fred's son. The ordinary businessman who wanted to work, and couldn't, not without paying off.

"Their crimes," the judge is continuing, "tear at the very heart of our civilized society and our form of representative government. . . . They can expect from this court only the gravest of sentences."

And with that, he sentences the former congressman-turned-mayor to ten years imprisonment.

Chapter Twenty-Six

"That Great Jewish Lawyer"
September 22–October 29, 1970

As our investigation in Hudson goes on, the bribers, or victims of extortion, if you prefer, stream into the office on a weekly basis. Williamson continues to sit in his office as they line up outside. "How much did you pay?" he asks each, for starters. The answers range from a few thousand to tens of thousands on each public contract in Hudson.

"Williamson is doing great!" Lacey tells me. "Wait 'til you hear this," he rumbles a laugh. "Bernie Murphy, the purchasing agent, hits everyone for ten percent. He took twenty-eight hundred eighty-four dollars," Lacey smiles, "and four cents."

"Who paid that?" I ask.

"A guy by the name of Hugh Platt, Jr."

"Everyone paid?"

"Everyone," Lacey confirms. "And that doesn't include the city workers who have to kick back three percent of their salaries."

I can't believe it. It is too ugly. Municipal workers. Civil servants. All forced to hand over three percent of their incomes? It is a feudal empire. It is almost "le droit du seigneur." But that, of course, dealt with more than just money.

"We've got a dozen and a half firms confessing to hundreds of thousands of dollars in kickbacks," Lacey continues. "But that's just the money we identified coming in. Firm by firm. We have found millions in their bank accounts and bond purchases from sources we have not yet pinned down."

"Fabulous," I say. And it is.

"The best one is that the IRS has traced $948,000 worth of municipal bonds, purchased for cash . . . by Congressman Cornelius Gallagher," Lacey smiles.

"Where did Gallagher get the money?" I ask.

"We don't know yet, but we intend to find out."

"Is the congressman part of the ring?"

"On the fringes," Lacey replies. "He gets his from the mafia, Joe Zicarelli, and . . . we hear that he is selling appointments to the military academies."

****

The FBI background check on Lacey is finished. His nomination is expected any day. But the choice of his successor is up in the air. Senator Case notified the White House he intends to send my name in. But his office reports that Justice will object. It's good old Henry Petersen, again.

****

The good news is that the IRS has traced $700,000 in bearer bonds that boss John V. Kenny has bought for cash. Kenny sent the chief of police, Fred Kropke, with the bagful of cash to William Sternkopf.

Sternkopf is a commissioner of the Port Authority of New York and New Jersey, which owns and operates the bridges and tunnels between New York and New Jersey, and built and owns the World Trade Center. John V. Kenny had the governor put Sternkopf on the commission, and Sternkopf reciprocated by turning Kenny's $700,000 in cash into bearer bonds of the Port Authority. Where are the bonds? An informant reports Boss Kenny has given them as presents to his children and grandchildren: $400,000 to his son-in-law, Paul Hanly; and $300,000 to his granddaughter, Margo Hermann.

We send the agents out with grand jury subpoenas; we want those bonds. Many people don't know it, but bearer bonds are just like cash. No names on them. Anyone can cash them in.

****

October 7

Kenny's granddaughter, Margo, and her husband, Elmer Hermann, go into the grand jury. Both take the Fifth Amendment about the $300,000 in bearer bonds. Lacey brings them both before Judge Wortendyke to compel them to testify. It is the first public proceeding in the Hudson County investigation.

Standing before Judge Wortendyke, with a crowded courtroom behind him, Fred lashes out at the Hudson machine, and its "plunder . . . unmatched by anything in my experience. You'd have to go back to the days of Boss Tweed to find its match."

I see the reporters writing furiously. "No contracts are let without placing a squeeze on contractors. . . . Even the suppliers of food to the hospitals have to kickback," Lacey tells Wortendyke.

At the end of the session, the young *Star Ledger* reporter, Bob Herbert, approaches Lacey. "Do you really believe that the Kenny machine rivals the Tweed ring?" the slender young reporter asks Lacey.

"You bet! Just wait. You'll see," Fred replies.

But we are running out of time. Before the end of the day President Nixon announces that he has sent Fred's name to the Senate to be confirmed as a United States District Judge.

****

October 8

The Hermanns and the Hanlys turn in the $700,000 in bearer bonds. The next day New Jersey's largest newspaper, the *Newark News,* runs an editorial demanding that Nixon nominate me as U.S. Attorney. To my surprise other newspapers are following suit. Thirteen months ago I was not even a resident. I knew nobody. And still don't. I am not in the New Jersey bar. Now, the senior United States senator is pushing me, Fred is publicly endorsing me, and the newspapers are screaming for me.

I have only two problems. The first is Henry Petersen. He is blocking Justice Department approval. Without that, my name won't go to the White House. The second is the local bar and the local politics. They have their own interests.

****

The week of October 19 is a dandy. First, Senator Case calls a press conference and announces Justice is blocking my name. Standing before the press, the senator proclaims that it won't do the department any good, because he will not approve any other nomination. Under senatorial courtesy, that means no other nomination will be confirmed. Then he goes on the attack against Petersen, without naming him. He refers to Will Wilson's assistants "somewhere in the lower levels of the Justice Department . . . they don't like him." And, to add some gasoline, he adds, "and they are jealous of him."

"That's just what you need," Fred laughs as Jon and I sit in his office taking stock of where we are.

"Maybe I should go down to D.C. and see the senator," I suggest. "I've never even met him."

"I called Case," Fred responds. "He says it's not necessary. He will support you to the end. It's you or nobody."

"Did he say anything about Herb's speech?" Jon asks with a twinkle in his eye and a side glance at me.

"What speech?" Fred asks with a rumble in his voice, while I shake a "no" at Jon, telling him to stop.

"What speech?" Lacey rumbles even louder, turning to me.

"Well," I begin, "I was speaking before a conclave of police officers and social workers—a national conference at Point Pleasant Beach—when one of them asked about marijuana prosecutions."

"And what did you say?"

"Well . . . I told them that they should not be surprised when young people don't obey the drug laws when they see their parents openly violating other laws."

"What else?"

"If I remember right, I said that it was kind of silly to impose stiff penalties for mere possession of marijuana, and stigmatize kids as criminals, when we don't even know that a smoke of that stuff is any more harmful than smoking a Lucky Strike, which I do, or drinking alcohol, which I also do."

"You did!" Lacey stares at me.

"Why don't you show Fred the small item that was in the *Evening News*," Jon suggests, helpfully.

"Yes," Fred says. "I'd like to see it."

"I'll see if I can find it," I say, with no such intention.

"What are you doing?" I say to Jon, after we leave Fred's office.

Jon laughs, "Just having fun. Don't worry, Fred threw me a wink as we left."

****

One day later, October 22, here comes Jon Goldstein with another newspaper article. I don't like the way he is grinning.

"What you got?"

"An article," Jon smiles.

"Where from?"

"*The Jersey Journal.*"

"That rag! It's just a mouthpiece for the Kenny machine."

"Not so this time," Jon can barely contain himself. He looks like he is about to burst.

"You know Geoffrey Gaulkin, the young prosecutor of Hudson County?" Jon asks.

"Yes. So what?"

"Well, last night he made a speech to the so-called Citizens Committee of Hudson County, and he warned them about you."

"Me?"

"Well," says Jon, "it sounds like you. The article is entitled 'Corruption Probe is Likened to McCarthyism by Gaulkin.' Here's what he says. He says the assumption that everyone in public office is corrupt leads to the conclusion that it is all right to use any means necessary to root them out."

"What?"

"Oh, there's more. Much more. He speaks of 'the response of law enforcement officials seeking to ride the crest of this widespread belief by too much lecturing and screaming about crime instead of doing much about stopping it'! That sounds like Lacey, right?"

"That's crap! Anyway, he doesn't mention me."

"Here's the part I think is you," Jon cannot conceal his delight. "'An investigation can become an inquisition . . . a subpoena can turn into a source of harassment and a courtroom can become a platform for press releases.' He then recalled the McCarthy probe of alleged communists and said 'some very unfortunate things happened then,'" Jon concludes with a knowing nod. "That is you, I think. You're McCarthy."

"Sounds like he is campaigning among the pols to become U.S. Attorney," I say. "By the way, why don't you give up this newspaper reading?"

****

The last week in October the United States Senate confirms Fred as a federal judge. But Fred asks Justice to hold up his commission. He doesn't want to leave until the succession is decided. Senator Case again publicly nominates me, and attacks Justice for refusing to go forward. And John V. Kenny, the boss of Hudson County, goes on the offensive.

The state is in the middle of a campaign for the U.S. Senate. Harrison Williams, the Democratic incumbent, is running against Republican Nelson Gross. Gross put Nixon over the top in the 1968 presidential convention. He broke from Case, who had been holding the New Jersey delegation for Rockefeller. Now, two years later, Case is quietly supporting his Democratic colleague Williams. And Kenny, as the Democratic leader, is on the stump for Williams.

October 24

I am having breakfast in my New York apartment listening to the radio, when I hear a report of a street corner speech by Kenny. Infuriated by our seizure of the bonds from his family, Kenny shouts, "I wish I had Stern here so I could spit in his eye." I almost choke on my toast.

Five days later Kenny appears on the dais of the annual Hudson County dinner, where 3,000 have turned out to honor Senator Williams and the Democratic chairman of the county, Wally Wolfe. All the "boys" are there. Jersey City Mayor Whelan and City Council President Flaherty, as well as America's most corrupt congressman, Neil Gallagher, who calls us "a Gestapo stalking through our country." And then it is boss Kenny's turn. "I never knew that when you want to take care of children that is an offense against the U.S. Government," the leader shouts to the faithful. "If that displeases Lacey or that great Jewish lawyer Stern, well, that's just too bad."

Chapter Twenty-Seven

"Let Me Finish"
October 30–November 1970

October 30

Friday morning. I steam into the office and go straight to Don Williamson. "I want Kenny subpoenaed. I want him in the grand jury. I want him served today. I want him on the stand Wednesday morning."

"Who is going to question him?" Williamson asks in a way that tells me he wants it to be him, but guesses it's going to be me.

"I am."

He says it is all right with him, "under the circumstances." I don't like the sound of that. It sounds like he thinks this is *his* case. My next stop is Lacey.

"You'll have to watch him," Lacey says. "He has done a great job. We have a score of witnesses, thanks to him. He broke a lot of them. He's tough. But . . . maybe a little too tough," Lacey pauses, remembering, "I stuck my head in the grand jury when Williamson had Mayor Whelan of Jersey City on the stand," Lacey continues. "I never saw anything like it. Don was leaning over the witness box, his face about six inches from Whelan's, snarling questions. I turned and got out of there."

"What can we do?" I ask.

"I've thought about it," Lacey frowns. "I'm going to hang on here until the indictments come down in two weeks. Then I am going to announce that I will be leaving, and that you will try the case. After I go, you are on your own."

****

November 5

I walk across the street from our new offices heading for the grand jury room of the federal courthouse to rendezvous with John V. Kenny. I am with Bruce Goldstein, one of our new AUSAs. As we enter the elevator, I run smack into the seventy-eight-year-old Kenny, accompanied by his attorney, the dapper Walter D. Van Riper, with an ever-present flower in his lapel and fedora on his head.

Van Riper, like Kenny, is in his mid-seventies. Everyone calls him "judge," and many years ago he was one. Old school that he is, he greets me warmly. As for Kenny, I see why they call him "the little guy." I don't think he is more than five feet three or four inches. Kenny looks at me sheepishly, and says, "Mr. Stern, about the Jewish lawyer crack—"

"That's not what you said," I interrupt him, not wanting to hear his bullshit. "What you said was *great* Jewish lawyer.'"

Van Riper quickly steps between us. "Look, Herb, Mr. Kenny is going to take the Fifth. I gave him a card with the words to read. Why not just let us go? You know he has a perfect right to invoke the Fifth."

I figured Van would tell him to take the Fifth. All weekend I have been thinking about how to get Kenny on the record, without violating his rights. By now we are out of the elevator, at the door of the grand jury suite.

"Van," I respond, "I know he has the right to invoke privilege, but he has to do it on the record. Not in the hallway."

"All right," Van Riper sighs, and turning to Kenny, reminds him, "Johnny, I'll be right outside the room." Van Riper has to wait in the anteroom. As always, only the witness is allowed before the grand jurors.

Jon Goldstein and Williamson are waiting for us. Williamson, short, stocky, not more than a couple inches taller than Kenny, takes

Kenny by the arm and escorts him into the room and seats him in the witness box. Kenny can barely be seen above the rail that runs along three sides of the box. Once he is seated, I can see his hand reaching for his jacket pocket and, undoubtedly, Van Riper's prepared speech invoking the Fifth Amendment. If that emerges, I am done.

My plan is simple. I will warn him. And warn him. And then warn him some more. Then I will ask a question that may stimulate an answer. Just one answer—that's all I need—and we will be under way. I know enough about the man to figure out that there is one question that he will find impossible to resist answering: Did he lie to the press when he said the bonds were his? I figure an old-time politico will be tempted to defend his press statements. If not, then it's over.

I begin the warnings. It goes on for a while.

"May I read a statement?" Kenny interrupts.

"Just let me finish," I reply.

"Oh yes," he responds. "I thought you were finished."

Back to the warnings about the use of testimony against him. Then on to his right to counsel. "You have the right to an attorney, and I understand that Judge Walter Van Riper is your attorney out in the grand jury waiting room."

"That's right," Kenny responds.

And now the "question." After all the warnings, he either invokes privilege, or we are on our way.

"Mr. Kenny, you issued statements to the press that the $700,000 in bearer bonds was purchased in cash by you. Are those statements issued by you to the press *true*?"

I see he is indignant at the suggestion he lied to the press.

"I don't know how much bonds the government has."

"Did you purchase these bonds?"

"Certainly I did."

"Did you purchase them for cash?"

"Yes."

We are on our way. Now I question him about the source of the cash. "I am glad you asked me how I got the cash," Kenny states. "I had a contract with Penn Railroad for forty years." Except then he agrees that the most money he ever made in one year was $80,000.

"Where did you take the cash from?"

"My home."

"Where did you keep it in your home?"

"In a cellar. In a clothes cabinet."

When I get on to how big the cabinet is, and the use of the chief of police to carry the cash to the broker, Kenny brings down the curtain. He snaps back in his chair, remembering what Van told him and, as I watch with a sinking feeling, his hand reaches for his side jacket pocket. Out comes Van Riper's prepared card, and he begins to read, concluding, "I must respectfully decline to answer questions on the ground that to do so might tend to incriminate me." That ends it. But too late. The most influential politician in New Jersey says he keeps hundreds of thousands of dollars in greenbacks in his basement.

Later, in the grand jury waiting room I see a very attractive young woman. I ask Williamson who she is, and he tells me it is Kenny's girlfriend. She looks about fifty years younger than Kenny. "What is she doing here?" I ask Williamson.

"I subpoenaed her," replied Williamson.

"Why?"

Williamson tells me that she kept a diary. I don't see the relevance of that. Williamson then takes Kenny by the arm and marches him over to the young woman. "Have you two met?" he says with a sneer. "I'd like to introduce you to each other . . . Mr. Kenny, I'd like you to meet—"

"Christ," I break in. "Let's get the hell out of here," I tell Jon and Bruce.

Chapter Twenty-Eight

"The President is Entitled to the Lawyer of His Choice" November 4–16, 1970

WE ARE GETTING close to an indictment in Hudson. We have to be. Lacey is getting pressure from Attorney General Mitchell to leave. Senator Case keeps hammering Justice to clear my nomination. We don't have enough to indict, yet. And yet, we can't wait much longer. When Lacey leaves, and if I go, it may all fall apart.

The press knows that the indictments are close and are all over me. On November 14, the Newark *Star Ledger* interviews me. When Lacey goes, will I stay? What if Nixon does not want me? In the end I tell them the only thing that I can: "I'm simply delighted to have the sponsorship of a man like Senator Case." But I also tell them that I recognize that "the president is entitled to the lawyer of his choice," as though Nixon could care less about who is U.S. Attorney in New Jersey. When the reporter suggests that Nixon wants to appoint Nelson Gross, who just lost his senate race against Harrison Williams, I have to laugh. Gross, whom Case despises, has no chance of senate confirmation.

****

My father is worried about me. He keeps calling. He wants to know what is going to happen to me. "Are you going to get the job?"

"I don't know, Pop."

"What about the New Jersey bar exam? Are you going to take the exam?"

"Yes."

"When?"

"In February."

"How are you going to pass? You have been out of school almost nine years."

"I'm going to take the bar review course here at night."

"Can you manage all that?"

I'm not sure that I can. By the time Lacey leaves I will be running the office, finishing the Addonizio briefs in the Court of Appeals and preparing to argue. I will be getting ready to try the biggest criminal case in the country, and going to school at night. But I don't tell him that. He dropped out of grade school to support his mother and sister, and then went to high school at night, completing it in a year and a half. Then straight to law school at night, because then you did not have to go to college first. I'm making no complaint to him.

****

November 16

We are about to announce the Hudson indictments. Goldstein, Williamson and I walk into Lacey's office. Seated at his desk, he looks up and peers at us from behind his heavy black-framed glasses. "Are you ready?" he asks us. I am not at all sure that we are. It's only been six months since the first of the subpoenas went out. But we march out together to our library, which is crowded with all kinds of press. It is one fifteen in the afternoon.

We file in and seat ourselves behind the large conference table, our backs to the wall, facing a room full of cameras and reporters. "The United States Grand Jury has just indicted twelve men, including the mayor and the president of the city council of Jersey City, the Democratic chairman of Hudson County, the chief of police of Hudson, the purchasing agent of Jersey City, the commissioner of the Port Authority of New York and New Jersey, and others." Lacey holds up the indictment. "You will find all twelve names here in the indictment. We have copies for each of you."

The press shouts questions. Lacey knows he can't answer them, because he can't go beyond the words of the indictment. But he can't resist praising the IRS, who made the investigation with our office, and taking a shot at the FBI, who refused to assign agents. "A very significant factor has been the close cooperation with the Internal Revenue Service," he tells them.

Jon leans over to me and whispers, "Wait 'til the bureau hears that. Fred just pulled their nose." Our attention is drawn back to the press. "When will the case be tried?" one of the press shouts out.

"We will ask for a trial date in the spring."

"Will you stick around to try the case?"

"No. I will leave before the end of the year. The chief prosecutor will be Herb Stern, my first assistant, who, I hope, will have been nominated by the president by the end of the year, when I leave. Mr. Williamson and Mr. Goldstein will assist Mr. Stern."

Chapter Twenty-Nine

The Commission
November 16–December 31, 1970

T HE "HUDSON TWELVE," as the press now calls them, have all been arraigned. The trial is scheduled in May. Six months for both sides to prepare. For us, the preparation involves finding more witnesses and evidence.

The pressure is mounting on Lacey to leave. He was nominated by the president and confirmed by the Senate back in mid–October. He has hung on until the indictment. On November 24 Attorney General Mitchell summons Fred to Washington. The next day, the Newark *Evening News* headlines, "Mitchell prods Lacey." And Lacey, Goldstein, and I powwow. "What happened?" I ask.

Lacey shakes his head. "He told me I am now a judge. Nominated and confirmed. My commission is on Nixon's desk. He said they will send the commission up as soon as I set the date of the swearing-in," Lacey shrugs. "Looks like time has run out."

"Have you set the date?" Jon asks.

"No. I told Mitchell I need some minor surgery, which I do, and—"

"What surgery?" Jon and I break in together.

"Just a gall bladder operation," Lacey laughs at our obvious distress. "Piece of cake. I go in on the weekend, December 4, and when I come out I'll resign and set the date for my judicial swearing-in."

"What did you tell Mitchell?" Jon asks.

"Just that. And by the way," Lacey adds with a grin, "I thanked him for increasing us from eighteen assistants to thirty in just one year, and told him you are going to need a bunch more."

"Amen," I say. "And also a presidential nomination."

****

The editorials are flying. They all want Stern. Senator Case is calling the editors and publishers of every newspaper in the state. And there is an enormous number of papers from the tip of Cape May in the south up the length and breadth of New Jersey. I have no time to worry. But I have to get ready to argue the DeCarlo appeal on December 4.

The day before the DeCarlo argument I go to Philadelphia, where the Third Circuit Court of Appeals sits. By coincidence, the same panel of three judges that will hear DeCarlo will hear the Colonial appeal the day before. So I go a day early to listen to the Colonial argument, but only as a spectator. Because of Lacey's representation of Bechtel at trial, I am disqualified from representing the government as long as I work under him.

The panel of judges is composed of Collens Seitz, Harry Kolander, and Ruggiero Aldisert. Mayor Zirpolo is not before the court, so Ed Williams is not there. The rest of the gang, Rifkind, Toolan, Brill, and the others, argue. It is great to see them. What is not so great is the way the court is treating the government, represented by the departmental lawyer assigned by Henry Petersen. I don't like the tone of it, particularly the attitude of Judge Aldisert.

The next day is worse. It's the same panel for the DeCarlo appeal. And I'm in trouble. But, to my surprise, the trouble is not Saperstein's letter from the grave. As I argue, I hear Judge Aldisert mumbling, "They killed him." He looks like he will reverse because the jury heard about arsenic poisoning. I always thought that the arsenic would lead the jury to conclude suicide. After all, you have the letter posted on the way to the hospital by a man who knows he is about to die. But if Aldisert thinks the arsenic poison spells murder, we could be in trouble for implying that crime to the jury.

****

December 4

I am back in the office, saying goodbye to Fred. He is on his way to the hospital. He expects to be back Monday to set the date for his induction.

"If you need me, I'll be under the name Smith."

"Smith?"

"I'm going to be helpless in bed after the surgery. I'll be more likely to survive as Smith than Lacey."

****

It turns out that Fred Lacey may not survive under either name. A few days later my phone rings. It's Tom Campion, Fred's former law partner at his old firm, Shanley & Fisher, and one of his closest friends. Tom has been helping us, unofficially. When we needed counsel for Zelmanowitz during the trial, Tom did it. Didn't charge anything either. That's Tom. He looks like a banker. Very proper. He rarely speaks and uses few words when he does. This time is no different.

"Fred's in trouble."

"What!"

"He's sick. I am getting him out of New Jersey. My cousin, Dr. Kevin Cahill, is admitting him to Lenox Hill Hospital."

"When?"

"The ambulance will be here in an hour."

"So will I."

Campion and I are in the street when the ambulance arrives. We see them take Fred out on a stretcher. He is unconscious, or maybe dead. I can't tell. His large form is unmoving, eyes closed, no color.

"What happened?"

"Infection," Tom answers in a word.

"Will he be okay?"

All I get from Tom is a shrug.

****

Lacey has been operated on. I go to the hospital as often as I can. He is in bad shape. It's been a week.

Jon, Tom, and I meet in my office. "If he is in trouble," I tell them, "it will be better for him to be sworn in as a judge. I checked it out with the administrative office of the courts. Even if he has to retire immediately, after he is sworn in, he and Mary will get half the pay of a federal judge for the rest of his life. And Mary gets survivor benefits if it goes really bad. But Justice is holding up his commission."

"Why?" Tom asks.

"They say they don't want him sworn in on day one and taking medical leave on day two. That's what they say, but," I add, "I'm not sure that's what they mean. It may be that this is a way to stop me. And you know the Criminal Division doesn't want me."

"Nothing to be done," Campion says.

"No," I reply. "I have done something. I called Dick Kleindienst, the deputy attorney general, and I have an appointment to see him tomorrow. I'm going to offer my resignation if they agree to send up Fred's commission so he can take the oath."

"I'll go with you," Tom says.

The next day we are on the Eastern Airlines shuttle, sitting side by side. As we fly, it comes to me that much as I would like to have Campion with me, I can't bring him into a meeting with the Deputy Attorney General of the United States. "Tom," I begin, "I've been thinking about the meeting. You know this is Justice Department stuff . . ."

"Okay, I'll wait outside the building."

****

Kleindienst does not keep me waiting. The deputy AG's office has a fireplace. I don't know if it works, but it looks nice. Kleindienst himself looks in his mid-forties, a little portly, grey hair and a ruddy countenance. Outside the department he is a favorite target of the press, viewed as an arch law-and-order conservative, which he is. But in the department, everyone loves him. From file clerks and secretaries to department lawyers, everyone calls him Dick. He is a man without airs, with an ebullient love of life. I haven't seen him often but we get along. I don't care about his politics. I'm a professional prosecutor, not a politician.

"Dick," I tell him, "the White House or the department is holding up Fred's commission.

"That's right," he says.

"If I'm the problem, and even if I'm not, I want you to know that I will resign if you send the commission up and let him take the bench."

Kleindienst looks at me and breaks into his wide, toothy grin, "Herbie," he laughs, "that will not be necessary."

He tells me that he will send "Woody," his executive assistant Harlington Wood, up to New Jersey to evaluate Fred's health. If the report is okay, he will make sure the commission is released.

When I get outside to where Tom is waiting, I do a Campion on him. "It's okay," is all I say. He just nods. I tell him not to tell Fred or Mary Lacey about the trip. Another nod.

****

December 22

Lacey is out of the hospital. He announces that he will resign "next month," once he recovers from surgery. The same day Attorney General Mitchell announces that he is appointing me "Acting United States Attorney." But he refuses to announce whether they will have the president appoint me. This angers Senator Case, whose office publicly states that some "of Stern's older colleagues in Washington are a bit jealous." He means Petersen, of course. When Petersen reads that, and I'm sure he will, there will be more trouble.

There is one piece of good news. On December 30 the Court of Appeals affirms Weber's conviction. The end of the year marks the end of the mission that brought me to New Jersey. Five years ago.

Chapter Thirty

Acting U.S. Attorney
January 1–31, 1971

TO BE **ACTING** U.S. Attorney does not mean that you can act like one. I've got lots of ideas for the office. I want to build an institution. But I have no time for new initiatives, even if I had power to implement them.

With Fred out the month of December, and now January, I have thirty AUSAs in three offices to supervise, and an additional ten slots to fill. Fred has gotten us up to forty AUSAs. We are now one of the largest offices in the country, right behind Washington, D.C., Chicago, and the Southern District of New York. I have the most important criminal case in the country to try in May, and we are still investigating like crazy. The appellate briefs are due in the Addonizio appeal. I will argue the appeal in February. The pretrial motions in the Hudson County case are to be briefed in January. I have to argue those motions. When I can, I run over to New York to visit Fred in the hospital. At night I sit in a classroom in Rutgers Law School, crowded with recent graduates attending a bar review course.

We study trusts, wills, and contracts. Just what I need. All of us, the "kids" just out of law school and the "old-timers" like me are there because we have little chance to pass the bar exam without a bar review course. My classmates are amused to see the United States Attorney studying with them. That wears off quickly. The fatigue doesn't. Pretty soon I'm falling asleep in class. But if I don't go every night, I can't possibly pass the February exam. If I flunk, my friends in D.C. will have a picnic, and I will be out.

Woody, Kleindienst's assistant, has finished his investigation of Fred's health status, and clears Fred to serve on the federal bench. We have the commission. Fred has set February 1 as his induction. But he is still in the hospital. I visit him when I can. He looks terrible. He must have lost forty or fifty pounds. He tells me he is on the mend and I hope that is true. When he takes the judicial oath, there will be a vacancy in the office. The way the law reads, if the president has not selected a United States Attorney by then, the federal district judges fill the vacancy—until the president acts, *with* the advice and consent of the Senate.

Lacey and Senator Case have been lobbying the judges. Case had appointed several of them, and Lacey will be their colleague. Fred tells me that they have voted to seat me as United States Attorney, to take office immediately after Fred is sworn in as district judge. I will then no longer be "acting." I will be the USA. Once I am court-appointed, Senator Case intends to prevent any other presidential appointment. Then we can form our institution.

****

I am exhausted. My nightly studies have been overwhelmed by the press of work, particularly as Williamson has refused to brief me on the Hudson County investigation. He insists that he has a right to present important witnesses at the trial. If I don't promise him specific witnesses, then he will not share what he knows. He tells me that he will not allow me to steal his case.

In an effort to defuse the situation, I ask Bruce Goldstein, one of our new AUSAs who worked on the investigation, to see Williamson. Bruce has a pleasant, non-threatening personality that goes with his wide smile. His outer softness belies his determination. He reaches out, but Williamson refuses to meet. Williamson refuses to recognize my authority to require the debriefing, insisting that he works for Fred Lacey, not me. The situation is disintegrating.

****

Lacey is better, but is still in the hospital. After ascertaining that he is well enough, Bruce Goldstein informs Fred of Williamson's refusal.

From his hospital room Fred calls Williamson and orders him to meet with Bruce and brief him. Williamson says yes, but when Bruce goes to him, Williamson refuses to provide information. He tells Bruce that Stern "is stealing my case." He will give no information to anyone without an ironclad guarantee as to the witnesses he will question at the trial. In an effort to catch up, I am poring over files attempting to replicate what Williamson had done. Bruce is even shuttling back and forth to Lacey's hospital room with documents to debrief Fred.

It is now impossible to continue my nightly attendance at the bar review course. That means I cannot take the February 3 bar exam. Better to be the United States Attorney who never took the bar than the one to flunk it while in office.

BOOK IV

THE LEVER

Chapter One

United States Attorney
February 1–19, 1971

February 1

The ceremonial courtroom is full. It had been half empty when Fred took his oath as U.S. Attorney just seventeen months earlier. Then, only Senator Case attended. Now the former and the present governors, Hughes and Cahill, U.S Senator Williams, New Jersey Chief Justice Joseph Weintraub, New Jersey Attorney General George Kugler, and every county prosecutor in the state who can manage a ticket are at the head of an overflow crowd. What a difference a year makes!

Senator Case is here, of course. We are seated near each other. As our eyes meet, he smiles. It is the first time we have actually seen each other, face to face. Given the events of the past months, the ludicrousness strikes us and we both laugh.

Fred looks gaunt. The attendees conceal their reaction, but their surprise at his appearance is palpable. The seriousness of his illness has never been made public; now it is self-evident. The courtroom ceremony is mercifully brief. When it concludes, the dignitaries leave. Then Fred and I go back into Chief Judge Augelli's chambers to swear me in as the court-appointed United States Attorney.

When we emerge from the Chief Judge's Chambers, I am the United States Attorney for the District of New Jersey, but not a member of the New Jersey bar. Court-appointed USAs make eighty percent of the salary. So I'm up to $28,000 a year. Even so, it's a temporary salary and maybe a temporary job. But I'm no longer "acting." For better or worse, I am the head of the office.

Head of the office. The enormity of it hits me. I suddenly feel penned in by responsibilities. People are all over me. Congratulating. Pumping my hand. At once my collar feels too tight. I have the sense of being suffocated. I have to break out. Pushing my way steadily through the throng, I finally reach the cold air outside. I need to be alone. I climb into my car and head for the apartment in Manhattan, which I have kept even after moving to New Jersey.

A few hours later, after I have pulled myself together, I make my way back; there is no alternative. Jon and I are on our own, and that is the way it is going to be. By late afternoon we meet to plan the organization of the office and we go to work. I make Jon first assistant. "Jon, we're not going to prosecute routine bank robberies and stolen car cases any longer. I want to limit our involvement in prosecuting local crimes."

"The bureau won't like it. Hoover uses those statistics to justify his budgets," Jon reminds me.

"It's bullshit. In the typical bank robbery, the bureau makes an arrest after the locals have caught the robber. Same with stolen cars that cross state lines. In an extraordinary case, sure we'll take it, if the bureau really made it. But we have too few assistants and far too few judges to tie up the office and the courts with stuff the locals are perfectly adequate to handle. This state has to be fumigated. We are the only ones who can do it."

"You know," Jon points out, "the volume cases do give our young people experience in the courtroom. A kind of training. Useful as they move up to more serious cases. And we can use the volume statistics to get more people out of D.C."

"I know we will lose all that. But we can solve part of the problem by hiring more people out of local DA offices, like Hogan's, who can already try a case. And if we keep making big cases, like Newark and Jersey City, we'll continue to get all the help we want."

"What are you going to do about Williamson?" Jon brings up the biggest problem.

"I am issuing a written order to him today as the United States Attorney. He will have to give me a memo laying out all he knows about Hudson by February 19. I figure he'll refuse."

"And if he does refuse?"

"I'll fire him. It's for the best. He should not be here."

As Jon gets up to leave, I tell him, "The bar exam begins the day after tomorrow. On Wednesday."

"So?"

"Just wanted you to know that I asked one of the men to prepare a motion to the Justices of the Supreme Court of New Jersey to admit me on motion without the exam. I'm having it filed today."

"What did you say?"

"I told them that I wanted to take the bar, but my duties have made that difficult. Last January I tried DeCarlo, so the February bar was out. I could not take the June bar, because I was trying Addonizio, and I am overwhelmed now on the cusp of the two-and-a half-day February bar exam."

"You know, Herb, no one has ever been admitted on motion to the New Jersey bar. The bar here is very protective, what with the proximity of hundreds of thousands of lawyers in New York and Philadelphia."

"I know."

****

My secretary, Nancy Scardo, tells me that Chief Justice Joseph Weintraub is on the telephone. I have never spoken to the man before.

"I have the votes. It's not unanimous," he chuckles, "but I have the votes."

"Yes, sir."

"Come to my office, and I will swear you in."

"Yes, sir. And thank you very much."

****

I am a full-fledged, card-carrying member of the New Jersey bar. The chief justice personally gave me a certificate, but already there are rumblings from the bar. Weintraub could not care less. I think he did it to keep the work of the U.S. Attorney's office going, because he tells me that he called "Cliff Case" to give him the good news. Later I find out how close the vote was. Four justices voted yes, three voted no.

****

The Third Circuit court has scheduled two full days for the argument of the Addonizio appeal. It is unheard of in a court where affording one side more than half an hour is considered wildly generous. What does this portend?

February 18 and 19

Accompanied by Gary Brown, I make the arguments on the Addonizio appeal for the United States. There are scores of issues, including one that is a mirror image of the defendants' argument in Colonial. Newark public officials claim that they did not commit extortion, but that they were instead bribed. Just the reverse of Colonial, where the corporate givers defended themselves by claiming they were not bribers but instead victims of extortion. I try to make the court see that under the Hobbs Act, when a public official takes money "under color of official right," he commits *both* bribery *and* extortion. I sure hope that the court agrees, because that is the same theory that the Hudson County case rests on. I argue that all payments to public officials are extortion, because extortion is defined as taking under "color of official right" in the statute. If I lose on that, the Hudson case could be dead.

If I have any lingering doubt about the haunting nature of this bribery-extortion specter, it is resolved when I walk out of the Addonizio appellate courtroom. A deputy clerk of the court is waiting for me in the hall. He hands me the opinion of the Third Circuit reversing all the convictions in the Colonial case. Standing in the corridor, I read only the one word, reversed. Exhausted from two days of appellate argument, I stand transfixed, unable to move.

"What's wrong?" Gary Brown asks.

"I'll read this on the train back. I'll tell you then."

On the train, I finish reading. There is not one word about bribery versus extortion. Judge Aldisert has avoided the issue entirely. Speaking for himself and Judge Kolodner, they reverse because there were not enough women on the grand jury that indicted in Colonial. He finds that at the time of the Colonial indictment, grand jury selection in New Jersey was unconstitutional. It's all different now, he says, so no other prosecutions are in danger, unless someone in an open old case preserved the point. And no one ever has. To top it off, Aldisert writes that because the statute of limitations has run, we cannot re-indict any of the defendants. We apparently have an opinion written for just this one case, and a direction not to bring it again.

"Was it unanimous?" Brown asks.

"Yes, and no. Kolodner signed Aldisert's opinion, but Collins Seitz did not join because he recused himself."

* * * * * *

I am crushed. Years of work washed out. Plainly guilty businessmen and public officials have their convictions wiped clean. All because the grand jury pool was statistically deficient in women prospects. And Aldisert writes that we are forbidden from re-indicting them. And even worse, this is the same panel that heard the DeCarlo appeal. What's next, I wonder. By the time I get to my office in Newark, I am despondent.

Jon Goldstein is waiting for me.

"You heard?" I ask.

"Yes," Jon is grim. "The press called and read the opinion to me. It's on the wires."

"What a disaster. And Aldisert says they can't be retried."

"Well," Jon laughs, "he's wrong."

"What do you mean?"

"I mean that there is a specific federal statute that says when a case is dismissed because of a grand jury defect, the statute of limitations is tolled, and the defendants can be re-indicted. The Court of Appeals is wrong. They can't ignore this specific statute."

"Then, Aldisert is all wet?"

"We can re-indict," is all the conservative Jon will give me.

"Great!" I say. "We can also re-indict Zirpolo." Zirpolo had been retried before Judge Wortendyke. With me recused, Ed Williams had his partner Ray Bergen try it. Henry Petersen sent one of his men up from Washington to prosecute. The jury convicted, but Judge Wortendyke threw out the conviction because of improper remarks by Henry's man in both his opening and in his summation.

"Who do you want to handle it?" Jon asks.

"Your pick."

"Let's give it to Dick Shapiro." Shapiro is one of our new crew, someone Jon particularly favors.

"Agreed."

Chapter Two

Washington, Trenton, and Paris
February 19–March 31, 1971

February 19

Williamson is supposed to give me his memo by today. He doesn't. I figure he never will, but I give him until March anyway. I know he has to go. The scene with old man Kenny and his young mistress was disgraceful. That, together with his nastiness with witnesses, and insubordination compel the conclusion that he should not be here.

What I don't figure on is his call to Petersen. Williamson spends two days with Petersen in Washington, proclaiming that he alone knows the case, and that I am unprepared to try it.

In the end I appeal to Kleindienst and Wood, who step in again and authorize me to terminate Williamson. Now Petersen cannot save Williamson. But Petersen has an excuse to question my fitness to try the case. He calls me to say that he has assigned one of his men, a guy named Hantman, to debrief Williamson, and to be "the department's supervisor of you on the case."

"Henry," I tell him on the telephone, "does that mean I am not to try the case?"

"No," Petersen says. "But he will supervise you."

"Supervise me? This is after Colonial, Weber, DeCarlo, and Addonizio? He is going to supervise me!"

"That's right."

I know Petersen wants me to blow. Instead, I laugh, "Well, Henry, this guy Hantman must be one great trial lawyer."

Hantman comes and hangs around. But he eventually goes, which is fine with both of us.

****

March 10

As we get ready for trial, the Third Circuit strikes again. A panel reverses the conviction of Sam the Plumber DeCavalcante. This time it is not us.

It is a strike force case, but it hurts nonetheless. Judge Adams writes the opinion, with Judge Rosen, and Judge Aldisert on the panel. Two down. Colonial and now DeCavalcante, with the appellate DeCarlo decision yet to come. My bad feeling is getting worse. I have no reason to doubt Judge Aldisert's integrity, but he doesn't seem to like our cases. So far we are 0 for 2 with him. And my guess is he will preside on DeCarlo. I can still hear his mumbling during the argument, "They killed him."

****

Jon and I feel surrounded. Our relationship with Petersen and the Criminal Division could not be worse. The strike force, located in our building, using the same investigatory agencies, reports directly to Henry Petersen. They do not tell us what they are investigating. They even lie to us about their activities. For months Lacey had been complaining about their irresponsibility and even mendacity. His written complaints to Kleindienst were referred to Petersen. And that was the end of that. The chief of the strike force, John Bartels, and I barely speak.

May 1

It breaks out into the newspapers. "Five men were arrested yesterday for allegedly plotting to sell $1 million in stolen treasury certificates . . . The agents were so secretive about the matter that at about 7:00 p.m.

U.S. Attorney Herbert J. Stern said he had just been told of the arrests which had been made before noon. Stern said the organized crime strike force had not even passed a copy of the complaint to his office. Strike force head John Bartels admitted the arrests had been made by Secret Service agents yesterday morning."

"Henry has what he wants," I tell Jon. "He wants control in as many districts as he can, with his own people reporting directly back, going around the U.S. Attorneys. That's what he started with us, in Colonial. Now he has offices in Detroit, Buffalo, and here. And the agencies have their own fiefdoms and agendas. They can pick between the strike force and us. The IRS is the only one that will take direction from us. And I don't know how long that will last."

"As long as we make the cases," Jon smiles, "they will be with us."

"Maybe. I'm not so sure. What we need to do is hire our own people. Our own investigators, an office squad, like we had when I was an ADA in Hogan's office. Guys who directly report to and take orders from us."

"The only way would be to get the other big offices behind it, Southern District of New York, and Eastern," Jon says. "If we can get Woody on board we have a chance."

"I agree," I say. "I'll call Mike Seymour in Southern, Bobby Morse in Eastern, and Jim Thompson in Chicago. I know just the investigators I want to hire."

"Who's that?"

"Two guys who made my first arrest. Henry Cronin and Joe Feeley. You should have seen them. They locked up this guy Kingsley, who was scamming a couple of opera stars…"

"Okay," says Jon, who has heard my stories. "But the bureau will go nuts. When I see it, I'll believe it."

****

My admission to the bar by the New Jersey Supreme Court in the midst of the bar examination causes an uproar. Those taking the test are heard from, loudly. I don't blame them. They got the news as they walked into the exam. The bar associations are something else. They want to protect their exclusive prerogatives, and do not want an out-of-state

U.S. Attorney. The Sussex County Bar Association passes a resolution condemning my admission as "unfair to all other attorneys in New Jersey and an infringement on their rights." Then the trustees of the New Jersey State Bar Association weigh in. "No other person has been so admitted in the history of our bar. His petition was filed February 2, 1971, the same date as the order of admission . . . a precipitate action taken without consultation with the Board of Bar Examiners, when the applicant was seeking an appointment. This required the court's abstention from action having partisan overtones." But the public press supports my admission. The *Newark Sunday News* editorializes, "If the Supreme Court discriminated, it was not against bar candidates who must take the test, but in favor of the public interest."

My favorite anti-letter appears in the *New Jersey Law Journal.* "I would submit," this guy writes, "that the United States of America in appointing a United States Attorney who is not a member of our bar demeaned the state of New Jersey and the bar of this state." I am sure this guy will get his back slapped repeatedly with lots of free drinks at his next bar association gathering. I have no interest in attending. My very appearance might "demean" these right thinkers and sound viewers.

This seems an excellent moment to assume control over the Newark chapter of the Federal Bar Association. Why not create our own local federal bar? The existing chapter of the Federal Bar Association is but a half dozen federal career employees who meet for lunch twice a year. After a brief recruiting drive, during which a bunch of my boys join, we outnumber everyone in the association. Not surprisingly, I am elected president by a landslide. We are a small bar now. Maybe forty members. But that is going to change.

****

April 5

My secretary, Nancy Scorpo, tells me a supervising customs agent is on the telephone.

"He says one of his inspectors, Lynn Polletier, has just made an arrest."

"So tell him to call the duty assistant. Who has the duty today?" I ask.

"I think that you will want to take this yourself," Nancy insists. So I take the call.

I'm told that a customs inspector in Port Newark discovered ninety-eight pounds of pure heroin under the floorboards of a Volkswagen camper bus, which arrived from France. She called for backup, and waited for the consignee to arrive—a Frenchman named Roger DeLouette. When he showed up, he was immediately placed under arrest. He also immediately "broke." He confessed to being a member of the French SDECE, the Service de Documentation Extérieure et de Contre-Espionage (Foreign Intelligence and Counter Espionage Service), the French equivalent of the CIA.

"Is this bullshit?" I ask.

"No. We think this is true."

"Why?"

"First, he has SDECE identification hidden under the carpet in his hotel room."

"That means nothing."

"Second, he was told he could contact the SDECE man at the French Consulate in New York. He was given the name Donald McNabb."

"And?"

"And we checked. There is a Donald McNabb assigned to the consulate."

"And?"

"And our sources at the CIA tell us that McNabb is the SDECE man at the consulate."

"Holy shit! Did this DeLouette tell you who sent him over here with the heroin?"

"Oh yes. He says it was a Colonel Paul Fournier."

"And do we know who he is?"

"DeLouette says Fournier is the head of the SDECE, that's their CIA. We are trying to check it out."

In ten minutes, Jon Goldstein is in my office. We have to assign this DeLouette matter to someone to lead the investigation.

I run over our current assignments. "You, John Barry, Bruce Goldstein, and Marc Dembling, and Dick Langway are our trial team on Hudson. We pick a jury in just five weeks. The best man for this is Don Merkelbach."

"But he is slated to retry Tony Boy Boiardo," Jon objects.

"It will never happen. Tony Boy will get sick again. Don came out of Lordi's office and has more trial experience than our new guys. He did a great job on Addonizio. He deserves this."

"I'll tell him," Jon says, as he leaves my office.

Chapter Three

"An X Will Be Fine"
March 31–May 17, 1971

WITH JUST FIVE weeks until the Hudson trial, we get an enormous break. We have been cracking company after company. No one did business in Hudson without paying. I could put dozens of businessmen on the stand who paid. But the businessmen did not make direct payments to the big boys, to Mayor Whelan or to city council President Flaherty, and certainly not to boss John V. Kenny. Instead, the givers all paid to collectors: Bernard Murphy, purchasing agent in Jersey City; John J. "Jack" Kenny, former Democratic chairman of Hudson County (no relation to John V. Kenny); and Frank Manning, who served as engineer, first for Jersey City, and later for Hudson County. It was the collectors who funneled money up a chain of errand boys to the bosses. The givers never saw the ultimate recipients.

We have only one witness who can link the businessmen's cash payments to the big guys: Frank Manning. Williamson and Fred Lacey had persuaded Manning to turn before we indicted. The case against the three top men, the mayor, the city council president, and the Boss, depends entirely on Manning.

Frank Manning had worked in Jersey City and later in Hudson County. When with the city, he collected ten percent on city contracts; with the county, ten percent on county contracts. On the Little Guy's "orders," Manning distributed cash to the mayor, to the president of the city council, and, of course, to John V. Kenny himself. Manning's evidence was more than sufficient to indict on. But it is still just a one-witness case. Then Donald A. Robinson, J.J. Kenny's lawyer, calls on me and tells me that the former county chairman is prepared to testify against Whelan, Flaherty, and . . . John V. Kenny.

"But," Robinson says, "we will take no plea. The charges have to be dismissed. Jack Kenny has to be immunized. Transactional immunity."

"Can your client give us John V. Kenny?" I want to know.

"Yes," Robinson laughs, "and something very concrete. Very, very physical."

"What?"

"The boys know that Manning is your witness. The Little Guy gave Jack $50,000 in cash to hire investigators to discredit Manning."

"Does he still have the cash?" I ask.

"You bet," Robinson smiles. "Every dollar. You make the deal, we turn the cash over to the government."

"You have a deal," I nod. "When do I meet your client?"

"As soon as you wish," Robinson laughs. "But not here. He won't come near this building. You have to prepare him in a hotel room."

"When did you say I can get the money?"

"Day after tomorrow," Robinson laughs again. "I'll get a room in the Gateway Hotel, across from the train station."

****

April 21

I set out for the hotel alone. Robinson insists that J.J.'s flip be held close, even in my office. Only Jon Goldstein is permitted to know, and he has other business today.

As I leave, Jon alerts me about the Frenchman DeLouette. The case has been assigned to Judge Fred Lacey. As the Frenchman is an indigent and without counsel, the court assigns an attorney to represent him. And Lacey assigns a former law partner of his from Shanley & Fisher, none other than Donald A. Robinson. Interesting. Fred does not know that J.J. is about to flip. Now one lawyer controls two very important witnesses, in two very different cases.

J.J. Kenny and Robinson are in the hotel room when I get there. A large shopping bag is on the room's only bed. Kenny, a handsome man in his late forties, with a florid face and wavy grey hair, nods hello to me as I enter. Then he nods at the bag. We need no introduction. He has been under indictment since November. We saw each other at his arraignment.

"Dump it," I tell him, pointing to the bag.

As he turns the bag over, money cascades out. It covers the bed. I can see bills of various denominations. Not just hundreds, but also twenties and even tens. And the bills are old. Some, very old. There are bills signed by Henry Morgenthau, Bob Morgenthau's father, when the old man was Roosevelt's secretary of the treasury, thirty or more years ago.

"Sign them," I tell Kenny.

"You mean the bag?"

"No, the bills. Each one, with your initials and the date."

"Why?" asks Kenny, surprised.

"Because money is fungible, and these bills are going into evidence at the trial. I want to prove the chain of possession, from you to me, and then me to the court," I explain.

"Can I just put an 'x' on each one?"

"An 'x' will be fine," I decide.

After Kenny leaves, Robinson reminds me that J.J is also under indictment by the state on a corrupt land deal. I tell him I know, but the only immunity his client is getting is on the existing federal indictment. Robinson wants more.

"You know," Robinson says, "if you ask him questions about the state indictment while he is on the stand, he will be immunized. The state will not be able to prosecute."

"I know," I acknowledge. "But I can't do that. Matter of fact, before trial, I am going to tell the attorney general that your man is our witness."

"But not too soon," Robinson pleads.

"No, shortly before trial," I assure him. "I expect to see Attorney General Kugler at the Legislative Correspondents Dinner in a few weeks. I'll wait until then."

* * * * * * *

Over the next few weeks, J.J. Kenny enriches us with information. As Democratic chairman in Hudson County for five years, he extorted money from Hudson County contractors by simply withholding their checks until they paid off. There were so many that he cannot remember all of them. There was $5,000 from the builder of a firehouse and $50,000 from a sewage construction firm. He tells us about $225,000 in kickbacks from Sarubbi Construction for work on Pollak and Mental Health Hospitals. But the big gift he gives to us, and the problem that he causes us, is J. Rich Steers Construction. We had not heard of Steers before.

Kenny tells us Steers paid $50,000 for turnpike work, $30,000 for work done for the Port Authority, and $150,000 for a bridge in Jersey City. All great. But when Bruce Goldstein goes to Steers, they not only confirm J.J. Kenny's story, they also tell Bruce they paid off Robert Burkhardt with $30,000 when Burkhardt was Governor Hughes's secretary of state. The problem is that Burkhardt is not one of the Hudson County defendants. So the case against Burkhardt is a new case. There is no way Bruce can bring it home on the eve of the Hudson trial. It will have to wait.

****

DeLouette, the Frenchman with the heroin, will have to wait as well. We are learning a great deal about the French Secret Service. Don Merkelbach is doing a fine job.

May 12

Five days before the Hudson County trial, I go to the legislative correspondents dinner. I go, but I do not intend to stay. It's New Jersey Attorney General Kugler I want to see. I seek him out. I tell him the news will soon be public: J.J. Kenny will be severed as a defendant and will testify for us.

"Will you keep away from our indictment?" he asks.

"Absolutely," I tell him, "but you know, I can't control the cross." He seems satisfied.

Kugler's seeming acquiescence doesn't last. Every day before trial he calls me. I have to repeat my promise not to immunize Kenny from the state's case. Not satisfied, the day the trial opens, he sends me a letter to memorialize our conversations and my agreement "to avoid questioning our Kenny" on matters in the state indictment. It's a "Dear Herb" letter expressing "gratitude" for the agreement and extolling our cooperative efforts. Its real purpose is to make a record, and make sure I keep my word.

The lack of trust between his Division of Criminal Justice and our office is palpable. Jon and I are convinced that Kugler's director of criminal justice, Evan Jahos, is egging Kugler on. The repeated demands for assurances, now in writing, do not bode well. Nonetheless, I write Kugler back on May 19, a week before Kenny is to testify, in the most cordial terms, again promising to keep away from the subject matter of the New Jersey accusations, but reminding him that I can't control what defense attorneys do on their cross examination of Kenny

Chapter Four

"A Way of Life"
May 17, 1971

THEY CALL IT "a way of life." The obscene, embedded, systematic tithing to public officials by everyone who works for Hudson and its constituent cities, Bayonne, Union City, Hoboken, West New York, North Bergen, and its jewel, Jersey City, is summed up by the phrase coined sixty years ago: "A way of life." We are going to break it for all time.

I have no illusions. Whatever we do here, we cannot change human nature. There will always be graft, but, I swear, never again will it be so deeply entrenched in Hudson County. I have only one regret—I have been forbidden to prove that the municipal and county employees are forced to kickback three percent of their salaries. They are, in fact, forced to do so, but Judge Shaw has ruled that these kickbacks are outside of the scope of the indictment. He's right. It doesn't fit, legally, but when we end the public lives of these men on trial, that graft, too, will end forever.

In the weeks before trial, a reform movement sought a recall vote on Mayor Whelan and Flaherty, president of the city council. It failed. Not by much, just a few hundred votes. Still, it failed. It's Addonizio all over again. But in Newark, eventually most of the citizens came to their senses. We are determined not to fail in Jersey City. I have reluctantly decided to open, close, and handle all the witnesses, on direct and cross, myself. If this case is to be lost, I will be the one who loses it.

We have developed our trial strategy. Again, it is to buttress and protect our main witness, the one who, if believed, will ensure conviction. Potentially, we have two, J.J. Kenny and Frank Gerard Manning. But of the two, the centerpiece must be Manning. He is the better witness. More important, as city engineer, he collected on city work; as county engineer, he collected on county work. Plus, he was the secret principal of Gerard Engineering, and his company also paid to work. He dealt directly with every level of the conspiracy. If he is believed, all the defendants will be convicted. If he is discredited, the case is lost.

The way must be prepared for him. First, we'll put on the witness stand a bevy of contractors who paid Murphy, J.J. Kenny, and Manning. Then, J.J. Kenny will testify, to spread the money upward. Then the money itself: The secret purchases of bonds for cash, using Fred Kropke, the corrupt chief of police of Hudson County as a messenger boy between John V. Kenny and Sternkopf, commissioner of the Port Authority, who served as financial advisor to the conspirators. Then, with the stage set, we will bring forth Manning, near the end of the case, when his credibility will have been so buttressed in advance that, we hope, successful cross-examination will be impossible.

Some trial lawyers would be tempted to put Manning on first, to outline the scheme, and then use the others to corroborate him later, but I will not go that route. Past mistakes in Colonial will not be repeated here. Manning will go on *after* the others.

But first we must pick a jury.

Chapter Five

Trashcans and Florida Bank Accounts
May 17–31, 1971

THE HUDSON COUNTY corruption trial will be held in Newark, but Judge Shaw brings us down to Trenton to pick a jury from the middle of the state. He does all the questioning so it only takes a day, and then, like DeCarlo and Addonizio, the jurors are confined to a hotel in Newark until the trial ends.

The jury looks okay. We have eight women and four men. The defendants use all their challenges. We only use one: I excuse a Republican committeewoman. A different party and a different county, true, but I cannot take a chance. In New Jersey the party lines are not what they seem.

Manning and J.J. Kenny, the state's witnesses, have been severed from the trial. Another defendant has pled guilty: James Corrado, who was the administrator of Pollak Hospital, and whose office the conspirators used as a headquarters. That leaves eight defendants. The press already calls them "the Hudson 8."

John V. Kenny attends court in a wheelchair. He is plainly preparing to exit the trial on grounds of ill-health just as soon as he can. He has had elective hernia surgery and complains of other ailments. He has a full-time nurse, in full uniform, white cap, cape, and all, in constant attendance. Nothing I can do about it.

After the jury is selected, Judge Shaw gives us two days off to get organized back in his Newark courtroom. I am to open to the jury on Thursday morning.

****

May 19

"Proceed, Mr. Stern," Judge Shaw growls.

"Thank you, Your Honor." It is so crowded in the old courtroom that the collective body heat threatens to overwhelm the air conditioning. As I walk forward, I see Mary Lacey, Fred's wife, in the front spectators' row. She is wearing a red, white, and blue dress. I don't know where she got it, but she looks great to me. She beams at me, and I grin back.

For an hour and a half I take them through the defendants, the charges, and the proofs. I name sixteen companies who were extorted by the defendants, "who did in fact extort from many engineers, suppliers, contractors, and firms who sought to do business with Jersey City and Hudson County; and that they did their extortion both by fear and by misuse of their public office."

I follow the plan. Payment after payment from firm after firm is detailed to the jurors. Then I turn to the fear of apprehension which drove John V. Kenny to order the return of some of the graft. "There came a time when the then U.S. Attorney Frederick B. Lacey began to investigate; when books and records of Gerard Engineering were subpoenaed by Mr. Lacey's office."

"Then," I tell the jurors, "the defendants became afraid. Because of this fear, the leader, John V. Kenny, ordered the wheels of conspiracy to crank in reverse." They began to return cash to businessmen. We shall prove to you that the defendant Walter Wolfe, the Democratic Chairman of Hudson County, took Mr. Merrigan into a men's room of a restaurant and gave him back $18,000 in cash. Not to keep, just to hold, so he could explain what he had done with some of the cash that has been raised." Similarly, the conspirators used Chief of Police Kropke to deliver cash back to Ashland Oil.

I focus on this return of money not merely to show guilty knowledge, which it does; nor even to add to the case against Wolfe and Kropke, which it also does; but also because I am going to introduce those very greenbacks into evidence and let the jurors touch them, if they want to.

****

The defendants' openings are the usual reminders about presumption of innocence and reasonable doubt. All but one. Jack Noonan, Wally Wolfe's lawyer, appears to be making an insanity defense. He tells the jury that a head wound Wolfe suffered as a Marine on Saipan in World War II affected Wolfe "in certain ways" and that he did not have any criminal intent because he did not fully understand what was going on.

I whisper to Jon, sitting next to me, "Can you believe it? Wolfe, the Democratic chairman of Hudson County, is defending on the ground of insanity!"

"*Someone* is nuts," Jon whispers back, "but we better get Wally examined by a psychiatrist of our own."

****

After the defendants open, the payers troop was brought onto the stand to testify to payments to purchasing agent Murphy. From the biggest to the smallest.

C.J. Lagenfelder, Baltimore Contractors, wished to bid on a $40 million reservoir project. They sent the company plane. Bernie Murphy boarded, and over cocktails he demanded a seven percent cash kickback, $2.8 million. James R. Crawford of Lagenfelder testifies that when he got the demand he decided not to bid.

Hugh Platt, Jr., of Ray Palmer Associates, had been broken by Williamson. He testifies that Murphy hit him up for ten percent of a sewage treatment contract, which came to $2,884.04. "I had little choice, if we were going to be paid."

"What did you do with the $2,884.04?" I ask.

"I took it down to Mr. Murphy's office," Platt replies.

"Including the four cents?"

"He rejected it."

"He took the cash and gave you back the pennies?"

"Yes."

Herman Silverman, of Sylvan Pools, testifies he kicked back $6,000, ten percent of his pool contract. Aaron Groveman, of Adsley Construction, testifies to paying $10,000 for the contract to rehabilitate Jersey City's Roosevelt Stadium. After half a dozen, I figure we have enough to set the stage for J.J. Kenny. Only I don't figure on Attorney General George Kugler and his Division of Criminal Justice.

****

May 26

I am about to call J.J. to the stand, but before the jury enters, Richard B. McGlynn, chief of the state's division of criminal justice trial division, comes striding into court.

"What's he doing here?" Jack Barry asks me. "Didn't you have a deal with Kugler?"

"You bet. And in writing. Kugler insisted on it in writing. We will not ask any questions on the state indictment. I told him I could not control the defendants who—"

I have to break off because McGlynn is speaking. He marks the state indictment of J.J. as a court exhibit and tells Judge Shaw that the state will prosecute this indictment in spite of the federal immunity.

Apparently, Kugler and company not only distrust me, they have forgotten who Iron Balls Shaw is. I watch as Shaw's face goes from red to purple. Pointing his finger at McGlynn, the judge lambasts him. He tells him that the state attorney general has no standing in his court. "I will not permit any state official to interfere with the trial of this case, in any manner." Then, glaring at McGlynn, Shaw says ominously, "And anyone who thinks he can do it will be before me for appropriate proceedings."

Jack Barry leans over from the middle of our table. "This is fantastic. They must have gone nuts in Trenton. They look like they are trying to stop J.J. from testifying."

"I really don't think that's their aim. They're just paranoid about us. They think I'm going to sabotage their case," I tell Jack.

"Either way, it's nuts."

Before the end of the day, Judge Shaw orders federal marshals to protect J.J. Kenny from the state. "This is terrible," I tell Jack Barry. "The state guys will think we did this."

I take Kenny through his direct. A poor witness, he nonetheless manages to describe payment after payment. Hour after hour, I plod through the records. I get what I need, but barely. It's like trying to dance with a partner who's wearing concrete shoes. I speed up to reach my finale: The $50,000 given to J.J. Kenny by Boss Kenny.

I go up to J.J. with a closed bag. As he tells about receiving $50,000 in cash from John V. Kenny to discredit Frank Manning, I open the bag and spread out the money. J.J. identifies it. I gather the money in my arms and walk over to the defense table. "I offer these into evidence," I say, as I dump the money on their table. With their loud objections and motions for mistrial ringing in the courtroom, we at least have an interesting finish to my direct.

****

The first cross-examiner is J.V. Kenny's lawyer, the dapper Van Riper. And the first thing he does is to pick up the state indictment that McGlynn had marked as a court exhibit. Van Riper then methodically questions J.J. about the state indictment, line by line, effectively and efficiently immunizing him from prosecution on the state charges.

Judge Shaw, calling us up to the bench, says softly to Van Riper, "You definitely clinched the matter that he has immunity from state prosecution."

"Why did Van Riper do that?" Jack Barry whispers as we return to our seats. Before I can say "I don't know, " Van Riper shows us why.

Referring to all the kickback money J.J. testified to collecting, Van Riper asks whether J.J. had given any of that money to John V. Kenny. Leaning forward on his seat, J.J. replies, in almost a shout, "I never gave Mayor Kenny a dime in my life!"

Now we know why Van Riper went out of his way to get J.J. off the state hook. A little good old Hudson County horse-trading. But Van Riper is not through with us. He brings out that we prepared J.J. to testify in a hotel room in New York. He does not, of course, bring out why we needed to get out of New Jersey. Van Riper asks what he did in the hotel room.

"We talked about women and things happening in New York and New Jersey . . ." J.J. smiles benignly as the courtroom titters. "And," he continues, "Mr. Stern talked continually about corruption. He appeared to be against it."

******

At the recess Jon, Jack Barry, and I lick our wounds. "Did you really talk about women?" Jack deadpans.

"I have my own problems with all these Jon's, Jack's and John's. Not to mention you, a Jack J., talking about another Jack J."

"My name is John," Barry says.

"We've been calling you Jack for years."

"I know. But my name is John."

"Alright. So it's another John J."

"That settled, what are we going to do with this nut on the stand? We have to get him off as soon as possible."

"Right," Jon Goldstein says, "except Ray Brown gets to cross him first."

******

Raymond A. Brown is the best cross-examiner in New Jersey. That's my opinion. It's also the opinion of most of the trial bar. Tall. Elegant. A black man with skin so light that folks don't know he is black. But he lets everyone know as quickly as he can. His efforts in the civil rights movement are legendary. I admire him. I'm also scared about his cross of the unstable John J. Kenny.

As we wait, a young AUSA comes running over from the office. He's all excited. The IRS has just discovered that Whelan and Flaherty have joint, numbered bank accounts in Miami Beach.

"How much?" I ask.

"I'm told one million two hundred twenty-two thousand four hundred thirty-three dollars, mostly in bearer bonds, some in cash."

"The money is there?"

"No. The bank says Whelan and Flaherty sent a Jersey City cop with a suitcase to pick up the bonds and the money on June 12."

"Last year?"

"Yes."

"That's a few weeks after we issued the first round of subpoenas to Hudson and Jersey City," Jon recalls.

"Where is the loot now?"

"No one knows."

"John," I turn to John Barry. "I need you to go to Miami. *Today.* I need you to get copies of those records and be back here *ASAP.*"

"But we can't use the photocopies that way," John says. "We have to subpoena the bank officer to bring them up and put him on the stand."

"I know. And we will. But please, believe me. We will need those records tomorrow. Monday the latest. Take any of the boys you want. But go *now.*"

****

Ray Brown's cross of J.J. Kenny is as devastating as I expected, particularly when he asks Kenny—my Kenny—where he kept his own loot. Just like what I did to John V. Kenny in the grand jury.

J.J. tells Brown he kept his money in the basement. "Where in the basement?" Brown inquires.

"In a garbage can," Kenny responds.

"Oh, yes," says Brown, "A garbage can. Very good."

After a recess, Brown comes in carrying a shiny new garbage can. He plunks it down in front of J.J., and asks him if this garbage can is similar to J.J.'s.

"It is," replies J.J., his face turning red. The jury is tittering.

"How much of the can did the money fill up?" Brown asks as he lifts the top of the can, and thrusts his hand in.

"Well," Kenny struggles, "it covered the bottom of the can."

There are snickers in the courtroom. Even crusty Shaw is smothering a smile.

Brown then takes my $50,000 and inserts the bills. "About that high?" he asks the hapless J.J., who now must peer into the bottom of the can.

"About a fingernail lower," he manages to respond, turning even more scarlet.

A glance at the jurors shows me what I don't want to see. They are laughing with Brown at J.J. Kenny.

Brown is done. After the jury leaves the room, Brown pulls the can away. I object. It has been used as an exhibit. I demand that it be marked for identification and remain in the courtroom. I have plans for that garbage can.

When the jury returns, the atmosphere in the courtroom has lightened. It's because of Brown's cross, and the general weakness of J.J. Kenny as a witness. J.J. has been so flakey that one attorney requests a psychiatric evaluation of him.

****

While John Barry goes to Florida, I put more payers on the stand. I get money into the hands of Bernie Murphy, J.J. Kenny, and Frank Manning. Every time I do, I put Ray Brown's trashcan in front of the particular witness. I am implying to the jury that all collectors had their own garbage can. I do it over and over, until Brown objects and finally gets his garbage can out of the courtroom. As we go into our weekend recess, I hope we have removed at least some of the sting of Brown's cross.

****

Over the weekend, John Barry returns from Florida with the bank records.

"Tell me," I ask John.

"It's fantastic. In 1968 Flaherty went to the Miami Beach First National Bank on recommendation of a Jersey City banker. He met Senior Vice President Dennis Clum and asked if he could open a numbered account that did not show his name. When Clum said yes, Flaherty opened a bag and handed over $523,000 in cash and bearer bonds. Then Flaherty came back later with Whelan, who put in $502,000 in bearer bonds."

"Wow, this is dynamite!" I exclaim.

"Wait until you hear the rest," Barry continues. "The boys then brought their wives in and executed agreements which authorized the men and their wives to transfer money in or out of each other's accounts."

"You mean Flaherty and his wife could withdraw from Whelan's account and vice versa, with Mayor and Mrs. Whelan having the authority to withdraw from Flaherty's?"

"You bet. The mayor and the President of the City Council. Total partners in crime," Barry laughs.

****

May 31

First thing Monday, I hand out copies to Ray Brown, Whelan's lawyer. He looks at me, then rifles through the records.

"What are these numbered accounts?" Ray looks up at me.

"Those are your client's banking records. His and Flaherty's. Joint accounts," I answer.

"Joint?"

"Joint."

"How much?" Brown sighs.

"Over one million two hundred thousand."

"Joint accounts?"

"That's right."

"I see," says Brown quietly.

I'm sure he does. It is the end of any hope he may have had for a successful defense. I can see the resignation. I don't expect any more trouble from him. Now all he can do is go through the motions. It's what I aimed to achieve. As a competitor, I am elated. As a professional, I'm sorry.

Chapter Six

The Boss Is Out
May 31–June 22, 1971

I AM HOLDING THE $700,000 in bearer bonds that John V. Kenny bought for cash, using Chief of Police Kropke as a messenger. Kenny actually bought $782,000 worth of bonds, so I guess that after he gave the $700,000 to the grandkids he kept $82,500 for himself. I put the physical bonds into evidence. So far, so good. The jury has seen the $50,000 he gave to J.J. and the other $700,000 he gave to his family so lots of cash coming out of him, But nothing going in to him. No witness has put any kickbacks directly into J.V.'s hands, J.J.'s words still linger at trial: "I never gave Mayor Kenny a dime in my life." A good old-fashioned Hudson County payoff, in the courtroom. But I am not concerned. Frank Manning will soon take the stand.

When Manning had cash from city work, he would call Kenny and report he had a "city resolution." A county kickback was a "country resolution." If he had a lot of money, he reported a "lengthy resolution." But I am defeated by bad health, again.

June 10

Kenny has fallen ill. Even our doctors confirm it. He requires prostate surgery immediately. There is nothing I can do. Judge Shaw severs Kenny from the trial. Manning goes on the stand. But the drama is gone. The task is to finish putting in the rest of the case as quickly as possible.

June 22

I have the courtroom swimming in Kenny's bonds, Kenny's $50,000 cash gift to J.J., tens of thousands Kenny ordered given back to businessmen through party chairman Wolfe and Chief Kropke when we started investigating. Not to mention the Florida bank records of the $1.2 million. The courtroom is awash in ill-gotten gains. With that, I close the government's case. Now let's see what the defense can do.

Chapter Seven

"Quite a Saver. Quite a Housewife."
June 22–July 3, 1971

WITH KENNY GONE, the top defendants are Jersey City Mayor
Whelan and president of the city council Flaherty. They cannot take the stand, not with their Miami bank records to explain, and
no way to explain them. Same for Bernie Murphy, one of the "collectors." He would have to deal with a dozen witnesses putting cash into
his hands, with no way to rebut them. The three defendants who may
pose some challenge for us are Sternkopf, commissioner of the Port
Authority of New York and New Jersey; Fred Kropke, chief of police of
Hudson County; and my favorite, Wally Wolfe, the incumbent chairman of the Hudson County Democratic party, who is defending on the
basis of insanity, occasioned by a war wound on Saipan. He claims not
to know right from wrong, and an inability to control his conduct. His
lawyer, Jack Noonan, has two experts, both doctors. Both testify that
Wolfe meets the legal test for insanity. First, I cross Dr. Ralph Panzer.

"Now, you say in your medical opinion Mr. Wolfe lacks the substantial capacity to conform his conduct to the requirements of the
law."

"On the basis of my test, I said that, yes," the doctor responds.

"Let me put it this way, Doctor: in your medical opinion, does
Mr. Wolfe know the difference between right and wrong?"

"Yes."

"In your opinion, does Mr. Wolfe know the nature and the quality of the acts which he does? Does he know when he's opening a window that he's opening a window?" I continue.

"Yes."

"Does he know that when he's opening a door he's opening a door?"

"Yes."

"Does he know that when he's going into a men's room he's going into a men's room?"

"Yes."

"Suppose the evidence here establishes that Mr. Wolfe accepted $20,000 in United States currency from a contractor, would you say he knew, if that were the facts, that it was money?"

"He knew it was money, on the basis of my data," the doctor admits.

"And he knew the difference between right and wrong. You have told us that."

"I did."

"Is it your testimony that he lacked the ability to control himself when he took the money?" I ask.

"No, that's not my testimony."

So much for Dr. Panzer.

****

After the cross, I am in the hall with Jon, Bruce Goldstein, and John Barry. "Where did you get that stuff about opening doors and windows?" Barry asks.

"The DA's office, right?" says Jon.

"Yes. There was a great lawyer there, Vince Dermody. I saw him do that when a homicide defendant tried an insanity defense."

"Dermody? Irish?" Barry wants to know.

"Sure." I begin to expound. "There was Dermody and Keenan. There's Hogan and Lacey. The Irish and the Jews dominate the courts. Morgenthau and Rifkind; Williams and Toolan; the two judges who helped break me in, Quinn and O'Brien; there's two Goldsteins and John Barry; Stern and—"

"It's time to go back into court," says Jon, which is a good thing. I would not know what to do with Bissell, Brown, Dumont, and Langway, except claim that they changed their names.

****

Noonan's next expert witness is his big gun, Dr. Stanley L. Portnow. This gentleman actually has outstanding credentials. He has an office on Park Avenue in New York City. He is a diplomate of the American Board of Psychiatry and Neurology. He is the chief of forensic psychiatry at Bellevue Hospital in New York City. He has been director of psychiatry for the Department of Corrections in New York City. And lots more. He has testified many times, and he carries his exhibits with him from case to case. Including a model brain. Pedantic and pompous, Dr. Portnow is here to tell us that as a result of wounds received while on Saipan, Wolfe is legally insane.

"Are you within the realm of reasonable medical probability, Doctor," says Jack Noonan, "satisfied that at the time of committing any prohibited act charged in this case that the defendant Walter Wolfe, as a result of mental disease or defect, lacked substantial capacity to conform his conduct to the requirements of the law which he is alleged to have violated?"

"This conduct requires the formation of an intent, and because the capacity of intent is dependent upon comprehension, judgment, reasoning, which is impaired in this type of brain damage, I would have to say no. My opinion is that he did not have the substantial capacity to conform his behavior."

To illustrate his testimony the doctor uses his plaster model of a human brain with moveable parts, which the doctor manipulates as he testifies to Wolfe's injuries. Noonan marks it into evidence as Exhibit DW-24.

I can't wait to cross-examine this very self-assured gentleman. He is not only highly credentialed, but as he sits smiling at me, it is clear that he is confident that he can handle me. I decide to begin with his role in the case.

"Doctor, you are giving us the benefit of your independent medical expertise, is that not so?"

"That is correct," he responds.

"And you are not an advocate in this cause, you are not partial to one side or another, is that so?" I continue.

"No. I view my role as an objective observer."

"When you said on direct you were examining Mr. Wolfe 'for his defense' what you meant was you were examining him to see whether or not you could come to testify on his behalf?"

"I was examining him at the request of Mr. Noonan," answers the doctor.

"That was the phrase you used, 'examining him for his defense'?"

"Yes. Mr. Noonan is his defense lawyer."

"You say you were surprised when Wolfe seemed readily agreeable to come to you at any hour you wished him to come, is that right?"

"Yes."

"Notwithstanding that you were examining him 'for his defense'?"

"Yes."

"It seemed to you evident that his judgment, understanding, abstract reasoning had been reduced because this man was agreeable to see you any time you wanted to see him when you were 'examining him for his defense,' is that so?" I ask.

"Yes. In my experience in examining defendants, they don't usually come at ten thirty at night or on Sunday or holidays, or something like that," Dr. Portnow explains.

"But Mr. Wolfe was willing to do it and that means there is something *unusual* about him?" I press.

"It is just one facet I used as a suggestion," Portnow wants to move away.

"And the other patients you were examining, Doctor, these were all men of sound mind?"

"Not all of them."

I see a few jurors smiling. Now the real fun. Wally Wolfe occupies two public offices, and Dr. Portnow has evaluated Wolfe as incapable of exercising any significant degree of comprehension, judgment or reasoning.

"He is incapable of exercising any degree of reasoning, judgment, is that so?" I ask the doctor.

"I said any *significant* degree."

"Is it your testimony, Doctor, that he has been able to serve as a freeholder in county government for ten years without any *significant* degree of comprehension, judgment, or reasoning?"

"Did you say that is my testimony?"

"Yes."

"I don't understand your question," he complains.

"Don't you? You are telling us that Mr. Wolfe is a man who is incapable of forming any *significant* degree of comprehension, judgment, or reasoning, aren't you?"

"Yes."

"And you know that for the past ten years he has been an elected official in the county legislature, right?"

"If freeholder is a county legislature, yes. I would say relatively speaking his comprehension, judgment, reasoning, and thinking occasioned by his brain damage is not the same as perhaps the other freeholders who might be sitting with him."

"Didn't you say he was unable in any *significant* degree to have comprehension, judgment, or reasoning?"

"Yes."

"Is your testimony, Doctor, that this man is so mentally incapacitated that he lacks the substantial capacity to conform his conduct to the requirements of the law?"

"Insofar as his thinking, reasoning, judgment, and comprehension are involved, I would say that it is not possible."

"It is not possible to what?"

"Would you repeat the question?"

"Not possible to what?" I insist.

"I must have the question read back to me," Portnow sounds desperate.

"What are you saying is not possible?" I insist, again. Portnow has his mouth open, but nothing emanates. He glances up at the bench.

"Doctor, have you forgotten the question?" Judge Shaw gives him a rare smile.

"I have, Your Honor."

"Read it back," Shaw orders.

After it is read the good doctor says, "Yes."

"No further questions."

Now the doctor wants the plaster brain back, but Wolfe's attorney has marked it into evidence. "Do you need the brain back, Doctor?" I ask.

"I do. I can let you have it for a day or two."

"You can take your brain," I say magnanimously. As the doctor leaves, brain under his arm, a fair number of the jurors are openly laughing.

I feel it went great. But there's one piece of Portnow's testimony that I expect will haunt me. During the doctor's testimony, he described the wounds Wolfe received as a Marine in Saipan: "multiple gunshot wounds of the face, skull, arm, thigh, and chest."

I can't help glancing over at Wolfe with respect. And I can see some jurors do the same. I know it technically has nothing to do with the case, but it has a lot to do with the man. And therein lies the difficulty. Noonan has moved some jurors.

****

Fred Kropke, Hudson County chief of police, is up on the stand. A police officer for much of his adult life, Kropke is an experienced witness. Perched in his witness chair, Kropke is not ill at ease. He has a square jaw and a large bulbous red nose. Although wearing civilian clothes, the sixty-year-old Kropke appears completely relaxed. He knows there is a fundamental weakness in our case against him, and he intends to highlight it for the jury.

He cannot deny that he owes his appointment to John V. Kenny. The "Little Guy" actually pinned the badge on Kropke's chest when he took the oath. And Kropke cannot deny taking bags of cash to brokers for Kenny's investments. But no contractor has testified to giving him any cash for himself. No count in the indictment charges any act of extortion by him. On the stand, he categorically denies any role in exacting any money from anybody. He finishes his testimony with tears in his eyes. "I never took a dollar from anyone," he sobs, as he pleads for his acquittal. With that, the trial week ends.

****

My weekend is consumed with a day-by-day examination of four years worth of Kropke's bank and insurance records. Every check, every cash deposit, every share of stock purchased for cash. No one can do this for me. I have to be able to handle the records at a fast clip on the cross.

Even more important are the bank and brokerage records of Kropke's wife. In the words of the notorious bank-robber Willy Sutton, "That's where the money is." On Monday morning, I am ready.

****

I stand before the chief of police with the jurors on my left. They seem expectant. Kropke is perfectly relaxed.

"You were her sole support?" I ask Kropke about his wife.

"Yes."

"You were giving her all her money, weren't you, Chief?"

"Mrs. Kropke got all her money from Chief Kropke," he says angrily.

"That," I say, "is exactly my point. How much do you give her?"

"I give her $500 every two weeks."

"Where did you get the cash from?" I inquire.

"Mr. Stern, I get $26,000 per year and you," pointing his finger at me, "you can sit here until doomsday and never find a contractor to say he ever gave me a dollar."

Well, he's right about that, but I can show a ton of dollars coming out of him. I talk him through all of his deposits and cash purchases, month by month.

"In December of 1967, you paid $13,000 in cash to purchase a lot?"

"Yes, sir."

I take each month of 1968: cash into the bank, cash for stock purchases every month. We reach October.

"In just one month, in October 1968, you and your wife deposited $6,900 in cash?"

"Yes, sir."

"And the next month, November, your wife deposited $1,400 in cash into her checking account?"

"Yes, sir."

Then I show him the records of a diamond ring purchase for $6,800, a mink coat for $4,800, and thousands of dollars of stock his wife purchased for cash.

"Your wife doesn't work, does she?"

"No, sir," Kropke shakes his head, and then with his head lowered he mumbles, "but she is quite a saver. Quite a housewife."

The jury refuses to look at him when he leaves the stand.

****

Sternkopf is up next. He is a commissioner of the Port Authority, put there by John V. Kenny. Before that, Kenny had made him a turnpike commissioner. He is an older man, with iron-grey hair, yet slim and obviously in good condition. He carries himself like a banker, which in a sense he is, the banker for the mob.

As I get ready for his testimony, Bruce Goldstein briefs me. "We have one rotten deal that Sternkopf did personally. He got together with a man named D. Louis Tonti, executive director of the New Jersey Highway Authority."

"What's that?" I ask.

"That is the Garden State Parkway, in official language," Bruce smiles.

"Got it."

Bruce continues, "The two of them got together and secretly bought 80 acres of land for $90,000 and then turned around and sold it to the Parkway—headed by Tonti—for $300,000 to build the Garden State Arts Center."

"So Sternkopf is burying money for Tonti, just like for Kenny?"

"Yes. Sternkopf sent Tonti's end, $110,000, to a Giovanni Paolini in Rome, who then put the checks into a Swiss bank account."

"I don't know if Shaw will let me cross-examine Sternkopf on this," I tell Bruce. "It is unrelated to anything here."

I make my offer of proof to the judge. For the press, it's a bomb-shell that sends them running from the room to the telephones. For Judge Shaw, it's a dud. He won't let me use it on cross. He does let me show that Sternkopf controls three corporations whose only function is to own three safe-deposit boxes for John V. Kenny, and that Sternkopf helped Kenny to turn cash into bearer bonds.

And with that, testimony in the case is over. Summations by the defense will begin. There are eight of them. I am not scheduled to deliver mine until July 5. So we have some time for other business.

Chapter Eight

He Built the Garden State Parkway
July 3–4, 1971

JON, **B**RUCE, **D**ICK Langway, John Barry, and I meet to go over where we are. We've got this guy Tonti. He just issued a statement that my allegations are "Hogwash." He goes into the grand jury next week, on July 7, where he can explain the checks he sent to Italy and then on to Switzerland.

"Who will put him in to the grand jury?" Jon asks.

"Either you, Bruce, or me, as long as the Hogwash man goes in next week. Second, they say this guy built the Garden State Parkway. We know he did this rotten deal with Sternkopf, so the bet is he grabbed contractors building the parkway as well. Bruce, you're head of special prosecutions. Subpoena the firms that worked on the parkway. Look for cash. If we find some, we will find Tonti."

I can see that Bruce is delighted. But he is going to have more. I continue, "Burkhardt, the former secretary of state—J. Rich Steers says they paid him off. Get a subpoena out for Burkhardt." They say Burkhardt took $20,000 for himself and $10,000 for the Democratic Party. Let's schedule him for indictment next month, August."

"So fast?" asks Bruce.

"I don't know how much time we have left," I tell him.

Washington is not going to let this go on indefinitely. I either get the job or the axe. I figure whatever comes will be shortly after the trial.

And that brings me to Atlantic City. So, I tell Jon, "Every time we turn around, we bump into another corrupt pol. We've taken care of the Dems in Newark and the Dems in Jersey City. It's time for the Republicans in Atlantic City and Atlantic County."

I tell Jon Goldstein that this is his baby. We have no evidence. No witnesses. But we will do just what we did in Hudson County. Jon will send agents down to Atlantic City to catalogue successful "bidders" for contracts at city hall. After that, the subpoenas will go out for their records. Then will come the cash. And then the harvest. "So, get the agents to start swarming over Atlantic City. As names of successful bidders come in, have subpoenas go out.

"What's going on with the Frenchman with the drugs?" I ask Jon.

"Don Merkelbach has been handling it. He's debriefing DeLouette. He's also been preparing to try Tony Boy Boiardo. But Tony Boy's trial, as you know, has been put off again. Too sick."

"And the Colonial case?"

"Dick Shapiro is getting ready to indict."

"When?"

"Next month."

"I want to finish the Congressman Gallagher business, too," I tell Jon.

"We will. Let's catch our breaths!" Jon protests.

"Trouble is, Jon, I don't know how many breaths we have left," I repeat.

We entered the office with Lacey less than two years ago, but already some of our young lawyers are preparing to leave. They have fulfilled the two-year commitment they made to Fred. Jack Bissell wants to leave at the end of the year; Ted Margolis, chief of appeals, is leaving, too, as well as Hunt Dumont. So I will have openings for the executive assistant and deputy chief of Criminal. Dick Langway will be chief of criminal, with John Barry as head of appeals. We have a great team, if we are allowed to remain. But Washington remains silent. Joe Hayden, my former adversary in the Weber case, and a true gentleman, has written Attorney General Mitchell urging my appointment. I am eternally grateful.

Chapter Nine

Heroes
July 3–4, 1971

FOR TWO DAYS I listen to summations. Much of mine has been prepared. It was done on a daily basis during trial by excerpting testimony. I can plug in whatever I want as I outline my argument and answer the defendants'.

Nothing in the summations of six of the defendants troubles me. But there are two that do. Kropke's lawyer keeps asking the jurors, "What is a police officer doing in a case like this?" highlighting the fact that no one kicked back any cash into his hands.

I know I can make an answer about his delivering money for John V. Kenny. I can talk about his own cash. But how do I tie him to the overall extortion conspiracy? In the elevator leaving our building on the way to court to sum up, I tell my problem to John Barry. He has more candle power than the rest of us.

"Well, you have to—you have to—" John has the habit of starting twice when he is thinking deeply, "you *have* to own the chief of police to run a county as corrupt as Hudson."

I love it! One phrase and it's done. And I use it, almost word for word. "You can't run a city and a county the way these men ran Jersey City and Hudson County unless you own the chief of police. They did own that chief of police. John V. Kenny personally pinned his badge on him," I tell the jurors. I believe I see a nod here and there.

Surprisingly, my biggest concern is Wally Wolfe, in spite of his crazy defense. I have seen the jurors sneaking peeks at him, particularly when his wounds were described. In summation, Jack Noonan plays on that obvious sympathy. In a different case, without a claim of mental disability caused by a gunshot wound, he could not do it. Perhaps even in this case I could stop him, but I haven't the heart to try.

"Remember a June night many years ago on a foreign Pacific Island. Recall that Wally Wolfe was a young man remaining outside a foxhole," Noonan says softly as he strides before the jurors. "He was outside that foxhole because there was only room for two men. Wally, decent, honest, loyal," he pauses after each descriptive, "Wally remained outside that foxhole, firing his BAR at the enemy, and they in turn indelibly and permanently marked his brain and forehead."

Noonan turns his gaze onto Wolfe, and the eyes of the jurors turn with him. "You can see that scar today. He is still an honest, decent, loyal guy. Let him walk out that way. Don't," he shakes his head, "don't you add another mark to his brow."

I can't help but look at the spot on Wolfe's brow that the jurors are staring at as well. When I turn back to them, I see two women openly crying and some male jurors brushing at their eyes. And I remember the newsreels I watched as a kid of the landings on beaches of godforsaken islands like Saipan.

The human heart is larger than logic. All my clever little cross-examinations of Wolfe's experts come to nothing now. This is beyond that. The "science" doesn't matter. And if I try to harp on the expert testimony now, I will sink my case.

Why is it, I wonder, that genuine heroes, two Marines like Bob Jacks and Wally Wolfe, or an infantry captain with a Silver Star, like Hugh Addonizio, or a naval officer with a Bronze Star, like Tom Whelan—why is it that such heroes come home after saving our country, only to wound it? Is that what they fought for? As I stand before the jury, I know I must say just that.

"Mr. Wolfe served this country honorably and well. I honor him for it. We all *must* honor him for it. He served on Saipan, and he was wounded. But," I add, "he also left some friends on Saipan. They did not stay there so he could return and collect $20,000 from Steers and pass $18,000 to Merrigan in a men's room. That's not why we sent people overseas, why some were wounded and some did not come back. I honor him for his service, but it is no license for what he did here."

I finish on Saturday, July 3. We are off on Sunday, which also happens to be Independence Day. The judge will charge on Monday. Then it is up to the jury.

Chapter Ten

"Do You Want Me in This Job?"
July 5, 1971

July 5, Monday

Judge Shaw sweeps through the red curtain behind the bench, to the usual "All rise." He is carrying his jury charge. When everyone is settled, the judge calls for the jury. Again the "All rise" rings out and we all stand for the jurors, the judges of the facts. When everyone is settled again, the judge begins his reading.

There is nothing duller than the reading of a charge to a jury at the close of a criminal trial. Jurors are uniformly alert at the outset, expecting to acquire legal information necessary for their decisions. By the end of the forty minutes or so of monologue, they have received either too much or too little information to be useful. They usually are forced to conclude that they are on their own.

After the charge is finished, and all the attorneys' objections are heard at side bar, the deputy clerk collects the exhibits and leads the jurors out of the room. "All rise," he cries, as the jurors rise. As they go, we are all left behind, standing, with no idea of when they will return.

We are not left for long. Three hours and thirty-five minutes later, they are back, having filled out the 239 guilty or not-guilty boxes on the verdict sheet, after first having had their lunch. The verdict is quickly read. All defendants are convicted on all counts except for a minor player, Kunz, the business manager of Jersey City, who is convicted on only 12.

Courtrooms are quiet places—or should be. Robert Shaw's certainly is. So, the celebration does not begin until we are outside the building. Then we can cut loose. Microphones and cameras surround the exit of the building.

"It was Judge Lacey who personally spearheaded the investigation into what was a long-entrenched bastion of corruption," I say to the press as our team emerges from the courthouse. "This is the end. If only the public will dare to fight as witnesses, fight as jurors, and fight as voters against venal city halls, we can guarantee that principles established 195 years ago will endure for today, for tomorrow, and forever."

As we walk across the street to our office, I say to Jon, "Should we take the staff out to celebrate?"

"Absolutely!" is Jon's enthusiastic response.

But first, I have two calls to make. It's a legal holiday, so I call Fred Lacey at home. "Herb, I heard! It's on TV. Great! They were out less than four hours, less than the Addonizio jury, right?"

"Fred. This one is yours, too," I tell him.

I don't know how to reach Senator Case, I don't have his home number. But he solves the problem by calling me, just as I am about to leave. "Remarkable achievement," he says. "That county has been a blemish on the whole country even before I was born," he chuckles. "Remarkable. Please give my congratulations to the team."

"I will, Senator. Is there any chance you would visit our office?"

"I would be most delighted."

Then I figure I should tell him that we are now going after his own party, the Republicans in South Jersey. I figure he should know, because he will be standing for re-election next year.

"Wonderful!" he exclaims. "The rotten bunch is almost as long entrenched as the Hague-Kenny organizations. I remember Nucky Johnson down there many years ago. The present gang is no different. Can you get them?"

"I don't know, sir, but we are sure going to try." When I hang up, I go quietly to join my party. The entire trial team, lawyers and agents, are in the restaurant. We are celebrating when the manager comes running over, spluttering. "The White House is on the phone. For you," he tells me.

I pick up the telephone with no idea how whoever is calling found me. It's John Mitchell, the attorney general. He is either at the White House or using their switchboard. "Herb, I just wanted to call and congratulate you on this magnificent victory."

"Thanks. Do you want me in this job?"

"Why do you say that?" he replies, like he has no idea what I am talking about. There seems little point to pursuing this, so I let it end there and return to the party.

Chapter Eleven

"You Have Eighteen Months"
July 7–August 18, 1971

July 7

I do not know how much time we have left in this office. I know we must not waste a moment of it. Two days after the verdict, we have Tonti, the man who built the Garden State Parkway before the grand jury. The "Hogwash" man takes the Fifth. I must make sure that subpoenas go out to the contractors who built the tollbooths on the Garden State Parkway—our old motto, "Cherchez la cash." I am sure this guy collected tolls for himself. We'll see how much hogwash we come up with.

****

To our distress, the state insists on prosecuting John J. Kenny. I hold no brief for the man. He is totally corrupt, undeniably guilty of the state charges, and he betrayed us on the stand after we immunized him. But—we did immunize him. We simply cannot be silent while the state prosecutes a federally immunized witness. Kenny's lawyer, Don Robinson, has moved before Judge Shaw to enjoin the attorney general of New Jersey from proceeding. He has requested that we join in. If we do, it will bring us into direct conflict with the state.

Jon, Bruce, John Barry, and I meet to try to come up with a decision. It is a solemn moment around our big conference table. "If we do it—" says Barry, "if we do it, Shaw will grant the injunction. But, I think the circuit will vacate it on appeal."

"Why?" I ask.

"They'll rule that he first has to present his application to state court. They will defer to see if the state courts uphold or override the federal immunity grant." And, Barry adds, "We will be going against the Cahill administration in court. These are Republicans. They'll use it against Case's efforts to get you nominated."

"You forgot to add," I say, "that all this would be for a bum who sold us out on the stand."

When the laughter subsides, we agree. Fruitless or not, bum or not, we gave our word. So we will file and take the consequences. We submit our brief on July 29.

****

August 5

The Third Circuit strikes again. John Barry strides into my office. "The Circuit just reversed DeCarlo's conviction."

"What? Was it Judge Aldisert again?"

"Yes," Barry says. "Aldisert. You argued it back in December, right?"

"Yes."

"Well, it took him eight months, but he did it," John says.

"Unanimous?"

"Yes."

"Kolander I can understand, but Collins Seitz, too?" I ask.

"Yes," says John. "And here is what Aldisert says," Jon reads, "'Incurably prejudicial error . . . extortion charge was turned into a murder trial.'"

"Why? Because we proved that Saperstein died of poison, when he mailed the letters on the way to the hospital?"

"Yes," Barry tells me.

"This is bullshit," I explode. "The guy killed himself, after begging the bureau to protect his family. The state of mind of Saperstein is relevant in an extortion case. The fact that they drove him to suicide is highly relevant to the terror they inflicted. We are going back to the

Circuit. I need to draft a petition for rehearing and for a rehearing en banc, before all the judges."

Three strikes. First Colonial—not enough women on the grand jury, and a prohibition against re-indicting; then Sam the Plumber DeCavalcante, a strike force case; and now Gyp DeCarlo— "prejudicial" evidence of poisoning. Enough is enough. We are going back on this one.

With Barry still there, I call Jon into the office. "Is Shapiro ready to re-indict Colonial?"

"I believe so," says Jon.

"Aldisert says we can't. Well, we will. Right away. I want that indictment in one week!"

August 12

We re-indict all the Colonial defendants.

****

August 13

The next day we indict former New Jersey Secretary of State Robert Burkhardt and state Senator Willard Knowlton for taking bribes.

August 14

We are back before Judge Shaw for the sentencing of Whelan, Flaherty, and Sternkopf. The judge listens to Ray Brown and the other defense attorneys. Ray is always eloquent, but it does not aid him this time.

Judge Shaw addresses the defendants. "It taxes the imagination to speculate on the amount of money involved in ten percent of all public contracts of Jersey City and Hudson County." Judge Shaw glares at the defendants. "Cities become impoverished, unable to relieve the excessive burden of taxation, because of a rotten system pouring money into pockets of corrupt politicians." Shaw taps his gavel, "Whatever compassion and sympathy there may be," Judge Shaw shakes his head, "should be brought in the direction of the public. The money that would have lifted a burden from a citizen's back was diverted into the pockets of avaricious politicians." Whelan and Flaherty get fifteen years each, Sternkopf gets ten. Chief Kropke gets five years.

****

A few days later, I am back before Judge Shaw for the sentencing of Wally Wolfe. I guess that even Iron Balls Shaw, tough as he is, was moved by Wolfe's military service. He gives Wolfe a suspended sentence. I am surprised, but not miffed. The message went out with the Whelan and Flaherty sentences. And Wolfe was a bit player. Truthfully, there is something about that Saipan business that gets to you. It obviously got to Shaw. Well, if the bad things we did in life should exacerbate a sentence, why not the other way around?

****

Senator Case makes his promised visit to our office. We assemble the entire staff. Every person who works in our three offices is in our large library to greet him. It is a rare moment for us and, I think, for him.

As he walks into the room, everyone stands and spontaneous applause breaks out. If the senator were not such a dignified figure, I think our people would have been cheering. "I want to thank you, each of you," the senator beams at them. "First under Fred, and now Herb, in less than two years you have compiled an unheard-of record in law enforcement. I mean law enforcement anywhere, at any time. I know," he laughs, "I can count on you to continue until, as I said at Fred's induction, the rascals are not only 'on the run,' but run out of town!" With that, the senator insists on personally greeting every lawyer, every secretary, and every intern.

An hour later, he and I are alone in my office. "You will be nominated soon," the senator tells me. "After this last win in Hudson, the department and the White House have no choice. They know that I can keep you here. If they keep things as they are, with you court-appointed, and me preventing anyone else from assuming the position, and you keep going as you have, the administration will get no credit. In fact, it will continue to be criticized. So you will get the call soon."

"That's great news," I respond.

"Yes," Case smiles, "it is. But . . . there is an election coming up next year. The president is up. So am I. If Nixon loses, Senator Williams will have the new president replace you. If Nixon wins and I lose, Nixon will replace you. You have eighteen months, until January 1973. After that . . . who knows.'"

When I tell him of my troubles with the Cahill administration, Case just smiles. "Do you what you have to do," he says.

Chapter Twelve

South Jersey Republicans and Lefties
August 18–September 1971

August 18

We are in the federal courthouse in Camden, New Jersey, before U.S. District Judge Mitchell Cohen on a life-or-death motion to our startup investigation of Republican Atlantic City.

Our grand jury subpoenas have been challenged in a clever way. The South Jersey businessmen who did business with Atlantic City have moved to quash our subpoenas, contending that the investigation of Atlantic City should be run from the Camden grand jury, in the south, rather than the Newark grand jury. We have only a skeletal office in Camden. If Judge Cohen grants the motion, it will effectively hobble us.

Mitchell Cohen is the most debonair of the New Jersey federal bench. Wealthy, he was one of the original investors in *My Fair Lady* the Broadway play. He holds the title of "Commendatore"—some kind of knight—that he received from exiled King Umberto of Italy. Judge Cohen is a Republican who has ambitions to join the Third Circuit, which sits in Philadelphia, where Cohen actually resides. But he is a solid jurist, and practical.

It is Jon's investigation, but I race down to the Camden courthouse with him. The head of the office has to argue this, to send a message to Judge Cohen.

The courtroom is stuffed with South Jersey press that know that this is the first step in the kind of investigation that resulted in the indictments in Newark and Jersey City. They figure it is Atlantic City's turn. And they are right.

Standing before the judge, I argue that the intent of the motion to shift between grand juries is nothing less than an effort to "thwart and impede the public interest." I can see that the judge really gets it. "Motions denied," he rules, smiles at me, and off he goes.

On the long drive back, I tell Jon that I am done. "From now on," I tell him, "it's your baby." I can see that this does not trouble him at all.

****

August 22, Sunday

My telephone awakens me at 6:00 a.m. "Wha—?" I croak into the phone.

"This is Bob Mardian," a voice says. Mardian is the assistant attorney general in charge of the Internal Security Division in the Justice Department in Washington. These are the boys who chase the "leftists," the antiwar and antinuke demonstrators. This is a big priority in the Nixon administration. During the Johnson days, when Ramsey Clark led the department and Earl Warren was chief justice, Nixon campaigned against the Dems based on their liberal records. Slogans like "Impeach Earl Warren" abounded. Strong treatment of leftists and antiwar demonstrators were big issues in the 1968 Presidential election.

After the Republicans won, they set up a special unit in the Internal Security Division under a lawyer named Guy Goodwin, who runs around the country prosecuting "flower children." Their cases have numbers, like the "Chicago 7," the "Seattle 8," and the "Milwaukee 14." And then there are the "grave security risks," the Catholic priests allied with Father Berrigan.

"What's up?" I ask Mardian, trying to wake myself up.

"We just arrested twenty-eight people in Camden," Mardian replies. "A bunch of them are Catholic priests–part of the Berrigan group."

"Oh . . . what for?" I ask.

"They broke into a Selective Service office to destroy draft records, tried to stop the draft."

"How did this happen?" I ask again, mystified.

"We had an informant. We put surveillance on them for weeks. We used Judge Cohen's chambers as a lookout post."

"You did?"

"Yes. And Herb,"—big pause—"we used your two assistants in Camden, Subin and Finnegan, to work the case."

"You did?"

"Yes. And we told them not to tell you," Mardian admits.

"You did?" I seem to be repeating myself.

"Yes. And we don't want you to be mad at them. They were under orders."

"Of course not," I say, wondering if he is for real. "So, why are you calling me now?"

"Well, the Berrigan people have to be arraigned, bail set, and then there's the grand jury presentation . . ."

"Well, I'll tell you what," I say. "You guys have done such a great job I think you should keep on doing it. Who supervised the arrests, Guy Goodwin?"

"Yes."

"I think he should stay with it," I say, as I break off.

Subin and Finnegan. Interesting. Now that bears some thought.

Chapter Thirteen

"Still Want the Job?"
September 1971

THE **FRENCH ARE** a problem. Don Merkelbach is convinced that DeLouette, while working for the SDECE, ultimately delivered a hundred pounds of pure heroin to Port Elizabeth in New Jersey. I believe Don is correct in his assessment.

Roger DeLouette joined French Intelligence in 1946, serving in Greece, Cuba, Algeria, and the Ivory Coast. His code name was "Delmas." He had direct contact with the head of the French Secret Service, whom he identified as Colonel Paul Fournier. On one occasion, Fournier ordered him to transport counterfeit American currency. Then, on December 15, 1970, Fournier recruited DeLouette to transport the heroin to the United States. DeLouette was promised 300,000 francs, approximately $50,000, to deliver the drugs, and he was given about $5,500 to purchase a Volkswagen camper, which he picked up on March 1.

Fournier called DeLouette and directed him to a meeting in a forest, the Forest of Rambouillet, outside Paris. There, DeLouette met another agent. This second agent took two suitcases full of heroin from his own car and distributed the drugs under panels in DeLouette's truck, after removing the panels with tools from his kit. On March 17, DeLouette drove to Le Havre and shipped the camper to Port Elizabeth. On Sunday, April 4, he flew on a TWA jet from Paris to New York. He was arrested the next morning when he claimed the camper.

Throughout April the French denied that DeLouette had ever been an agent of the SDECE, or that there was any such person as Colonel

Fournier. As the weeks passed, however, the French protests changed. The story became that DeLouette was a *former* agent who had been discharged, and that he was now making up a story in revenge. As for Fournier—they still denied that there was such a man. But a few months later their story changed yet again.

September 14

Don Merkelbach and I attend a meeting at the U.S. Bureau of Narcotics and Dangerous Drugs in New York City. The French are in town. We meet with Max Frenet, in charge of the French detectives; Honare Gevauden, assistant director of the Police Judiciare; and his assistant, Claude Shaminades. They now admit that Colonel Fournier exists, but they steadfastly deny that Fournier has been involved in shipping the heroin to the United States. They claim the matter has been fully investigated and that the charges are simply false.

"Your entire investigation, gentlemen," I tell them, "apparently lasted just four days, from April 6 through April 9. That is no investigation."

The French are indignant. They insist that DeLouette is lying and that Fournier is innocent. "All right," I say. "Here is my proposal. We will administer a lie-detector test to DeLouette. Your representatives can be present. You can submit questions. If DeLouette fails the test, I will personally see to it that he spends most of his remaining life in prison." I see smiles break out on the faces of our guests. "But," I add, "if he passes, I expect you to bring proceedings against Fournier in France."

The French agree. They are surprised to learn that we have anticipated the issue. Don Merklebach, as a former assistant prosecutor, has already arranged with his old office, Joe Lordi's office, to schedule the lie detector test for one week away, September 21. When the French see that we have it all set, they look very unhappy. But what can they do? They have already agreed!

****

When I get back to my office, I get a telephone call from Attorney General Mitchell. "Herb," he says as soon as I pick up, "do you still want the job?"

"Yes," I say quickly.

"I thought I'd ask," he chuckles, "because the president is going to nominate you tomorrow."

Chapter Fourteen

Fiat Justitia Ruat Caelum
September 15–28, 1971

September 15, 1971

Six years after I left Hogan's office, Nixon nominates me to be U.S. Attorney for the District of New Jersey, which I effectively have been for nearly a year. Now, finally, Jon and I can build what we hope will become an institution, as independent as possible on its watch for the public interest.

Watching out for the public is not enough. You have to be equipped to fight for it. We know how to investigate. And, because we have grown, we have the people to conduct the investigations. But our "old hands" are leaving, and many of the attorneys on our staff are young, with limited trial experience. In fact, many of our young lawyers have never tried a case.

There are only two things we can do. The first step is to institute a series of in-house lectures on trial practice. This we do at night. Attendance is mandatory, of course, since I am the lecturer. The lessons of Dermody and Kennan and of Rifkind and Williams are passed on as best as I can. The second step is more effective, because it is more direct: We begin to recruit from Hogan's office. If we are to do what the senator has promised the people of New Jersey, we have to get a move on.

****

September 21

Don Merkelbach had prosecutor Joe Lordi's office administer a lie-detector test to Roger DeLouette. The French came to observe. They brought questions for DeLouette, but, in typical style, they arrived too late for their questions to be included. So Don Merkelbach scheduled another test. DeLouette passed the first test, including the questions "Were you recruited by SDECE? Were you directed by Fournier to receive $17,000 in counterfeit currency? Was the smuggling of heroin done according to the instructions of the man sent by Fournier?" And, "Did Fournier give you a contact in the French Consulate in New York?"

In order to accommodate the French, we give DeLouette the second test using their questions. He passes them all, except one. He is found to lie in denying that his girlfriend was involved in the smuggling. The test is obviously valid. I don't see how the French can get out of the deal, but I am sure that they will try.

September 27

I sign a letter drafted by Merkelbach to the French, demanding that they fulfill their promises, and prosecute Colonel Fournier. "Do you think they will make good on their word?" Jon asks in my office, reviewing the letter before we send it.

"Not a prayer," I respond. "Not many people investigate themselves—or those they think of as themselves. Did I ever tell you about the Patrolman Crowe case? The guy who mowed down Julius Ofsei when I was in Hogan's office—"

"Yes," says Jon quickly.

I guess he gets tired of my stories. We don't have time for them anyway. We have to run to court. Someone pops in and tells us that Judge Wortendyke has issued a surprise announcement. With no notice, he is resigning. He has just declared that this is his last day on the bench. Jon and I race over. We don't want to miss it.

Wortendyke's courtroom, the large, elegant, ceremonial chamber with inlaid ceiling and wall sconces, is nearly empty. Wortendyke sits alone on the bench, hearing his last motions. Some few attorneys who have heard he is leaving have dropped by. But most of the spectator benches are empty.

As I push through the swinging doors and survey the scene, a feeling of sadness envelops me. I have learned so much in this room. The shadows of Rifkind and Williams, Brill, Toolan and Lacey, Hayden and Bliablias haunt the place. But most of all, I shall miss the kind, grandfatherly figure who will sit no more upon that bench. "The only objective towards which a man's conduct should be aimed is the satisfaction of his conscience." That is what he said, how he lived, and that is how he judged.

As the judge rises to leave, Don Robinson, representing the bar, rises along with him. "If it please the court, Your Honor, we would like you to remain."

Wortendyke shakes his head ruefully, "I am in my seventy-seventh year. My memory is not as sharp. I am finding it harder and harder to remember names. I am, frankly, going to miss it. But it is time to go." With that, he walks out.

As he goes, my eyes fall on the front of his bench. There is a motto engraved on the wooden face: *Fiat Justitia Ruat Caelum*—"Let justice be done though the heavens fall."

I turn to Jon, "We can't let him go quietly. The Federal Bar Association will want to give him a tribute."

Jon nods, "We will see to it." There is nothing more to say. I want to get out of the room before someone notices that my eyes are leaking.

Chapter Fifteen

The Jersey Shore
October 1–November 2, 1971

"Sludge? What's sludge?" I ask Jon Goldstein, who has come into my office along with Dick Hill, one of our assistants.

"'Sludge' is what the shore communities collect in their sewage systems during the summer months," Hill responds. "They keep it in tanks until it hardens. Then between December 15 and March 15 of each year, they add water to it and pump billions of gallons through pipes into the ocean, less than 1,000 feet from their beaches."

"Okay, Dick. But what is sludge?" I repeat.

"It is the hardened mass of metal particles and human feces which is then sufficiently liquefied to pump it out through the pipes," Hill explains.

"Disgusting," I say.

"It's more than that," Jon emphasizes. "It's extremely dangerous to the public's health. That stuff breeds disease. The EPA says it washes up on the beaches. Those beaches are 'the Jersey Shore' that hundreds of thousands use in summer."

"But," I ask, "Isn't it gone by the summer?"

"A lot of it is," Dick responds, "but a lot isn't."

"Okay, but how is this our business? Doesn't the state regulate this?"

"They do, but they don't," Dick responds. "So if we don't, no one will."

"I still don't get how this is our business. I know we have been cleaning up cities, but beaches?" I can see that neither Jon nor Dick is amused. It is just different stuff than what I am used to. Give me a murderer, or a corrupt pol, and I know what to do. What do you do with nineteen New Jersey shore communities who pollute their own shorelines in the winter and live off them in the summer? "How do we have anything to say about this?" I ask.

Jon and Dick explain that there is an old statute, the Refuse Act of 1899, that makes it illegal to discharge anything into a navigable body of water.

"So do we have jurisdiction?" I ask.

"Well," says Dick, "the statute exempts municipal 'sewage' passing from a municipal sewer system."

Somewhat relieved, I say, "Too bad. So I guess we are out of it." I am anxious to get on to the next item on our agenda, the DeLouette and Fournier investigation.

"Well," Jon smiles, "Dick and I think that pumping dried-out sludge is not the same as pumping liquid sewage. As we see it, the shore towns are forcing solid waste out into shoreline water. That is a violation of the statute."

"If you are right, that this 'sludge' is not 'sewage'—"

"Yes," says Jon.

"I give up. What do you want to do?"

They produce a draft letter that they want me to sign, addressed to each mayor of the nineteen shore communities, demanding that they dispose of the sludge at least twelve miles out to sea, rather than the present 1,000 feet from their beaches. My letter threatens to go to court if they don't. They have me saying, "I am not an advocate of ocean dumping. I am also aware that New Jersey may require that any ocean dumping be considerably further out to sea than twelve miles. For an interim period, however, it is certainly more desirable to discharge sludge twelve miles out to sea rather than 1,000 feet from beaches, which are used by so many people."

"Dick," I ask, "what if they don't comply?"

"We can go to court and seek an injunction."

"Is that a civil case?"

"Yes," Dick smiles.

"Do you know how to do that?" say I, who have never tried a civil case.

"Yes," Dick is trying not to laugh.

"Okay. I'll sign the frigging thing."

After he leaves us, I express my concern to Jon. "You know, as Butterfly McQueen might have said, 'I don't know nothing about birthing no civil case.' What are we getting into?"

"Don't worry, Herb. That's why we have Dick Hill and a whole civil division."

****

I may know nothing about how to stop the shore towns from shitting on their own beaches, but I do know how to deal with the French polluting us with heroin. The French have reneged on their deal. I will indict Colonel Fournier, the head of the SDECE. It will be a bombshell. Will it compel the French to prosecute? I doubt it. But, it will certainly prevent future shipments from that source. But this is one I can't do on my own. It will cause an international explosion. I have to clear it with the Justice Department—if I can.

Right now the department's criminal division is in turmoil. The assistant attorney general in charge, Will Wilson, has resigned under fire. He is accused of past misconduct as a lawyer in Texas. And guess who will now head the criminal division?—Henry E. Petersen.

Henry has come far since we first met: from deputy chief of organized crime to chief of organized crime, to deputy assistant attorney general, and now to assistant attorney general. Although not great for me, in all fairness, as they say, he deserves it. He is a consummate bureaucrat who has made many contributions, although I don't know if he has ever tried a case.

A week after Wilson's departure, I reach out to Deputy Attorney General Richard Kleindienst on the DeLouette-Fournier case. I have no intention of going through Petersen—not unless I want to get strangled in his bureaucratic maneuverings. I go over the facts with Dick, including the breach of the agreement by the French. When I'm done, Dick says, "Okay. Hit him." It's on.

Chapter Sixteen

Jersey City; Atlantic City; Paris, France
November 2–15, 1971

THERE ARE ENCOURAGING signs of progress in New Jersey. In Jersey City, the reformers have put up a candidate, Dr. Paul Jordan, a physician, to challenge the Kenny machine in the mayoralty race to fill Tom Whelan's seat. And, in South Jersey, we hear that State Senator Hap Farley, the Republican boss, is in trouble in his bid for reelection. He is the last of the bosses: Kenny in Hudson, Wilentz in Middlesex, and Farley in Atlantic County. Although his candidacy has been endorsed by his fellow Republican, Governor Cahill, our probe of Atlantic City has spotlighted how corrupt that county is. We look forward to the election results with some enthusiasm, hoping that it will be a big day for progress in New Jersey.

November 2

Finally, Election Day. And a great one for New Jersey! Dr. Paul Jordan has beaten the Kenny machine. He will take office as mayor of Jersey City. Dr. Joseph McGahan has beaten Senator Hap Farley in Atlantic County. As the editorial in the *Star Ledger*, New Jersey's largest paper, says:

> A bright new era in Jersey politics was etched into history yesterday, as voters turned their backs on a fossilized chapter of old-line political machines.

The voters in Jersey City and Atlantic County were given an unparalleled opportunity to break with an era of machine politics . . . .

There is little doubt that a federal grand jury investigation provided a pivotal impetus in the decisive switch of voter sentiment, unbroken for decades, dating back to the late Enoch (Nucky) Johnson, the flamboyant boss of Atlantic politics.

I know I can't influence elections by campaigning or endorsing candidates. But I sure can go after scoundrels in office. And I'm going to keep on doing that, although we are always accused of political witch hunts. To that I respond, "You'd be amazed at how many sons of witches we can catch."

For one, we are going after Little Pussy Russo. By September 9 we finally get clearance from the IRS to indict Little Pussy Russo for tax evasion. It is somewhat anticlimactic—Russo is already in state custody for refusing to answer questions before the State Commission of Investigations. Jon assigns the tax prosecution to AUSA Gary Brown. We want Russo tried the next month.

As to Tony Boy Boiardo, it looks like we will never get him to trial. Tony Boy is genuinely sick. On the other hand, he can no longer function as a mobster. He is done. If Gary Brown can take Russo out, and if I can reclaim DeCarlo's conviction, the boys on the FBI tapes will be finished. If not, then I guess we will just have to wind up and begin again.

There is one "son of a witch" I still can't touch, however: John V. Kenny. He has literally taken up residence in a room at Pollak Hospital. He claims to be too ill to leave. But he is not too sick to use a telephone or to receive "visitors." With Kenny pulling strings from his hospital bed, the Hudson political machine still lives—and it will continue to function until he is taken out of the picture.

* * * * * * *

Three days from indicting Colonel Fournier, Dick Kleindienst calls me. "I want you to go to Paris," he says.

"Why?" I ask.

"The United States ambassador to France has asked to meet you. He wants to be briefed on the case."

"Dick, that means he wants to shelve it."

"Probably," Kleindienst admits.

"I don't want to go," I tell him.

"But you will," Dick assures me. "He has offered to put you up in the residence with his family. By the way, do you know who he is?"

"I have no idea. And I don't care," I respond, emphatically.

Kleindienst ignores me. "He is Arthur K. Watson, everyone calls him Dick." He continues, "He is also the son of Thomas Watson, former president of IBM, and the brother of Thomas Watson, the current president of IBM, who has just been appointed ambassador to Russia. Dick himself was president of IBM World Trade, headquartered in Paris, before his appointment as ambassador to France."

"Great. I am the son of Sam Stern from Fourteenth Street and Avenue A, New York City, a not distinguished graduate of Stuyvesant High School."

Kleindienst roars with laughter. I get the sense that he, too, was not born to the purple. When he quiets down, he tells me I must leave tomorrow night. So, of course, I do.

****

November 5

I leave for Paris. The car with the flags is waiting when I land in the morning. It sweeps me through the city directly to the embassy, where Watson is waiting in his office, seated at a desk before a fireplace where a low fire is burning. It's a wet, damp day.

Watson looks up from signing documents and smiles warmly at me. "You know what I'm doing?"

I say the only thing I can. "No."

"I am making the only investment that I can in this job." He pauses, as though waiting for me to guess. "I am buying an island off the coast of Maine for my children."

Lucky children. Actually, I think he may have said, "An island for *each* of my children," but I'm not too sure.

"Come on," he says. "I want to hear about the case. But not in here," he looks quickly around the office. "Bugs. Come with me." With that he takes me to the corridor, pulls back a curtain which shields what appears to be a small closet door, opens the door and ushers me into a room made of what looks like plastic. I mean, you can see through the walls, floor, and ceiling. The room is long and narrow, in the shape of a cigar. It is obviously bug-proof, because nothing can be hidden inside.

The room has a really long conference table, which looks like it could host twenty or more people. It's kind of weird, since Dick— he tells me to call him "Dick"—and I are alone in this enlarged fishbowl.

As I expect, at first Dick tries to persuade me that DeLouette is a liar and that Fournier is innocent. "I have been given personal assurances at the highest level of the French government," he tells me solemnly. But by the time we finish going over the facts, he has become convinced that Fournier is guilty.

He suggests lunch. The car with the flags takes us to Maxim's in Paris, where the maitre d' and the captains bow nearly to the ground when he walks in. And I have the best meal I've ever tasted

For the next two days, we go around Paris together, meeting with high-ranking officials whom Watson tries to persuade to proceed against Fournier. We fail, of course. But I have to go through this effort before I can indict.

In the two days Watson and I spend together, I'm living with him and his family in their residence, a structure built before World War II. I get to kind of enjoy the man. Watson is a good-natured sort.

As I get ready to fly back to the USA, he becomes a little maudlin. "You know what my father said to me when he was on his death bed?" Dick asks me.

"No," I say, and I wonder what the legendary Thomas Watson's last words were.

Dick looks at me gravely. "Clothes do not make the man," Dick pauses, "but they make the businessman."

Shortly after my return from Paris, on November 15, we indict Colonel Fournier of the SDECE for shipping one hundred pounds of pure heroin into the United States.

I expect all hell to break loose. So does the State Department. To keep the affair at a lower level, when Kleindienst authorizes the indictment he says I am to be the only spokesman to the press on behalf of the United States.

****

I already have trouble enough at home. When I get back from France, I learn that the mayors of the shore communities are resisting a ban on sludge dumping. Something has to be done.

"Where are we on this?" I ask Dick Hill and Jon Goldstein.

"We are no place," Jon reports. "The shore communities say they have no place to put the sludge except to dump it."

"Is that true?" I ask Dick Hill.

"No, it is not true. They could pump it out, truck it to barges, and then dump twelve miles out," he responds.

"But they won't?"

"No," he shakes his head.

"I understand you have a film," I nod over to a projector that Hill has set up. We turn off the lights and close the blinds, and Hill rolls the film.

"As you can see, we pushed yellow dye through the pipes that usually push out the sludge," Hill explains. "See where the dye winds up?"

I can see. Within twenty minutes of the pumping, the yellow dye winds up on the beach. "The next sequence shows an actual pumping of sludge," Dick explains. "We let one community pump out for a few minutes. Watch what happens."

I see flocks of birds drawn to the immediate vicinity, alighting on the water and feeding on the fecal and other material as it flows onto the beach.

"All right," I interrupt. "That's enough. Maybe it's a stretch under the 1899 statute, but we can't let these fools spread shit all over their beaches. What do you need for your civil suit?"

"We need to hire chemists to do a toxic analysis of the water after flushing to document the hazard, in addition to what we already have from the EPA," Dick answers me.

"Do it."

Chapter Seventeen

Come and Stand Trial
November 15–December 3, 1971

MY ATTENTION TIME for the effluent flowing onto the Jersey Shore is limited, given the toxic publicity flowing at me from Paris. The French are furious at my announcement of the indictment of Colonel Fournier and my accusation that elements of the French Secret Service are shipping heroin into the United States. The French are on the attack. Through direct statements, and by not-for-the-record briefings, and by not-for-attribution leaks, they are hitting back at DeLouette, and at me.

The French have gone from asserting that DeLouette was never an agent of their Secret Service and that no such person as Colonel Fournier exists, to claiming that DeLouette was terminated from the SDECE by Fournier for misconduct and that he now seeks revenge. As for me, I am described alternately as a political hack and as a tool of the American CIA. In all capacities, I am branded a liar.

But as the French press begins to dig into the story, more details begin to emerge about Colonel Paul Fournier, whose real name is apparently Paul Ferrer. Ferrer has been in the French Secret Service ever since he joined De Gaulle's Free French in 1941. Fournier-Ferrer is summoned to an examining magistrate in Paris at the end of a day when no one is usually around. But the French press is waiting for him. When a photographer snaps the colonel's picture, a police officer seizes the camera. Asked if he is there on the DeLouette matter,

Fournier snaps, "I don't know what you are talking about. I am here on a personal matter." When the authorities leak to the press that I met with Fournier and gave him a lie-detector test that he passed, I brand the story a lie. The French press prints my statement, verbatim. The press in Paris, it seems, are okay. Just like here, they don't buy official bullshit.

Colonel Roger Barberot gives a radio interview in Paris. He is director of the competing French Intelligence Service, the "Bureau for Agricultural Production Development," a cover for secret operations overseas. Barberot, a former French ambassador and naval officer, left France after the Germans invaded in 1940 and joined the British Eighth Army in North Africa. He then joined De Gaulle's Free French forces. Much later, he served as a colonel in the French army in Algeria. He resigned in protest of the torture abuses by French forces. He identifies Fournier as Ferrer, confirms that DeLouette was an agent—first for his own organization, then for Fournier in the SDECE.

Every day the exchanges between various French spokesmen and me become more heated. Michel Debré, the minister of defense in President Pompidou's cabinet, takes to the TV. He denounces me as an ambitious politician who has created "a serialized novel." He then authorizes "Colonel Fournier" to issue a statement to the press, addressed to me. "If I am guilty, Mr. Stern," the colonel says, "you prove it!"

The press, of course, immediately call me for a response. Appearing before a bank of cameras, I say, "If you are innocent, Mr. Fournier, come to this country and stand trial. You are assured of a fair trial. Do not hide behind international borders."

That is apparently too much for the French. The next morning, I get a call from Dick Kleindienst. "It's over, Herb. No more comments. President Pompidou has just telephoned President Nixon. If there is any more, he is calling off a scheduled meeting between the two of them in the Azores. Anyway, we've made our point. Fournier is finished. He will go. And we are getting assurances of greater French efforts on the Marseilles labs."

I tell Jon and Dan Merkelbach that we have to roll it up. And we do. There will be some cleanup. The French will pretend to investigate. But nothing will come of that, except Fournier, or whatever his name is, and a few others will be eased out. For our part, we will get DeLouette the minimum sentence, five years. The guy should get more. One hundred pounds of pure heroin is a lot. But you have to pay for what you get, and we got a lot in shutting down the operation in Paris.

BOOK V

A PLACE TO STAND

Chapter One

Full Salary
December 3, 1971

THE PRESIDENT HAVING nominated me, the Senate having confirmed me, I am finally ready for an induction ceremony. The fact that I have been doing the job for almost exactly one year—since the day Fred Lacey entered the hospital—does not dim the moment for me, or for my father.

Wortendyke's courtroom—I always think of it as his—is filled. There are fifty-two AUSAs now, and it looks like they are all here. Judge Wortendyke is not present, but the entire active bench is, including Fred Lacey. Lots of public officials have shown up, but only a few that I care about. Senator Case, of course; Chief Justice Weintraub; and the new mayors of Jersey City and Newark, Paul Jordan and Ken Gibson. They represent the hope for the future. I hope they fulfill it, although we are beginning to hear disquieting rumors about some in the Gibson entourage.

Attorney General Kugler attends and speaks graciously about our office. He seems a very decent man. I don't understand why our official relationship is not better. Perhaps it will be, once we put the J.J. Kenny dispute behind us.

Fred speaks. Draped in his judicial robes, his deep bass voice rumbling from the bench where he sits among his colleagues, he says, "This powerful office is now in the hands of a man of great character and unbounded courage . . ." It is a high moment for me.

Chief Justice Augelli tweaks me, as he notes the number of my "junior G-men," calling them the most recent crop of Phi Beta Kappas. He smilingly adds, "With all this talent you've attracted, Mr. Stern, yours must be a simple job."

Unfortunately, he has that wrong. Far from simplifying, the influx of new assistants has greatly complicated things. I have all these people running around, with chiefs and deputy chiefs, and no way to keep abreast of the details of their activities, certainly not if I am going to keep hands-on in courts and grand juries.

Lately, in an effort to keep informed, I adopted Hogan's practice of having the office's incoming mail screened by my secretary and by Jon's, with problem pieces brought in to either one or the other of us. But the omnipresent fear remains that somewhere, down deep in our engine room, some junior lieutenant is pulling out the seacocks and we will be sunk before we even know we are taking water.

I think we were at our best at twenty-five assistants, using a rifle to hit selected targets. Now we are fifty-two in number, and, because it is in the nature of things, one day the office will be double or triple that. And at that size, it will be taking cases that others could and should handle, and it will move relatively glacially. It is already beginning to happen with us. But I am determined to speed up what Lincoln, speaking of his generals, called "the slows."

At the end of the ceremony it is my turn to speak. I promise "to conduct this office so that the people of the state may look to it with hope, pride, and expectation. We are going to fight the pollution of public office, the pollution of our beaches, and the pollution of our civil rights."

When we get back to our office, Jon reminds me that I am now entitled to my full salary of $32,000, rather than just eighty percent. "Oh, that's right," I agree.

"Well," he says hopefully, "that should help unblock the top supervisors here."

"Don't be greedy," I respond with a laugh. But, actually, I have already taken care of it—my colleagues will also be getting a raise.

The next man into my office is Dick Hill. According to him, the next pollution battle is going to be on the beaches. The mayors of the Jersey Shore communities have decided to fight.

Chapter Two

Newsmaker
December 3, 1971–January 15, 1972

THE DAY AFTER my induction not all the comments about me in the press are entirely flattering. One anonymous source remarks, "It is like having a loaded gun in there in the hands of a gorilla, you can't be sure it won't point at you." But maybe that's flattering in its own way. I am getting used to publicity, favorable and not-so-favorable.

I notice that the more publicity you make, the more you get. You become a "newsmaker," so whatever you do becomes presumptively newsworthy. Then the prizes and awards start coming, to induce appearances. More appearances, more news, and so it goes. I like it some, and don't like it some more. I appear on TV talk shows and give a lot of speeches and interviews. It is vital that we maintain public support. Aside from an aging senator, the support of the press is all that we have. And, I have to admit, it's heady stuff when people recognize you on streets and in restaurants. But it is also a pain in the ass.

"TV personalities" ask me ridiculous questions on the air, questions that I don't know how to answer. One morning, I drive into New York at the crack of dawn to go on the *Today Show*. Sitting in front of a national audience, Joe Garagiola asks me, "Is the gambling in Puerto Rico honest?"

"How should I know?" I answer. "Ask the U.S. Attorney for Puerto Rico."

I go on Bill Beutel's show on ABC, and he says, "You got some very important defendants, but we know you did not get the top people." I look at him and say, "Oh, yeah, and who would they be?" He starts sputtering, and I don't get invited back.

But most of my experiences are of a better sort. Unlike the "stars," the working press are not showmen. They are idealistic types. Sure they get cynical, but that is because their idealism is often frustrated. That feeling strikes a chord with me. We have no press officer or spokesman in our office. Jon and I do our own answering to the press. It's better. With no buffer between us, the reporters can make better judgments.

There is one thing I have learned to be careful about, however. They teach these folks in journalism school, or maybe in city rooms, that their stories should be "balanced." That means that even in favorable stories, a reporter feels that his own credibility depends on finding something unflattering to say. It shows his objectivity. But the object of the "objectivity" can get upset. All in all, I do the press thing because it is good for business. The rest of the time I try to stay out of the way.

I am a private person. I stay out of the social columns and away from parties, unless they relate to my office. I don't even know what to say at cocktail gatherings. I can make a speech in front of a thousand people, but I have trouble making small talk over a drink. Most people find me boring.

In the weeks following my induction, the prizes, plaques, invitations to accept honorary degrees accelerate. I am even selected one of America's Ten Outstanding Young Men by the United States Jaycees in a ceremony in Indianapolis. There, Mayor Richard Lugar gives me the key to the city. I have to go on tour for the Jaycees, and I get the key to Chattanooga, Tennessee. In Alabama, Governor George Wallace makes me an Honorary Lieutenant Colonel in the Alabama National Guard. That's one award I will keep in the carton when I get back to Newark. The press points out that Nelson Rockefeller, John and Robert Kennedy, Henry Kissinger, and even Nixon have won the award. Senator Case, in his paternal way, takes pride in putting the publicity about the award into the *Congressional Record.*

Of course, this publicity stirs talk about my political future. I want none of it. I don't want to be a governor, forced to go to every sewer opening, and expected to be a member of a "party," required to support a party leader and a "party line." As for the Senate, there is all that, and worse. Imagine having to sit and listen to what Cliff Case has to listen to? No, thanks. I know that's a selfish position. After all, if the senator had never run, there would have been no me. But deep down there is another reason I do not want to seek elective office. I do not want anyone to think for even a moment that the object of our efforts were for personal political advancement. I desperately want the office to continue to be above all that.

So now we try to direct press attention to Jon Goldstein and to Bruce. They are the office's future. In my capacity as a past honoree, I nominate Jon for next year's Ten Outstanding Young Men. I also put him in for every department award there is. He wins them all. I hope we can replicate for Jon what Fred did for me. Senator Case has assured me that he will support Jon's candidacy when the time comes. We can't last forever. But, perhaps, for at least one more generation.

One party I will make. In my capacity as president of the Newark Chapter of the Federal Bar Association, we schedule a luncheon for December 17 in honor of Judge Wortendyke. I persuade Dick Kleindienst to come up. I figure the judge will like that. And he does.

❦ ❦ ❦ ❦ ❦ ❦ ❦

The day after Wortendyke's testimonial gathering, Jon Goldstein hustles into my office with a clip from *The New York Times.* "They just fired Bob Meyer, the U.S. Attorney in Los Angeles."

I read the article. "It says he resigned."

"What's that you usually say?" Jon smiles.

"Oh, yeah." I laugh. "Bullshit."

As I read the article, it looks like a repeat of what happened to me with the "Camden 28." Meyer's case has become known as the "Pentagon Paper Case"—the criminal case brought against Dr. Daniel Ellsberg for stealing the Pentagon papers and delivering them to *The New York Times.*

"Last June," the article says, "Mr. Meyer refused to sign a two-count indictment that charged Dr. Ellsberg with illegal possession of the Pentagon papers and converting them to his own use."

421

I look up from my reading. "Listen to this, Jon. See if it sounds familiar. 'Mr. Meyer felt "upstaged" by lawyers from the Internal Security Division of the Department of Justice, who flew to Los Angeles, . . . presented evidence to a grand jury, and sought an indictment without consulting very extensively with Mr. Meyer.'"

Looking up again at Jon, I remark, "Meyer was lucky. I'd just as soon they had upstaged me by not calling at all. They can keep their fine cases to themselves."

****

Of course, we can't avoid the Criminal Division, with its strike force. Nor do we want to. We remain insistent that our office, as appointed by the president, is the chief law enforcement office for the district. Yes, we report to the attorney general. Yes, he has the right and power to set national guidelines and standards for United States attorneys. And sure, he needs bureaucrats to do that, and even divisions, with specialties like anti-trust and tax. But sending teams of lawyers into districts to set up offices separate and apart from the USAs, teams which report directly back to bureaucrats who take over functions of the United States attorneys—that is something else. And that is what Henry Petersen has achieved, brilliant super-bureaucrat that he is. He now has more than a dozen offices in different districts.

But opposition is building among the leading USA offices. Mike Seymour in southern and Bobby Morse in eastern New York and I have been meeting on the strike-force issue. We plan to get together with other USAs. Dick Thornburgh of western Pennsylvania is a valuable member of our group.

****

January 12

For weeks John Barry and I have been finalizing our briefs on the DeCarlo re-argument before all the judges of the court of appeals. Most of the work has been his, and it is brilliant. Together, we go to Philadelphia and I argue before all the judges of the circuit in their large ceremonial courtroom. Aldisert goes after me, as I expect. But John tells me he thinks I gave as good as I got. Time will tell.

January 14

We file our lawsuit against fifteen Jersey shore communities, seeking to enjoin their pumping sewage sludge onto their own beaches. This is the kind of lawsuit that a USA for a district can bring with some hope of success. On the other hand, if a strike force from D.C. were to sue these communities, the D.C. attorneys would get no local help.

Chapter Three

"Foaming at the Mouth"
January 15–March 27, 1972

WE HAVE SUCCESSFULLY recruited two experienced ADAs from Hogan's office—Mel Krakov and Ed Plaza. I hope to turn over the evening trial practice sessions, probably to Mel. He seems to like to teach. And with Dick Kleindienst's help, we have hired three investigators to work directly with us. My first choice: Henry Cronin, the New York detective who made my first arrest, not counting the pickpocket.

Jon wins one of the ten Arthur S. Fleming awards presented each year in the entire federal service nationwide. A luncheon in his honor is scheduled in Washington on February 17.

****

February 18

Judge Barlow gives his opinion. Jon and Dick Hill have done an extraordinary job. They proved, Barlow holds, that the sludge was solid, not liquid; therefore, not sewage protected from our reach by the 1899 statute. "Adding water in order to pump it out to sea does not reconstitute it as raw sewage," Barlow rules. And because he credits our evidence that the sludge contains "live viruses associated with poliomyelitis, infectious hepatitis, and meningitis," he finds irreparable harm and permanently enjoins the pumping. Forty-two years of flushing sludge ends.

And we are going to keep it that way. Not that I had anything to do with the court proceedings personally. I would not begin to know how. I am not even in town for the decision. I am in Philadelphia on February 18 arguing the appeal in the Hudson County case.

****

My biggest fear is that we have become swollen with success and bloated by size. We must keep up the pressure on our staff and on ourselves. We can't regard this office as a career. Time is not a luxury, it is an enemy. I am not satisfied that we have the same momentum in 1972 as we did in the two previous years.

"Where are we with Tonti, with Gallagher, with the Atlantic City investigation?" I push the two Goldsteins, Jon and Bruce, when I return to the office.

I know that we have established that Tonti, the "Hogwash" man, and his former chief engineer took nearly $200,000 from the engineering company, Frederick Harris, Inc., and from Automatic Toll Systems, when they built the parkway. But I want to know, "When will the indictment on Tonti be ready?"

"Next month," Bruce says. "By mid-April."

"Good. But why so long?" I press.

"Didn't Jon tell you?"

"Tell me what?"

"Between the sludge case in Trenton and you in Philadelphia," Jon breaks in, "I haven't had a chance."

"When we broke the Harris company last month, they admitted that they also paid off former State Treasurer John A. Kervick," Bruce continues.

"Kervick? Former Governor Hughes's state treasurer?"

"Yes," Bruce nods.

"That means we have Burkhardt, Hughes's secretary of state, and also his state treasurer?"

"Yes."

"Okay, how much did Kervick get?" I ask Bruce.

"Over $113,000," Bruce smiles.

"The one that should be accountable is Hughes's attorney general, Arthur Sills," I say. "He presided over this mess."

"What about the Republicans in Atlantic City?" I turn to Jon.

"We have enough payoffs, maybe, to indict," John reports. "But I want to wait. More come in every week."

"The election there is May 9. If we have enough to indict, I want to do so before the vote."

"If we do that," Jon tells me, "we will be accused of interfering in the election."

"Sure. And if we could indict, and we don't, if we keep quiet and say nothing, how is that not influencing an election?" I argue.

Jon shrugs, "Whatever we do, we will be wrong."

"Right," I say. "So let's be wrong letting sunlight in, rather than keeping the curtains closed."

I turn to Bruce again. "What about Congressman Gallagher? Are we ready to go?"

"Yes. The IRS has finished. Tom Greelish, one of our new AUSAs, has put it all together."

"Where are we?"

Bruce explains, "We have, as you know, $942,000 in municipal bond purchases. All for cash, all in phony names, but all with the congressman's initials, in reverse. G.E.C."

"What kind of names?" I ask, fascinated.

"'George E. Connors,' for example. We traced $408,000 of what he bought into the Whelan-Flaherty account."

"So he bought those to accommodate Whelan and Flaherty?"

"Right. We can prove he personally cashed $201,000." Bruce continues. "That leaves about $333,000 still in his possession, or somebody's."

"Let's go," I say. "Send him a grand jury subpoena for about ten days from now. We have to get going. We are getting big, and slow—"

"By the way," Jon interrupts, I think deliberately, "Did you hear about your friend Ambassador Watson?"

"No, what?"

"He apparently got drunk and went nuts on a Pan Am flight. He started stuffing money down the blouses of the stewardesses, yelling for more Scotch, until he passed out, sprawled across the first-class lounge, foaming at the mouth."

"What!" I am staring at Jon.

"Yes. He was apparently chewing some kind of tablets," Jon informs me. Well, the thought of that picture gets my mind off of my own troubles, which is probably what Jon intended.

Chapter Four

"Why that's Bullshit, Mr. Gallagher."
"Try to Prove it, Mr. Stern."
March 27–April 14, 1972

March 27

Congressman Cornelius E. Gallagher shows up with his subpoena. But instead of going to the grand jury room on the fourth floor of the Post Office-Courthouse, he reports to my office on the fifth floor of the federal building across the street.

"Congressman Gallagher is here." My secretary, Nancy, sticks her head into my office.

"Keep him there," I say. I heave myself out of my chair and follow her into the waiting area just outside my room. Gallagher is there. He is immaculately dressed, pencil-thin and fit, with pure white hair that he keeps long; a handsome man. On the outside. I notice he is carrying an attaché case.

"I would like to see you," he says, nodding towards the door of my office.

"But I don't want to see you," I reply. "Why don't you just go across the street to the grand jury waiting room? It's on the fourth floor."

A half hour later, I go across. As I enter the building, the congressman is standing near the elevator. As I pass, he says, softly, "What do you want?" I make like I don't hear him. I remember Fred Lacey and

DeCavalcante. I don't need to make myself into a witness. I am going to prosecute this bastard.

When I get him before the grand jury, he puts his briefcase on the table, snaps it open, and displays a bunch of municipal bearer bonds.

"What is the face value of the bonds that you have in that suitcase?" I ask.

"I haven't counted them," Gallagher replies. "I think it is about three hundred and fifty thousand dollars, or three hundred seventy."

"That's just like money, isn't it, Mr. Congressman?"

"Mr. Stern, you know it is like money."

He tells the grand jurors that the bonds belong to the Hudson County Democratic organization; that they were given to him to hold in trust for the party by a Mr. Ben Schlossberg, who happened to die in 1968. So poor Congressman Gallagher has been holding onto them, he says, waiting for someone, anyone, to tell him what to do with them. But, unfortunately, no one came around.

"Now, I just want to say this, Mr. Stern," the Congressman continues. "I am a trustee of these bonds. I don't know what to do with the bonds because Mr. Schlossberg is dead. I don't know who to contact. I don't know whether the party still exists . . . the Democratic Party has been totally devastated in New Jersey."

I can't believe my ears. I am going to indict this man for perjury as well as tax evasion. I ask him, "Now, Mr. Schlossberg died in 1968. That is a fact?"

"That is a fact."

"Now, you say you were the trustee of these bonds, is that right?"

"Yes, sir."

"Now, in 1968 when Mr. Schlossberg died, who was the head of the Democratic Party in Hudson County?"

"All I know—" Gallagher begins.

"Answer the question," I tell him.

"Mr. Kenny" comes the answer.

"In 1969, with your problem of who to turn the bonds over to, who was the head of the Democratic Party in Hudson County?"

"Mr. Kenny" Gallagher answers again.

"Congressman, all the time that you had these three hundred and seventy thousand dollars worth of bonds after Schlossberg died, you were troubled by the fact that you didn't know who to give them to?"

"That's exactly right, Mr. Stern. I am still troubled. I don't know whether I am doing the right thing or not in regards to my trust," Gallagher answers solemnly.

"Who did you make contact with in the Democratic Party in order to find out about that?"

"Nobody."

"You told nobody in the Democratic Party?"

"I don't know who the Democratic Party is anymore."

I can see the grand jurors with their faces screwed up in disgust at the obviousness of his lying. We usher him out of the room. The bearer bonds stay behind.

April 4

Seven judges for the United States Court of Appeals for the Third Circuit reverse the Aldisert opinion and reinstate DeCarlo's conviction. Chief Judge Collins Seitz reverses himself. Judge Aldisert and Kolodner dissent from their colleagues.

****

April 11

Two weeks after his grand jury appearance, the grand jurors indict Congressman Cornelius Gallagher for tax evasion and for perjury. A few days later, some wits—newsmen, I think—create lyrics to a song formerly called "Mr. Gallagher and Mr. Sheen." They call it "Mr. Gallagher and Mr. Stern":

> "Oh, Mr. Gallagher. Oh, Mr. Gallagher.
> There's a briefcase full of bonds you must explain.
> Tell us who you have to thank
> At the Hudson County Bank
> Where you tried to hide behind a phony name."

"Oh, Mr. Stern. Oh, Mr. Stern.
Those securities are none of my concern.
I just held them for a guy
Who was kind enough to die."
"Why, that's bullshit, Mr. Gallagher."
"Try to prove it, Mr. Stern."

Chapter Five

Under Attack
April 11–21, 1972

CONGRESSMAN **G**ALLAGHER **HAS** gone on the attack. So has State Attorney General Kugler. My office—really I—am the target of both.

"This is a political indictment aimed specifically at discrediting me at a time when congressional redistricting is the major issue in New Jersey," Gallagher says to the press. A few days later he takes the floor of the House of Representatives. "My family and friends have been subjected to a terror equal only to the oppression in Nazi Germany."

"So now I'm a Nazi," I say to Jon. "I don't get these guys. Did you know that Neil Gallagher was a captain commanding a rifle company in General George Patton's Third Army? That he was wounded three times and decorated eight times? For Christ's sake, I couldn't even drive a truck right when I did my six months. Then this guy goes back and does a year in Korea. Under different circumstances, I'd ask for his autograph. But then he comes back home, hooks up with Bayonne Joe Zicarelli and John V. Kenny, and enters a bum-of-the-year contest."

"We have other trouble," Jon says. "Did you hear what George Kugler said in the Third Circuit last week?" I hadn't. We kept out of the appeal that Kugler took from Judge Shaw's order enjoining the state from prosecuting John J. Kenny. John Barry said we had no standing. In any case, we don't want to fan the flame between the state and us any further.

"Did Kugler argue it personally?"

"Yes," Jon reports. "Kugler told the judges that he was not told before we called John J. Kenny to the stand and immunized him."

"What!" I almost shout. "I met Kugler a week before trial and told him. Then he wrote me a letter. Then I wrote him back. It was all lovey-dovey. Dear Herb, Dear George, cordially, all that stuff."

"Well," Jon shrugs, "he told the court," he glances at his notes, "'We were never notified when the proceedings would be held, and by then, even if we were notified, we had no standing in federal court.'"

"But he sent McGlynn into the courtroom. He had McGlynn introduce the state indictment into the record before J.J. testified. Van Riper questioned J.J. from McGlynn's exhibit!"

"I know," Jon says mildly. "I was there."

****

April 14

Any hope of reconciliation between the New Jersey attorney general and us is shattered. David Biederman, a former deputy state attorney, makes a complaint to Bruce Goldstein, our chief of special prosecutions. He claims that Attorney General Kugler and Evan Jahos, the director of criminal justice, covered up a crime committed by the second most powerful man in the state, Paul Sherwin, who is not only the incumbent secretary of state of New Jersey, but Governor Cahill's closest friend.

Bruce has prepared a memo with documents brought in by Biederman. They lay out Sherwin's effort to obtain a state contract for Manzo Contracting, which had made a $10,000 contribution to the Republican Party, and promised $40,000 more. Sherwin, the secretary of state, actually directed the commissioner of transportation, John Kohl, to throw out all the bids, as a favor to second low bidder Manzo so the project would be bid again. Incredibly, Sherwin put this request in writing to the commissioner. "In this particular case, I would prefer that you reject the bids and request a rebidding, and if you will telephone me on Tuesday, I will be glad to give you the reasons for my request."

When Commissioner Kohl called, Sherwin told him of Manzo's contribution to the party. Kohl revealed all this to Biederman, Attorney

General Kugler's deputy, who served as counsel to the Department of Transportation. Biederman hit the ceiling. He protested to Kohl. When commissioner Kohl said that he would obey Secretary of State Sherwin's request, Biederman went directly to Attorney General Kugler.

Kugler refused to intervene. Biederman made a memo: "I discussed this matter with the Attorney General and advised him that in my view Mr. Sherwin's action was in derogation in policy of the bidding statutes. I further advised the Attorney General to take the matter up with Mr. Sherwin. His reply was that he would not do so, but thought my Commissioner could do so . . . Mr. Sherwin's request could be considered as part of a conspiracy to violate the bidding statutes."

Biederman's screams finally produced action. The bids were not disturbed and the contract was awarded to Centrum, the original low bidder.

A memo from Kugler to Biederman, two weeks after Biederman's, is a killer to Kugler, who signed it with his initials:

> November 4, 1970
>> RE: Manzo Contracting Company
>> Neither the Director of Criminal Justice nor I feel there is any
> further action required in the above action.
>> GFK

I call for a meeting with Bruce and Jon. "You know what this will do if we get involved?" I ask rhetorically. "It will end any law enforcement cooperation between us and the state."

"What choice do we have?" Jon asks in reply. "Do nothing?"

"Well," I say, "I'm not sure there is any federal jurisdiction. What is the federal crime?" I ask hopefully.

"If we look, I'm sure we'll find one," Jon says.

"If we look," I say, "this will spread beyond the secretary of state. There will be no way it doesn't come out that Sherwin committed a state crime—it's there in black and white—and that Kugler stuffed it back into the box. Bruce," I turn to him, "who is Biederman? Is he still a deputy AG?"

"No. He quit months ago. And—you are going to love this—the AG's office has prepared an ethics complaint against him for representing a company that he had investigated while he was a deputy AG. Apparently, that is why he is here, almost two years after the Manzo thing with Sherwin. Biederman wants revenge."

"Oh—"

"Wait, the part you'll love is that the client was Mal Brothers, one of the companies that kicked back to Addonizio-Boiardo, through the Kantor account."

"That is unbelievable."

"Right," says Jon, who obviously has already been briefed. "They will say that he came here seeking revenge and, if we go ahead, they will say that we are striking back over J.J. Kenny. So," he asks, "what shall we do?"

After a moment, I say, "We are in the uncovering, not the covering-up business. We go ahead. Before we do, I have to call Henry Petersen. This is going to start a shitstorm."

****

April 17

I appear before Fred Lacey. Don Robinson representing DeLouette, of course wants a suspended sentence. That is not possible. I fulfill my promise by asking for the five-year minimum sentence. Fred accedes and imposes the minimum. However, over all of my "objections," which Washington required me to make, Fred releases the transcripts of all of the DeLouette interrogations by the French *juge d'instruction*, Roussel. It is all public now a la DeCarlo. What a pity.

****

And then there's D. Louis Tonti, the "Hogwash" man who built the Garden State Parkway, taking tolls for himself as he built it. On April 20 we indict Tonti and Philip May, his former chief engineer, for collecting nearly $200,000 in bribes from Frederick Harris, Inc., and Automatic Toll Systems. We are careful to wait until the income tax indictments are also ready. The Tonti case came from the Kenny case, which was investigated by the IRS because the FBI lacked any interest in the investigation. We cannot expect the IRS to continue to staff bureau cases—which was virtually all we had in Newark and Jersey City—if we do not at least prosecute the crimes for which the IRS does have jurisdiction.

****

April 21

An interesting criticism rears its head in an editorial in the *New Brunswick Home News*. Referring to Tonti, it suggests we failed in prosecuting just the public officials. "Four firms have been identified as involved in the bribery, extortion, conspiracy charges. We think bribery and extortion require two parties, those who take and those who give. . . . We applaud the energy and devotion of Herbert Stern . . . At the same time, we think that the New Jersey business community had better look to its own morals. . . . The problem is larger than just punishing those who demand bribes, it also includes those who give bribes. As long as the latter exist, there will be those in high places who are willing to join the ranks of the former."

Jon brings the editorial in to me. This is serious stuff. Sure, in an ideal world you would go after both sides of the deal. We did that in Colonial, and we tied ourselves up in knots.

"Jon," I tell him, through a cloud of cigarette smoke, "someone instigated this editorial. If the idea gets fashionable that you can't get one side of a corrupt deal without the other, we'll be out of business."

"I agree," Jon says. "When we can get both, we do. We have. But businessmen are not going to talk if they know that if they do they will be prosecuted and/or put out of business. Sure, in theory, if they knew that they would get caught and punished, they would not do the crime. But it doesn't work that way."

"Yes," I say with a grin, "remember Rifkind at Leuty's sentencing? 'The computers have been clacking out don't do what poor old Leuty did.' Well, it's bullshit. Threats of big punishments don't deter. The true deterrent is certainty of detection, and a requirement to prosecute both sides will only help to insulate both sides. Who is giving the push to the paper?"

"Remember Tom Dunn, the mayor of Elizabeth, the one who was mentioned by DeCarlo on the tapes?"

"No." I draw a blank.

"Well, he was. That paper is around his area. We hear he does not like us much."

"Let him take a number."

****

The cases are building up: Gallagher, Burkhardt, Tonti, the Kervick and Sherwin investigations; not to mention trying to get the old boss, John V. Kenny, on trial. He is still in Pollack Hospital, still weaving his webs. It is infuriating.

Then there is Jon's investigation of the administration of Atlantic City. The election there is less than thirty days away

And I've got old cases, like Colonial and Boiardo. Moreover, I want to open up other counties. We have grabbed the state by the neck and shaken it. I want to keep on shaking. But my head is swimming.

Chapter Six

"I'll Have to Investigate"
April 21–26, 1972

W**HEN I REACH** Petersen to tell him about the Sherwin-Kohl-Kugler cover-up, he offers no objections. I think Henry kind of likes the facts. He authorizes the investigation and suggests I go to see Kugler and give him a heads-up. I'm not crazy about that idea, but maybe Henry is right. We have no potential federal crimes committed by Kugler. It is not a federal offense to refuse to prosecute a state crime. But, of course, our investigation will upset him. It makes sense to try and draw the sting, rather than to send the bureau in cold. So, I make an appointment with Kugler.

April 26

Jon and I are in Kugler's office. Rather than make a speech, I hand him Biederman's documents. I watch him as he reads. He is in obvious distress. He is a big man, well over six feet, but he seems to shrink as he goes through the package. When he puts the papers down, he looks up and says, "This is the only time there was any difficulty with Sherwin, and Garven stopped it."

Pierre Garven is Governor Cahill's counsel. The meaning is clear. Sherwin put the muscle on Commissioner Kohl to throw out the bids to repay Manzo for his contribution, and Biederman complained, repeatedly. Then Biederman went to Kugler. Kugler, after pushing him away, went to Garven, and Garven stopped Sherwin. No harm, no foul. Except, there was a foul. A crime had been committed, and the AG did not want to do anything about it.

"George," I tell him, "I have to investigate."

"I know you do," he says. Then, perking up a bit, "This fellow Biederman. Do you know that we made an ethics complaint against him? That's undoubtedly why he came to see you."

"Yes, George. I know. But I still have to investigate."

"I know," he says, with resignation. "I have to tell the governor, of course."

"That's up to you," I say. And with that, Jon and I leave.

"Jon," I tell him as we walk, "please memo that conversation." He nods, still taken by the moment. After all, it isn't every day that a United States Attorney has a conversation with a state attorney general involving misconduct by a secretary of state, which the governor's counsel had to step in and fix.

Shortly after our visit to his office, Kugler telephones to tell me that he has spoken to Governor Cahill. They have decided that, given the circumstances, the U.S. attorney's office should investigate Sherwin without state involvement.

I call Bruce in. "Send your grand jury subpoenas out to Manzo. The game's afoot."

Chapter Seven

A Nation of Men as Well as Laws
May 1972

L AW DAY. THERE are celebrations throughout the nation, and New Jersey is no exception.

It is fun to watch the pols pontificate about how we are a "nation of laws and not of men," as though laws are self-executing and don't need discretion in application. But any talk of discretion makes people nervous. It is seemingly inconsistent with our theory of government. We repeatedly talk discretion out of existence. I do it myself. When asked, I deny that prosecutors use discretion in enforcement. We have to, or the moral police get after us. And no one can win that debate. The rule of law always trumps, philosophically.

Mayor Tom Dunn of Elizabeth, who is also a state senator, uses his Law Day speech on the "government of laws" to go after our office. He says we use discretion to oppress people. I hear it on the news, and I read about it.

"We are in desperate shape," Dunn tells the people of New Jersey:

> Accusation is virtually identical to conviction . . . The evidence needed for conviction can be purchased . . . Widespread granting of immunity to lawbreakers results in arbitrarily selected more 'attractive targets'. . . To grant immunity to the crooked businessman in order to convict or destroy the public official he

schemingly corrupted is to say that the 'weak are worse than the guilty' . . . The public official is frequently underpaid and over-worked . . . To make categorical statements about never granting immunity to a public official is to make a political judgment . . . Under the Rule of Law, this should not be an arbitrary decision...I have personally suffered from the abuses...The Rule of 'Law' can-not endure when we substitute the arbitrary 'Rule of Men.'

Bruce, Jon, and I promptly confer. "What's with him?" I ask the guys.

"Don't you remember?" Jon says. "I told you he was mentioned fre-quently on the DeCarlo tapes. The mob guys said he would do them favors."

"Is this true?"

"We don't know," Bruce says.

"Well, I can see where he might be pissed off about that, *if* it's not true, but he is plainly trying to stop us. Imagine casting people like Addonizio and Kenny as helpless, weak, underpaid, overworked lambs corrupted by demonic businessmen—"

"Herb," Jon interrupts, "it's only a speech."

"Yes, but he is trying to start a thing going," I contend. "Remember that editorial —he wants to stop us immunizing businessmen to get tes-timony against the pols. And he is right about one thing. I will NEVER give immunity to a public official unless it's to get a higher one, as we did with Manning and J.J. Kenny—"

"We know, we know," Bruce stops me.

****

May 2

Hoover is dead. The announcement is a shock. An era, actually several eras, are over. He was his own Justice Department; a national, profes-sional policeman, almost never accountable to anyone. He used his professionalism and his longevity for nearly forty years to control the successive short-term political appointees who occupied the top three levels of the Justice Department. Only Bobby Kennedy could com-mand him, and not always at that.

The Camden 28 case is an example. After I made it clear to Bob Mardian of the department's Internal Security Division that I wanted nothing to do with the case, Hoover, anxious that our popular office conduct the prosecution, demanded that AG Mitchell order us to take the case on. I assigned it to John Barry.

"John," I told him, "you will do your duty, of course. But," I paused, "I want no incidents. No confrontations. Just put in our case and let the defendants say whatever they want. Then let the jury call it." I had learned that the case had been virtually procured by an FBI informant, Robert Hardy, who had encouraged the antiwar activists to commit the break-in to destroy draft records, and provided the wherewithal.

A few weeks later, when the defendants were scheduled to appear before Judge Larry Whipple, John got wind that they were planning to refuse to rise when the judge entered. John told Whipple who, as he entered the courtroom, said, "Please remain seated."

Well, Hoover is dead. And for all the bureau's failings, for all that it would not do, and for all that it did that it should not have done, Hoover's FBI is a magnificent organization. I don't want it to lose *all* of its independence. That could be disastrous. As Fred Lacey used to say, "You could never take this country over without first taking over the FBI." Still, with Hoover gone, perhaps now it will become more responsive to the department without losing its integrity. Maybe we won't have to scrounge labor agents—as I did in Colonial—or IRS agents—as Fred did in Addonizio and Hudson, to do the bureau's work. Unfortunately, the Camden 28 case remains ours, rather than the Internal Security Division's, because that is the way Hoover wanted it. Even though he is dead, I cannot change this assignment.

****

May 4

Jon tells me he is ready to indict in Atlantic City. But we are only five days away from the Atlantic City elections. The papers have been full of news of our investigation for weeks, while the target, Mayor William T. Somers, has denied any wrongdoing.

I refuse to withhold the indictment because of an election. A choice must be made, and I pick informing, rather than withholding information from the public. That is what we did with Addonizio in Newark. I admit that is not what we did in Jersey City, where as members of a Republican administration, we would have been crucified had we indicted the Democratic machine a week before elections. Inconsistent? Maybe. Even probably. Nonetheless, this time I will not delay the indictment.

The "Atlantic City 7" defendants include the Republican incumbent Mayor Somers; his predecessor; the public works director; the director of public parks; and three other officials. Our theory, as in Jersey City, is that the defendant public officials committed extortion both by threat and by color of office, which requires no threat— another lesson from the Colonial prosecution. In a separate indictment, we charge Patrick J. Doran, the Atlantic County engineer, for extorting $162,000. Two indictments mean two trials to be added to the pending cases.

May 9

The voters go to the polls in Atlantic City. Somers and his crowd are resoundingly defeated. The trial will be early next year. The case will be Jon's and whomever he picks to help him. If we lose, we will be attacked on the timing of the indictment. If the defendants are convicted, we will hear nothing more about it.

****

Former Secretary of State Burkhardt has pled. Tonti will be Bruce's baby. We still have an ever-increasing backlog of cases: the old Colonial case, the investigations of former State Treasurer Kervick and of present Secretary of State Sherwin, as well as tons of the mundane stuff that an office of over fifty lawyers is deep into.

One of these other cases is the ODALE—the Office of Drug Abuse Law Enforcement program.

****

A few months ago, Nixon announced a program to combat the illegal heroin trade. He brought the USAs of the major offices to the White

House for a meeting in the cabinet room. Dick Kleindienst, as deputy AG, had brought us over to the White House in a bus. When we were seated, he told us, "Remember, when the President walks in, you all stand." I guess I would have figured that out, but I was grateful for the tip.

Nixon walked in, we all stood, and he gave us a talk. He took me by surprise. I didn't like the guy then, and I still don't, but it was a different Nixon than the one you see on TV. His limbs were not crossed like they were holding his body together, and he joked around with us.

"I understand they brought you over in a bus," he said. "I've always opposed busing. The fumes, you know. Then," he flashed us a smile and said, "there is always the issue of who sits in the front or the back." We all laughed.

He really didn't mean anything racial by it, just making a joke. I guess he was trying to get people relaxed. He seemed relaxed. I suppose he felt he was with his own people. Anyway, he introduced this very intense young guy, Egil "Bud" Krogh, Jr.

Krogh told us that the idea was to end the narcotics problem by attacking it on the street level. Standing before an easel, with a pointer, he gave us statistics and then the plan. We USAs would put some of our AUSAs into a task force in our communities. They would merge with local police, customs, IRS, narcotics, and even secret service agents, to fight street-corner sales.

I noticed right away that Hoover had enough brains and clout to keep the bureau out of this cockamamie project. I wish I had enough of either to keep my people out. In my view, putting the limited resources of USA offices to fight any kind of street-level crime is nuts. I fought with the bureau to let my office decline ordinary bank robberies and stolen-car cases in favor of local prosecutions. We need to husband our resources. Now we are supposed to fight street-corner pushers?

I know it can't work. I spent too much time in the criminal courts in Manhattan, dealing with street-level addicts and pushers, watching drying-out addicts puke in holding pens while awaiting arraignment. I saw the playwright Eugene O'Neill's son Shane throw himself on the floor kicking and screaming when, at his family's request, I asked the judge to hold him without bail after he broke into his doctor's office to get a fix.

I know that you could load the entire American consumption of heroin onto one deuce-and-a-half-ton truck just large enough for eleven men, the kind of truck I drove in the army. Given our coastline, it is almost, no not almost, actually impossible to keep the tens of thousands of miles of unpoliceable borders sacrosanct. All you have to do is look at a map with the ins and outs of coastlines, and a myriad of harbors, not to mention the Mexican and Canadian land borders, to know that. Our borders cannot be completely secured. Sure, I got the Frenchman unmasked who sent the Volkswagen camper into Port Newark, and I would have put him in jail, too, if I could have. I did it because he was a criminal. But I knew I could not stop street-level addicts and pushers.

We can't stop the drug trade. We have wasted fortunes trying to prosecute it out of existence. There is too much profit in it. Funny thing about drugs, they are cheap to produce. Cost almost nothing. The high price to addicts is based on the illegality of the sale. Addicts must pay their pushers, and where do they get that money? Why, they extract it from us—from the burglaries of our homes. Janice Wylie and Emily Hoffert would not have been butchered in their apartment, if Robles had not needed fifteen dollars for a fix. We have to remove the profit to the pushers by decriminalizing the substances. Only that will inhibit the trade.

How would it work? There are lots of things we could try. But I do know that where we are now is a bad place. Making criminals out of addicts has not worked. I know that the staggering amount of money we have spent in law enforcement to punish pushers, wholesalers, and manufacturers has not worked—not for the last seventy-plus years; and that we *have* to try something else. That's why I go around and gently suggest that we consider decriminalizing marijuana, which is no more harmful, and probably less addictive than alcohol. It would at least be a start. But, with all our office's popularity, I can't sell this idea in New Jersey. Anyone who suggests decriminalization of any kind of drugs is labeled soft on crime, or pro drugs. We are too desperately in need of public support for our fight against abuse of public office to squander it on a lost cause.

So we will support the ODALE program as best we can, because it's what the President of the United States wants. And in the end, maybe I am wrong. I hope that I am wrong. I hope it works.

****

May 12

Robert Burkhardt, former secretary of state and Democratic state chairman, pleads guilty before Judge Kitchen in Camden. He takes a plea to accepting a $20,000 bribe. Bruce goes down to Camden to take the plea.

I am happy to stay home, because we have gotten a break on the John V. Kenny prosecution. We are finally going to get Kenny out of Pollak Hospital.

I am negotiating with Kenny's counsel, Walter D. Van Riper, for Kenny's plea. For months I have been chasing the Little Guy, trying to get a trial date, while he has been living and operating out of the hospital, claiming to be too ill to stand trial. If this case goes to trial, it is one I would have to try personally; but, if Kenny enters a plea, I will be freed up to try Congressman Gallagher.

The good news is that, by the middle of the month, Van Riper calls and says that J.V. Kenny will take a plea. He still won't plead to extortion, but he will take six counts of tax evasion, each punishable by three years. The seventy-nine-year-old Kenny can get eighteen years. This makes the IRS delirious with joy, and they are entitled to it. They did all the heavy investigating because the FBI was not interested. Of course, that was a while ago. The bureau has since become more responsive to our needs, that is after we obtained the convictions in Newark and Jersey City. Not to mention Hoover's death.

May 18

The old boss of Hudson County is wheeled into the courtroom. It is a charade, of course. Sure, he is elderly. But while he does have physical problems, I know he has been running the remnants of his organization from his hospital room. However, I figure that with eighteen years available to him, Iron Balls Shaw has adequate scope for punishment. And the judge has heard the evidence of Kenny's years of graft in the earlier trial.

With the nurse in costume by one side, and his doctor by the other, Kenny enters his six guilty pleas to tax fraud for each of six years. Judge Shaw sets next week, May 23, for sentencing and tells Kenny that on that day he is going right to jail. "Come prepared for immediate execution of sentence," Shaw leans over the bench. "There will be no stay. Come prepared!"

"Can I say something?" the diminutive figure in the wheelchair asks.

"Yes," Shaw responds.

"You know those years of tax evasion I just pled to?"

"Yes," Shaw rasps.

"I just received a refund check of $2,986 for one of those years."

The New York Times reports, "Mr. Stern looked unhappy with that revelation. Mr. Van Riper suppressed a grin." Now, there is some very accurate reporting.

Chapter Eight

A Stench Lingers
May 2–23, 1972

I **WALK INTO MY** office and find Mayor Tom Dunn, the man who in his Law Day speech accused me of political prosecutions, sitting in the waiting area near my secretary. "Can I see you?" he says.

When I take him inside and we are seated at my desk, he says, "All right, I'm here."

"Yes, I can see that," I observe.

"No. I mean, go ahead and arrest me or put me in the grand jury," says Dunn.

"What are you talking about?"

"The press and the radio say you are investigating and are about to indict me," Dunn tells me.

"What!" I exclaim.

"Yes," Dunn asserts. "We are in a political campaign and those are the reports. I'm going to lose the election. What you do doesn't matter. I'm not a lawyer. I have no other profession. I've had two heart attacks. I have my jobs as mayor and state senator. When those are gone, that's it. So you might as well go ahead."

"Mayor, like I said, I don't know what you are talking about. The only thing I know about you personally is that stupid Law Day speech you made." I can see Dunn slump forward in obvious relief. The man looks pathetic.

I pick up the phone and intercom Nancy. "Have we gotten any press calls about Mayor Dunn?"

"Yes," she says. "Don't you remember? It was the local radio station and the newspaper, the *Red Bank Register*. You said it must be about Law Day. You did not want to respond to Mayor Dunn's speech and did not call them back."

I turn back to Dunn. I can't help feeling sorry for him. Even if I had returned the calls, all I could have said in response to questions about an investigation would be "no comment." Prosecutors never confirm or deny investigations. But, as I look at the man, I can't help feeling that a mere "no comment" is unfair. So I ask him, "Mayor, would you mind stepping outside for a moment?"

"Okay," he says and leaves to wait by Nancy. While he is gone, I get on the telephone. I call Bruce Goldstein, then the bureau, then the chief of IRS intelligence, and finally the strike force. No one has any investigation going on the guy. It's a blank.

When I'm finished, I ask Dunn back in. "Mr. Mayor, I've checked the agencies. There are no investigations of you."

His whole demeanor brightens. "Thank you, thank you, Mr. Stern," he says as he gets up to leave.

"Just a minute," I stop him.

"Yes," he says apprehensively.

"How would you like me to call the press and tell them that?"

"Like it! I would kiss your feet."

"That is not necessary, sir." And in his presence I call the paper and the radio station and spike the story.

The next morning, Nancy buzzes me, "There is a police officer here from Elizabeth to see you."

The cop is very spiffy, his leathers—belts, cap, boots—all shined up. He hands me an envelope. When I open it, there is a thank-you card from Mayor Dunn. There is also his original Law Day speech, with his handwritten notes. Finally, there is a long yellow sheet of paper— the kind lawyers use. On it is written, fifty times, front and back, "I am sorry I gave 'that' speech on Law Day, 5/1/72."

****

May 22

Spectacular news: The Third Circuit affirms the Whelan and Flaherty convictions. Most important, Judge John Gibbons's opinion for the court endorses our "extortion under color of official right" theory—that whenever a public official takes money, he commits both bribery and extortion, irrespective of the voluntariness of the payment.

Never again will a public officeholder be able to defend a Hobbs Act prosecution for extortion on the ground that he was instead bribed. AUSA Tom Greelish and I had written a law review article, "The Unnecessary Distinction between Bribery and Extortion," for the *Seton Hall Law Review*. We did not cite it in our briefs. Neither did the court. But it was there. Was that cricket? Why not? I take it that a bit of scholarship is always timely. No prosecution should have to go through what I did in Colonial when a briber defends that he was extorted, or an extorter defends on the theory that he was bribed.

****

In Boss Kenny's case, we get some information that will be useful in the sentencing. For several months we have been gathering evidence that John V. Kenny has been hiding out in Pollak Hospital, pretending to be too ill to stand trial, while still pulling political strings from his hospital room. Now we are able to prove it. Assemblyman David Friedland calls and gives me information that leads to our obtaining affidavits from three Hudson County assemblymen, Christopher J. Jackman, Michael P. Esposito, and David Friedland himself. The assemblymen swear that Kenny continues to control their votes and all the patronage in Hudson County, including sending two names for judgeships, and a replacement for Sternkopf on the Port Authority. Secretary of State Paul Sherwin actually got the two men their judgeships. Kenny even authorized these three Democrats in the assembly to switch votes and make Republican Thomas H. Kean Speaker of the Assembly, so that Friedland could get a powerful committee chairmanship. Kenny did all this string-pulling from his hospital room after his severance from trial, while publicly claiming to be too sick to be retried.

Now his sentencing is on for May 23. Not only do I intend to use these three affidavits, but I also intend to force Assemblyman Friedland to take the stand. While it is true that we learned of the other two assemblymen because Friedland had called my office, the reason for his call was to persuade us to tap his own telephone in the legislature to catch Kenny's manipulations. After I hit the roof about the eavesdropping, the slimy fellow gave up on the other two assemblymen. I now have affidavits from all three. But I want him, in particular, on the stand.

John Barry, Bruce Goldstein, and I meet to prepare our position.

"What are we going to do at that sentencing hearing?" Bruce asks.

"We are not going to let this creep Friedland just whisper in my ear and hang back," I declare. "You know what happened when he called and suggested a wire tap? I said, 'Why don't you just testify in the grand jury?' He said 'No. The people of Hudson County would not understand.' Imagine that! Well, they are going to understand. I want him subpoenaed for the sentencing hearing. The nerve of him, asking me to tap the assembly's telephone lines! We haven't used electronic surveillance in any of our cases."

"We got the information from him that got us the affidavits," Bruce reminds me.

"I know. But he goes up. I want him exposed."

"How come Sherwin is listening to Kenny in making appointments? And what is this business with Assemblyman Kean?" Bruce asks.

"Remember," John Barry says, "Kenny had his Democratic organization quietly support Republican Cahill for governor over Democrat Bob Meyner, whom he hated. I don't . . . I don't know anything about the Friedland-Kean deal."

"And I don't care. It's none of my business," I say. "Why Kenny did what he did is not our affair. The fact that he sat in a hospital, ducking trial on grounds of illness, while pulling the strings from his hospital room, that *is* our business. And we are going to make it the public's business. The public is going to know that the 'stench in the nostrils' that the senator spoke of at Fred's induction still lingers. Get a subpoena out to Assemblyman Friedland for the sentencing hearing."

As John Barry and Bruce leave my office, John turns back and says, "By the way, did you see the article about Bill Subin leaving?"

"No," I say.

"Well, I think the press is onto the trouble over the Camden 28 case," John tells me.

"What trouble?" I ask. "He was my AUSA keeping information from me, while he worked with Goodwin and Internal Security."

"Well, he says in the article that his resignation was caused by 'an internal matter' and he would comment further later," John continues.

"Really? That will be interesting."

****

May 23

We have a dandy of a sentencing hearing. Kenny, nurse, doctor, wheelchair—all are there. But the theater belongs to Friedland.

When David Friedland takes the stand, I let Van Riper examine him first. It is the only time I ever root for the defense in one of my cases. Van and I play ping-pong, with Friedland as the ball. Van Riper brings out that Friedland was playing a double game with both the reform movement of Mayor Paul Jordan, and the old organization now run by Kenny from Pollak Hospital.

"I met with Mayor Jordan to pledge my support to him. . . . Subsequent to that, I met with Mayor Kenny to gain his support for the Democratic leadership in the assembly," Friedland is forced by Van Riper to admit.

"You switched your allegiance to the Jordan organization?" Van Riper prods.

"Not publicly. Privately."

"Did you hide it?" Van Riper lowers his voice to a near whisper.

"Yes," admits Friedland.

"You went to Mayor Kenny about getting back on the assembly ticket?"

"I realized that the only way to get the leadership was to approach Mayor Kenny, which I did, and that was January of 1972," Friedland answers.

"You wanted Mr. Kenny's support to make you speaker of the House?" Van Riper's last words are very loud.

"That is right."

"Where did you approach Mr. Kenny?"

"In the hospital."

"For the past several months you have been the leader of the so-called Hudson County block in the assembly, have you not?" prods Van Riper.

"Yes, sir."

"And on behalf of that block did you trade with the present speaker of the house?" Van Riper accuses him.

"Of course I did."

"Did you trade for making yourself chairman of the powerful conference committee?"

"That was definitely part of the trade."

After Van Riper finishes smacking Friedland around, it is my turn. I point out that he had called our office in April, got the duty officer and asked him to place a wiretap on his legislative office.

I continue, "Shortly thereafter I returned your call?"

"You did, within about ten minutes," Friedland laughs.

"And I told you that, if you had any information that this man was deceiving the court, I wanted you before a grand jury?" I am not amused.

"Yes, you did."

"You told me you did not want to go before a grand jury?" I press on.

"I said I preferred to speak privately," Friedland answers.

"And that is how you came to make your April 28 affidavit?"

"That is right."

"When you first telephoned the office of the United States Attorney in April, you knew that we had been trying to get Mr. Kenny into a courtroom for more than a year, to try him on federal indictments?" I insist.

"Yes, sir."

"Did you know, Assemblyman, at that time he was claiming he was too ill to stand trial?"

"Yes, I did."

"You had many conversations with John V. Kenny in his hospital room at Pollak Hospital between November 1971 and January 1972?"

"Yes," he says.

Friedland is forced to concede that he knew that from his hospital room Kenny submitted two names to Sherwin for state judgeships, and that the governor made the appointments.

"Did you at any time report that to the office of United States Attorney?"

"No, I did not."

"Did you tell us about meetings with Kenny for the past fourteen months?"

"No, I did not."

I do not know if the Friedland testimony advances the ball against Kenny, but I sure hope it helps fumigate the assembly. I want to wash after just looking at this guy, the chairman of the conference committee. When Van Riper and I finish with Friedland, Van Riper speaks on Kenny's behalf.

The elegant Van Riper, flowered boutonniere in place, begs Shaw for leniency for Kenny. "There is no need to punish this man. He is already punished," Van Riper gently points over to Kenny, sitting lost in his wheelchair. "He has already suffered humiliation, he has suffered disgrace, he has suffered degradation and, finally, he has suffered downfall."

I make no speech. The issue is not in doubt. Shaw will send Kenny to prison. There is no need for me to grandstand. Kenny himself has nothing to say.

Judge Shaw imposes the full eighteen-year maximum sentence on Kenny and sends him to Springfield Medical Facility in Missouri for medical evaluation. The judge makes it clear that after the 90-day medical evaluation, Kenny will be returned for final sentencing, which will undoubtedly be less than the full eighteen years.

As our team leaves the courthouse, two reporters, Alex Michelini of the *New York Daily News* and Bob Rudolph of the *Star Ledger*, grab us. They tell us that Secretary of State Paul Sherwin just confirmed that he did get the names of the two judicial candidates, but says that all he did was merely pass them on to Pierre Garven, the governor's counsel.

When we are back in the office, sipping coffee at my conference table, Jon reclines in his swivel chair. "You know, Herb, it's been about two and a half years since we came into office with Fred."

"Yes, I know. Actually, two months longer than that," I observe, "which reminds me. It's time to open up Mercer and Bergen Counties. Same technique, we subpoena—"

"That is not what I meant!"

Chapter Nine

A Matter of Privilege
May 23–July 1, 1972

WITH KENNY INCARCERATED, another era has closed, at least in New Jersey. But we are still knee-deep in the Sherwin investigation when Frances Henderson, the senator's administrative assistant, telephones. "Senator Case wanted me to call you and report that several days ago he got a call from Governor William Cahill, asking for an appointment."

"Oh?"

"And yesterday the governor and Secretary of State Paul Sherwin flew down to Washington on the state plane to meet in the senator's office. I was in the room," she continues.

"Ah?"

"The governor began to tell Senator Case that Paul was under investigation by you and—" she pauses.

"Oh?"

"—and the senator stopped him cold and asked him . . . I have my notes . . . yes, here it is . . . he asked, 'Bill, if I was called into a grand jury, would this conversation be privileged?'"

"Great! Great! What happened next?"

"Oh, Cahill and Sherwin immediately got up and left."

"Did they say anything else?"

"Not a word." With that I break into laughter.

"Well, whatever," the dignified Frances says. "I have a memo of the meeting for our files." Frances rings off.

****

That is not the only attempted interference by the state into our investigation. Bruce Goldstein tells me that he and his agents are stumbling over state investigators in interviewing Manzo, the contributor who Sherwin tried to help get a contract. Both Pete Richards, my former Justice Department colleague, and Ed Stier, the former AUSA who had broken Zelmanowitz, now both deputy state attorney generals, are subpoenaing Manzo's records and questioning witnesses.

Bruce comes to me upset. "I thought Kugler told you that we were to investigate alone?"

"That's what he said."

"Then what's going on?"

"Find out," I tell Bruce. "Call down to the state division of criminal justice. You can speak to Pete and Ed. They are good people."

After Bruce checks he reports that Manzo, outraged that his $10,000 contribution had not gotten the contracts rebid, actually brought a lawsuit to get his money back. On May 30, just days ago, during the trial, a witness told the state judge that Manzo had given the money "to have the job thrown out, and he promised he would give between twenty-five and fifty thousand if it was bid again." The judge immediately notified the division of criminal justice. But Kugler, away on a European vacation, had not told any of his staff of his decision to leave the investigation to us.

June 13

I am happy to convert our investigation into a joint one with the state—I'm perfectly comfortable working together with Pete and Ed. We all meet in my office and agree on strategy. Fifteen days later, Kugler and I jointly announce the state and federal indictments of Secretary of State Paul Sherwin.

****

On the same day that Sherwin is arraigned, former Secretary of State Robert Burkhardt is sentenced by Judge John J. Kitchen in Camden.

Bruce calls me from the courthouse with the news. "You won't believe this!"

"What?"

"Judge Kitchen just gave Burkhardt probation," Bruce announces.

"Probation?" I am astounded.

"Yes. Wait 'til you hear this. He fined him $5,000 and—"

"Five thousand?"

"Yes." Bruce assures me. "Five, and the judge is allowing Burkhardt to pay in installments."

"This is total bullshit," is my reaction.

"True enough. The press, or at least some of them, are going nuts," Bruce tells me.

****

Back in February, John Mitchell resigned as attorney general in order to run the Committee to Re-Elect the President—hard to believe they chose a name that yields the acronym CREEP. Since then, Dick Kleindienst has been acting AG. He has been up for confirmation for quite a while.

I have spoken in public support of Kleindienst's confirmation. In the words of the trade, he has been our "Rabbi." We could not have accomplished what we did without him. It is the only public endorsement I have ever made, if it can be called that.

June 12

Dick is confirmed and appointed Attorney General of the United States.

June 17

Five men are caught trying to break in and wiretap the Democratic headquarters on the sixth floor at the Watergate office complex.

****

By the end of June the matter that first brought me to New Jersey is in the papers again. All of the corporate defendants in the old Colonial case plead guilty in state court to the indictment that mirrors ours in federal court. Only relatively small fines are involved. The pleas cover charges in both courts. This plea deal is great for us. Now, only Jacks and Zirpolo remain in the case.

Chapter Ten

"Sealed with a Kiss"
July 1–August 1, 1972

July 1

Gil Spencer, the editor of the *Trentonian*, a newspaper covering the middle of the state, has been writing blistering editorials supporting our efforts. Today, he writes a doozy, excoriating Judge Kitchen for the Burkhardt sentence. Bruce comes racing into my office to show me Spencer's latest. He is laughing so hard he can hardly speak.

"Listen to this," he chortles, as he reads Spencer's editorial. "'It is hardly likely that the betrayers of public trust in New Jersey will have a testimonial dinner for federal Judge John J. Kitchen. But God knows, they should,'" Bruce is strangling with laughter. "'They should spirit him to the dais on their shoulders . . .'" Bruce is now spluttering and I am listening with open mouth, "'. . .on their shoulders, singing and sobbing their gratitude and scattering lilacs and lilies in his path.'"

We are now both doubled over with laughter. "It's titled," Bruce reads, "'Sealed with a Kiss,' because in it he says, 'The judge sealed the Burkhardt episode with a kiss, or to put it another way, probation!'"

"Bruce," I say, between gasps, "that man deserves a Pulitzer Prize."

****

July 1

The attorney general's office has made a big mistake. Their press people have leaked a false story designed to make it look as though

459

the attorney general and our office launched a joint investigation of Secretary of State Sherwin back in June, after the state judge, Judge Stamler, forwarded the May 30 testimony to both of our offices. This press release is designed to cover up the cover-up of Sherwin's misdeeds. "After testimony was taken, Superior Court Judge Stamler sealed the transcript and sent it off to both the U.S. Attorney's offices and the State Attorney General," the release reads. It is of course a lie.

Within days, an enraged Biederman fires back. His charges are headlined in the *Bergen Record*:

> *A COVER UP FOR SHERWIN CHARGED*
> Biederman says he is willing to testify that top-ranking New Jersey officials covered up corruption charges against Secretary of State Paul Sherwin. He says he warned Attorney General George F. Kugler about two years ago of a conspiracy involving Sherwin . . . . He took his information to Kugler, Evan Jahos, Chief of the Division of Criminal Justice, and Commissioner Kohl, Transportation Commissioner. When the three did not act, he says, he went to U.S. Attorney Herbert J. Stern who convened a grand jury.

"There is going to be hell to pay," I say to Jon, when I get him alone.

"What can we do?" he wonders.

"The only thing we can. Tell the truth."

"Biederman is lying, too," Jon points out. "He did not come to us because Kugler did not act for two years. Biederman came to us because they made an ethics complaint against him."

"If we're asked, we will say that too."

****

And of course we get asked, over and over. And we tell the truth. Our investigation began in April, when Biederman came in, not June after the judge sent the transcript. The newspapers are screaming for an investigation. The New Jersey legislature refuses. The State Commission of Investigation refuses. Governor Cahill, who has been busy expressing confidence in his secretary of state, is now issuing statements in support of his attorney general who, in direct contradiction of what he told us in his office, and in the memo, denies that he ever knew of Sherwin's activities until the state judge forwarded the testimony.

Interestingly, no member of the opposition Democratic Party calls for an inquiry, only the press.

Just when it seems it will blow over, one Republican maverick, Senator James H. Wallwork, obtains the memos from Biederman and releases them to the press. That does it. On August 1 Kugler, caught in the hurricane of renewed publicity, orders the SCI to reverse itself and conduct an investigation. He hopes this will put out the fire. But it does not.

Chapter Eleven

Ghosts
August 1–November 9, 1972

I T'S STILL NOT over. The press, egged on by Senator Wallwork's cries of cover-up is demanding the appointment of a special state prosecutor for the Sherwin case. Attorney General Kugler, yielding, asks Chief Justice Weintraub to appoint one.

The chief justice appoints Matthew Boylan. A tall man, lean of frame, he is a real trial lawyer. He had better be, because if he loses in the prosecution of Sherwin, the Cahill administration will turn its guns on me. "This unjust accusation was made by Stern to embarrass us," they will say if Sherwin is acquitted. The trial has been set for October 16.

****

Judge Shaw is dead. He died July 10. When Kenny returns from his ninety-day medical study, a different judge will pronounce the final sentence. I am sure it will be reduced. Kenny has already suffered a heart attack in the prison hospital.

We must not let Judge Shaw's passing go unnoticed. Little in stature, Shaw was a towering presence in our cases. His decision to release the DeCarlo tapes was in itself a life-changing event in New Jersey's body politic. I have decided to name our office library in his honor. I invite Mrs. Shaw to hang his picture on our wall. I tell the assembled staff that the public owes a great debt to the judge, one our office should not forget. "All in all, we will not see his like again."

While true enough, I have no illusions about his remembrance. In time it will fade, then extinguish. In a short while, as these things go, new young AUSAs will encounter Shaw's photograph and wonder who he was, and why it is in "their" office library. But, perhaps, there will be one who will inquire, who will take pains to peer into the past to learn. Lucky indeed will be any who do, for they will learn much of what it means to be a judge. And a great deal about the history of their own U.S. Attorney's office.

****

The days fly. They become weeks, then months. They see successes, and some failures, too. I still can't get my people to open up investigations of Republican Bergen and Democratic Mercer counties. My colleagues want to finish chewing what is in their jaws now, before taking more bites.

But time has also removed some of our backlog. I no longer have to worry about a retrial of Jacks and Zirpolo, the last of the Colonial ghosts. These two schmucks have been arrested, can one believe it, *passing* a bribe of $30,000 to a Monroe Township official to obtain a zoning change for a housing development. The official notified the county prosecutor of the solicitations, who arrested Jacks and Zirpolo as soon as the money changed hands. They are going to learn that it is not more blessed to give than to receive.

****

The ghost of DeCarlo, the Salerno case, is ready for trial. This is the ring that Zelmanowitz, on the stand, revealed stole millions in bonds from a Boston bank. The names came out under cross-examination by DeCarlo's lawyer, Querques. When Zelmanowitz broke after his month-long journey from Miami to Newark, the deal he made with then-AUSA Stier was to give up DeCarlo. Nothing more. During his cross-examination, we were stunned to discover from Zelmanowitz's testimony that the leader of the stolen bonds ring was "Fat Tony" Salerno.

Salerno is bigger than DeCarlo, bigger than Boiardo. Salerno is at the top of the Genovese crime family with a home in Miami Beach, Florida; a hundred-acre horse farm in New York; and an apartment in Manhattan. He goes back to the origins of the family, to the days of Lucky Luciano and Meyer Lansky. He controls all the numbers in Harlem.

Dick Langway, chief of the Criminal Division has prepared the case for trial.

Gerry Zelmanowitz has been brought back from his "relocated" location to testify at Salerno's trial. Zelmanowitz has been given a new name—Paul Maris, a new social security card, and a false employment history with the super-secret Atomic Energy Commission. With typical Brooklyn ingenuity, he has already used his new identity to take over a 350-employee dress company, which now bears the name "Paul Maris Company." I guess you can't hold a bad man down.

Langway tells me he is ready to go with an "air-tight" case against Fat Tony. This will strike a great blow at the mafia in New York and be quite a feather in the cap of New Jersey!

****

"Dick Langway needs to see you immediately," Nancy's on the intercom.

"Where?" I ask.

"He is standing outside Judge Garth's courtroom on the fourth floor of the courthouse," Nancy tells me. "He says to hurry."

I race to the elevator and run across the street to the courthouse, then into another elevator, loping down the hall. I find Langway outside Judge Garth's courtroom. He looks like he has tears in his eyes.

"What happened?" I am at his side.

"Zelmanowitz –" says Dick, catching his breath. "Zelmanowitz just testified that the defendant Salerno in the courtroom is not the man who was introduced to him as "Fat Tony" years ago when he fenced the stolen bonds. Zelmanowitz now claims that someone else had apparently used Salerno's name, and that he," says Dick, pointing to a fat man with a cigar clenched in his teeth, standing down the hall with a defense attorney, "is not the man who was involved in the stolen bonds."

"He did, did he!"

"Yes," Dick shakes his head in disbelief.

I look over at Salerno, who has been watching us. Although out of earshot, he obviously knows what Langway is saying. He strides a few step closer, chuckles and without even bothering to remove his cigar, he bows in my direction.

I can feel the blood rising to my head. "Where is Gerry?" I ask.

Langway takes me to a room we have for witnesses. There he is, Gerald Martin Zelmanowitz, master con man, utterly composed, sitting deep within an armchair.

"It's been a long time, Gerry," I greet him.

"Two and a half years," he agrees. "It's been a long time for me, Herb, hiding out from the mob. And for my wife. And for my daughter."

With that, he gives me a knowing smile. Knowing, because he knows I will get it, that I will understand that he has just bought his peace from the mob. He doesn't care that we have a jury sequestered because Salerno is a defendant. He doesn't care about the co-defendants. He will testify against them, and we will gain some convictions. But we will not get a conviction against Salerno. That is the price for Gerry's freedom from fear for the rest of his life.

I turn on my heel, saying nothing because there is nothing to say.

"Herb, I'm sorry," Langway is distraught as we leave the room.

"It's okay," I tell him. "Not your fault." And it isn't.

I wait until the judge is ready and I go into the courtroom, so that I can personally move to sever Salerno. Langway should not have to do that. It really wasn't his fault. Maybe it isn't even Gerry's fault. The deal he made was for DeCarlo, not Salerno.

It goes hard, but sometimes you just lose. I just did.

Chapter Twelve

Looking Ahead
September 1–November 9, 1972

A **FEW WEEKS INTO** September, my secretary buzzes me, "The senator is on the telephone." For me, there is only one senator. So I promptly get to it.

"Herb," he says, "I'm sorry."

"Sorry about what, sir?"

"I want to recommend you for Judge Shaw's seat on the court, but the American Bar Association wants federal judges to have at least fifteen years in practice and you, I think, have only ten, right?"

"Yes, sir," I respond, completely surprised by the conversation.

"Well, I called the department and asked if they would submit your name, but they said no. I'm kind of stymied."

"Senator, I am more than grateful to even be considered—"

"Well," Senator Case breaks in, "you've earned it. And we don't have to worry about succession in the office. Nixon is certainly going to win over poor George McGovern now, with the Eagleton thing, on top of everything else. And it looks like I will not have any problem in my reelection, so I can guarantee that Jon Goldstein will succeed you. But I could not get you past the department this time."

"I read the department just indicted the Watergate burglars, including a couple of White House aides," I remark.

"Yes. It is unbelievable. The president couldn't lose this election if he tried. What his people are doing with a penny-ante break-in of a Democratic campaign office defies imagination."

"You must know McGovern pretty well."

"I do. George is a good man. A very good man. But," he gives his famous giggle, "don't quote me. I'm supposed to be running with the other guy."

****

I am surprised that the senator would even consider me for a federal judgeship so early. But on reflection, I see his point. My role here has changed. I am no longer running from court to court. I still go, but Jon is doing most of that now. I seem to be spending more and more time meeting with the public and the agencies and pushing the AUSAs to move investigations. It is wise for the senator to look ahead and provide for the next four years.

The public forums have been revealing. I have been speaking out In favor of the notion of instituting public financing of political campaigns. Our prosecutions throughout the state provide generous footnotes of the bona fides of the need for change in the way we fund our politics. While it is clear that no change of any kind is acceptable yet, we are making inroads.

The drug issue is something else. I can't return to the idea of the decriminalization of drugs, not even starting with marijuana, not with the president's ODALE program in full swing and my AUSAs involved in rounding up street-level pushers. As a matter of fact, we USAs just met with Nixon in New York to discuss our progress—which is little or nothing. So I guess we will continue "punishing" addicts, filling our jails with users and low-level sellers while we both fill the pockets of international drug conspirators and . . . empty our own.

I have begun to suggest at least cutting back, if not totally eliminating, capital punishment. But I am a total flop. The public is too wedded to gas chambers and electric chairs. As popular as our law enforcement efforts and achievements are, many of our most ardent fans refuse to believe that capital punishment does not deter murder or protect society, but instead brutalizes it. I just can't get it across.

I could talk about the Wylie/Hoffert murders—the young girls butchered while bound back to back—and about George Whitmore, an innocent young man who narrowly escaped paying for their deaths with his own. I could tell them about the kid that I interviewed in a police station who had been primed with all the details of a gruesome rape-murder of an elderly woman, and who may not have committed the crime.

Sure, we want the blood of the men who did those crimes, and of men like Joseph Michael Donohue, who are professional killers; but the satisfaction that brings—if satisfaction is the proper word—we pay for with our Whitmores. Yes, it's true that all punishments run the risk of error. But capital punishment is different. The difference in the degree of the punishment makes it different. And if we allow the punishment we want for the Donohues, for the man who killed Wylie and Hoffert, even for the Hitlers and the Himmlers to justify the widespread use of capital punishment, we enable these monsters to kill more and more people, by our hands in their names.

These are the things I want to say, but I can't. I cannot give my audiences the benefit of my life experience in the few minutes I have to speak to them. I cannot describe the scene, the very smell in a police station at 2:00 a.m. when you arrive to see a kid, friendless and alone, who has been interrogated for hours and who has confessed to a crime that he, *maybe*, committed. You can't describe that, and if you start to, there will be few who would even want to listen.

So I do what I can by nudging in a direction rather than pushing the final destination. I argue for limiting capital punishment to the murder of policemen to avoid apprehension during commission of another crime, and for crimes against humanity, just as I have in the past suggested getting rid of laws against the use of marijuana as a precursor to decriminalizing all currently illegal drugs. Even so, I am not having much success.

So, at thirty-five, too young for a federal judgeship, and promoted out of trying cases, I occupy myself doing my best to manage the office. From crisis to crisis.

****

October 17

The trial of Secretary of State Paul Sherwin begins in state court. This is the one case I simply cannot afford to lose, and my office is not going to try it. If the prosecution loses, the Cahill Administration will demand my head.

It takes ten days. Then it is over. On October 26, after four hours and fifteen minutes of deliberation, the jury renders its verdict: Guilty.

What's next? As the *Times* account puts it, "The State Investigation Commission will now look into allegations by Republican state senator James H. Wallwork that the state attorney general's office sat on the Sherwin case for more than a year."

November 7

President Nixon and Senator Case score overwhelming reelection victories.

November 9

The SCI announces that its hearings into Wallwork's charges will be "private."

Chapter Thirteen

A Private Inquiry and a Christmas Gift
November 9–December 1972

"**W**HAT'S A 'PRIVATE' inquiry?" I ask.

"One you don't want people to hear," Jon gives me the helpful literal definition. Then, seeing my face, he continues, "Look, we are ahead. Imagine if Sherwin had been acquitted. Then the Cahill crowd would have crowed, 'See? There was no cover-up because there was nothing to cover up.'"

"So now they are going to cover up the cover-up?"

"What else do you expect?" Jon responds.

****

Jon and I testify before the SCI behind closed doors. We testify to Kugler's statement that this was the only time they had trouble with Sherwin, and Garven stopped it. That testimony, along with Biederman's contemporaneous memo, establishes that Kugler personally knew about Sherwin's efforts to influence the bidding. Jahos, the director of criminal justice whom Biederman also memoed, Kugler, and Pierre Garven, the governor's counsel, as well as Biederman himself also testify.

Recently retired state Supreme Court Justice John Francis has been hired as special counsel to conduct the inquiry. His questioning foreshadows the conclusion of his "investigation." The only question is when and how, not whether he will exonerate the Cahill administration.

We are too busy to dwell on the SCI, or at least Jon is. He hustles down to Camden, along with Gary Brown, to try Patrick J. Doran, the Atlantic County engineer, for extorting more than $160,000 from businesses doing business with the city. On November 14, Gary opens to the jury describing "a well-oiled graft machine." Democrats in Hudson County, Republicans in Atlantic. The story is the same. Jon presents the witnesses. In ten days, Doran is convicted of taking payoffs on every major highway contract for the past five years. The jury was out one hour and fifty-five minutes, a new record. Jon has surpassed both Fred and me.

****

November 22

Sherwin is sentenced to two years in prison by state Superior Court Judge Francis Crahay. Gil Spencer, the remarkable editor of the *Trentonian*, writes:

> It is difficult to think of the Sherwin bribery case without thinking of the Burkhardt bribery case . . . Sherwin was sentenced to jail because the judge is obviously a man who understands what corruption can do in high places—no geographic area of the world, including Singapore in the 1920s—can top New Jersey's record for official betrayal. Mr. Burkhardt was sentenced by a judge whose concept of judicial responsibility is obviously tantamount to a screwdriver.

I show the editorial to Bruce. "Take a look. This guy is great. He should get a Pulitzer," I observe, not for the first time.

"Do they give those out to smaller newspapers?"

"Don't know. But they should," I reply.

****

November 27

More ghosts are laid to rest. Jacks and Zirpolo plead guilty to receiving the Colonial bribes and to attempting to pay a bribe to the Monroe

Township official. The same day, federal Judge Clarkson Fisher imposes the final sentence on John V. Kenny, reducing the eighteen years to eighteen months. The eighty-year old Kenny, still in the prison hospital, waives his right to be present.

****

I know it is immodest, but I have wondered why no one in law enforcement in the United States has ever come to us to study the techniques we have developed to burn out corruption in public office. At the end of November, that changes—we hear from our first student.

"There is a George Beall on the phone," Nancy intercoms me. "Says he is the U.S. Attorney for Maryland."

All I know about the guy is that he is the younger brother of the United States Senator for Maryland, J. Glenn Beall, Jr. It is not hard to figure out how he got the job. His qualifications as a USA seem suspect. No law-enforcement background. But, of course, I take the call. Within five minutes, I am very glad that I did.

"I'd like to come and see you," he says. "I know that Baltimore County is totally corrupt. I want to do something about it."

"Okay. Do you have any evidence?" I inquire.

"No. No, I don't. That's what I want to see you about," he answers. "Our IRS chief of intelligence here tells us that you people have gone into counties cold and cleaned them up."

"IRS? Not bureau?"

"Right."

"You are on the right track," I tell him. "Come on up. We'll help all we can."

****

December 11

Beall, AUSAs Barry Skolnik, and Russell T. Baker, and IRS Chief of Intelligence Robert Browne come to our offices in Newark. Beall is an impressive young man, in my view. He seems to have already figured out that to have any hope of success, it is the IRS, not the

FBI that must be his lead agency. Sure, the IRS doesn't have primary investigative authority over bribery and extortion, but where such activity exists there is always an IRS violation.

Our Maryland visitors spend the day with us. Beall and his people wow us. It's a lesson to me. No one path to a prosecutorial appointment is the "right" way to pick. Look at Bobby Kennedy. It is not the resume that counts. It is the character and the commitment.

We give Beall and his colleagues "the lecture." Go in cold; subpoena the county records; subpoena the contractors' records; look for the cash. Bruce sits with them, going over subpoenas we used in Hudson, Atlantic, and Newark. He gives them briefs we used when the subpoenas were attacked. When they say goodbye, we tell them that we are absolutely confident that if Baltimore County is as corrupt as they say, they will hit pay dirt and very soon at that.

****

Ten days after Beall leaves, U.S. Congressman Cornelius Gallagher pleads guilty to income tax evasion. There is no doubt in my mind that Judge Garth will sentence him to at least two years in jail.

And that is the end of the last case I was scheduled to try—I mean, tried by me, personally. Tonti is Bruce's. Atlantic City is Jon's. Maybe I will do former State Treasurer Kervick, once we get around to indicting him. It is time to open up Bergen and Mercer counties, but the boys insist on waiting until Jon finishes the Atlantic City case, which he starts January 9. I say okay, but I tell them that is the last deadline.

****

December 22

Our office Christmas Party. We have much to celebrate and to be thankful for, and it's the season to show it. We have taken over an entire restaurant. We have to, given our size with AUSAs, staff and agents and press invited.

I am having drinks with the staff as I move around the room. I encounter several reporters. "Did you hear?" one of them shouts above the din.

"Hear what?" I ask.

"President Nixon just commuted Gyp DeCarlo's sentence. He let DeCarlo out of jail."

"What did you say?" I thought I misheard. The guy then repeats the news and tells me that the word on the street is that Frank Sinatra, DeCarlo's cousin, arranged for the commutation through his pal Vice President Spiro Agnew.

"What are you going to do about it?" asks the reporter. A good question, I think as I shrug it off. Talk about a way to ruin a good party.

Chapter Fourteen

"Mr. Stern and his Staff
Merit Cooperation"
January 1–9, 1973

FRED MCMAHON, THE bureau case agent on DeCarlo, is in my office, responding to my request for an investigation into Nixon's commutation of DeCarlo.

"I tried, but your request was bounced back by headquarters in D.C."

"Did they give a reason?" I ask him.

"Yes. They say that the bureau will not investigate the White House without a written order from the attorney general."

"And?" I prompt

"And they say that they forwarded your request over to the department, and we have to wait."

****

Shortly after the Gallagher plea, *The New York Times* editorializes:

> After months of protesting his innocence, Representative Cornelius E. Gallagher has now entered a plea of guilty . . .
>
> The recent record is abysmal. The mayors of Newark and Jersey City have been convicted of bribery and extortion crimes. Two former mayors of Atlantic City have been indicted and are awaiting trial. Both the present and former Secretaries of State have been

convicted. The former Speaker of the New Jersey Assembly has been jailed.

What this record reveals is the appalling spread of corruption and official wrongdoing. It also shows the impact of vigorous law enforcement work by Herbert J. Stern and his first-rate staff of investigators and lawyers. Under Mr. Stern's vigorous direction, his office has amassed a remarkable record. Mr. Stern and his staff merit the cooperation of everyone interested in restoring honesty to government in New Jersey.

What the *Times* could not know is that, within two weeks of that editorial, we will indict John A. Kervick, Governor Hughes's state treasurer; that D. Louis Tonti will plead guilty to shaking down contractors on the Garden State Parkway and squirreling the money into a Swiss bank; or that Attorney General Kugler, perhaps stung by these successes, instead of heeding the *Times*' call for cooperation with our office, will announce an action which threatens to stop all of our investigations cold.

****

January 9

Kervick, former Governor Hughes's state treasurer is indicted for taking $113,000 from the Frederick Harris Engineering firm, one of the firms that paid off Tonti.

The indictment adds gasoline to the New Jersey corruption story and, with the conviction of Former Secretary of State Burkhardt, is damning to the former administration of Governor Hughes.

At the announcement of the indictment, there is a feeling of frenzy in the air. The word on the street is that former Governor Hughes will himself be indicted next. It's not true; indeed, we don't have even a single allegation against Hughes personally. But that is the drumbeat on the street.

At the press conference, a reporter shouts out, "We hear that Governor Hughes came within just one vote of an indictment by the grand jury."

"That's nonsense," I respond.

"Well, you are investigating him, right?" the reporter asks.

There it is again. Just like Mayor Dunn. What do you do with a question like that? No prosecutor confirms or denies investigations. "No comment" is the invariable response. If I do a "no comment," there will be banner headlines, "Stern refuses to confirm or deny investigation of Governor Hughes." I will look great in the paper, and I will never have to produce anything. After all, it's just a "no comment." On the other hand, what if I deny it and something turns up later?

"The rumor is *totally* false," I say. "We are not investigating Governor Hughes, and we have *no* reason to do so." The hell with it. That's the truth. I wish I could have said the same thing in just one word—"Bullshit!"—but I guess the message got across.

Anyway, a couple of days later Attorney General Kugler announces that firms like Fred Harris Engineering, who have paid off public officials like Kervick and Tonti, will henceforth be barred from any future state work, even if they testify for us at trial. They will be blacklisted whether or not they cooperate.

Well, that ought to make it just about impossible to get businessmen to cooperate, immunity or no immunity. I figure that if I get any more cooperation like that announcement from the state AG, I might as well shut down and leave town.

I really don't want another argument with the man. But what can I do? This fight I must do alone. My good right arm is missing. On January 8, Jon began the Atlantic City trial in Camden.

Chapter Fifteen

"We Will Summon the Wind"
January 10–February 28, 1973

January 25

Kugler publicly responds to my entreaties not to bar businessmen from public contracts after they testify. "They're not heroes," he tells *The New York Times.* He points out, "These business representatives become witnesses in order to avoid going to jail . . . What insurance does the state have that they won't pay off again?"

It's a tough argument to counter. I am not sure I can get the public behind an effort to protect government witnesses who have paid off, but I have to try. A state rule of debarment would double and triple the difficulty in finishing the cleanup of the most corrupt state in the nation. So I let fly to the press.

> In every one of our cases it has not been the businessman who solicited misconduct. In New Jersey, corruption has become such a way of life in certain metropolitan centers that every businessman knew he simply could not work unless he kicked back.

The argument gets more heated. It is one that I cannot afford to lose if we are to keep our investigations going. Finally, I take to the TV talk-show circuit. When asked about our cases, I respond, "My office uncovered all the corruption you are talking about. These cases were not brought by the state, which has laid back and now is trying to put us out of business by putting our witnesses out of business. Just as we protect our witnesses against physical reprisal, we have to try and protect them against economic reprisal."

To my surprise, the fight is short-lived. The TV stations and newspapers editorialize strongly against Kugler's position. For example, from WNBC-TV, "For three years U.S. Attorney Herbert Stern has been diligent uprooting corruption in New Jersey. Now he is being sniped at." And *The New York Times* hits the nail on the head: "The State's Attorney General is proposing an anti-corruption rule that actually threatens to undermine effective law enforcement work."

Kugler retreats. The press, our only friend other than Senator Case, has once again rescued us.

****

But there is one controversy that plagues and haunts me: John J. Kenny. The attorney general has had his way, in spite of Kenny's federal immunity grant. J.J. Kenny has been tried, convicted, and sentenced to six years in state court. It's not that he didn't deserve it, all of it. He did. But the state had no legal right to try him. Ironically, I can't abide the man. But, because I defended our immunity grant, the state has made it seem as though my effort to protect Kenny is the cornerstone of my disputes with Kugler.

Jon is trying two former mayors of Atlantic City in Camden. John Barry is picking a jury in the Camden 28 case on February 8 in the same courthouse. That means he and his team will be out for about two months.

****

February 14

It is just Bruce and me when, on February 14, the State Commission of Investigation releases the findings of its "private investigation." Rejecting Jon's and my sworn testimony, the SCI publicly exonerates Kugler of any cover up in the Sherwin matter. The 95-page report has 1,700 pages of testimony attached. The whole magilla is dumped on the public.

In exonerating Attorney General Kugler, the SCI says he knew nothing of Sherwin's efforts to dump the bids. It mildly rebukes Director of Criminal Justice Jahos for not paying attention to his own files, where Jahos failed to "discover" Biederman's memo until after Jon and I went to Kugler.

As for Jon's and my testimony that Kugler admitted to us, "This is the only time there was any difficulty with Sherwin, and Garven stopped it"—which Kugler denies—the Commission discounts our sworn word.

Referring to the "vagueness of human recollection," and to the "ephemeral quality of recollection," and to the "frailty of recollection," our testimony is dismissed as "obviously inadvertent misstatements." Why did Jon and I show up with our "dim" recollections? The SCI finds that there is bad blood between Kugler and me, stemming from my use of J.J. Kenny in the Hudson County trial. Kugler testified that he and I had a "bad fight" before the Hudson trial about the use of J.J. Kenny. Kugler swore to the SCI that he was "furious" at me; that before trial "Stern kept waving the United States flag and playing the national anthem to me. We had a very bad fight and I went to Washington over it."

I can't believe my eyes. First, Kugler sent the head of his trial section to court before Kenny ever took the stand. Then, in the Third Circuit, Kugler said he had no advance notice of the immunity to be given J.J. Kenny before the trial, that "nobody told me anything." Now, he says I told him in advance, but we had a fight, even though he sent me a letter before trial saying, "Dear Herb, This is to tell you how very much I appreciate your contacting me concerning your plans to grant immunity to John J. Kenny. This certainly indicates a desire on your part to continue the splendid cooperation between the state and federal authorities . . . I appreciate immensely your agreement with me to make every effort to avoid questioning Mr. Kenny concerning the state indictment."

I am so mad I cannot see straight. What kind of a cesspool is this state, that a former Supreme Court Justice could write, and the Attorney General could testify to such bullshit?

When Bruce comes into my office with his copy of the report, he finds me striding around the room with smoke coming out of my ears.

"Have you read it?" I ask.

"The report? Yes. All the testimony? No."

"Did you see the immediate press reaction?" I ask him.

"Yes."

"The articles make it sound like I am busting up the nursery with my hotheaded misbehavior by making accusations against my play-mate . . . Listen to this," I pick up a paper. "The headline from *The New York Times*: 'Stern-Kugler conflict seen harming fight against crime and corruption.'"

"I saw that," Bruce admits.

"You did! Well, did you see what our fine public leaders had to say?" I go on, without waiting for an answer. "Listen to this, this crap: 'One leading state official said that the dispute could destroy the kind of trust essential for vigorous prosecutions of political corruption.' Imagine that!"

I can see Bruce trying to speak to calm me down, but I'm not hav-ing any part of it.

"Listen to the quote from the Speaker of the Assembly, Thomas H. Kean – remember him? He's the guy who made the deal with David Friedland and Boss Kenny to become speaker—he says, 'There is no question that the open breach between the top state and federal pros-ecutors could create a lack of confidence among New Jersey citizens.'"

With that, I stop pacing and slam down the paper. "Lack of confi-dence? I'll show them lack of confidence!"

"What can we do?" Bruce asks.

"Do? We have one friend in this state—I mean besides Senator Case—the press. And they can summon the wind. These politicians are just windmills. When the press pulls the report apart and digests the testimony, there will be a whirlwind. Then the pols will twirl the other way around."

"Do you think the press will read a 95-page report and 1,700 pages of testimony?"

"No. Not at first," I admit. "And that is what the SCI is counting on, the press not slogging through. That is why all the testimony was behind closed doors. But we will make sure that the press does read the backup testimony. I want excerpts of the report put next to excerpts of what Kugler told the Third Circuit, next to his letters to me. I want it all tied up in a package. If we give the press a head start, they'll do a thorough job."

It takes a week. But by its end, just about every paper in the state has nailed the SCI and Kugler to a cross in both news accounts and editorials. The public legislators have stopped decrying the "feud" and become quiet. *The New York Times* editorial, for example, is captioned, "Whitewash in New Jersey."

But it is Gil Spencer of the *Trentonian* who issues the big blast:

> "The State Investigation's Commission prostituted itself, vilely and nauseously, by affixing its name to a one-sided, occasionally malicious, politically oriented, pseudo report."

February 23

Nine days after the release of the SCI report, Kugler issues a statement. "I am disturbed by published reports that there has been less than full cooperation between my office and that of the United States Attorney . . . while there have been differences of opinion, this has never detracted from the excellent working relationship between the United States Attorney and myself."

After I read that, I put my feet up on my desk and light my first cigar in a week.

****

Shortly after the Kugler statement, I get a call from Dick Kleindienst. "Governor Cahill called me," he reports.

"He did?"

"Yes," Kleindienst pauses. "He said to me, 'Stern is trying to destroy my attorney general.'"

"I see," I say, waiting for the blow to fall.

"I said," Kleindienst pauses for an even longer moment that seems an hour, "I said, 'Herbie wouldn't do that!'" Then he dissolves in a wave of laughter.

****

From Fred Lacey I get a note, "*Oderint Dum Metuant.*" Because he knows that, unlike him, I do not read Latin, he provides a translation: "Let them hate so long as they fear"—a motto attributed to the Roman emperor Caligula, who was himself a pretty scary character.

My father is concerned at what he has been reading. He just can't understand it. There he is, in Manhattan, an assistant attorney general for New York State since 1943. He is about to retire after thirty years of service. He says he has never seen anything like this. He called during this past week, and now he calls again. "How will this all end?" he worries.

"It's over Pop. All done," I assure him.

"You really think so?"

"Sure. They declared victory and left."

"Is all this conflict necessary?" he wants to know.

"No. No, it isn't necessary . . . if they leave me alone."

"But you say it's over?"

"Yes," I tell him, once again.

"Good. Please don't forget the retirement luncheon they are giving me."

"Dad, I wouldn't miss it for the world."

What I don't tell my father is that while this fire has been put out, I have one blazing in South Jersey where Jon is trying a passel of Republican former officeholders, including two former mayors of Atlantic City—one of whom lost reelection because we indicted him. If Jon does not prevail, the state Republican crowd will be at us again, lickety split.

******

In the same Camden courthouse, I have John Barry trying the Camden 28—actually down to 17 now, because of severances—the priests and other war protestors who broke into the Selective Service office. If we lose that one, the Nixon law-and-order society will grind their teeth; and if we win Atlantic City, they will grind their teeth. Based upon what I see going on in Washington with this Watergate business, "law and order" stops at crime in the streets. "Crime in the suites," as Ralph Nader calls it, is a whole other thing.

Chapter Sixteen

Off to the Races
March 1–20, 1973

March 7

Jon is victorious, again. All of the Atlantic City defendants are convicted. The jury was out two days. We were sweating it out by the second day. But they came in with a clean sweep.

I am exhilarated. The boys can't hold me back any longer. I meet with Jon and Bruce to launch our new campaign: Republican-controlled Bergen and Democratic-controlled Mercer counties.

"Bruce, how about you take Mercer. Jon, you put a team on Bergen. Okay?" I want to be sure that they agree.

"Bergen County includes Fort Lee, Englewood, Hackensack, Ridgewood, Oradell, Paramus, and about sixty other cities and towns," Jon dryly observes.

"Yes, I know," I say, with assumed assurance. I don't really know, because I still don't know that much about the geography of New Jersey. I've only been living here about three years.

"But let's start with the county records, going back—let's say—six years. The contracts. The bids. You know the drill. Bruce," I add, turning to him, "you did a great job on Tonti. So your decks are clear for Mercer, right?"

"Right," Bruce says with his usual laugh.

Just last week Bruce appeared before Judge Barlow on the Tonti sentencing. Barlow said to the former commissioner, "You are no different from a common thief," and sent the "It's all hogwash" man off to prison for three years.

When the guys leave, I sit back, content. The next surge is under way. Finally.

****

I go to New York for my father's retirement luncheon. There is a bit of stir among the New York AG crowd when I arrive, what with all the recent publicity. It's a little odd to me, coming back to a New York function in such different circumstances, but it's great for my dad. He has a ball taking me around.

The next day, still luxuriating in my newfound ease, I receive a telephone call from a lawyer who identifies himself as Lewis B. Kaden. He claims he represents a detective state trooper who has "information" he wants to disclose. They want to come in after hours to preserve confidentiality.

"Not again!" I say to myself. But what can I do, refuse to see him? I can't do that. I make an appointment with Kaden and his mystery trooper for late on March 19.

As it turns out, I can't keep the appointment. I am notified by the Third Circuit that the Ivanov-Butenko spy case will be argued the morning of March 20 in Philadelphia. Igor Ivanov, a Russian spy, corrupted Butenko, a defense-industry worker, into passing real secrets. The case was tried and the men convicted years before Lacey and I came into the office. But the conviction was remanded to the Third Circuit by the Supreme Court to decide the question of whether the President of the United States can order warrantless eavesdropping on suspected foreign spies, foreign embassies, and so forth. Washington has asked me to argue it.

I must go down to Philadelphia the night before the argument, which is the nineteenth. So, I ask Bruce to cover the appointment with Kaden.

****

March 20

When I return to the office, I find Jon and Bruce waiting for me. They look grim. "What?" I say to them when I walk into my office.

"You are not going to believe this," Jon begins.

"Try me."

"Tell him," Jon turns to Bruce.

"This Kaden," Bruce begins, "is a young lawyer with political ambitions. He ran unsuccessfully for Congress. He is in a New York labor law firm, Ted Kheel's firm—"

"So," I interrupt, anxious to get on with it.

"He represents a state police detective named James Challander. He brought the trooper with him, along with photostats of documents and checks. In 1969, when Cahill ran for governor, his campaign raised over $100,000 on the sly. It had contributors write checks to a public relations firm, name of Writer's Associates. In return, the contributors got phony invoices for PR services, so they could deduct the checks. That gives our IRS guys jurisdiction."

"Jurisdiction over what?" I ask. "How did that help the Cahill campaign?"

"That's the dandy part," Jon joins in. "The PR firm cashed the checks at racetracks and gave the cash to the Cahill campaign."

"Racetracks? Why racetracks?"

"That's the very best part," Bruce chuckles. "You know who owns the Garden State and Monmouth racetracks here in New Jersey, and the Hialeah track in Florida?"

"No."

"Eugene Mori. Do you know who he is?"

"No."

"He is the father-in-law of Governor Cahill's state treasurer, Joseph S. McCrane! Detective Challander says the AG's office does not want to go to a grand jury with this."

"McCrane? Governor Cahill's former state treasurer? He did this—he washed the money?"

"Looks that way. By the way, McCrane resigned last November, the same day that Sherwin did."

"Oh shit," I groan. "Here we go again."

"You want to forget about it?" Jon asks.

"Bullshit. Get grand jury subpoenas out to this 'Writer's Associates.' Let's see who used the account and how much in checks they cashed."

"Do you want to call Attorney General Kugler and inform him," John deadpans.

"Are you kidding!"

Chapter Seventeen

"We are Going to Tell the Truth"
March 20–April 1973

April 7

Detective Challander's allegations are deliberately leaked by the Democrats. The state senate minority leader, J. Edward Crabiel, at a press conference, says he is "outraged by reports of the federal investigation. Reliable sources have informed me that the Cahill administration tried to cover up the investigation."

****

"How did this happen?" I ask at a meeting with Bruce and Jon. "This is a timed release. It's orchestrated. This Senator Crabiel is an announced candidate for the Democratic nomination for governor. What is going on?"

"We are being used, obviously," Bruce shrugs. "The primaries are on May 5, less than a month away. The D's are after Governor Cahill. All of a sudden, we are getting support for a cleanup."

"Tell me about this guy Kaden."

"All I know is that he is an active Democrat. Ran for the nomination for Congress. And that's all I know," Bruce answers.

"Looks like he's pulling our strings," Jon shakes his head.

"Well," I decide, "I don't care if he is Geppeto, just like I didn't care if Biederman was out for revenge when he brought us Sherwin. We have the checks and the bills from Writer's Associates. We are bringing in the companies that used the PR company's bills to hide the contributions and take the tax deductions. McCrane will have to account. As for Kaden, I don't care if he makes himself president. Jon, how is John Barry doing on the Camden 28 case?"

"It's been two months, and John thinks another month or six weeks."

"Everything quiet?" I ask.

Jon answers, "Quiet? Well, the defendants are playing guitars in the halls on breaks."

"But we are leaving them alone, right? No trouble?"

"They are pretty well-behaved, actually."

"Good!"

"What about the story?" Bruce asks.

"We have no comment, of course. God only knows how Kugler and company will respond to Trooper Challander's accusations."

****

Kugler issues a statement calling State Police Detective Challander a liar. Kaden responds, "If Mr. Kugler had been as courageous and concerned with the truth as Detective Challander, it would never have become necessary to bring information about an investigation the state refused to pursue to Mr. Stern."

Then Kugler does another foolish thing. He claims that our federal investigation was not begun by Challander's complaint, but that the IRS had been working on it for months with the state.

"There is no truth to the stories that the investigation by federal officials was started as a result of a disgruntled state trooper," Kugler says. And then he challenges me, "I now call upon U.S. Attorney Herbert Stern to issue a statement that these rumors are unfounded and that federal and state authorities have been cooperating in this investigation."

When the press asks him about the propriety of cashing campaign checks at a racetrack, Kugler says he is "not shocked campaign checks were being cashed at a racetrack. Checks are cashed in many places. Some people go to a bar, others go to banks and other places as long as there are funds to cash them, even if it is a political contribution."

I know the Democrats are trying to start another war between me and the Cahill administration for political purposes. I know that I can avoid a mess by just a "no comment." But I just can't do it. It would be tantamount to a lie. We are going to tell the truth.

****

The press is having a field day. The best of the best, of course, is Gil Spencer, the editor of the small *Trentonian*:

> KUGLER AND STERN AGAIN
> New Jersey Attorney General George Kugler can be consid
> ered somewhat sensitive to cover-up charges. Of course, he's not
> as sensitive as he would be if the dauntless State Investigations
> Commission (SIC) hadn't done a running quadruple back-
> ward somersault and lovingly exonerated him of any impropriety
> involving the bribery-conspiracy case against subsequently con-
> victed Secretary of State Paul Sherwin. But he is sensitive. Thus
> little imagination is needed to picture his reaction to this week's
> new reports picturesquely suggesting that an unhappy State Police
> detective had gotten federal officials to investigate alleged corrup-
> tion in the financing of William T. Cahill's 1969 campaign for
> governor...

And then, in the final blow, the leadership of the 1,100 member state troopers association issues a statement in support of Challander: "Without Detective Challander's courage and Mr. Stern's diligence, this important investigation would never have gone forward." The spokesman for the association is none other than, Lewis B. Kaden.

****

In the midst of these back-and-forths, and of the headlines about a new fight between the attorney general and the United States Attorney, Judge Brendan T. Byrne of the Superior Court goes to Trenton to announce his judicial resignation and his candidacy for the Democratic nomination for governor of New Jersey. He is supported by none other than . . . Lewis B. Kaden.

Chapter Eighteen

"Don't Tell Me That!"
April–May 15, 1973

HAVING SUBPOENAED THE Writer's Associates records, Bruce discovers the names of the businessmen who used the PR firm's false bills to make secret donations to Cahill's 1969 gubernatorial campaign. He brings these businessmen in, one by one. They all break and admit the secret payments, except one. William H. Preis, the CEO of Stop and Shop Corporation, wholly owned by Grand Union, testifies that the Writer's Associates bill for $5,000 and his company's check were all legitimate. He testifies that he can't imagine why the check was cashed at a racetrack. On April 24 we indict him for perjury. Shortly thereafter, Preis hires Donald Robinson to be his lawyer.

******

Two weeks later, Robinson, the man who had represented J.J. Kenny and Roger DeLouette, pays a call on me. Here we are again. Robinson wants a deal, for cooperation. He tells me, "Preis wants to plead guilty, go back into the grand jury, and tell the truth."

"Good. But no deal. We have Preis cold," I say. "We have plenty of evidence without him."

Robinson replies, "But he is going to tell why he did it and who told him to lie to the grand jury."

"Why he did it? We know why he did it. To pass money."

"True," says Robinson. "But you don't know who pressured him to make the payment. And you don't know who pressured him to lie before the grand jury."

"Pressure. What pressure?" I ask. "By whom?"

Robinson smiles, "His lawyer, Nelson Gross."

"No! Don't tell me that!" I protest.

"Yes. Nelson Gross," he repeats. "Gross was Grand Union's lawyer, and solicited Preis for the contribution to Cahill in the 1969 campaign, when Gross was Republican state chairman. He had asked for $25,000, but Preis would only do $5,000. Then, when your subpoena came, Preis went to Gross, who put the wood to him to lie—he told Preis, 'Say it was legitimate. They can't prove anything.'"

"Oh, no," I am shaking my head. This is what I really don't want to hear. Gross is the sworn enemy of Senator Case, going back to Gross's break with Case over the Nixon nomination. Now I am going to have to indict Gross, and the pundits will spread the lie that I am acting as a hatchet man for Case.

****

May 14

Preis pleads guilty. On May 22 we indict Gross for subornation of perjury and for tax charges.

****

Of course, we immediately fall under attack about the Gross indictment. Some news commentators assert that the indictment springs from Gross's feud with Senator Case. Britt Hume, who succeeded Jack Anderson, calls. He wants a comment. I try to persuade him that the feud story is bullshit, but he tells me that the fact that people are saying it is itself newsworthy, and he goes with the piece. All in all, however, most of the working press know nonsense when they see it.

Chapter Nineteen

"Cleansed Climate"
May 15–June 5, 1973

May 15

The Atlantic City public officials have received sentences ranging from two to six years from Judge Cohen.

May 20

The Camden 28 case is over. The jurors announced their unanimous verdict: Not guilty. It was quite a trial. The defendants were given every opportunity to say whatever they wished to the jurors. They demonstrated that the FBI itself facilitated the raid—the bureau supplied money, burglar's tools, and all else necessary for the break-in to its own informant, Robert Hardy. Hardy wound up called to the stand by the defense. The defendants produced a memo from FBI files urging agents to interview New Left and anti-war dissidents frequently to "enhance the paranoia endemic in these circles and [to] further serve to get the point across that there is an FBI agent behind every mailbox."

At the end of the trial, Judge Fisher charged the jury that if the government participation in the break-in had gone "to intolerable lengths . . . an offense to basic standards of decency . . ." they could acquit. And acquit they did.

As the jury foreman read the verdict, the spectators and the defendants sang a chorus of "Amazing Grace." Then the courtroom erupted.

Judge Fisher, removing himself from the courtroom, was discovered in the hall by the elevator, where the crowd swirled around him, saluting and cheering him.

John Barry immediately announced that the remaining eleven defendants would not be prosecuted.

This case represents a plain, open instance of jury nullification. We are not supposed to talk much about jury nullification, raising as it does the specter of "lawlessness." It is the old tension between doing law and doing justice. But as long as we preserve the right—or at least the ability—of jurors to do justice there will be limits to how far the state or the nation can go in the name of the law.

One of the jurors, Samuel Braithwaite, an Atlantic City cab driver, left a letter with the clerk of the court, with instructions to deliver it to the defendants after the trial. He wrote:

> "Well done for trying to heal sick, irresponsible men who were chosen by the people to lead them . . . men who failed the people by raining death and destruction on a helpless country. To you . . . with God-given talents, I say 'Well Done!'"

****

May 24

We indict former state treasurer Joseph McCrane. At the press conference, I am asked about Governor Cahill. "Was the governor involved in the improprieties in his 1969 campaign?" I reply that we have made no such allegation, "It would be wrong for anyone to make those charges." We have nothing on Cahill and, as with former Governor Hughes, I feel morally bound to make that clear.

Although there is more to be done, we have effectively brought the investigation to a conclusion in just over two months from when Detective Challander and Kaden first came to us.

****

And so, the month of May ends with an editorial by the *Ledger*, New Jersey's largest newspaper, which summarizes more than just the month. It marks what should be the beginning of the end of my time in the office.

CLEANSED CLIMATE

The enforcement breakthrough in Atlantic County is significant by itself, for this was an area considered sacrosanct, dating back to the halcyon period of Enoch (Nucky) Johnson, the political boss.

But it would be misleading to isolate the Atlantic City crackdown . . . the U.S. Attorney's Office has moved swiftly whenever there was evidence of possible wrongdoing, an approach that has not been consistently evident at the state level . . . it has inspired an atmosphere of confidence in the Garden State that has not been apparent in many years...

And this may be one of Mr. Stern's most commendable achievements—a radically changed climate in which the Garden State no longer can be denigrated as a sanctuary for the corrupt official and a haven for syndicate crime figures.

What Senator Case had called "the stench in the nostrils" of the nation has been dissipated to a major degree. Oh, I know we have not ended corruption in office —we can't do that without changing human nature. But we have broken the teeth of the political machines. It is their functionaries who are now afraid. While there is more work to be done and strict vigilance to be maintained, the day of wholesale selling of public contracts in New Jersey is over. Businesses no longer enter the state expecting to have to tithe.

It is time for me to think of leaving, to pass the leadership on to Jon, while we still can. Perhaps after that, to Bruce. It is a way to cement our standards into a tradition for the office. I know that Judge Garth is being considered by Senator Case for the Third Circuit. His seat on the district court will be open. There might be that opportunity; or, if not that, then there is always private practice. My still-perfect cousin, Arthur Greenbaum, one of the leaders of Cowan, Liebowitz & Latman, in New

York, has indicated that the firm might find a place for me, even with my lack of civil trial experience. It is just the kind of firm I would want, if private practice is what is next for me.

****

Five days later, on June 5, the world turns upside down. Governor William Cahill, whom Senator Case refused to endorse, loses the Republican primary. His own party has refused to renominate him. Congressman Charles Sandman, a conservative South Jersey Republican, defeats him. According to an editorial in the *Bergen Record*, "Charles Sandman's victory in the Republican gubernatorial primary was a triumph not so much for himself as for United States Attorney Herbert J. Stern."

This makes me uncomfortable. We did not do what we did to help Sandman or to hurt Cahill. I want no credit for the governor's defeat. Truth be told, I would rather vote for Cahill, whom I regard as progressive on social issues, than for Sandman. As the editorial notes, "Mr. Sandman's notions of public policy are straight out of the last half of the nineteenth century. With few exceptions, his positions are hardline conservative or reactionary."

June 5 has also been a memorable day in Washington, D.C.

Chapter Twenty

Watergate and Washington
May 15–June 5, 1973

"**P**ETERSEN FACES AN inquiry on his Watergate actions"—page one of the June 5 edition of *The New York Times*. As I read the story, I marvel. How did it come to this . . . Henry? . . . Under investigation?

The responsibility for the investigation into the Watergate break-in of the summer of 1972 had been in the hands of Henry Petersen. As assistant attorney general, head of the Criminal Division, Henry was in overall charge.

When presidential candidate George McGovern alleged cover-up, it was Henry Petersen who assured the public that the Watergate investigation was "among the most exhaustive and far-reaching in my twenty-five years in the department." He must have known that his statement was an exaggeration, at best. Months before, White House counsel John Dean had told Petersen, "This matter could lead directly to the White House." Dean asked Petersen to confine the investigation to the burglary itself, and Petersen agreed. Furthermore, Petersen did not disclose this conversation with Dean—not to the FBI, or the United States Attorney for the District of Columbia, whose office was handling the investigation.

Thereafter, Petersen kept Dean advised of the progress of the investigation until the November 1972 elections. Henry, of course, in charge of the Criminal Division, not only had access to all of the investigation's findings, but he also could and did direct and limit its focus in order to avoid involving the White House.

Why would a man like Henry draw a *cordon sanitaire* around the White House? I ask myself, as I read the newspaper report.

I do not believe it is because he is a corrupt man, a party man, or a political animal. Henry is an ex-Marine, accustomed to discipline and obeying orders. He is not a maverick. He is no boat-rocker or apple cart upsetter. He is a bureaucrat, a believer in authority and in the chain of command of an organization. These attributes served him well within the bureaucracy that he chose as his home for twenty-five years. His devotion to duty permitted him to rise to the position of assistant attorney general of the Criminal Division—and he attained this high rank without political patronage, within a system that had never before allowed in such a high position one who was not politically appointed.

By Petersen's lights, he used his promotion within the department to achieve the "good end" of centralizing Washington's control over the United States Attorneys. He transformed the notion of a strike force from its initial conception based on the Colonial Pipeline model—a temporary entry into a district to deal with a specific problem, presumably beyond the ability of the local United States Attorney to handle—into what he viewed as its final form—a permanent satellite office staffed by employees selected by the Criminal Division.

Petersen now has nearly a score of these permanent "strike force" offices in districts around the country, reporting to his chief of the Organized Crime and Racketeering Section in Washington. These strike forces, staffed by several hundred Department attorneys, are totally independent of the local United States Attorneys. But within a year, Henry's supreme bureaucratic achievement has started to crumble, because of a burglary of an office in the Watergate complex, and because of revelations that the White House cover-up has spread even into the Department of Justice.

By April 15, 1973, the limitations on the scope of the Watergate investigation that Henry agreed to with John Dean have been breached. Through the work of the bureau and the AUSAs in Washington, D.C., the root of the crime, and the efforts to cover it up, have been traced to the White House itself. And Earl Silbert, the assistant United States Attorney leading the investigation, complains about Henry's attempts to limit their investigative efforts and, even worse, Henry's funneling information to the White House.

What has largely been known only behind the scenes begins to emerge when Kleindienst and Petersen go to the White House and inform Nixon that former Attorney General Mitchell and members of the White House staff are involved in the scandal. Kleindienst, who does not want to investigate his former patron, Mitchell, immediately recuses himself, signaling his intention to resign his office. From April 15 until May 18, the day a special prosecutor is appointed, Petersen continually fills Nixon in on the prosecutors' progress.

On April 30, Kleindienst resigns as attorney general. To Kleindienst's outrage, for he has had nothing to do with Watergate, the president simultaneously accepts the resignation of his two top aids, H.R. Haldeman and John Ehrlichman—who are both implicated in the affair—and also fires White House counsel John Dean. Now the public fires are burning, illuminating the arrival of a new attorney general.

Nixon asks Elliot Richardson, his newly appointed secretary of defense, to become attorney general in place of Kleindienst. Richardson agrees and during his confirmation hearing promises the Senate to appoint an independent prosecutor to investigate the Watergate incident and cover-up, without interference by Justice. On May 18, overruling objections from Henry Petersen, Richardson appoints his old Harvard Law Professor, Archibald Cox, as special Watergate prosecutor.

Up to that point, Henry, ignoring protests from the United States Attorney's office in the District of Columbia, has repeatedly been meeting directly with Nixon, filling him in on the progress of AUSA Silbert's investigation. Silbert, concerned about Petersen's role, advises the new attorney general that Henry is a conduit of information to the White House. On May 4, even before he appoints Cox, Richardson decides that the special prosecutor must not work under Henry Petersen, but must instead be truly "independent."

Soon after his appointment, Cox and James Vorenberg of his staff meet with Petersen. On the night of May 29 they question him, with a stenographer present, to get up to speed on the progress of the investigation thus far. And then they effectively terminate Petersen's contacts with the investigation.

On June 5 the story of Petersen's removal from the case breaks in *The New York Times*. Two weeks later the *Wall Street Journal* reports, "Henry Petersen is distraught. . . . Mr. Petersen has been relieved of the Watergate case by Special Prosecutor Archibald Cox . . . Mr. Petersen believes that the department's career staff are suffering unfairly for the sins of higher ups . . . according to the journal, the effect on morale has been devastating to the Strike Force . . . half-a-dozen chiefs of 'Strike Forces' have left their posts in recent months."

Chapter Twenty-One

Law and Order
June 5–30, 1973

WE HAVE, OF course, been aware of the turmoil in Washington, although not the behind the scenes details, at least not until the *Times* story of June 5. We now follow the progress as best we can from newspaper accounts.

How do I feel about Henry's predicament? My feelings are mixed. Henry has been no friend to me, at least not for the last four years or so. There is a temptation to gloat. And yet, Henry has in a sense been trapped, caught between his duty as a law enforcement officer and his position in an administration that he thinks he must defend, or at least obey even as he investigates it. In a sense, George Kugler repeatedly faced the same dilemmas. And, repeatedly, both men refused to relinquish either the role of prosecutor or the role of loyal member of an administration—and so in the end made a hodge-podge of both. Now, unfortunately, sooner or later, both Petersen and Kugler, each of them basically decent and honorable men, will leave their offices with their reputations gravely wounded. This much is clear: Friends and political allies cannot investigate each other. A *totally* independent prosecutor *must* be appointed in any and every such circumstance.

Are there any institutional changes that our government, state and federal, can make to resolve these conflicts? More to the point, are there any institutional changes that can better prosecutorial performance? In the end, I think not. It always comes down to questions of courage and independence. And while these can be exemplified, they cannot be institutionalized. On the state level, more independently elected, rather than appointed local district attorneys and state attorneys general might help some. But not much. Not until the public is educated to expect more from the DA or whatever that office is called in the community. We must learn that the DA, as the chief law enforcement officer of the jurisdiction, is more than a courtroom prosecutor. He must be more than a loyal member of an "administration." He is charged with investigating and uncovering the kinds of crime that generally elude the police and agencies working alone. When the public measures performance of prosecutors against that standard, the standard of Dewey, Hogan, Morgenthau, and Lacey, then law enforcement will undergo a sea change throughout the United States.

****

The Cahill administration is still in office, but its days are numbered. In November a new governor will be elected and he will take office in January. My troubles with the Cahill crowd are over. Soon enough, they will be cleaning out their desks. But we have other problems.

Major cases are backing up for trial. Republican former State Treasurer McCrane, Republican State Chairman Gross, and half a score of lesser lights remain to be tried. And there are the active investigations into Bergen and Mercer Counties to move along.

Fortunately, on June 12, former State Treasurer Kervick pleads guilty. On June 15 Congressman Gallagher is sentenced to two years in jail by Judge Garth.

****

Before the month of June closes, Attorney General Richardson discovers the communication from the FBI, forwarding my December 1972 request for an investigation of Nixon's commutation of DeCarlo's sentence. Richardson authorizes the FBI to proceed with an investigation, which he assigns to Archibald Cox. Cox, in turn, tells Richardson that my office should do the investigation and that I should report my findings to both Cox and Richardson personally. So, it is now up to me to determine how a notorious murdering criminal persuaded the President of the United States to grant him a commutation of sentence.

****

A few days after Congressman Gallagher's sentencing, I receive a telephone call from Cox. Nancy buzzes me. I pick up the phone. "Herb Stern speaking."

Archibald Cox's secretary's voice comes over the line. "The special prosecutor wants me to inform you that this call will be recorded."

"Okay." What else can I say?

"Herb," I hear a rather uptight voice on the other end. It seems to go with the pictures I have seen of a lean, stiff looking, Boston Brahmin type, with a bow tie and half-glasses perched on his nose.

"Hi, Archie," I say. "What is this about recording our conversation?"

"I have to. The Senate has been immunizing witnesses, and I am trying to keep a record to show that none of my evidence is tainted by the immunity grants."

"Great," I say, although I don't think it is so great. But since he is recording, I lace the conversation with phrases like, "Archie, we have to stick to bedrock principles." I figure, if I am speaking for the ages, I might as well sound as good as I can.

Anyway, we discuss my investigation of the DeCarlo commutation. We agree that I will send the bureau out to interview all the possible witnesses, including the pardon attorney in Justice, the people in the White House, Vice President Agnew, and Frank Sinatra, in order to determine whether Sinatra used his connections with Agnew to obtain a White House commutation of DeCarlo's sentence.

****

FBI agent Fred McMahon is a very happy man when he and I meet to plan our strategy for the investigation. This is the moment that this bulldog agent has been waiting for. Now he is rarin' to go.

"How are you going to run it, Fred?" I ask him.

"I am flying down to Washington. First stop, the Justice Department. I am going to put the pardon attorney under oath, after I warn him of his rights, and then—"

"Whoa!" I break in. "You are going to travel? The bureau will let you travel?"

"On this one, they will," Fred smiles broadly.

"Great." And I send Fred on his way.

The plan is not elaborate. Everyone gets interviewed. And every relevant scrap of paper will be reviewed and copied. And then we'll see.

****

Judge Garth has not yet been nominated for the Circuit, but his ABA evaluation is well under way. He is well respected, so he's a cinch to clear the ABA hurdle and be nominated before the end of July. Senator Case has decided to submit my name to the new attorney general, Elliot Richardson, to fill Leonard Garth's seat on the district court. The senator tells me, "We'll try again now. It's a year later, so you are older, thirty-six, right? So we will push it."

****

I am now about to do a dumb thing, at least that is what my colleagues tell me. I have been invited to be the speaker at the Lawyer's Division of the Anti-Defamation League dinner at the Waldorf Astoria in New York. An enormous attendance of the leaders of the New York bar is expected. For example, my old boss, Frank Hogan, will be there. Accepting the invitation is not my problem. What I intend to say, that's another thing.

Last month, Governor Rockefeller pushed through the New York legislature what he described as the "toughest drug laws in the nation"—providing mandatory minimum 15-year sentences for relatively small amounts of narcotic sales, up to mandatory life sentences. Rockefeller assured the people of New York that imposing Draconian punishments will curtail drug trafficking.

In my opinion, this is arrant nonsense. The punishments are brutal. They will fill the jails, but they will not stop the drug trade. I have no doubt that the passage of those laws will be regretted in years to come.

My colleagues do not disagree with me. But some think I should keep my mouth shut, particularly at the moment when Senator Case is pushing me for a federal judgeship.

June 13

I deliver what may be my swan song before a packed house of lawyers:

> One of the most serious problems we face today is that in the mind of our fellow citizens, the scales of justice do not weigh true. "Law and Order" has come to mean one thing to the poor, the weak and the friendless, and quite another to the wealthy, the powerful and the well-positioned. . . .
>
> We must determine whether we have been emphasizing those considerations, which bring us closer to equality before the law, or those which drive us farther apart.
>
> For example, we hear much today about increasing the penalties for crime, with the attendant justification that increased deterrences will automatically thereby result in fewer criminals. We must reject such panaceas to our problems of crime control, for there are no panaceas . . .
>
> Simply put, it does not really matter what you threaten a man with, if you cannot persuade him that you will be able to deliver it. . .
>
> I suggest to you, my fellow members of the Bar, that if we will have law, if we will have order, then we are going to have to start by imposing them on the "top" of society, not on its "bottom," and that, in the end, the only true path to our imposing it on others is by imposing it first upon ourselves.

The applause at the end is hardly deafening. Then again, I did not expect that it would be. But apparently Senator Case did not disapprove. When he reads about the speech in *The New York Times*, he calls me for a copy. Then, on the last day of the month, June 30, he inserts it verbatim into the *Congressional Record* of the Senate.

Chapter Twenty-Two

"Something Smells"
July 1–September 1, 1973

AGENT **F**RED **M**C**M**AHON has been running all over Washington, questioning anyone and everyone who touched the DeCarlo commutation. Washington being the sieve that it is, word leaks to the press. That starts a torrent of calls.

Simultaneously, Senator Henry Jackson, a Washington State Democrat, writes a letter to Attorney General Richardson, demanding access to Department of Justice records and interviews of former Attorney General Kleindienst and White House Counsel John Dean.

"Something smells, and I want to know what," Jackson says, as he releases his letter to the press. All this hits the newswires on Friday, July 6, and continues over the weekend.

The next week I am in Elliot Richardson's office in the Justice Department, bringing him up to date on both the DeCarlo investigation and the leaks to the press.

To me, Richardson looks like Clark Kent. Square jaw, straight hair combed back, narrow black horn-rimmed glasses. He looks very fit. If he took the glasses off and changed clothes, he could be you-know-who. Smart, too, with superb academic and professional credentials, including president of the *Harvard Law Review*, and law clerk first to Learned Hand of the Second Circuit and then to Felix Frankfurter of the Supreme Court. He had been U.S. Attorney for Massachusetts during the Eisenhower years, and later attorney general and lieutenant governor of Massachusetts. Not to mention Secretary of Defense, just before becoming U. S. Attorney General. I don't impress easy, and titles don't do it for me at all. But this is an impressive man. I mean this guy even landed on Normandy on June 6, 1944—D Day!

"The long and short of it is," I tell him, "it looks like there isn't anything dirty in the DeCarlo commutation."

"What happened?" he asks.

"Simply this. DeCarlo is on his last legs, suffering from terminal cancer. The warden in the Atlanta Penitentiary, which you know is a maximum security prison, became nervous about DeCarlo dying in his prison. It was the warden who initiated the request for executive clemency, so he could die at home."

"That's it?" asks Elliott.

"That's it," I answer.

"How extensive was the investigation?" he wants to know.

"Complete!" I assure him. "The agents interviewed everyone, including the pardon attorney. They even placed him under oath and warned him of his rights."

"And Sinatra?"

"No involvement. The agents even interviewed Sinatra's mother."

"His mother?"

"Yes. She and DeCarlo are related. All she had was that when DeCarlo was little she babysat for him."

Richardson and I both laugh. He tells me to prepare a report for Archibald Cox. I tell him I will do so next week.

I think the meeting is over, when Richardson says, "Are you ready to take the veil?"

I know what that means. Senator Case's recommendation of me for a judgeship is on Richardson's desk. It will now be up to him whether to move it.

"Yes, I am," I say quickly.

"You know you will have to clear the Committee of the ABA and their rule is that a candidate must have fifteen years' experience. You have, as I understand it, less than twelve...about eleven and a half?"

"Yes," I am forced to agree.

"Well . . . have you tried a lot of cases? Perhaps that would help."

"Oh, yes! I was an ADA in New York. Tried lots of cases there. Then as a department attorney and in the U.S. Attorney's office, I tried a number of major cases . . ."

It occurs to me that Richardson might be impressed with some of my adversaries, particularly Williams. "I even tried a case against Edward Bennett Williams," I go on.

And then, to footnote the bona fides of my claim, and dimly remembering that Richardson had been U.S. Attorney in Massachusetts when Williams represented the famous Bernard Goldfine there, I say, "Williams told me the story how, when Bernard Goldfine consulted Williams, Williams said to him, 'You don't have a defense,' and Goldfine replied, 'Defense? If I had a defense, I'd use my regular lawyer, Slobodkin.'"

I figured that should get a laugh out of Richardson, who had prosecuted Bernard Goldfine for tax evasion and had dealt with Williams. Goldfine was a famous figure—he caused a sensation when it came out that he had given a vicuna coat to Sherman Adams, President Eisenhower's chief of staff and a former governor of New Hampshire. Because of his close relationship with the president, Adams was arguably the second most powerful man in the country. The story was that the revelation of Goldfine's gift of the vicuna coat forced Adams to resign.

But Richardson is not laughing. Not even smiling. Instead, he looks at me grimly, then down at his papers, and grunts out, "All right, I'll send it forward."

In a minute I'm out of there, wondering what happened. Maybe, I figure, he heard the story before. Anyway, I'm on my way back to New Jersey.

****

The next week I telephone Cox to report, as Richardson had requested. When his secretary comes on, there is no announcement about recording, and I figure I know why. On Monday July 16, Alexander Butterfield blew the lid off of things when he testified before the Senate committee that President Nixon had a taping system throughout the White House.

When Cox gets on the telephone, I say, "Archie, not taping anymore?" I laugh, but he doesn't. Doesn't even reply. No sense of humor,

I guess. We do agree, however, that the DeCarlo thing is a dry hole and that that is what the press will be told.

****

A few days later, I get some insight into the lack of humor among the D.C. higher-ups. Edward Bennett Williams comes in for a pretrial meeting with Jon and me. Ed represents Walter Jones, under indictment for bank fraud. Ed comes sweeping in, in typical Williams style. Effervescent, bubbling with stories.

The first thing he wants to talk about is Watergate.

"I'll bet you think this Watergate is a big deal." Ed looks at me.

"Well, it looks like it to me, it—"

He talks right over me. "I can tell you it's nothing compared to Sherman Adams and Bernard Goldfine. You know I represented Goldfine?"

"Yes, you told me years ago, how you explained to him he had no defense and he said—"

Ed continues as if I had not spoken. "Everyone thinks he only gave Adams a vicuna coat. But there was actually hundreds of thousands of dollars in cash."

"What!" I had never heard of this.

"Yes. Cash. And Goldfine had a secretary named Mildred Paperman and she kept a record of every cash payment."

"She did?"

"Yes. She did. And when Goldfine wanted to talk to help himself, I took the records to the then-U.S. Attorney for Massachusetts, Elliot Richardson—"

"What!" I am starting to get the picture.

"And Richardson got the IRS going, and the IRS contacted Adams's landlady in Washington. He rented a brownstone when he was at the White House. And this cheap Yankee paid his rent by cashier checks. And," Williams chuckles, "his landlady hated him. She made a record of each check: the amount; the bank; and the check number. So the IRS had the cash going in to Adams from Mildred Paperman, and cash going out to the landlady. And then . . ." Williams pauses.

"Then . . ." I echo, mesmerized.

"Then the administration changed. Kennedy came in. And Eisenhower contacted Jack Kennedy and made a deal. If the new administration didn't indict Adams, then he, Eisenhower, would never criticize Kennedy's foreign policy decisions. So, Jack told Bobby to fold the case."

It's stunning. I can't believe it. A few days ago I told Richardson what I thought was a funny story. Now this! I sit wondering if Richardson thinks I was kind of blackmailing him.

"I'll bet you think Adams is dead," Williams jogs me out of my funk.

"I . . . I don't know," I stammer.

"He runs a ski resort in New Hampshire," Williams laughs, finally ready to talk about the pending trial of his client.

****

The Williams meeting haunts me for days. At first, I worry about what Richardson thinks I was trying to do. But soon what really gets to me is the arrogance. The arrogance of power, of position, if Williams's story is true. And I have no reason to doubt him, as he was Goldfine's lawyer and well-connected in Democratic circles.

What strikes me is the obscene perversion of our system of justice. Imagine, men like Kennedy and Eisenhower summarily deciding that a man like Adams, who sat at the pinnacle of power in the White House and sold his office, should not be prosecuted because Eisenhower liked him and Kennedy wanted to store up a favor.

I hope the story isn't true. I do not want to believe it.

****

On the local scene, as now former Congressman Cornelius Gallagher goes off to prison, he lays claim to the $300,000 plus in bearer bonds that he originally denied were his. So ends that hypocrisy. And it ends well. Over $200,000 goes to the IRS and the court for taxes, penalties, and fines. The rest is seized by his lawyer, Charles McNellis, leaving nothing for Gallagher.

Within a few weeks, before the end of August, word leaks from the department in Washington that I am being put forward for a federal judgeship. And that, in a sense, marks the beginning of the end of my time as the head of the office. The task now is to leave with Jon in succession, in a position to continue the work. And, equally important, to further cement into an enduring structure what Fred Lacey and Clifford Case started in 1969.

Chapter Twenty-Three

DeCarlo Still Speaks
September 1–October 22, 1973

THE CONSTANT PRESSURE from United States Attorneys to curtail, if not eliminate, the strike forces is finally bearing fruit. I am sure that Henry Petersen's weakened standing has a role.

September 20

Richardson has empanelled a committee made up of sixteen United States Attorneys to evaluate the strike forces and make recommendations. Now that we have an attorney general who was himself a United States Attorney and who understands the tensions caused by two separate Department of Justice offices in the same district, we have the chance to reunify the authority.

Richardson has placed Dick Thornburgh, the U.S. Attorney in Pittsburgh, as head of the committee. I am not on it, nor, as a short-timer, should I be.

Henry's strike forces have caused havoc around the country. His objective was to increase law enforcement by bolstering it beyond what he viewed as the capacity of "political" U.S. Attorneys. But these strike force offices had the unintended effect of weakening law enforcement by diminishing the office of the United States Attorney. And, in the final analysis, only a United States Attorney can launch a statewide cleanup, such as Fred Lacey did in New Jersey, or as Jim Thompson did in Illinois. Yes, a strike force can do a Colonial Pipeline case. But you need a strong, fearless, locally respected U.S. Attorney like George Beall to do what he is doing in Maryland, and beyond.

****

October 10

George Beall has been going great guns in Maryland. He uncovered numerous payoffs to Vice President Agnew, commencing when Agnew was governor of Maryland. What we hear behind the scenes makes its way into the public. The rumors, then the press leaks, then the columns, then motions filed in court culminate today, when Agnew strides into federal court in Baltimore to plead *nolo contendere* to one count of income tax evasion. The year selected is 1967, the year *before* he became vice president. And the deal is that Agnew gets no jail. And what does the government, that is, the people of the United States get? Agnew's resignation. That's it!

Richardson is concerned that Nixon's possible impeachment or resignation might result in Vice President Agnew becoming president. For that reason, Richardson is so determined to get Agnew out of office that, by any rational standard, Agnew makes out like the bandit that he is. True, Richardson files a lengthy recital of the evidence against the vice president. And true, that does hurt Agnew. But Richardson's insistence that Justice file a full statement of the evidence against Agnew also hurts the department. The evidence conclusively demonstrates Agnew's guilt of bribery and extortion. Had the decision been mine, I would either have taken a plea of guilty, or gone to trial. But I guess the country is better off without me as attorney general—at least if Richardson's approach is what the country truly needs—because I would not have let the bastard off.

****

October 20

Whatever else Elliot Richardson may have done, or not done ten days ago, tonight he sails off into legend. Folks are already calling it the Saturday Night Massacre. Richardson has resigned rather than obey

Nixon's order to fire Archibald Cox. Then his deputy AG, William Ruckelshaus, resigned rather than fire Cox. Finally, Nixon ordered Solicitor General Robert Bork, the last man in the chain of command, to do it and, what do you know, he does! Well, Richardson did an honorable thing. As for Bork, he can find lots of reasons to do what he did, in order to "save the country" or the department, but I would not have done it.

But I wonder, suppose Richardson had just said "No. I will not." Would Nixon have dared fire him, and then move on to Ruckelshaus, and then on to Bork, and after him who—Henry Petersen? Whatever. Richardson has earned a distinguished place in history.

****

And me? I have cleared the ABA. They even gave me a "well-qualified" rating, one higher than the "qualified" I needed to pass. The FBI background investigation is no problem. But I do have a problem with some South Jersey Republican politicians. They are holding me up in the White House.

To my amusement, Brendan Byrne, the Democrat nominee, has been running on flyers that proclaim he will fight corruption "the way Herb Stern fights corruption." He is also using the DeCarlo tapes, which mention him, when he was Essex County prosecutor, as a man who could not be bought. DeCarlo is dead. Riddled with cancer, bedridden for months, he died October 20. But he still speaks.

This amazing month is far from over. We have had the vice president resign from office after pleading "nolo" to tax evasion. That was October 10. Ten days later, the attorney general and his deputy resign, refusing to follow the president's order to fire Cox.

October 22

The New York Times calls me. Is it true, they want to know, that Peter Rodino, a Newark congressman who now serves as chairman of the Judiciary Committee, is associated with the mafia?

Martin Tolchin of the *Times* is on the telephone. "We are doing a 'Man in the News' piece on Rodino. His committee is getting ready to consider impeachment proceedings against the president. And we are hearing some pretty bad things about him."

"What is that?" I ask.

"That he is associated with organized crime," Tolchin tells me.

"Who says that?"

"You know I can't reveal my sources."

Then he reads excerpts to me from the DeCarlo tapes, with DeCarlo talking about Dennis Carey, Democratic chairman of Essex County, where Newark is located. DeCarlo is saying, "Carey double-crossed me. We gave him plenty of money, but we didn't get one thing from him. A lot of it was Tony Boy's. The only favor we ever got were off Hughie (Addonizio) and Rodino."

Tolchin also tells me that Rodino used to share an apartment in Washington with Addonizio when Addonizio was in Congress.

Someone has given Tolchin very precise information. It seems likely to me that the White House is trying to undermine the House Judiciary Committee by impeaching its chair, even before the committee gets started on impeaching the president. They are spinning stories in a town that rotates like a carousel, with the figures on it twirling, rising and falling in the wind of the moment.

So, what am I to do? I know nothing about any unseemly, much less criminal activities of Rodino. But, am I supposed to be a reference for him? I am the United States Attorney, not the Better Business Bureau. And my name is in the White House for a federal judgeship, with Senator Case laboring to get it out. What do I need this for? All I have to do is a Pontius Pilate with a "no comment."

But I can't. The vice president has resigned. Rodino is presently presiding over the investigation of Gerald Ford to replace Agnew, and he may soon be presiding over the impeachment of the president. I will not allow the confidence of the American public to be further eroded by the conversations of Gyp DeCarlo. Not when there is no evidence I know of that Rodino did anything wrong. I cannot vouch for Rodino's whole life, but I can and I will vouch for him today.

"Today, in my opinion, Rodino is an honest man, and a fine public servant," I tell Tolchin. Before the end of the day, I get similar calls from others in the national press, and I make roughly the same statement. Some print it. Some don't. The *Times* does.

Chapter Twenty-Four

The Flaming Pen
October 22–31, 1973

ON THE TWENTY-FOURTH, my favorite newspaperman, Gil Spencer, does another of his fabulous editorials. This one salutes the first of the indictments from our Mercer County investigation:

THE LIST KEEPS GROWING

Mercer County Superintendent of Public Works Larry Marinari, who was indicted last Friday by a federal grand jury for extortion and filing a false tax return, is the 168th New Jersey public official charged and-or convicted since 1969 when a concerted state and federal campaign to clean up the state was launched. But who's counting, you ask.

Well, Herbert J. Stern, for one, the U.S. Attorney who has established a reputation as one of the nation's most successful corruption fighters. Of course, he had help from a number of sources, not the least of which was an assigned territory—New Jersey—so rich in flagrant corruption that his job could almost be compared to shooting fish in a barrel . . . have public officials learned their lesson? Well, there is reason to believe they are frightened as they have never been before, but no proof corruption has been eliminated and it may never be. The greatest danger is that we will again accept such abuses of trust as something "we can't do anything about because everybody does it." Or, just as alarming, that there won't always be dedicated and fearless prosecutors to expose the corrupt and make them pay for their crimes.

The odd thing is that I have never met or even spoken with Gil Spencer. Not even once in all these months. So I pick up the telephone and call him.

"You!" he says. "I can't believe it." And we both chuckle.

"Have they cleared you yet for your judgeship?" he wants to know.

"No. Not yet. I'm not sure they will, given the Rodino business," I tell him. "But I wanted to call and thank you. In my opinion you are right up there with crusading newspapermen of yesterday, like Lincoln Steffens and Ida Tarbell. You may have a smaller stage, with a little newspaper in Trenton, New Jersey, but you have had a great impact here. You deserve a Pulitzer Prize."

"Thanks. But they don't give that out to people like me."

"Well, maybe I'll nominate you," I reply.

"You can't. You're not in the club. You have to be a journalist."

I'm not sure Spencer is right. So, I call Columbia University.

"Are nominations accepted only from newspapers?" I ask.

"No," I am told. "Anyone can nominate." So that's what I do. Jon and I collect a bunch of Spencer editorials to submit to Columbia University, so we can nominate Gil for the Pulitzer.

****

The month of October drags to a close. Still no presidential nomination. Word has begun to circulate in the political world that my nomination may be in trouble. Before the end of the month, I receive a call from Mayor Dunn of Elizabeth, the author of the famous Law Day speech.

"Mr. Stern, I don't know if you are aware of it, but I was National Co-Chairman of Democrats for Nixon last election."

"No, Mayor. I had no idea."

"Well, I was," Dunn continues. "After the election, the president brought me to the White House for a private dinner. Just him and me. And he told me, 'Tom, if you ever want anything, just pick up a phone and call me direct.' And, Mr. Stern, if you want me to, I will call the president for you."

"I am so deeply appreciative of your kindness," I say, thunderstruck. "But I think it would be best if we let Senator Case handle it."

After we end the conversation, I am left staring at the phone. And I reflect on how the DeCarlo tapes continue to ripple through so many lives. The people who were recorded. Those who were mentioned. The good and the harm done by the tapes' public filing. The alert they sounded. The pain that they caused. The evil they exposed. The innocent they may have besmirched. Was it worth it? No enduring answer comes to me.

But this much is very clear. Acts of generosity and kindness are often returned.

Chapter Twenty-Five

I Want You to Be Attorney General
October 31–December 7, 1973

HE GUBERNATORIAL CAMPAIGN is in its final moments. There can be little doubt about the outcome. The Republican candidate, Congressman Sandman, is simply too conservative for New Jersey. Then there is the so-called corruption issue of the Cahill administration, which in my view is not very corrupt—certainly not in comparison to the preceding Hughes administration and the Democrat machines in Hudson and Newark. But the most recent disclosures of corruption have been Republican ones.

Election night is no surprise. Brendan Byrne becomes governor-elect. A few days later, Martin Greenberg comes to see me. A prominent attorney, Greenberg was elected to the state senate on Byrne's ticket. He had been an assistant prosecutor under Byrne, and later his law partner, and he is extremely close to the governor-elect.

"Brendan wants to see you," Greenberg tells me. "He would like you to come to his house in West Orange."

"Why?"

"He wants you to be attorney general," Martin tells me.

"But I am waiting on my nomination to the federal bench," I point out.

"If you want to be a judge, that could be arranged after your service as attorney general," Greenberg suggests.

So, I go to meet with Governor-elect Byrne. When I arrive at his home, I see that he lives in a modest house—now, of course, surrounded by a detail of state troopers.

I have never met or spoken to the man before, and I look forward to meeting him. I find a very attractive, articulate, and intelligent person. He tells me that he wants me to be his attorney general. I respond that I prefer to keep on the path I have taken.

"I hear you have some trouble," he says.

"Yes, but I think Senator Case can deal with it," I respond with more confidence than I actually feel.

"Well, I'll keep it open for you. At least for a few weeks," says the soon-to-be governor.

A few days later, Senator Case calls. He tells me, "The White House has released your name. You will be nominated within days."

The rest is pro forma. A trip to the Senate for a brief confirmation hearing, and then, on December 7, the Senate confirms the appointment.

****

In its last days, the Cahill administration has been making its own appointments. After Chief Justice Weintraub announces his retirement, Governor Cahill nominates former governor Hughes to replace him. Hughes will need confirmation from the state senate. He will certainly achieve it. He is one of the most popular figures ever to appear on the New Jersey scene. And, before he became governor, he was an able and respected judge. And yet . . . as governor, he certainly presided over the most corrupt state in the nation.

I guess Hughes is worried about me, concerned that I might make some public comment that could hurt his nomination. So he calls me on the telephone. "Why don't we go out and buy our judicial robes together?" he jokes. I know what he means. He wants to know that I will not attack him. But, as a prosecutor, I have nothing to attack him with. As far as I can tell, he committed no crime. I even defended his reputation when the press came after him when his state treasurer was indicted. I am still the United States Attorney. I do not comment on gubernatorial appointments. So I laugh and say, "Sure, Dick. That's what we'll do." He laughs back, knowing he will have no trouble from me.

But Hughes is not so fortunate where Gil Spencer is concerned:

> It was as if it never happened, that there had been no corruption in this state, that it had never touched the Cahill or Hughes administrations, that the arrest of top officials in both administrations was a figment of a lunatic imagination, that there had been no need for an awakening of the public political conscience, and that, somehow, we had all been spirited to a magic glade where Republican William Cahill could confer the nomination for Chief Justice upon former Democratic Governor Richard Hughes without the slightest fear of a complaint, contradiction or controversy. . . . For eight years, Governor Hughes presided over one of the most unspeakably corrupt states in the memory of man . . . as the immensity of the cancer slowly became evident, so did Mr. Hughes' reluctance to apply the knife. Festering infections in Newark, Jersey City and elsewhere were lanced by federal, not state, authorities.

Hughes's nomination for the state Supreme Court is overwhelmingly approved by the state Senate

Chapter Twenty-Six

A Promise
December 7, 1973–January 18, 1974

A JUDICIAL INDUCTION TAKES more than a day to prepare. Mine is set for January 18. It has to be a date convenient to the dignitaries who desire to attend, most importantly, Senator Case. Fred Lacey will be sitting on the bench with my new colleagues when I take the oath. Our new state chief justice, Richard Hughes, and Governor Brendan Byrne have indicated that they too wish to attend. Senator Harrison Williams found something else to do.

The judges have unanimously voted to fill the vacancy in the U.S. Attorney's office with Jon. I have told Chief Judge Cohen that I want Jon's induction as court-appointed U.S. Attorney to be one ceremony with mine. So the date also has to be convenient to his family. Senator Case has already sent in Jon's name for the presidential appointment.

I am more than ready to leave my life as a prosecutor. It has been exactly twelve years since December 11, 1961, when I stood near Robert Rifkind, under the eyes of our respective fathers, and raised an arm, draped in my green army private's uniform, to take the oath as an attorney. In a few days, after I take the judicial oath, the arm I will lower will be draped in black.

I entered the legal profession with great hopes and expectations. I began with the ideals of a young person. Some of those were blunted by the grinding experiences of the life I found, by the realities of the criminal courts of the city of New York; by the bureaucracy of the national government; by the corruption in the police; by the faithlessness of so many in public service. But in confronting all that, the abrading resulted in a honing, too; a sharpening of skills, of determination, of purpose, of a desire to change things, and to change myself as well.

Between then and now, I have been fortunate. I got to do pretty much what I wanted to do . . . often enough discovering that what I desired was not what I really wanted.

And what did I want? In retrospect, the answer becomes clear to me. I wanted to be free. I wanted to own myself. I did not want to "play ball" or "get along" or "go along."

Perhaps it is a form of arrogance, of self-love, this refusal to bend, to bow, and to depart from one's own judgment; to refuse to say something is blue, when in truth it is green; this abiding notion that to lie is to degrade oneself by denying one's self and that to deny one's self for power, prestige, much less for money, demeans the gain. I am convinced that it is precisely self-respect that separates policemen who won't take graft, from others who will. It is self-respect that explains why some refuse to yield to improper wooing, while others will; why some public officials will not ever accept a gratuity, while others demand bribes; why some prosecutors reach out to disturb the status quo, while others are content within the system. In the end, it comes down to how one views oneself. What was it that Judge Wortendyke said? "The only way a man should conduct himself, the only objective towards which a man's conduct should be aimed, is the satisfaction of his conscience."

Have I been able to achieve the satisfaction of my own conscience in all things? It would be a rarer life than mine that could withstand the intimate examination of a white glove. Just as my office has had its failures, for we did not win all of our cases, these twelve years have seen personal failures as well. Be that as it may, it is time to pass the mantle of prosecutor and go on to something in its own way even more formidable—to be the sort of judge that I have admired as a lawyer. A judge who wants to decide rather than avoid decisions. A judge who wants to at least nudge the law forward rather than cower in fear of reversal or criticism.

Judge Wortendyke is gone. So is Judge Shaw. In the basement of the courthouse, I locate Judge Wortendyke's old desk and ask that it be moved into my chambers. That is the desk I will use. And I will sit in Judge Shaw's old courtroom. These physical things will carry reminders of the spirit I want to emulate.

Dad has come up from his Florida retirement apartment to attend the induction. The night before the event, he takes a fall and cuts his head. He emerges from the hospital okay. Just a big bandage on his forehead.

On the morning of January 18, before a crowded courtroom, I take the judicial oath and, in Richardson's words, with it the veil. Jon and Fred Lacey have provided the robe. My father drapes it around my shoulders. Senator Case leads the speakers.

"I was joking with your father," the senator looks directly at me. "Joking about his weeping at your being sworn in as United States Attorney, and we wondered if we were going to have a Niagara today," Case pauses for the laugh he gets. "But he held up just beautifully and performed just as a fine, old, New York Republican assemblyman ought to perform." When the laughter is again stilled, the senator says, "I am not going to try to be serious because what we do, not what we say, is what counts. And sometimes things are too important and they are too close to you to be serious about them—if you know what I mean." And with that he turns directly to me, wishes me luck, and resumes his seat.

When all the speakers have finished, it is my time to utter my first words wearing the judicial robes. "It would be impossible to render a full accounting of all that I owe to so many in this room. . . . I hope it will suffice if I say to you that I am well aware of it . . ."

I say that I know that a judge must be circumspect in speaking. "But surely it must be permissible still to remark upon our very remarkable system of government, on our country and on its people."

My mind turns back, just a handful of years, to when Jon and I first arrived in New Jersey, friendless and alone. It is a moment to acknowledge the greatness of our country, of our system of government, and of our people:

> A country which is secure enough, a government which is free enough, and a people who are generous enough to make a stranger welcome, to provide him with bountiful opportunity and ultimately to embrace him and to elevate him far beyond his deserts.

I close the brief remarks with a promise, a promise on top of promises:

> The promises which are chiseled into the marble of all of our courthouses are written there only in stone. They are not indelible. Indeed, they will not even be truthful unless those who labor in the courthouses make them so. I now join with my colleagues to realize the phrase which appears on this very bench: *Fiat Justitia Ruat Caelum* – "Let justice be done though the heavens fall."

Afterword

The new Byrne Administration, inducted in January 1974, felt compelled to investigate Detective James Challander's charge that the Cahill Administration covered up the illegal fundraising during its first campaign. It seemed fitting, inasmuch as Byrne owed at least some credit for his election victory to the courageous whistle-blowing detective and to his lawyer, Lewis B. Kaden. Kaden himself was well rewarded. In January, he became a cabinet member, counsel to the governor, no less. So the auguries seemed well aligned for Challander, who had been reduced to driving a patrol car on the New Jersey turnpike, and whose lawyer was now counsel to the governor.

Led by First Assistant Attorney General Robert DelTufo, the investigation dragged on. It was begun in January 1974, and it did not conclude until October, when New Jersey Attorney General William F. Hyland announced the result. And the result was: there was no cover-up . . . it was just that the Cahill administration had viewed the situation "myopically," rather than with Challander's broader vision. The irrepressible Gil Spencer editorialized: "Attorney General William Hyland's report on the so-called Challander episode did everything but pop into a pinafore."

As for Challander, on November 13, 1974, after 18 months of driving the turnpike, he was finally transferred to the Criminal Justice Division to assist in preparing cases for trial.

The United States Attorney's office under Jon Goldstein continued the mop-up of New Jersey. Nelson Gross, former Republican state chairman, was tried and convicted. The prosecution was handled by Jon personally. Former State Treasurer Joseph McCrane of racetrack fame was also convicted after trial. Bruce Goldstein prosecuted that case. The Mercer and Bergen County investigations yielded indictments. From January of 1974, when Jon Goldstein took command, until January of 1977, the office continued to perform as it had since Fred Lacey's arrival in September of 1969.

Henry Petersen, under constant assault in news articles and in hearings before the congress, expostulated to the press, "I am not a whore." On November 1, 1974, he had had enough and submitted his resignation after twenty-seven years of service in the department. Upon his death in 1991, the department created a Henry E. Petersen award. It is the highest honor that the Criminal Division can bestow.

****

The election of James Earl Carter in November 1976 changed the landscape, by shifting control of the Justice Department into the hands of his victorious Democratic party in January 1977. The Democratic senator from New Jersey, Harrison Williams, demanded that Jonathan L. Goldstein be replaced as United States Attorney by a Democrat of Williams's own choosing. President Carter, in a handwritten letter, discharged Goldstein. At the recommendation of Senator Williams, President Carter appointed First Assistant Attorney General Robert DelTufo—author of the Challander report—as United States Attorney in 1978.

Senator Case, up for re-election in 1978, was challenged and defeated in the Republican primary by ultraconservative candidate Jeffrey L. Bell. As a result, former basketball great, Bill Bradley, a Democrat, was elected to Case's seat, with fifty-five percent of the vote. .

In 1981 Senator Harrison Williams was prosecuted for bribery, but not by the New Jersey United States Attorney's office. He was convicted in the Eastern District of New York, Brooklyn Courthouse. He received a sentence of three years imprisonment.

****

Assistant United States Attorneys during the time of this work were at the outset of their professional journeys. All of them went on to distinguished careers in the private and public sectors. For example, Jack Bissell and Gary Brown took the federal bench, and later became successive chief judges of their court. Jon and Bruce Goldstein, and John Barry—until his untimely death—became leaders of the New Jersey bar. Both Goldsteins are still in active practice, as are many of the others.

****

Some of the criminal laws—as we know them today—have also matured over these fifty years.

The blue laws are largely gone. Pornography prosecutions—where minors are not involved—are largely gone as well. It is inconceivable today to prosecute for the kinds of photos and films that we routinely prosecuted in the early sixties. An indictment of Lenny Bruce would be unthinkable. Pornography is now big business. Its "stars" have their own awards banquet. They are paid to perform sexual acts recorded on film, which, if done in private for money would lead to their arrest under criminal prohibitions for prostitution . . . statutes that for some reason we remain committed to enforcing.

Homophobia is greatly diminished. Prosecutions for "deviant" sexual activity are no more. Same-sex marriage is at a tipping point in recognition as a "right." Perhaps we shall even see the day when we simply keep our noses out of each other's bedrooms.

As for gambling, while criminal laws still forbid that activity, many of the states are such serious competitors through lotteries and off-track betting that the "illegal" industry has withered.

The notion that drug addicts are criminals is more and more suspect. The experiment of increasing penalties for drug use as a deterrent is more and more rejected. Filling our jails with addicts is more and more questioned. Even the idea that executing murderers deters murders is less and less credited. Capital punishment still flourishes in some states, to be sure. But, as a national phenomenon, compared to sixty or so years ago, it is a diminishing, not an expanding industry. As Robert Ingersoll told us in the nineteenth century, more and more we are learning that the hallmark of a civilized society is the way it treats its "criminals." No one looking over his shoulder can fail to see the progressive changes in the criminal laws over the preceding half century.

As Franklin Delano Roosevelt taught us in his fourth inaugural—
his last major address to the nation:

> "The great fact to remember is that the trend of civilization itself is
> forever upward; that a line drawn through the middle of the peaks
> and the valleys of the centuries always has an upward trend."

There is one dilemma we will never solve: the tension between doing
law and doing justice, when we are sure that those goals conflict. We
cannot invite anarchy. But neither can we sully our souls to totally
avoid it. The heart can mislead. But so, too, can the mind. Stacking
and expanding analogies eventually distort, even deform the original
principle. Differences in degree invariably lead to differences in kind. In
administering "justice" there is no formula, no comfortable "always" or
"nevers." There is only awareness.

End Notes

BOOK I: FOR THE PEOPLE

CHAPTER 3/The Criminal Court Bureau

22 Paul Hoffman and I immediately became life long friends. He authored a book, *Tiger in the Court*, chronicling the United States Attorney's Office for the District of New Jersey.

CHAPTER 6/The Homicide Bureau

43 It is plain to me that I was saved from having to participate in the Bruce persecution by the lucky passage of time that saw me out of Kuh's Bureau and into Homicide. In later years I read that my slightly junior colleague, Nick Scopetta, refused the assignment to assist Kuh in the prosecution. I hope I would have as well. Poor Vince Cuccia who did take it on later publicly stated: "I feel terrible about Bruce. He didn't harm anybody. He was punished because of the words that he used. It's the only thing I did in Hogan's office that I am ashamed of."

CHAPTER 9/Time to Move On

60 Years later, after his conviction and incarceration, Robles gave a jailhouse interview to Selwyn Raab of *The New York Times*. He described in detail how he broke into the apartment searching for money to support his $15-a-day heroin habit. He encountered Wylie and raped her. He bound her and was leaving when Hoffert came home. He took $30 from her, but as he was binding her, Hoffert said, "I'm going to remember you for the police. You are going to jail." Robles said when he heard that he, as he put it, "went bananas" and slaughtered the two helpless women. As a result of the Whitmore case, New York State banned capital punishment.

CHAPTER 11/The Murderers

68 I learn much later, after I leave the DA's office, and even after the trial, that Coyle misled me. After the shooting, Roberts threw a chair at Hagen-Hayer, slowing his escape. In return, Roberts got a bullet through his jacket. There is a well-known

531

photograph of Malcolm lying on the stage with a man bending over him administering mouth-to-mouth resuscitation. That man is Roberts, the undercover cop. The police department was apparently willing to mislead our office, and even withhold information during the trial, to maintain Roberts's undercover status. He was not revealed until years later, when he testified for the DA's office in the Black Panthers trial. The defendants in that case were acquitted.

74 Funny thing about life. Less than nine years later, I am a federal judge in New Jersey and by chance I am assigned a civil case brought by the estate of Malcolm X. The estate is suing a record company for using Malcolm's voice, which, during a song, comes on repeatedly interrupting the music saying "No surrender." When the case is called, I see Betty Shabazz, Malcolm's widow, who as the executrix of the estate is the plaintiff. She is sitting in the back of the room. I finish settling the case with the lawyers, we put it on the record, and then I call her up to the bench. I wave the two lawyers back out of earshot, so it is just she and I, right at the bench. I lean forward and say, "Do you remember me?" "I certainly do," she says, "and you're more mellow now." We both burst into loud laughter in the courtroom, while the lawyers, out of earshot of our conversation, look at us in wonder. Unfortunate woman, she later died as a result of a fire set by her grandson; and one of her daughters was arrested for plotting to kill Louis Farrakhan. Back in 1965, he was known as Louis X, and he eventually succeeded to the head of the Black Muslims. Apparently, the daughter believed that Farrakhan was involved in the death of her father. I wish I knew. Unfortunately, our investigation could never get beyond the shooters.

BOOK II: FOR THE UNITED STATES

CHAPTER 1/The Department of Justice

85 The "area men" initiative will later be expanded by Henry Petersen, Chief of the Section, who will create "strike forces" staffed and directed from Washington. Their stated rationale will be to enhance coordination between the separate law enforcement agencies. Their main purpose, in truth but not stated, will be to enhance the direct control of Washington Department attorneys over investigations and cases in selected districts.

CHAPTER 2/Peter Weber

89 In later years, George Schultz and Casper Weinberger, respectively, Secretary of State and Secretary of Defense in the Reagan Administration, would become its officers.

CHAPTER 4/Operation Pipeline

96 In later years, both companies changed names, merged, and moved.

CHAPTER 8/The Best Lawyers in America

118 In one year Williams will win both the Super Bowl and the World Series, while being universally acknowledged as America's finest trial lawyer.

CHAPTER 10/Voir Dire

128 And yet, as the years have gone by, I have come to believe that this sort of demonstration of power is a mistake. Such a revelation only makes an advocate's job harder by revealing that he is so smart that the jurors have to watch him closely.

129 Over the years I have come to the conclusion that Williams refrained because he understood the harm an advocate does to himself when he harps on those legal loopholes—these self-protective arguments at the outset of a case—rather than appearing as the truth-giver in the courtroom.

BOOK III: BATMAN AND ROBIN—THE FULCRUM

CHAPTER 1/Jersey Boys

226 As those who followed David Chase's remarkable television series *The Sopranos* may recognize from the names, these mobsters were models for the show. The name "Pussy Russo" was actually used—Tony Soprano was loosely based on Tony Boy Boiardo.

CHAPTER 9/"An Efficient and Effective Government"

260 In later years, such proceedings are held *in camera*—which means behind closed doors. The theory of the change is that this protects grand jury secrecy. I think the change is unwarranted. A public official certainly has the right to invoke the Fifth. He may even be able to do so without forfeiting his public position. At least that is what the Supreme Court says. But, in my view, he ought not to be allowed to do so in secret.

BOOK V: A PLACE TO STAND

CHAPTER 2/Newsmaker

421 He wins. Then we nominate Dr. Paul Jordan, Mayor of Jersey City. He wins, too.

422 Several years later, Thornburgh, as Assistant Attorney General succeeding Henry Petersen in the Ford Administration, effectively terminated the strike force program by transferring strike-force attorneys to the direct supervision of the USAs.

CHAPTER 7/A Nation of Men as Well as Laws

441 Hoover was Director of the Bureau of Investigations, the FBI's predecessor, from 1924 until 1935, when the FBI was established. His power did not reach its full scope until after 1935.

444 Krogh, it later turned out, was Chief of the White House "plumbers," the Nixon squad that did dirty deeds in Watergate and before. Later Krogh arranged the break-in of Daniel Ellsberg's psychiatrist's office. Of course, none of this had yet occurred at the time of the meeting.

CHAPTER 11/Ghosts

465 A fuller account of the confrontation with Zelmanowitz – from his point of view – is related by Fred Graham in *The Alias Program*, Little Brown and Company, 1976.

CHAPTER 13/A Private Inquiry and a Christmas Gift

473 A partial account of this meeting is recounted in *A Heartbeat Away* by Richard M. Cohen and Jules Witcover. On January 4, 1973, the first wave of subpoenas went out to the county government and to the 27 firms doing the most business with the county. Within seven months, Beall had assembled enough evidence to indict Vice President Agnew. In October 1973, less than one year after Beall opened his investigation, Vice President Agnew pled nolo contendere to tax evasion and resigned from office.

CHAPTER 15/"We Will Summon the Wind"

479 In later years, J.J. Kenny's conviction was reversed by the New Jersey Appellate Division, 2 to 1, because of the federal immunity grant. The state appealed to the Supreme Court of New Jersey, which unanimously, 7 to 0, affirmed the ruling of the Appellate Division, and ordered all charges against J.J. Kenny dismissed.

CHAPTER 16/Off to the Races

485 Months later, the opinion came down. I lost before the three-judge panel. I then asked the best lawyer in our shop, John Barry, to brief and argue the appeal before the entire court *en banc*. He won, reversing the panel, and establishing the right of the President to electronically surveil suspected foreign spies without first seeking a warrant.

CHAPTER 19/"Cleansed Climate"

494 In November we do indict the three New Jersey racetracks and Florida's Hialeah for tax fraud.

CHAPTER 21/Law and Order

502 Even today, Gyp DeCarlo is treated better than he deserves in the Tony Award musical, Jersey Boys, in which he is portrayed as a kindly, benevolent, Godfather-type figure.

CHAPTER 22/"Something Smells"

510 Williams shortly thereafter became national treasurer of the Democratic Party.

CHAPTER 24/The Flaming Pen

516 But, unfortunately, the evidence is persuasive that it is true. There are at least two principal sources of confirmation. Arthur Schlesinger Jr.'s monumental work, *Robert Kennedy and his Times*, documents the IRS investigation, including that the Service did obtain the cashier's checks that Adams had used to pay his rent with the cash Goldfine had given to him. Adams was interviewed by the head of the Organized Crime Section, Bill Hundley, then Henry Petersen's boss. Adams admitted receiving cash from "donors," whose names he could not recall – while denying it was Goldfine. According to Schlesinger, a Kennedy apologist, "In the end, gaps remained in the evidence…people might always arise to swear that they had given the money to Adams out of disinterested patriotism." Page 386. According to Schlesinger, that is why the tax case was dropped.

This evaluation makes no sense. In a tax case for unreported income, Adams could hardly defend on the ground he received the unreported income from persons – other than Goldfine – whose names he says he cannot recall. Unreported income is unreported income. The objective fact is that Goldfine and Mildred Paperman informed the IRS about the cash, the IRS did trace the cashier checks that Adams purchased for cash and used to pay his rent, and the Tax Division of the Department of Justice did refuse to bring the case.

But what of the allegation that the reason for the declination was President Kennedy's order to Justice to kill the case as a favor to former President Eisenhower?

Schlesinger admits that he did hear that was the reason. "It is said, although I have been unable to verify the story," he writes at page 386, "that John Kennedy sent the incriminating data to Eisenhower at Gettysburg…according to the story, Eisenhower, after looking at the Adams dossier, sent a message back to Kennedy expressing fervent hope that Adams be spared further humiliation." Page 387. And what does Schlesinger cite as the source of the story that he heard, but was unable to verify? He footnotes none other than President Kennedy himself. "John Kennedy, in whatever mood of truth or teasing, told such a story to Joseph Alsop." Then Schlesinger adds, "No one in the Department of Justice with whom I discussed the story had heard of it."

Schlesinger's assertion that no one who had worked in Justice at the time had heard of the Kennedy-Eisenhower deal on Adams seems far-fetched when one considers that Schlesinger himself cites to Bobby Baker's book, *Wheeling and Dealing*, published in 1978, which details the dealings between Kennedy and Eisenhower in respect to Adams. Although Schlesinger mis-cites the pages in the Baker book, and Baker himself used a fictitious name for Adams – who was still alive in 1978 – the details of the deal are completely set forth at pages 97-99, and Schlesinger knew well enough who Baker was referring to. In any event, Williams, who told me about the deal in 1973, had been both Goldfine and Baker's lawyer, and, knowing Williams as I did, was likely telling me something he had already repeated numerous times.

517 Spencer won the Pulitzer for editorial writing in 1974. He left the *Trentonian* to become editor-in-charge of the *Philadelphia Daily News*. In 1984, he became editor-in-charge of the *New York Daily News*.

518 Some months later, Peter Rodino telephoned me. It was the first time we had ever spoken. He asked me to take the position of Chief Counsel to his Judiciary Committee hearings into the impeachment of President Nixon. I respectfully declined. To accept would have required my resignation as a federal judge.

CHAPTER 26/A Promise

524 My father had run for the New York State Assembly in the 1930s, but was defeated. The Senator graciously ignored the returns.

Acknowledgements

Many people made this book possible. Martin Levin, Arthur J. Greenbaum, and Denise Penna Shephard provided enormous help and guidance. Without them, there would have been no book. Alan Marcus was inspirational throughout the entire process. The editorial advice of Clyde Feil, Otto Feil, and Audrey Peterson was indispensible, as well as my publisher's editor in charge, Jason Katzman, who was a benevolent guide. I would also like to recognize and thank my "readers" who suffered throughout early drafts and advised me as I went along: Thomas F. Campion, Ken Gantz, Martin Garbus, Bruce Goldstein, Jon Goldstein, Marc Himmelstein, Bill Jaffe, Kevin M. Kilcullen, Judy Marcus, Hew Pate, Toby Pell, Don Robinson, Willa Speiser, Peter Sudler, and Alan Winter.

Index

A

ADA (assistant district attorney), 3–5, 7–9, 19, 35
Addonizio, Hugh, 93, 122, 228–229, 239–240, 250, 260, 285, 290, 295–296, 302, 305, 312
Adoption process of baby, 15
Agnew, Spiro, 474, 503, 513, 515
Aldisert, Ruggiero, 335, 349, 352, 391–392, 430
Appeals Bureau, 30
Assistant district attorney. *See* ADA
Assistant United States Attorneys (AUSAs), 84, 86, 224, 246–247, 283, 289, 292, 315, 328, 339–340, 369, 417, 444, 463
Atlantic City, 384, 395–396, 406, 425–426, 437, 442–443, 473, 475, 477, 479, 483–484, 493–495
Atlantic County, 384, 406–407, 443, 471, 495
AUSAs. *See* Assistant United States Attorneys

B

Baby selling investigation, 15–17
Bar exam, 32, 332, 339
Barlow, 290, 292, 298, 300, 303, 309, 312, 318, 424, 484
Barry, John, 224, 292, 313, 316, 356, 367–372, 376, 383–385, 390–392, 422, 442, 451, 483, 488, 494
Beall, George, 472–473, 513
Bechtel, Stephen, Jr., 108
Bechtel Corporation, 89–90, 95, 98, 105, 107–109, 115, 120–121, 140, 150, 163, 173–174, 181, 183–184, 187–189, 198, 200, 247, 335
Bergen County, 463, 484, 528
Biederman, David, 433–435, 438–439, 460–461, 470, 480, 488
Big Inch, 89
Bissell, Jack, 247, 264, 283–285, 290, 292–293, 384, 529
Black Muslims, 65–66
Bochman, Ralph, 105
Boiardo, Anthony (Tony Boy), 93, 226, 229–230, 239, 242, 254, 257, 262–263, 283–284, 292, 299, 303, 307, 310–311,

407
Boiardo, Ritchie (the Boot), 93, 226–227, 256
Brown, Gary, 263, 283, 290, 292, 348–349
Bruce, Lenny, 42, 57
Burgess, Roy, 100–103
Burkhardt, Robert, 360, 383, 392, 443, 446, 457, 459, 471, 476

C

Cahill, William, 250, 391, 394, 406, 439, 451, 455, 460–462, 469, 482, 486, 489, 491–492, 494, 496, 502, 519–521, 527
Camden 28 case, 421, 442, 451, 483, 488, 493–494
Capello, Dominick, 94
Career Girls Murder Case, 58–61
Case, Clifford P., 241–242, 243, 313, 321, 323, 325, 331, 335, 338, 340, 345, 388, 393, 417, 420–421, 455, 466, 481, 492, 495–496, 504–505, 507, 515, 518, 520, 522, 524, 528
Castilian Room murders, 36–42
Challander, James, 486, 487–489, 527–528
Cohen, Mitchell, 395, 397, 493
Colonial Pipeline case, 91–94, 135–140, 162–167, 186–191, 192–193, 194–198, 199–201
and special grand jury, 104–110
examination of witness in, 148–152, 153–156, 157–161, 202–203
exhibits, 171–175
hire of best lawyers, 115–118
motions and riots of, 119–125
operation pipeline, 95–99
verdict, 177–181, 213–215
Colonial Pipeline Company, 89, 112–113
Complainants, 5, 26–27, 96, 158, 165
Complaint Bureau, 3–14
Compliance officer, 95
Cox, Archibald, 499–500, 502–503, 507–508, 514
Criminal Court Bureau, 18–24
Cronin, Henry, 6–7, 353, 424
Crowe, Patrick, 49, 51–57, 61

D

DA (district attorney) office, organizational plan of, 7

DeCarlo, Angelo, 93, 226–227, 229
Swiss bank accounts of, 237, 264, 270–274
DeCarlo case, 235–236, 235–238, 241–251, 248–250
cross-examination of witness in, 275–279
sentencing, 290
tapes of, 239–240, 246–247, 267–269, 270–272
DeCavalcante, Simone Rizzo, 94, 225–226, 229–230, 238, 242, 250, 281–282, 352, 392, 429
DeLouette, Roger, 355, 358, 360, 398–399, 401, 404, 409, 411–413, 435, 491
Department attorneys, 84–85
Department of Justice, 83–86
Dermody, Vincent J., 47, 78–79, 376
Dewey, Thomas E., 4
District judges, appointment of, 84
Donohue, Joseph Michael (robber and paid killer), 35–42, 44–46, 75, 78, 468
Doran, Patrick J., 443, 471
Drug case, 12–14, 18, 443–445
Dunn, Tom, 440, 448–449, 477, 517

E

Enemy Within, The (Kennedy), 88
Exclusionary Rule, 14

F

Farley, Frank S., 94, 406
FBI, 41, 44, 79, 85–87, 90, 92, 105, 165, 184, 225, 227–228, 233, 235–236, 333, 407, 442, 493
Feeley, Joe, 6, 353
Feldman, Karl, 115–117, 136–137, 147–151, 164, 168, 173–174, 176, 181, 184, 188, 192, 217–220
Fifth Amendment, 109, 247, 259, 261, 262, 283, 322, 329
First Amendment, 21, 23
Flaherty, Thomas, 326, 357–358, 362, 369, 371–372, 375, 392–393, 426, 449
Fourth Amendment, 11, 14
Fourth Commandment, 43
Frauds and the Rackets Bureau, 30

G

Gallagher, Cornelius E., 94, 321, 428–431, 432–437, 473, 475–476, 510

Gambling, 8, 9, 11, 94

Giles, Glen, 96, 115–117, 137, 147–152, 163, 166, 173–174, 176, 182–184, 188, 190–193, 212

Goldstein, Bruce, 328, 340, 360, 376, 382, 433, 449, 451, 456, 527, 529

Goldstein, Jonathan L., 83, 104–105, 107–109, 111–112, 115, 163–164, 167, 170, 205, 223–224, 231, 243, 261, 280, 287, 297, 311, 316, 324, 328, 349, 358, 376, 421, 527–528

Goldwater, Barry, 89

Gordon, Philip, 254–255, 259–260, 262, 311

Government travel requests (GTRs), 91

Gross, Nelson, 242, 325, 331, 492, 502, 527

H

H.C. Price Company, 89, 95–98, 96–97, 100–103, 101–103, 163, 188

Herman, Alexander, 34–36

Heroin, 12–13, 302–304, 355, 360, 398–399, 401, 405, 409, 411, 443, 445

Hobbs Act, 348, 450

Hogan, Frank S., 4, 19, 21–22, 42–43, 55, 60, 79

Homicide Bureau, 30, 34–43, 47, 58–59

Hoover, J. Edgar, 83, 85, 92, 441–442, 444

Hudson County, 94, 224, 227, 292–294, 297, 305, 313–314, 315–316, 322, 324–325, 332, 339–340, 348, 357, 359–360, 362–363, 364–366, 368, 375, 425, 429, 446, 450–452, 480

Hughes, Richard J., 122, 225, 229, 247, 273, 476–477, 494, 519–521, 522

Hundley, William G., 87

I

Illegal gambling organizations, 8

Indictment Bureau, 7, 15–17

J

Jacks, Robert, 108–110, 112, 116–117, 119–120, 129, 136–138, 140, 145–146, 154–158, 160–161, 230, 247, 463, 471

Jersey boys, 223–230

Jersey City, 93–94, 224, 292, 294, 297, 316, 346, 360, 362, 366, 369, 384–385, 392, 396, 406–410, 443, 521

Joyce, James, 90, 120, 183, 211

Joyce Construction Company, 90, 120, 183, 200

K

Kantor, Irving, 263, 283–285, 287, 298–301, 303–304, 311–315, 435

Keenan, John F., 48

Kennedy, Bobby, 85, 87–88, 89, 200, 203, 207, 209, 225, 233

Kennedy, John F., 89

Kenny, John J., 357–361, 363, 368, 370–371, 432–433, 479–480

Kenny, John V., 94, 224, 227, 294, 321–322, 325–326, 328–330, 364–365, 368, 373–374, 382, 446–447, 450–454, 472

Kervick, John A., 425, 437, 443, 473, 476–477, 502

Kleindienst, Richard, 252, 405, 499

Kropke, Fred, 321, 363, 365, 373, 375, 380–382, 385, 393

Kugler, George, 251, 360–361, 367, 417, 432–434, 438–439, 460–461, 470, 476–477, 478–482, 486, 488–489, 501

Kuh, Richard H., 19, 20, 42–43

L

Labor racketeering, 83, 87–90

Lacey, Fred, 105–107, 223–224, 241, 242–244

LaMorte, Anthony, 254, 261–262, 306, 308

Langway, Dick, 383–384, 464–465

Leuty, Ben, 115–117, 129, 136–137, 141–144, 147–149, 151, 165, 166–167, 173–174, 181–184, 217–220

Life magazine, report on mafia, 225–228

Lilley Commission Report, 225, 228

Lippe, Larry, 83

London, Ephraim, 21–23

M

Magistrate court, offenses in, 8

Malcolm X, murder of, 62–74

Manning, Frank, 316, 357–358, 363–364, 368, 371, 373

Mapp v. Ohio, 239

Mardian, Bob, 396–397, 442

McClellan Committee, 89

McCrane, Joseph S., 486, 488, 494, 502, 527

McMahon, Fred, 236–237, 239, 280–281, 282, 475, 503, 506

Mercer County, 463, 484, 516–518, 528

Misdemeanor cases, 18, 25

Muhammad, Elijah, 65–67

N

Napp-Grecco Company, 90, 96, 188, 193

Nation of Islam (NOI), 65

Newark, 93–94, 121–123, 225, 229, 240, 250, 254–255, 257–260, 283, 285–286, 292–294, 297–300, 304, 305–306, 316, 319

Newsmaker (1971-1972), 419–423

New York County, 4, 18, 34, 71, 22, 56

New York Times, 22, 273–274, 293, 297, 421, 447, 475, 478, 479, 481

Nixon, 241, 242, 252, 322, 331, 396, 412, 443–444, 474, 499, 514

O

Obscenity, 9, 18, 20–21, 42, 57, 79, 230

Office of Drug Abuse Law Enforcement program (ODALE), 443, 445

Opera singers case, 6–7

Operating Engineers, 88–90, 97, 204, 215

Operation Pipeline, 95–99

Organization of Afro-American Unity (OAAU), 65, 67

Organized Crime and Racketeering section, 83, 85, 87

Osage Construction Company, 90, 96, 193

P

Pentagon Paper Case, 421–422

Petersen, Henry E., 87, 90–94, 92–94, 104–105, 182, 231–234, 350–352, 405, 422, 438, 497–500, 501, 512, 528

Price, Harold, Jr., 96–98

R

Richardson, Elliot, 499, 502, 504, 506–510, 512–514, 524

Rifkind, Simon Hirsch, 141–146, 216–220

Rigo, Paul, 228, 248, 252, 254–255,

258, 262–263, 285, 298–299, 306–309, 306–312
Robbery case, 25–29
Rocha, Mitzi (Weber's private secretary), 89, 207–212
Russo, Anthony (Little Pussy), 94, 226, 316–317, 407
Russo, John (Big Pussy), 94, 227

S

Salerno, 291, 463–465
Saperstein, Louis B., 235–238, 248–250, 264–266, 270–272, 279
Satz, David, 105, 111–113, 223, 225, 229, 235–236, 238, 250, 283
Seat of government (SOG), 85
Shabazz, Betty (widow of Malcolm X), 70–74
Shaw, Robert, 249, 251, 260, 267–270, 274, 276–279, 280, 288, 290, 316–317, 362, 364–365, 367–368, 387, 392–393, 447, 462–463
Sherwin, Paul, 433–435, 438–439, 450–451, 453–454, 455–457, 460–461, 462, 468–469, 470–471, 479–480, 489
Sills, Arthur, 228–229, 241, 247, 426
Sludge case, 403–404, 410, 424–427
Somers, William T., 442, 443
Special agents in charge (SACs), relationship of USAs to, 85–86
Special Sessions Bureau, 7, 12
Sternkopf, William, 321, 363, 375, 382, 383, 392–393
Stone, Joe, 5, 6
Strike forces, 232, 352–353, 498, 512–513
Supreme Court Bureau, 7, 16, 30
Swindles, 5
Swiss bank accounts
of DeCarlo, 237
of Zelmanowitz, 264, 276

T

Tonti, D. Louis, 382, 383, 390, 425, 435–437, 443, 473, 476–477, 484
Trial part, 19, 25

U

United States Attorney (USA), 83
appointment of, 84–85
Herbert J. Stern as, 345–350
relationship of SACs to, 85–86
United States District Judges, 84

USA. *See* United States Attorney

V

Voir dire, 126–134

W

Watergate case, 466, 497–500, 509
Weber, Peter, 88–90, 91–94, 104–110, 114, 170, 204–206
illegal payments to, 95–98, 101–103, 120, 163, 183–184, 188
indictments against, 121–122, 182
testimony, 89
Wechsler, James A., 56
Westies, the, 36
Whelan, Thomas, 326–327, 357–358, 362, 369, 371–372, 375, 392–393, 426, 449
Whitmore, George, Jr., 59–61
Wilentz, David T. (boss of Middlesex County), 94, 105, 109, 111–113, 115, 147, 224, 247, 273
Willens, Phil, 83
Williamson, Donald J., 292, 320, 327–328, 330, 340–341, 351
Wolfe, Wally, 326, 365–366, 375–380, 385–386, 393
Worgan, David S., 4, 5, 14
Wortendyke, Reynier J., 122–124, 126, 146, 148, 152, 170, 172, 175, 177–178, 186–187, 199, 208–209, 214–215, 217, 289, 322, 350, 401–402, 421, 523
Wylie/Hoffert murders, 58–61

Z

Zelmanowitz, Gerald Martin, 237–238, 248–250, 264–266, 268–274, 275–277, 291, 463–465
Zicarelli, Bayonne Joe, 94, 228, 230, 432
Zirpolo, Walter, 108–110, 112, 116–117, 119–120, 129, 136–138, 140, 145–146, 154–158, 160–161, 230, 247, 463, 471